EIGHTH EDITION

Technical Report Writing Today

Daniel G. Riordan
University of Wisconsin–Stout
Steven E. Pauley

HOUGHTON MIFFLIN COMPANY   Boston   New York

Editor in Chief: Patricia A. Coryell
Sponsoring Editor: Michael Gillespie
Editorial Associate: Bruce Cantley
Associate Project Editor: Martha Rogers
Senior Manufacturing Coordinator: Priscilla Bailey
Senior Marketing Manager: Nancy Lyman

As part of Houghton Mifflin's ongoing
commitment to the environment, this text
has been printed on recycled paper.

Printed in the U.S.A.

Library of Congress Catalog Card Number: 2001093182

ISBN: 0-618-14016-6

23456789-DC-05 04 03 02

Contents

CHAPTER 4 Technical Writing Style 69

Section 2: Technical Writing Techniques

CHAPTER 5 Researching

CHAPTER 6 Summarizing

CHAPTER 9 Defining

CHAPTER 10   Describing

Section 3: Technical Writing Applications

CHAPTER 13   Developing Web Sites   322

CHAPTER 16   Proposals   419

Section 4: Professional Communication

Appendixes

APPENDIX A   Brief Handbook
for Technical Writers   540

APPENDIX **B** Documenting Sources

To the Instructor

The eighth edition of *Technical Report Writing Today* continues to change in order to reflect the dynamic new directions evolving in technical communication. The challenges of today's workplace require highly skilled writers able to produce a wide range of documents. *Technical Report Writing Today,* with its accessible style and abundance of exercises, will help students prepare for the writing demands they will face in college and on the job. While this newly updated edition features many changes—including a new chapter, "Developing Web Sites"—the book's basic structure and approach remain the same.

The structure of the book remains a sequence from theory and skills to applications. Early chapters present current information on how to handle the repertoire of technical writing skills from audience analysis through research and design. However, the chapters are organized as modules so that you may assign chapters in the sequence that best fills the needs of your course. For instance, you could easily begin your course with a discussion of audience and design, or you could start with applications such as descriptions or letters. Moreover, all the introductory chapters have extensive exercise sections so that students can either practice the concepts covered or go right into writing memos and short reports.

The approach of the new edition is also the same. The book's emphasis continues to be on such skills as definition and description and on such common writing forms as memos, informal reports, proposals, and letters of application. Each chapter is self-contained, asking the students to follow a process of creation that emphasizes audience analysis, visual analysis, and addressing problems related to creating the type of document under consideration. Each chapter contains exercises, assignments, models, planning sheets, and evaluation sheets designed to get students planning, analyzing, developing, and evaluating documents. Exercises provide a variety of strategies to help students learn. For instance, in the chapter on letters of application, students are encouraged to analyze and revise a letter, to create their own letter, or to follow an extended process of group interaction to create and test their letter.

The growing electronic, Web-based world of communication requires students to analyze new communication situations and to make their messages effective for different media and audiences. The eighth edition will help students do just that with practical tips on writing and designing for the Web. The basic question for a technical writing textbook is "How will it help teachers help students come to grips with the communication demands they will meet on the job in the near future?" The eighth edition blends instruction on traditional tools of the trade with new strategies and information to help your students develop not just their skills but their "savvy." This book will position students as effective communicators in the early 21st century and will position you and teachers like you as effective mentors for those students.

NEW TO THE EIGHTH EDITION

The changes to this new edition of *Technical Report Writing Today* reflect the authors' desire to make the book as current and as usable as possible.

The following list highlights some of the updates and revisions. Key additions include a new chapter on designing Web sites, new coverage of group work, evaluation sheets to complement the planning sheets, and new and revised examples and exercises.

▩ *Chapter 13, "Developing Web Sites."* Producing documents for the Web requires students to adapt their communication strategies to the new medium. Web writers must learn content creation, screen design, hyperlink navigation design, planning, and usability testing. This new chapter uses current thinking on Web communication design as well as professional and student examples to introduce students to the basics of effective Web site creation.

▩ *Focus Box on Electronic Résumés.* The Web has changed the traditional job search dramatically. Students now need to know strategies for creating effective electronic résumés. The new "Focus on Electronic Résumés" in Chapter 20 presents practical guidelines that help students take advantage of the Web as a job search tool.

▩ *Focus Box on Documenting Electronic Items.* Telling readers exactly where the information in a report was originally published has been complicated by all the new electronic sources now available, such as E-mail, and Web sites. The new "Focus on Documenting Electronic Items" in Appendix B contains information on the revised citation guidelines of major professional associations, like APA and MLA, so students can cite sources accurately.

- *Focus Box on Working in Groups.* Group work is a key aspect of today's work environment. This new "Focus on Groups" in Chapter 3 serves as a concise guide for students working in groups.
- *Useful Tips.* To make reference material easier to find, a new "Tip" feature has been added where appropriate throughout the text. These "Tips" explain how to handle such minor but important items as punctuating letters and using "a" and "the" in sets of instructions.
- *Evaluation Worksheets. Technical Report Writing Today* has, for several editions, contained planning worksheets. In response to requests from instructors, evaluation worksheets are now also included in key chapters. For example, Chapter 10 now contains both "Worksheet for Description" and "Worksheet for Evaluation of Description."
- *Many New Examples and Exercises.* New examples and exercises have been added to reflect the kinds of situations students are likely to encounter in future courses and on the job.
- *Change from "Model" to "Example."* A slight but significant change is that chapter-end documents are now called "Examples." An example implies one way of many to implement the principles, whereas a "Model" appears to many students to be the only way to implement the principles. Students need to realize that there are many ways to approach problems successfully.
- *Shortened and Rearranged Chapters.* In response to reviewer comments, the chapters on audience, process, and summaries have been streamlined. Material on organizing, previously found in Chapter 4, "Style," has been incorporated into Chapter 3, "The Technical Writing Process."

FEATURES

We have retained the features that have made *Technical Report Writing Today* the useful and popular text it is.

The following list highlights some of the features that have proven effective in previous editions of *Technical Report Writing Today* and continue to be highly praised by users of the book.

- Clear and Concise Presentation
  The chapters in this book are designed as "read to learn to do" material. The book assumes the reader is a student with a goal. By providing short paragraphs and clear presentation, the text helps the student achieve the goal of becoming an effective technical writer.
- Pragmatic Organization
  The text proceeds from theory to skills to applications, but teachers

may assign chapters in any sequence that fills their needs. For instance, teachers could easily begin their course with an application such as descriptions or letters. Because of the situational approach used in many chapters, students can start writing without having to read many theory chapters.

■ Helpful Chapter-Opening Features
Each chapter opens with two features to help orient students to the material to follow. "Chapter Contents" provides a brief outline of the chapter's main sections. "In a Nutshell" briefly summarizes the chapter's most important concepts.

■ Focus Boxes
The text contains numerous "focus boxes" (appearing at the very end of selected chapters), which discuss concepts that build on issues introduced in the chapter. These boxes discuss important topics such as credibility, strategy, E-mail, and bias in language, all of which students must master to become effective professionals.

■ Worksheets
Every major project has a worksheet that helps students organize their thoughts and prepare for the assignment. Each genre chapter also now has an evaluation worksheet, so that students working in groups have a basis for making helpful critical remarks.

■ Annotated Student Examples
The book contains over 100 sample student documents illustrating different writing styles and approaches to problems.

■ Numerous Professional Examples
Professional examples in the book illustrate contemporary ways to handle writing situations. Many students and teachers have commented on the helpfulness of the examples, which appear both within chapters and at the ends of chapters. Numbered examples at the ends of chapters (formerly called "Models") provide a greater level of detail than the necessarily brief examples within chapters.

■ Exercises
Appearing sequentially at the ends of all chapters, exercises, writing assignments, and Web exercises balance individual and group work, exposing students to different kinds of technical writing problems and solutions. Exercises appear in all chapters, even theory chapters, making it easy to get students writing. In many chapters the exercises are actually steps in the planning and drafting process required by the writing assignments for the chapter. As students complete the exercises, they will also be developing the project required for that unit.

▪ Situational Approach

Each of the genre chapters (e.g., proposals, instructions, job application letters) is built on situational principles. The student finds in the chapters all the necessary information, ranging from the audience to the rhetoric of the situation to the organization, format, and type of visual aids that work best in the situation. For instance, Chapter 15, "Recommendation and Feasibility Reports," includes a discussion of generating criteria. Chapter 16, "Proposals," includes a brief discussion of Gantt charts. Chapter 17, "User Manuals," includes a discussion of storyboarding.

▪ Appendixes

The book's two appendixes provide easily accessible material on grammar and mechanics (Appendix A, "Brief Handbook for Technical Writers"), and MLA and APA documentation (Appendix B, "Documenting Sources"). Appendix B now includes a focus box, "Focus on Documenting Electronic Sources."

OTHER MATERIALS FOR TEACHERS AND STUDENTS

▪ Instructor's Resource Manual

The Instructor's Resource Manual retains its chapter-by-chapter organization but offers more features to help teachers teach. Each chapter provides an abstract of a chapter in the book, teaching suggestions (including suggested schedules for sequencing an assignment), and comments on the exercises and writing assignments. The manual has always contained student examples, but in response to requests, the new edition greatly expands the selections, from nine to over fifty. These examples, all created by students responding to assignments in the text, will show your students how others have solved the problems posed in this book. The goal is to provide your classes with material that they can sink their teeth into. Use these examples as models or as the basis for discussions and workshops on effective or ineffective handling of the paper in the situation. You may photocopy these examples and use them as class handouts or create transparencies from them.

▪ Web Site

For the first time, *Technical Report Writing Today* is accompanied by a Web site. The site is divided into two sections, "Student Resources" and "Instructor Resources." The "Student Resources" section features chapter overviews, additional exercises, additional sample documents, links to professional technical writing organizations, and other materials that expand on the student text. The "Instructor Resources" section features an overview of the book, chapter outlines and abstracts, a transition guide outlining changes in the book since the previous edition, and other materials of use to instructors.

■ *The American Heritage Dictionary,* Third Edition
This standard reference is available in a hardcover, thumb-indexed College Edition or a briefer, less expensive, but still durable hardcover Concise Edition. Both dictionaries can be purchased at a deep discount when ordered in a shrinkwrap package with *Technical Report Writing Today.*

■ *A Guide to MLA Documentation,* Fifth Edition, by Joseph Trimmer
A Guide to MLA Documentation is a concise guide to the documentation system of the Modern Language Association of America. What makes this booklet so popular is that it is briefer, cheaper, and easier to use than the MLA's own handbook. *A Guide to MLA Documentation* includes numerous examples, a sample research paper, an updated appendix on American Psychological Association (APA) style, and helpful hints on such topics as taking notes and avoiding plagiarism. The booklet is thin enough to slip into a notebook and inexpensive enough to serve as a supplement for a main text. As part of the English Essentials series, the *Guide* responds to the growing need for texts that can be used by student writers at all skill levels. A complete sample research paper on Internet chat rooms is annotated with explanations of proper MLA format.

■ *Writing Online,* Third Edition, by Nick Carbone
Writing Online provides valuable resources, guidance, and activities that help instructors integrate on-line work into their courses. Introducing students into the on-line world, the text describes what it means to write on-line, gives brief and useful overviews of the main technologies and places for writing on-line, and offers a complete, rhetorically sound guide to conducting research on-line. The third edition includes additional information on graphic browsers, evaluating and citing Internet sources, and the research process, with updated screen shots throughout.

■ *Designing Effective Web Sites,* First Edition, by Johndan Johnson-Eilola
This concise handbook helps students across the curriculum build Web sites, a skill they can use both in college and the workplace. The guide covers two essential elements: usability and the structure of an effective site. Students learn the importance of determining a Web user's short- and long-term goals through surveys, interviews, and focus groups before developing and testing a site. In addition, students discover different methods of designing a site and creating devices for smooth navigation—plus the key concepts of structure and page layout. A fully integrated Web site provides summaries of

text material, further guidance on Web design, templates and graphics for constructing sites, and links to other sources. The site also advises instructors on how to use the book in composition courses and other courses across the curriculum.

ACKNOWLEDGMENTS

I would like to thank the technical writing teachers who offered valuable and insightful comments about the manuscript:

Tim Lindsley, Nicholls State University (LA)

Nedra Diane Lundberg, Kentucky State University

Nancy L. Webb, College of DuPage (IL)

In addition, my appreciation goes to the many students who over the years have demanded clear answers and clear presentations and who have responded with quality writing. For allowing their material to be reprinted in this book, my thanks to these students:

Jill Adkins	Mark Eisner	Kris Jilk
Kevin Albinson	Linda Elsing	Pat Jouppi
Dan Alexander	Louise Esaian	Kim Kainz-Poplawski
David Ayers	Craig Ethier	Cindy Koller
Sandra Baker	Curt Evenson	Mary Beth LaFond
Jennifer Baldini	Carol Frank	Chris Lindblad
John Bauch	Greg Fritsch	Chris Lindner
Rich Biehl	John Furlano	Jerry Mackenzie
Kim Bloss	Bret Gehring	Matt Maertens
Marie Brantner	Julie Ann Gotthardt	Todd Magolan
Karin Broekner	John Gretzinger	Tim Maple
Tony Bynum	Carolyn Hagemann	Brandon McCartney
Craig Cardell	Cheryl Hanson	Julie McNallen
Kevin Charpentier	Cynthia Hauswirth	Heather Miller
Nikki Currier	Tadd Hohlfelder	Jim Miller
Melissa Dieckman	Jodi Hubbard	Tracy Miller
Jim Duevel	Kevin Jack	Keith Munson
Tim Dunford	Rachel A. Jacobson	Jim Nord
John Dykstra	Karl Jerde	Mark Olson

Steve Prickett	Stacy Schmansky	Mike Vivoda
Steve Rachac	Chad Seichter	Andy Vold
Angie Ray	Mike Smith	Rosemarie Weber
Randy Richart	Brad Tanck	Michelle Welsh
Michelle Royer	M. R. Vanderwegen	Jeanne Wendlandt
Ed Salmon	Mike Vanderzanden	Marya Wilson
Jocelyn Scheppers	Steve Vandewalle	John Wise
Jim Schiltgen	Steve Vinz	David Zangl

Special thanks to Jane and Mary for their patient work with a difficult manuscript. For their insight and patience, I would also like to thank the following people at Houghton Mifflin: Dean Johnson, Michael Gillespie, Bruce Cantley, Elisabeth Kehrer, Martha Rogers, Marie Jackson, Cindy Graff Cohen, and Sandra Krumholz.

And finally, thanks once again to an understanding family who offered encouragement and support throughout this project—Mary, Jane, Simon, Nathan, Shana, and Clare Riordan, and Mike and Tim Riordan.

D.G.R.

Technical Writing Basics

1 Definition of Technical Writing

Chapter 1
IN A NUTSHELL

Here are the basics for getting started in technical writing:

Focus on your audience. Your audience needs to get work done. You help them. To help them, you must stay aware that your goal is to enable them to act.

Think of audiences as members of your community who expect that whatever happens will happen in a certain way and will include certain factors—your proposal is expected to include certain sections covering specific topics. When you act as members of the community expect other members to act, your message will be accepted more easily.

Audiences have experiences that may cause them to read your message in a different way than you meant.

Use presentational strategies. Presenting your message effectively helps your audience grasp your message.

- Use the top-down strategy (tell them what you will say, then say it).
- Use headings (like headlines in newspapers).
- Use chunks (short paragraphs).
- Establish a consistent visual logic by making similar elements in your document look the same.
- Use a plain, objective style that lets readers easily grasp details and relationships.

These strategies are easy to learn, but they take practice to use skillfully. They are your repertoire. Master them.

Assume responsibility. Because readers act after they read your document, you must present a trustworthy message. In other words, readers are not just receptacles for you to pour knowledge into by a clever and consistent presentation. They are stakeholders who themselves must act responsibly, based on your writing.

Technical writing is the practical writing that people do as a part of their jobs. Because it is practical, technical writing "aims to get work done, to change people by changing the way they do things" (Killingsworth and Gilbertson, *Signs* 232). Writing that gets work done is a key part of all professional occupations. Writing is frequent. Survey after survey has revealed that each week workers spend one to three days writing. In one survey, professionals in the aerospace industry revealed that they spend 68 percent of their work time—three and one-half days of each week—communicating (Pinelli et al. 9). Writing is important. Bob Collins, a corporate manager, put it this way: "The most critical skill required in today's business world is the ability to communicate, both verbally and in writing. Effective communication has a direct impact on one's potential within an organization."

The goal of this book is to make you an effective, confident technical writer. This chapter introduces you to the three basic concepts you need to know in order to be effective. All the rest of the ideas in the book stem from these three concepts: technical writing is audience centered, technical writing is presentational, and technical writing is responsible.

TECHNICAL WRITING IS AUDIENCE CENTERED

"Audience centered" means that the writing aims to help its readers. The common advice in this regard is: Be clear and concise. The idea is that clear, concise writing is easy to grasp and thus the best way to approach a reader. To be clear and concise, however, requires that you understand how writing affects readers and the interesting ways in which readers approach writing. Technical writing

- Deals with specific situations.
- Enables readers to act.
- Occurs within a community.
- Is interactive.
- Has definite purposes.

Technical Writing Deals with Specific Situations

Technical writing engages a specific audience that has specific needs. The customer who must assemble the computer workstation will receive the instructions that explain how to do it. The manager who needs to hear the results of the site visit receives the memo that explains them. A reader receives a document because he or she plays a role in a certain situation. If the reader has no role in that situation, he or she neither receives nor searches out the document. The writer's goal is to satisfy the audience's need. The audience approaches the exchange with definite expectations, and the writer fulfills them. See pages 25–26 for a memo directed to a specific audience with specific needs.

Technical Writing Enables Readers to Act

According to Killingsworth and Gilbertson, it is helpful to view technical writing as "writing that authors use to empower readers by preparing them for and moving them toward effective action" (221–222). "Effective action" means that readers act in a way that satisfies their needs. Their needs include anything that they must know or do to carry out a practical activity. This key aspect of technical writing underlies all the advice in this book.

Figure 1.1 illustrates this concept in a common situation. The reader has a need, a practical activity, that she must do. She must assemble a workstation. A writer, as part of his job, wrote the instructions for assembling the workstation. The reader uses the instructions to achieve effective action—she successfully assembles the workstation. This situation is a model, or paradigm, for all technical writing. In all kinds of situations—from announcing a college computer lab's open hours to detailing the environmental impact of a proposed shopping mall—technical writers produce documents that enable effective action. The writing enables the reader to act, to satisfy a need in a situation.

Technical Writing Occurs Within a Community

Action, however, occurs within a community, a loosely or closely connected group of people with a common interest. The key point for a writer to remember is that belonging to a community affects the way a person acts and expects other members to act (Allen; Selzer). In terms of writing, this concept means that readers expect writing—all communication, actually—to happen in a certain way, taking into account various factors that range from how a document should look to what tone you should use to address certain people. Effective writers use these factors, or "community values," to produce effective documents.

Figure 1.2 illustrates the community basis for writing. If you and I are employees of a company, we belong to the "community" of the company. We depend on each other to get our work done. We each have roles. In one of my roles, I visit job sites to investigate items our company has installed. In one of your roles, you oversee installation, interact with clients, and make decisions about the effectiveness of our product line.

When I visit a particular site, I perform research to carry out some of my responsibilities. I examine all the appropriate items, speak to the appropriate people, and take appropriate notes. However, my responsibilities also include enabling you to carry out your responsibilities. So, when I return from the site visit, I write a memo that will enable you to act after you read it.

FIGURE 1.1
Writing Makes Action Possible.

Need: To assemble object.

Writing makes possible…

…effective action (assembly).

FIGURE 1.2
Writing Occurs Within a Community.

Writer must research site information.

Reader needs site information.

Members have roles.

Writer delivers site information to reader, who receives it.

Writing joins members together.

As I write that memo, "community" values affect the way I write. I know that you expect memos to appear in a certain format because the company has a policy about format. I know, too, that you need the information I have found. Therefore, I will write the memo in the tradition that a person in this company expects, briefly but succinctly explaining what I found. You will read the memo, grasp what I have done, and then use that material as you do your job. You in turn may have to rewrite this material into a report to give to your supervisor, thus enabling that person to act, and so on.

The writing I do is deeply affected by my awareness of what members of my community need and expect. You need certain facts; you expect a certain format. You cannot know how to act on the facts I discover until I give them to you in a memo. Technical communication is based on this sense of community. "We write in order to help someone else act" (Killingsworth and Gilbertson, *Signs* 6).

Technical Writing Is Interactive

The key to all community exchanges is that they are interactive. Readers read the words in the document, but they also apply what they know or believe from past experiences. As the words and the experiences interact, the reader in effect re-creates the memo so that it means something special to her, and that something is not exactly what the writer intended. Figure 1.3 shows how this interaction works. The writer presents a memo that tries to enable the reader to act. Acting on an awareness of community values, the writer chooses a form (memo), mentions certain facts ("too much gapping"), and interprets those facts ("the pillars are incorrect").

The reader interacts with the memo, using the document's words and format and her past experiences to make it meaningful to her. With her personal meaning, the reader may take a different course of action from the one that the writer may have intended. The excessive gapping tells the reader that the pillars are correct, but because of a different report, that the machine that built the mat and molding needs repair. The problem also tells her that the legal department needs to be informed because there is a potential contract problem. The memo is more than a report on a problem. Because the memo is read interactively, the reader constructs a meaning that tells her how to act in a situation that the writer could not have known about.

This interactive sense of writing and reading means that the document is like a blueprint from which the reader re-creates the message (Green). The reader relates to certain words and presentation techniques from a framework of expectations and experiences and makes a new message (Rude; Shriver). Communication does not occur until the reader re-creates the message.

FIGURE 1.3
Communication Is Interactive.

Writer composes memo based on facts.

Reader filters information, incorporates previous knowledge,
and anticipates future problems.

Technical Writing Has Definite Purposes

Technical writers enable their readers to act in three ways: by informing, by instructing, and by persuading (Killingsworth and Gilbertson, "How Can"). Most writers use technical writing to inform. To carry out job responsibilities, people must supply or receive information constantly. They need to know or explain the scheduled time for a meeting, the division's projected profits, the physical description of a new machine, the steps in a process, or the results of an experiment.

Writers instruct when they give readers directions for using equipment and for performing duties. Writing enables consumers to use their new purchase, whether it is a clock radio or a mainframe computer. Writing tells medical personnel exactly what to do when a patient has a heart attack.

Finally, writers persuade readers with cogent reasons to follow a particular course of action. One writer, for example, persuades readers to accept site A, not site B, for a factory. Another writer describes a bottleneck problem in a production process in order to persuade readers to implement a particular solution.

TECHNICAL WRITING IS PRESENTATIONAL

Look at the sample page shown in Figure 1.4. You can tell immediately by the presentation, or format, that the message has two main divisions, that the first division has two subdivisions, and that the text in the second division is supported by a visual aid. Technical writers frequently use this kind of revealing presentation, often called simply "format," to make the message easy to grasp (Cunningham; Hartley). The basic theory is that comprehension depends on the reader's ability to grasp an overall structure quickly (Rude; Southard). Dramatic presentation, or format, helps the reader grasp the structure of the document as well as the individual units at a glance.

To make the structure of the document obvious, technical writers follow the old rule: Tell them what you're going to say; then say it. Although presentation has many strategies, the key ones are:

- Use the top-down method.
- Use headings.
- Use chunks.
- Use visual aids.
- Establish a consistent visual logic.
- Use plain and objective language.

Use the Top-Down Method

"Top-down" means putting the main idea first. Putting the main idea first establishes the context and the outline of the discussion. In Figure 1.4, the

FIGURE 1.4
Sample Page

Technical writing is the practical writing that people do on their jobs. The goal of technical writing is to help people get work done. This memo explains two key characteristics of technical writing: audience centered and presentational.

Audience Centered. Writing is audience centered when it focuses on helping the audience. To help the audience, the writer must help the reader act and must remember community values.

> **Help Act.** Writing helps readers get a job done or increase their knowledge so they can apply it another time in their job.

> **Community Values.** Everyone who belongs to any organization agrees with or lives by some of that organization's values. The writer must be sure to not offend those values.

Presentational. Technical writing appears in a more dramatic, presentational mode than many other types of writing. Presentational strategies help readers grasp messages quickly. Two key strategies are the top-down approach and the use of heads and chunks. Figure 1 illustrates the two methods. The first sentence is the top, or main, idea. The boldfaced words are the heads, which announce topics, and the x's are the chunks or ideas.

There are two methods: heads and chunks.

Heads
xxxxxxxxxxxxxxxxxxxxxxxxxx
xxxxxxxxxxxxxxxxxxxxxxxx
xxxxxxxxxxxxxxxxxxxxxxxxxx

Chunks
xxxxxxxxxxxxxxxxxxxxxx
xxxxxxxxxxxxxxxxxxx
xxxxxxxxxxxxxxxxxxx

Figure 1. Two Presentational Strategies

Remember, to be a good technical writer, always put your audience first and always present your material in a dramatic way.

entire introduction is the top because it announces the purpose of the document. In addition, the list at the end of the introduction sets up the organization of the rest of the document. When the reader finishes the first paragraph, she or he has a clear expectation of what will happen in the rest of the message. With this expectation established, the reader can grasp the writer's point quickly.

Use Headings

Headings, or heads, are words or phrases that name the contents of the following section. Heads are top-down devices. They tell the reader what will be treated in the next section. In Figure 1.4, the boldfaced heads clearly announce the topics of their respective units. They also indicate where the units begin and end. As a result, the readers always have a "map" of the message. They know where they are and where they are going.

Use Chunks

A chunk is any block of text. The basic idea is to use a series of short blocks rather than one long block. Readers find shorter chunks easier to grasp.

Use Visual Aids

Visual aids—graphs, tables, and drawings—appear regularly in technical writing. In Figure 1.4, the visual aid reinforces the message in the text, giving an example that would be impossibly long, and ineffective, to give in writing. Writers commonly use visual aids to present collections of numerical data (tables), trends in data (graphs), and examples of action (how to insert a disk into a computer). Documents that explain experiments or projects almost always include tables or graphs. Manuals and sets of instructions rely heavily on drawings and photographs. Feasibility reports often include maps of sites. More discussion of visual aids appears in Chapter 8.

Establish a Consistent Visual Logic

A consistent visual logic means that each element of format is presented the same as other similar elements. Notice in Figure 1.4 that the heads that indicate primary subdivisions ("Audience Centered" and "Presentational") look the same: boldfaced, the first letter of each word capitalized, and placed at the left margin. Notice that the heads that indicate the secondary subdivisions ("Help Act" and "Community Values") also look like each other, but differ from the primary heads because they appear indented five spaces. Notice the position of the visual aid, placed at the left margin, and the caption of the visual aid, italicized and in a smaller print size. If there were another visual aid, it would be treated the same way. The key to this strategy is consistency. Readers quickly grasp that a certain "look" has a particular significance. Consistent treatment of the look helps the readers grasp your meaning.

Use Plain and Objective Language

Technical writers typically use plain, objective language and terminology that the audience understands. Because their purpose is to inform, instruct, or persuade a reader about a specific practical matter, technical writers use words and sentence structures that focus the reader's attention on the relevant facts. As much as possible, the words should not prompt readers to make emotional, unusual, or unreasonable interpretations about the subject. Chapter 4 discusses objective language further. The key awareness for the writer is the meaning of the phrase "that the audience understands." If the audience understands the topic thoroughly, the writer can and probably should use specific terms that experts would know. If the audience understands the term "e flute," you can use that term rather than saying "the kind of cardboard that is like a sandwich with a flat piece on top and bottom and a wavy piece in between them."

TECHNICAL WRITING IS RESPONSIBLE

Earlier sections focused on the audience and the text, but this section focuses on you, the writer. It is not enough just to help people act and to be dramatically presentational. Because readers count on you to be their guide, you must do what you can to fulfill their trust that you will tell them what—and all—they need to know. In other words, technical writing is an ethical endeavor (Griffin). The key principle here is to take responsibility for your writing (Mathes).

You take responsibility because your readers, your employer, and society—each of these groups is called a "stakeholder"—rightfully expect to find in your document all the information necessary to achieve their goals, from assembling a tricycle to opening a factory (Harcourt). According to one expert, "Ethically it is the technical writer's responsibility to [ensure] that the facts of the matter are truly represented by the choice of words" (Shimberg 60).

In the text of your documents, then, you must tell the truth and you must do all you can to ensure that your audience understands your message. To achieve both, use language and format honestly; use visuals with precision; use simple, direct expression of ideas; and credit the ideas or work of others.

Use Honest Language

Suppose, for instance, that you are writing a manual for a machine that has a sharp, whirling part under a protective cover. This dangerous part could slice off a user's fingers. When you explain how to clean the part, you inform the reader of the danger in a manner that prompts him or her to act cautiously. It would be unethical to write, "A hazard exists if contact is made with this part while it is whirling." That sentence is not urgent or specific enough to help a user prevent injury. Instead write, "Warning. Turn off all power before you remove the cover. The blade underneath could slice off your fingers!"

However, the need for unambiguous language appears in other much less dramatic situations. Take, for instance, the phrase "When I click on the hyperlink, nothing happens." Anyone familiar with hypertext knows that this message is not accurate. Something always happens—a message window appears, the cursor moves to a point on the screen that you did not expect it to, or the original screen re-forms itself. The phrasing "nothing happens" is so imprecise that it does not allow another person to act in a helpful way. How can someone fix it if she does not know what is wrong? But that phrasing also indicates a moral stance—"I am not responsible. It is your job. I will not take the time and effort to right this, whatever inconvenience it may cause you." This kind of ambiguous use of language certainly is not dangerous, the way the previous example was, but it is a refusal to take responsibility in the situation. As such, the language does not help other people achieve their goals. It is wrong, not just because it is imprecise, but because it does not help the stakeholders.

Use Format Honestly

Suppose that in a progress report you must discuss whether your department has met its production goal. The page-formatting techniques you use could either aid or hinder the reader's perception of the truth. For instance, you might use a boldface head to call attention to the department's success:

> **Widget Line Exceeds Goals.**   Once again this month, our widget line has exceeded production goals, this time by 18%.

Conversely, to downplay poor performance, you might use a more subdued format:

> Final Comments. Great strides have been made in resolving previous difficulties in meeting monthly production goals. This month's achievement is nearly equal to expectations.

If reader misunderstanding could have significant consequences, however, your use of "Final Comments" is actually a refusal to take responsibility for telling the stakeholder what he or she needs. You should use something much more obvious in order to draw the reader's attention to the problem:

SAFETY PROBLEMS INCREASE

During the past two months, problems with safety have increased even as output has increased. We must form a total quality management team to analyze this trend.

Create Helpful Visuals

Suppose readers had to know the exact location of the emergency stop button in order to operate a machine safely. To help them find the button quickly, you decide to include a visual aid. The two examples in Figure 1.5 indicate an imprecise way and a precise way of doing so.

Use Direct, Simple Expression

Say what you mean in a way that your reader will easily understand. Suppose you had to tell an operator how to deal with a problem with the flow of toxic liquid in a plant. A complex, indirect expression of a key instruction would look like this:

If there is a confirmation of the tank level rising, a determination of the source should be made.

FIGURE 1.5
Imprecise Versus Precise Visual Aids

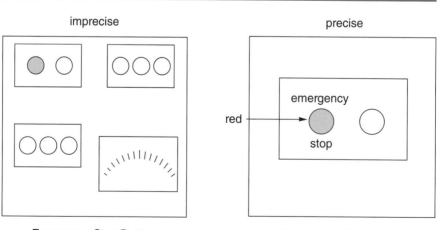

imprecise

Emergency Stop Button

precise

emergency

red

stop

Emergency Stop Button

A simple, direct expression of the same idea looks like this:

> Determine if the tank level is rising. Visually check to see if liquid is coming out of the first-floor trench.

Credit Others

Suppose a new coworker has found a way to modify a procedure and save the company money. You are assigned to write the internal proposal that suggests the change. Your obligation is to present the facts so that your manager understands who conceived the idea—and who gets the credit. To do otherwise would be to deny your coworker proper credit for the idea.

Throughout this book you will learn strategies for the clear presentation of language, format, and visual aids. Use these communication devices responsibly to ensure that your writing tells the audience everything it has a right to know. The audience trusts you because you are an expert. Be worthy of that trust.

Codes of Ethical Conduct

Many companies and most professional associations—Johnson & Johnson and the American Marketing Association, for instance—publish codes of conduct for their employees or practitioners. These codes provide guidelines for ethical action. They include a variety of topics, but several are typically addressed: fundamental honesty, adherence to the law, health and safety practices, avoidance of conflicts of interest, fairness in selling and marketing practices, and protection of the environment (Business Roundtable).

As a technical writer, you should be aware of the guidelines presented in the code of the Society for Technical Communication:

> As a technical communicator, I am the bridge between those who create ideas and those who use them. Because I recognize that the quality of my services directly affects how well ideas are understood, I am committed to excellence in performance and the highest standards of ethical behavior.
>
> I value the worth of the ideas I am transmitting and the cost of developing and communicating those ideas. I also value the time and effort spent by those who read or see or hear my communication.
>
> I therefore recognize my responsibility to communicate technical information truthfully, clearly, and economically.
>
> My commitment to professional excellence and ethical behavior means that I will
>
> ■ Use language and visuals with precision.
>
> ■ Prefer simple, direct expression of ideas.
>
> ■ Satisfy the audience's need for information, not my own need for self-expression.

- Hold myself responsible for how well my audience understands my message.
- Respect the work of colleagues, knowing that a communication problem may have more than one solution.
- Strive continually to improve my professional competence.
- Promote a climate that encourages the exercise of professional judgment and that attracts talented individuals to careers in technical communication.

■ EXERCISES

1. Make a list of several communities to which you belong (for instance, university students, this class, X corporation). Write a paragraph that explains how you used writing as a member of one of those communities to enable another member or members of the community to act. Specifically explain your word, format, and sequencing (which item you put first, which second, etc.) choices.

2. Explain a situation in which you would write to a member of a community to enable him or her to act. Identify the community and detail the kind of writing you would do and what the reader would do as a result of your writing.

3. Bring to class a piece of writing that clearly assumes that you (or the reader) belong to a particular community (good sources include newspaper stories on social issues like taxes, editorials, letters that ask for contributions). Point out the words and presentational devices that support your analysis. Alternate assignment: For a piece of writing given to you by your instructor, determine the community to which the writer assumed the reader belongs.

4. In groups of three, ask each other if the writing you do as a student or as an employee enables other people to do something. As a group, create a paragraph in which you list the kinds of people and actions that your writing affects. Use the Magolan memo (pp. 25–26) as a guide.

5. Your instructor will assign groups of three or four to read any of the following documents that appear later in this book: Bafflegab (pp. 87–88), Instructions for an Intermediate (p. 261), IMRD (pp. 296–298, 306–308, 309–311), or Informal Recommendation (pp. 298–300). After reading it, explain what made it easy or hard to grasp. Consider all the topics mentioned in this chapter. Compare notes with other people. If your instructor so requires, compose a memo that explains your results.

6. Choose one of the models at the end of a chapter in this book or a sample of writing you find in your daily life. Write a paragraph that describes how you interact with that piece of writing to gather some meaning. Describe your expectations about the way this kind of writing should look or be organized, what features of the writing led you to the main point, and any reactions to presentation language, visual aids, or context.

7. Write a paragraph that persuades a specific audience to act. Give two reasons to enroll in a certain class, to purchase a certain object, to use a certain method to solve a problem, or to accept your solution to a problem.

8. Write a paragraph that gives an audience information that they can use to act. For example, give them information on parking at your institution.

9. Draw a visual aid to enable a reader to act. Choose one of these goals: show the location of an object in relation to other objects (machines in a lab; rooms in a building); show someone how to perform an act (how to insert a disk into a computer; how to hold a hammer); show why one item is better than another (cost to purchase an object like a stereo or a TV or class notebooks; features of two objects).

10. Research your library's electronic card catalog. Write a paragraph that alerts your instructor to commands, screens, or rules that will give students trouble if they are not aware of them ("use ^u to go up on the screen"; "the log-in word must be typed in lower case"; "the library closes at 9:00 P.M. on Fridays").

11. Research a database available through your library's electronic catalog. Tell students about at least two types of material in the database (abstracts of articles, U.S. demographic information), and explain how that material will help them.

12. Analyze the following paragraph to decide who the audience is and what their need is; then rewrite it for a different audience with a different need. For instance, you might recount it as a set of instructions or use it to tell a person what objects to buy for this step and why.

The fixing solution removes any unwanted particles that may still be in the paper. This process is what clears the print and makes the image more "crisp." The photographer slips the print into the fixing solution, making sure it is entirely submerged. He or she will agitate the print occasionally while it is in the fixer. After two minutes, he or she may turn the room lights on and examine the print. The total fixing time should be no less than 2 minutes and no more than 30 minutes. After the fixing process is over, the print then needs to be washed.

13. Arrange the following block of information into meaningful chunks. Some chunks may contain only several sentences.

In response to a Technical Writing assignment, I interviewed UW-Stout's Athletic Trainer, Mike Raemaker, to gain insight on the types of writing encountered in the health professions. As a health care professional, I will have to be proficient in writing many types of documents to inform people who are on a variety of knowledge levels, thereby increasing their decision-making ability. According to Mr. Raemaker, health professionals are responsible for many forms of writing. I will have to write daily injury reports, progress notes, clinical evaluation, proposals for equipment, grants for funding, medical supply orders, and possibly articles for publication in magazines or journals. Daily injury reports include information on signs and symptoms of injury, how injury was sustained, observations of professionals, and a treatment regimen. Progress notes are sporadically added to the patient's file and deal with recovery progress and adjustments to the rehabilitation program. Clinical evaluations contain information on patients' past medical history, current chief health concern, and the diagnosis, and are used frequently in referral to other health specialists. Proposals for equipment and grants for funding are considered longer documents and are used to improve your facility with new equipment. Medical supply orders are used to maintain supplies, and published articles usually deal with your area of expertise. My writing will be directed at people who know more, less, or equal amounts of information about my subject. This information will give them information enabling them to make decisions. I will write to physical therapists, physicians, athletic trainers, health centers, pharmaceutical firms, patients, and "people with deep pockets." These contacts will have high levels of knowledge in their profession, and their insight will aid in the rehabilitation of a patient. For example, clinical evaluations are used to inform other professionals of a patient's overall condition, and they will incorporate this information in their future decisions and diagnosis. "People with deep pockets" refers to individuals in industries who are potential financial donors. Effective, clear written communication in the health profession is extremely important. A grant needs to be well written if it is to be clearly understood and accepted. Well-written grants and journal articles may go on my résumé and could aid in professional advancement. Writing to other professionals about patient concerns will give evidence of personal ability but will not promote career advancement.

14. In groups of three or four, analyze the following sample memo. Explain how the memo enables a reader to act, demonstrates its purpose, and uses specific practices to help the reader grasp that purpose. If your instructor so requires, create a visual aid that would encourage a reader to agree with the recommendation (perhaps a table that reveals all the results at a glance) and/or create another memo to show

how the memo is ethical. Your instructor will ask one or two groups
to report to the class.

DATE: April 1, 2004
TO: Isaac Sparks
FROM: Keith Munson
SUBJECT: Recommendation on whether we should issue bicycles to
the maintenance department

Introduction

As you requested, I have investigated the proposal about issuing bicycles
to the maintenance department and have presented my recommendation in this memo. I consulted with a company that has already implemented this idea and with our maintenance department. The decision
I made was based on five criteria:

- Would machine downtime be reduced?
- Is the initial cost under $5000?
- Will maintenance actually use them?
- Will maintaining them be a problem?
- Are the bicycles safe?

Recommendation

Through my investigation, I have found that the company could realize
substantial savings by implementing the proposal and still sufficiently
satisfy all the criteria. Therefore, I fully recommend it.

Would Machine Downtime Be Reduced? Yes. There would be less machine downtime if bicycles were used because maintenance could get to
the machines faster and have an average of 2 hours more per day to
work on them. This could save the company approximately $500 a week
by reducing lost production time.

Is the Initial Cost Under $5000? Yes. The initial cost of approximately
$1500 is well within our financial limitations.

Will Maintenance Actually Use Them? Yes. I consulted with the maintenance department and found that all would use the bicycles if it became
company policy. The older men felt that biking, instead of walking,
would result in their fatiguing more slowly.

Will Maintaining Them Be a Problem? No. The maintenance required is
minimal, and parts are very cheap and easy to install.

Are the Bicycles Safe? Yes. OSHA has no problem with bicycles in the
plant as long as each is equipped with a horn.

15. Interview a professional in your field of interest. Choose an instructor whom you know or a person who does not work on campus. Ask questions about the importance of writing to that person's job. Questions you might ask include

   ■ How often do you write each day or week?

   ■ How important is what you write to the successful performance of your job?

   ■ Is writing important to your promotion?

   ■ What would be a major fault in a piece of writing in your profession?

   ■ What are the features of writing (clarity, organization, spelling, and so on) that you look for in someone else's writing and strive for in your own?

   Write a one-page memo in which you present your findings. Your instructor may ask you to read your memo to your classmates.

16. Perform this exercise individually or in a group, as your instructor requires. Assume that you work for a manufacturer of one of the following items: (a) electric motors, (b) industrial cranes, (c) microprocessing chips, or (d) a product typical of the kind of organization that employs you now or that will when you graduate. Assume that you have discovered a flaw in the product. This flaw will eventually cause the product to malfunction, but probably not before the warranty period has expired. The malfunction is not life threatening. Write a memo recommending a course of action.

17. In groups of three or four, react to the memos written for Exercise 16. Do not react to your own memo. If all individuals wrote memos, pick a memo from someone not in your group. If groups wrote the memos, pick the memo of another group. Prepare a memo for one group (customers, salespeople, manufacturing division) affected by the recommendation. Explain to them any appropriate background, and clarify how the recommendation will affect them. Your instructor will ask for oral reports of your actions.

18. You have just learned that the malfunction discussed in Exercises 16 and 17 *is* life threatening. Write new memos. Your instructor will ask for oral reports of your actions.

■ WEB EXERCISE

Analyze a Web site to determine how it fills the characteristics of technical writing explained in this chapter. Use any site unless your instructor directs you to a certain type (e.g., major corporation, research and development site, professional society). Write a memo or IMRD (see Chapter 12) in which you explain your findings to your classmates or coworkers.

■ WORKS CITED

Allen, Nancy J. "Community, Collaboration, and the Rhetorical Triangle." *Technical Communication Quarterly* 2.1 (1993): 63–74.

Business Roundtable. "The Rationale for Ethical Corporate Behavior." *Business Ethics* 90/90. Ed. John E. Richardson. Guilford, CT: Dushkin, 1989. 204–207. Originally published in *Business and Society Review* 20 (1988): 33–36.

Collins, Robert C. Letter to Art Muller, packaging concentration coordinator, The Dial Corp. Scottsdale, AZ. 8 March 1994.

Cunningham, Donald. Presentation. CCC Convention. Minneapolis. 20 March 1985.

Green, Georgia M. "Linguistics and the Pragmatics of Language Use." *Poetics* 11 (1982): 45–76.

Griffin, Jack. "When Do Rhetorical Choices Become Ethical Choices?" *Technical Communication and Ethics*. Ed. R. John Brockman and Fern Rook. Arlington, VA: Society for Technical Communication, 1989. 63–70. Originally published in *Proceedings of the 27th International Technical Communication Conference* (Washington, DC: STC, 1980).

Hall, Dean G., and Bonnie A. Nelson. "Integrating Professional Ethics into the Technical Writing Course." *Journal of Technical Writing and Communication* 17.1 (1987): 45–61. Exercises 16–18 are based on material from this article.

Harcourt, Jules. "Developing Ethical Messages: A Unit of Instruction for the Basic Business Communication Course." *The Bulletin of the Association for Business Communication* 53 (1990): 17–20.

Hartley, Peter. "Writing for Industry: The Presentational Mode versus the Reflective Mode." *The Technical Writing Teacher* 18.2 (1991): 162–169.

Killingsworth, M. Jimmie, and Michael Gilbertson. "How Can Text and Graphics Be Integrated Effectively?" *Solving Problems in Technical Writing*. Ed. Lynn Beene and Peter White. New York: Oxford, 1988, 130–149.

Killingsworth, M. Jimmie, and Michael Gilbertson. *Signs, Genres, and Communities in Technical Communication*. Amityville. NY: Baywood, 1992. The material on community and interaction is based on ideas developed in this book.

Mathes, J. C. "Assuming Responsibility: An Effective Objective in Teaching Technical Writing." *Technical Communication and Ethics*. Ed. R. John Brockman and Fern Rook. Arlington, VA: Society for Technical Communication, 1989. 89–90. Originally published in *Proceedings of the Technical Communication Sessions at the 32nd Annual Meeting of the Conference on College Composition and Communication* (Dallas, TX: NASA Publication 2203, 1981).

Pinelli, Thomas E., Myron Glassman, Rebecca O. Barclay, and Walter E. Oliu. *Technical Communications in Aeronautics: Results of an Exploratory Study—An Analysis of Managers' and Non-managers' Responses*. NASATM-101625. Washington, DC: National Aeronautics and Space Administration, August 1989. (Available from NTIS, Springfield, VA.)

Rude, Carolyn D. "Format in Instruction Manuals: Applications of Existing Research." *Journal of Business and Technical Communication* 2 (1988): 63–77.

Selzer, Jack. "Arranging Business Prose." *New Essays in Technical and Scientific Communication: Research, Theory, Practice.* Ed. Paul V. Anderson, R. John Brockman, and Carolyn Giller. Farmingdale, NY: Baywood, 1983, 37–54.

Shimberg, Lee H. "Ethics and Rhetoric in Technical Writing." *Technical Communication and Ethics.* Ed. R. John Brockman and Fern Rook. Arlington, VA: Society for Technical Communication, 1989, 54–62. Originally published in *Technical Communication* 25 (Fourth Quarter 1978).

Shriver, Karen. *Dynamics in Document Design: Creating Texts for Readers.* NY: Wiley, 1997.

Society for Technical Communication. *Code for Communicators.* Washington, DC: STC, n.d.

Southard, Sherry. "Practical Considerations in Formatting Manuals." *Technical Communication* 35.3 (Third Quarter 1988): 173–178.

2 Defining Audiences

Chapter 2
IN A NUTSHELL

You write a different document based on how you define your audience. Because your understanding of your audience controls so many of your writing decisions, analyze the audience before you write. The key ideas are

- Who are they?
- How much do they know?
- What do they expect?

Find out who your audience is. Is it one person or a group or several groups? Are you writing a memo to a specific individual or instructions for "typical" workers?

Estimate how much they know. If they are advanced, they know what terms mean, and they understand the implications of sentences. If you are addressing beginners, you have to explain more.

Determine expectations. Expectations are the factors that could make an audience see the document differently than you intend. Will the document be interesting? Will it help them to perform a task? Will it conform to their sense of what this kind of document should look and sound like?

  Keeping a clear image of your audience as you write will help you decide how to handle the inevitable presentation and content problems.

Every piece of technical writing has an intended audience—the reader or readers of the document. Because the writer's goal is to enable that audience to act, the presence of the audience affects all of a writer's decisions, from planning, organization, and tone to visual aids, sentence structure, and word choice.

This chapter helps you make informed decisions about your audience and your document design. You learn to investigate the audience's knowledge level, its role in the situation, its attitudes, and its place in the organization, and to apply that knowledge in developing effective documents.

AN EXAMPLE OF TECHNICAL WRITING

The following memo illustrates how writers communicate. Todd Magolan performs routine inspections of thick rubber cargo mats that fit into the bed of special hauling equipment in manufacturing facilities. He reports on their performance to his supervisor, Marjorie Sommers. Sommers uses the reports to determine whether or not her company has met the conditions of its contract and to decide whether or not to change manufacturing specifications.

As you read the memo, note the following points:

1. The writer names the audience (Marjorie Sommers) and states the purpose of the memo for the audience (to deliver information on his impressions).

2. The writer uses objective language to focus on the specific parts of the cargo mat (trim lines, holes, kick plate) and to point out specific problems ("the front edge of vinyl/maratex still needs to be evaluated with a base kick plate"). Note that the writer uses the word "good" to mean "implements the specification exactly," knowing that his audience understands that usage.

3. The information is presentational, appearing in easy-to-scan chunks set off by heads. The writer sets up the document in the first paragraph by naming the three items—the 410, 430, and 480 mats—that he discusses in the body of the memo. He repeats these key words as section headings, presents information in a consistent pattern (vinyl/maratex, hole location, concerns) for each section, and numbers individual points within sections.

4. The writer uses a visual aid—the drawing—to convey a problem discussed in the 480 section (Figure 1).

5. The writing is responsible. The writer tells the stakeholder (Sommers) all that she needs to know to be able to do her job. In addition, the

memo treats other stakeholders properly. Magolan's company, for instance, has informed individuals handling its affairs. The customer has received honest treatment of the problem, allowing them to interact with Magolan's company in an informed manner.

Date:	3-15-03	
To:	Marjorie Sommers	Audience named
From:	Todd Magolan	
Subject:	Review of Mats at Oxbow Creek Plant	

After seeing the 410 and 430 Cargo mats, as well as the 480 Front mat, installed in the vehicles at Oxbow Creek, my impressions of each are as follows:

Introduction "sets up" discussion

Purpose

410 CARGO

Heading

1. The rear and side vinyl/maratex both fit. (The rear kick plate fits perfectly.)
2. All hole locations were good.
3. The front edge of vinyl/maratex was not evaluated because there was no base kick plate for the front.

Unemotional presentation

Assumes audience knowledge

Overall, I feel that the 410 Cargo mat fit was very good. However, the front edge of vinyl/maratex still needs to be evaluated with a base kick plate.

430 CARGO

Words repeated as section heads

1. With our revised vinyl and maratex trim lines, I feel the mat fit excellent. There was no pull out of the kick plate such as we noticed before.
2. All trim lines and holes are now good.

Chunking of information

It is my feeling that our proposed design is much more functional than the original design and should be incorporated if feasible.

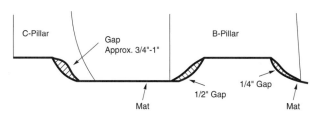

FIGURE 1
480 B-Pillar and C-Pillar Gap Problems

480 FRONT

Words repeated as section heads

1. All trim lines seemed good.

2. Hole locations were good. There was a little concern/suggestion that the rear group of holes (for the rear seat) be moved outward a few millimeters. The added lytherm seemed to bring them inward slightly.

3. The major concerns came in the B- and C-pillar areas (see attached sketch). There is much gapping between our mat and the molding. It is most evident in the C-pillar area. It is my opinion that our mat is correct in being molded to the sheet metal contour (in the C pillar) and that the pillars themselves are incorrect.

Chunking of information

If you have any questions or would like to discuss these findings further, please let me know.

This brief memo illustrates the skills and attitudes that technical writers employ. Although the memo is a straightforward report of a site visit, it is nonetheless a well-crafted document that effectively conveys the information that writer and reader need to fulfill their roles in the organization. To see a document that uses many of the same strategies to fulfill the needs of a much different audience, turn to the "Bafflegab" model on pages 87–88.

HOW MUCH DOES YOUR AUDIENCE KNOW ABOUT THE TOPIC?

Every audience has a *knowledge level,* the amount they know about the subject matter of the document. This level ranges from expert to layperson (or nonexpert). An expert audience understands the basic terminology, facts, concepts, and implications associated with the topic. A lay audience is intelligent but not well informed about the topic. Knowing how much the audience knows helps you choose which information to present and in what depth to explain it.

Finding Out What Your Audience Knows

Discovering what the audience knows is a key activity for any writer. To estimate an audience's knowledge level, you can employ several strategies (Selzer; Odell et al.; Coney).

Ask Them Before You Write. If you personally know members of the audience, ask them in a phone call or brief conversation how much they know about the topic.

Ask Them After You Write.   Ask the audience to indicate on your draft where the concepts are unfamiliar or the presentation is unclear.

Ask Someone Else.   If you cannot ask the audience directly, ask someone who knows or has worked with the audience.

Consider the Audience's Position.   If you know what duties and responsibilities the audience members have, you can often estimate which concepts they will be familiar with.

Consider Prior Contacts.   If you have had dealings with the audience before, recall the extent of their knowledge about the topic.

Adapting to Your Audience's Knowledge Level

You adapt to your audience's knowledge level by building on their schemata—that is, on concepts they have formed from prior experiences (Huckin). The basic principles are: *Add to what the audience knows, and do not labor what they already know.* If the audience knows a term or concept (has a schema for it), simply present it. But if the audience does not know the term or concept (because they have no schema), you must help them grasp it and add it to their schemata.

Suppose for one section of a report you have to discuss a specific characteristic of a digitized sound. If the reader has a "digitized sound schema," you can use just the appropriate terminology to convey a world of meaning. But if the reader does not have this schema, you must find a way to help him or her develop it. The following two examples illustrate how writers react to knowledge level.

For a More Knowledgeable Audience.   For a more knowledgeable audience, a writer may use this sentence:

That format allows only 8-bit sampling.

The knowledgeable reader knows the definitions of the terms "format" and "8-bit." He or she also understands the implication of the wording, which is that the sound will not reproduce as accurately if it is sampled at 8 bits, but that the file will take up more disk space.

For a Less Knowledgeable Audience.   A less knowledgeable audience, however, grasps neither the definitions nor the implications. To develop a schema for such readers, the writer must build on the familiar by explaining concepts, formatting the page to emphasize information, making comparisons to the familiar, and pointing out implications. You might convey the same information about sampling to a less knowledgeable audience in the following manner (Stern and Littieri 146).

In many ways it helps to think of digitized sound as being analogous to digitized video.	Explanation of concept
Digitized sound is actually composed of a sequence of individual sound samples. The number of samples per second is called the *sample rate* and is very much like a video track's frame rate. The more sound samples per second, the higher the quality of the resulting sound. However, more sound samples also take up more space on disk and mean that more data need to be processed during every second of playback. (The amount of data that must be processed every second is called the *data rate*.)	Highlighted text Implication of explanation
Sound samples can be of different sizes. Just as you can reproduce a photograph more faithfully by storing it as a 24-bit (full-color) image than as an 8-bit image, 16-bit sound samples represent audio more accurately than 8-bit sound samples. We refer to the size of those samples as a sound's *sample size*. As with the sampling rate, a larger sample size increases the accuracy of the sound at the expense of more storage space and a higher data rate.	Analogy Highlighted text Implications

To see more about writing for a less knowledgeable audience, refer to Chapter 9, "Defining."

▪ **EXERCISES**

---

1. Write three different sentences in which you use a technical concept to explain three situations to a person who knows as much as you do. (Example: "You can't print that because the printer doesn't have that font in memory." In this sentence, the writer assumes that the reader understands font, memory, font in memory, and the relationship of memory to printing.)

---

2. Rewrite one of the three sentences in Exercise 1 into a larger paragraph that makes the same idea clear to someone who knows less than you do.

---

3. Analyze one paragraph of the Bafflegab article (pp. 87–88) to determine the assumed knowledge level of the audience.

WHAT IS THE AUDIENCE'S ROLE IN THE SITUATION?

In any writing situation, your audience has a role. Like actors in a drama, audience members play a part, using the document as a "script." They perform actions after receiving the information in your document. Those who take the most active roles are users and decision makers. Users need a document that gives specific instructions for physically carrying out a process. Decision makers need documents that give them information they can use to come to an informed decision.

A good writer changes a document to accommodate different audience roles. The topic (and even the subtopics) may be similar, but the documents will be quite different because of the different roles of the intended audiences. To determine your audience's role, ask these questions:

- ■ Who will read this document?
- ■ What is the audience's need?
- ■ How does the writer's goal fulfill the audience's need?
- ■ What is the audience's task?

Who Will Read This Document?

The audience could be a single person (your supervisor), a small group (members of a committee), or a large group (the readers of a user manual). Sometimes you have both a primary audience, the person to whom you address the document, and a secondary audience, other people who could read it for information but not immediate action.

What Is the Audience's Need?

Why is the reader concerned with the content of the document? Marjorie Sommers needs Todd Magolan's memo to fulfill her role in the organization. She must be assured that the mats serve the purpose for which they were sold. She needs to be aware of possible problems so that she can keep the customer happy with the product and with the company's service. She must be able to explain to her supervisor how her department is functioning. She needs to know if she should talk to people in manufacturing about the fabrication of the part.

Sommers's need for the information itself, the content of the memo, is only one aspect of her needs. She must use that information in different ways with various people—the customer and other people in the company. In short, she needs the information to help her carry out her job responsibilities.

How Does the Writer's Goal Fulfill the Audience's Need?

As a writer, your basic goal is to enable your audience to act. You do so by creating a specific message that has a specific purpose. You need to answer two questions:

- What is my basic message?
- What is my purpose?

In general, your message is the basic facts you want to present; your purpose is to inform, instruct, or persuade your audience. The combination of the two is your goal. For instance, if your goal is to inform the reader of the results of a survey, you should write a memo that enables the reader to find the correct data. If your goal is to persuade the reader to act in a certain manner because of the data, you should write a report that clearly points out the significance of the data and the action they support.

As an example, Todd Magolan's purpose is to inform Sommers of the facts of the visit, and the message is that the product is performing as required by the contract.

What Is the Audience's Task?

What will the reader do after reading the document? *Need* is why the audience is involved in the situation. This involvement can have many factors, but a key one is a need for information that will allow the reader to carry out a task demanded by a role.

You can easily see the different effects of need by considering two audiences: operators of a machine and their department managers. Both groups need information, but of different kinds. Operators need to know the sequence of steps that make the machine run: how to turn it on and off, how to set it to perform its intended actions, and how to troubleshoot if anything goes wrong. Managers need to know whether to purchase the machine because it is a useful addition to the workstation. They need to know whether the machine's capabilities will benefit staff and budget. They need to know that the machine has a variable output that can be changed to meet the changing flow of orders in the plant; that the personnel on the floor can easily perform routine maintenance on the machine without outside help; and that problems such as jamming can be easily corrected.

Because the needs differ from the tasks, the documents directed at each are different. For the operator, the document would be a manual, with lots of numbered how-to-do-it steps, photos or drawings of important parts, and an index that allows the operator to find relevant information quickly.

For the manager, the document would contain explanatory paragraphs rather than numbered how-to-do-it steps. Instead of photos, you might use a line graph that shows the effect of the variable rate of production or a table that illustrates budget, cost, or savings.

Therefore, Marjorie Sommers will file the cargo mat memo for future reference in case a problem, especially with the 480, arises. First, though, she will alert her superiors to the problem with the pillars. Because Todd feels the problem is the customer's, Sommers will not ask manufacturing to change their process. But because she has been informed, she will have the facts she needs if she must act at a later date.

Is There More than One Audience?

Sometimes a document has more than one audience. In these situations, you must decide whether to write for the primary or the secondary audience. The *primary audience* is the person actually addressed in the document. A *secondary audience* is someone other than the intended receiver who will also read the document. Often you must write with such a reader in mind. The secondary reader is often far from the writer, so the document must be formal. The following two examples illustrate how a writer changes a document to accommodate primary and secondary audiences.

Suppose you have to write a memo to your supervisor requesting money to travel to a convention so that you can give a speech. This memo is just for your supervisor's reference; all he needs is a brief notice for his records. As an informal memo intended for a primary audience, it might read like this:

March 19, 2005
John,

This is my formal request for $750 in travel money to give my speech about widgets to the annual Society of Manufacturing Engineers convention in San Antonio in May. Thanks for your help with this.

Fred

Informal use of name

No formatting of document

If this brief note is all your supervisor needs, neither a long, formal proposal with a title page and table of contents nor a formal business letter would be appropriate. The needs of the primary audience dictate the form and content of this memo.

Suppose, however, that your supervisor has to show the memo to his manager for her approval. In that case, a brief, informal memo would be inappropriate. His manager might not understand the significance of the trip or might need to know that your work activities will be covered. In this new situation, your document might look like this:

Date:	March 19, 2005	
To:	John Jones	A more official
From:	Fred Johnson	format, including
Subject:	Travel money for speech to Society of Man-	formal use of
	ufacturing Engineers convention	names

As I mentioned to you in December, I will be the keynote speaker at the Annual Convention of the Society of Man-ufacturing Engineers in San Antonio. I would like to re-quest $750 to defray part of my expenses for that trip.

Orients reader to background and makes request

This group, the major manufacturing engineering so-ciety in the country, has agreed to print the speech in the conference *Proceedings* so that our work in widget qual-ity control will receive wide readership in M.E. circles. The society has agreed to pay $250 toward expenses, but the whole trip will cost about $1000.

Explains back-ground of request

I will be gone four days, May 1–4; Warren Lang has agreed to cover my normal duties during that time. Work on the Acme Widget project is in such good shape that I can leave it for those few days. May I make an appoint-ment to discuss this with you?

Adds detail that primary audience knows

As you can see, this document differs considerably from the first memo. It treats the relationship and the request much more formally. It also explains the significance of the trip so that the manager, your secondary audience, will have all the information she needs to respond to the request.

▪ EXERCISES

4. Write a brief set of instructions (three to six steps) to teach an audience how to use a feature of a machine—for instance, the enlarge/reduce feature on a photocopier or the proper method of moving the cursor on a computer. Then exchange your instructions with a partner. After in-terviewing the partner to learn the procedure, rewrite the instructions into a paragraph that explains the value of the feature to a manager.

5. Analyze either the memo in Exercise 14, Chapter 1 (pp. 19–20), or the memo in Example 15.2 (pp. 405–406) in order to determine the audience's need and task. Be prepared to report your findings orally to the class.

6. The site-visit memo on pages 25–26 is aimed at an audience of one. Rewrite it so that it includes a secondary audience who is interested in customer relations. If the subject matter of that memo is too unfamiliar to you, use a subject you know well (in-line fillers or a client's computer network).

WHAT ARE THE AUDIENCE'S COMMUNITY ATTITUDES?

Community attitudes are the expectations a reader has when he or she reads a document. They arise from the reader's role in the community, the social situation, and the feelings about the message and the sender. These attitudes powerfully affect the way readers read. These factors (based on Odell et al.) help you determine their attitudes:

- What consequences will occur from this idea?
- What is the history of this idea?
- How much power does the reader have?
- How formal is the situation?
- How does the reader feel about the subject?
- How does the reader feel about the sender?
- What form does the reader expect?

What Consequences Will Occur from This Idea?

Consequences are the effects of a person's actions on the organization. If the effect of your suggestion would be to violate an OSHA standard, your suggestion will be turned down. If the effect would be to make a profit, the idea probably will be accepted.

What Is the History of This Idea?

History is the situation prior to your writing. You need to show that you understand that situation; otherwise, you will be dismissed as someone who does not understand the implications of what you are saying. If your suggestion to change a procedure indicates that you do not know that a similar change failed several years ago, your suggestion probably will be rejected.

How Much Power Does the Reader Have?

Power is the supervisory relationship of the author and the reader. Supervisors have more power. Orders flow from supervisors to subordinates, and suggestions move in the reverse. The more powerful the reader, the less likely the document is to give orders and the more likely it is to make suggestions (Driskill; Selzer; Fielden).

How Formal Is the Situation?

Formality is the degree of impersonality in the document. In many situations, you are expected to act in an official capacity rather than as a personality. For an oral presentation to a board meeting concerning a multimillion-dollar planning decision, you would simply act as the person who knows about widgets. You would try to submerge personal idiosyncrasies, such as joking or sarcasm, for example. Generally, the more formal the situation, the more impersonal the document.

How Does the Reader Feel About the Subject?

The reader's feelings can be described as positively inclined, neutral, or negatively inclined toward the topic or the writer. If the audience is *positively inclined,* a kind of shared community can be set up rather easily. In such a situation, many of the "small details" won't make as much difference; the form that is chosen is not so important, and the document can be brief and informal. Words that have some emotional bias can be used without causing an adverse reaction.

Much the same is true of an audience that is *neutral.* A writer who has to send a neutral audience a message about a meeting or the results of a meeting might choose a variety of forms, perhaps a memo, or just a brief note. As long as the essential facts are present, the message will be communicated.

However, if the audience is *negatively inclined,* the writer cannot assume a shared community. The small details must be attended to carefully. Spelling, format, and word choice become even more important than usual because negatively inclined readers may seize upon anything that lets them vent their frustration or anger. Even such seemingly trivial documents as the announcement of a meeting can become a source of friction to an audience that is negatively inclined.

The cargo mat topic is of low importance to Marjorie Sommers now, because the inspection was routine. However, it could become very important if customer satisfaction with the mats diminishes and the legal implications of the contract are called into question.

Other factors may make even a neutral or a positively inclined audience more wary. For example, how important is it to their job responsibilities? Do they believe the topic is complicated by legal or personnel implications? If they regard the topic as important or complicated, they will pay more attention and you will have to be careful to adequately cover all aspects of it.

How Does the Reader Feel About the Sender?

A writer must establish a relationship with the reader. The relationship is affected by the writer's credibility and authority. As a technical writer, you are credible because of your role or your actions. If readers know that you are the quality control engineer, they will believe what you write on a quality issue. If readers know that you have followed a standard or at least a clear method of investigating a topic, they will believe you.

In addition, readers feel positively about a message if they feel that it is organized around their needs and if they "feel that someone has taken the time to speak clearly, knowledgeably, and honestly to them" (Shriver 204). Karen Shriver points out, in *Dynamics in Document Design*, that a group of African-American teenagers resisted an antidrug brochure because they felt, based on the comments and illustrations in the brochure, that the writers seemed to be only people who had noticed the problem, not people who were doing something about it. Once this values perception occurred, the document lost credibility and was negatively received (204).

Sommers is positively inclined toward Todd Magolan. Magolan knows that Sommers likes and trusts him because they have worked together for a while. Todd knows that Sommers is the supervisor and expects clear information without much comment.

Todd establishes credibility in the first paragraph by explaining his methodology—he inspected the site. He clearly feels that he has the authority to make evaluative comments that suggest future actions (incorporate the proposed design, not the original one). His tone is informal, using "I" and "you" liberally; notice, too, that he is comfortable enough to use a short, no-nonsense list structure. In short, Todd presents himself as a person whom the reader can trust.

Authority means that you have the sense that you can present messages that readers will take seriously. Basically you have the right to speak because you have expertise, gained by either your role or your actions. Naturally this authority is limited. Your report is authoritative enough to be the basis for company policy, even though you might not be the one who actually sets the policy. Developing the appropriate "sound," or voice, in the situation is difficult. The easiest way to begin to think about this concern is whether you want to sound informal or formal, use "I" and "you" or not.

What Form Does the Reader Expect?

Many audiences expect certain types of messages to take certain forms. To be effective, you must provide the audience with a document in the form they expect. For instance, a manager who wants a brief note to keep for handy reference may be irritated if he gets a long, detailed business letter. An electronics expert who wants information on a certain circuit probably won't want a prose discussion because it is customary to convey that information through schematics and specifications. If an office manager has set up a form for reporting accidents, she expects reports in that form. If she gets exactly the form that she specified, her attitude may easily turn from neutral to positively inclined. If she gets a different form, her attitude may change from neutral to negatively inclined.

Marjorie Sommers expects an informal memo that she can skim over easily, getting all the main points. She expects that this memo, like all that she receives reporting on site visits, will have the usual lines (Date, To, From, Subject) at the top and heads to break up the text. Todd knows that the message must be brief (one to two pages), that its method of production must be a word processor, and that it must appear on 8½ × 11 paper.

In this book each chapter explains a "usual form." The guidelines given will put you "in the ballpark" of how to write the type of document under consideration. However, you can and must be ready to adapt the usual form to the requirements of the readers and situation.

■ EXERCISES

---

7. Write a brief memo in which you propose a change to a more powerful, positively inclined audience. Use an emotional topic, such as eliminating all reserved parking at your institution or putting a child care room in every building. Before you write, answer the attitude questions on page 33. In a group of three or four, explain how your memo reflects the answers you gave to the attitude questions.

---

8. Analyze this brief message to determine whether you should rewrite it. Assume it is written to a less powerful, negatively inclined audience (Kostelnick). If you decide it needs revision, rewrite it. If your instructor so requires, discuss your revisions in groups of three.

   Thank you for your recent proposal on the 4-day 10-hour-a-day week. We have rejected it because:

   It is too short.

   It is too narrow-minded.

   It has too many errors.

---

9. In class, set up either of these two role-playing situations. In each, let one person be the manager, and let two others be employees in a department. In the first situation, the employees propose a change, and the manager is opposed to it. In the second, the employees propose a change, and the manager agrees but asks pointed questions because

the vice-president disagrees. In each case, plan how to approach the manager, and then role-play the situation. Suggestions for proposed changes include: switching to a 4-day, 10-hour-a-day week; instituting recreational free time for employees; and having a random drawing to determine parking spaces instead of assigning the spaces closest to the building to executives. After you complete the role playing, write a memo to the manager requesting the change. Take into consideration all you found out in the role playing.

10. In groups of three or four, agree on a situation in which you will propose a radical change, perhaps that each class building at your college contain a child care room. Plan how to approach an audience that feels positive about this subject. For instance, which arguments, formats, and visual aids would be persuasive? Then write the memo as a group. For the next class, each person should bring a memo that requests the same change but addresses an audience that is neutral or negative (you choose) about this subject. Discuss the way you changed the original plan to accommodate the new audience. As a group, select the best memo and read it to the class.

■ WORKSHEET FOR DEFINING YOUR AUDIENCE

❑ *Who will read this document?*
Name the primary reader or readers.
Name any secondary readers.

❑ *Determine the audience's level of knowledge.*
What terms do they know?
What concepts do they know?
Do they need chronological background?
To find your reader's knowledge level, you must (1) ask them directly, (2) ask someone else who is familiar with them, or (3) make an educated guess.

❑ *Determine the audience's role.*
What will they do as a result of your document?
Have you presented the document so they can take action easily?
Why do they need your document? for reference? to take to someone else for approval? to make a decision?

❏ *Determine the audience's community attitudes.*
What are the social factors in the situation?
Is the audience negatively or positively inclined toward the message?
Toward you?
What format, tone, and visuals will make them feel that you are focused on their needs?

❏ *What form does the audience expect?*

▦ WRITING ASSIGNMENTS

1. Interview one or two professionals in your field whose duties include writing. Find out what kinds of audiences they write for by asking a series of questions. Write a memo summarizing your findings. Your goal is to characterize the audiences for documents in your professional area. Here are some questions that you might find helpful:

    ▪ What are two or three common types of documents that you write (proposals? sets of instructions? informational memos? letters?)?

    ▪ Do your audiences usually know a lot or a little about the topic of the document?

    ▪ Do you try to find out about your audience before you write or as you write?

    ▪ What questions do you ask about your audience before you write?

    ▪ Do you change your sentence construction, sentence length, or word choice to suit your audience? If so, how?

    ▪ Do you ever ask someone in your intended audience to read an early draft of a document?

    ▪ Does your awareness of audience power or inclination affect the way you write a document?

    ▪ Does your awareness of the history of a situation affect the way you write a document?

    ▪ Do you ever write about the same topic to different audiences? If yes, are the documents different?

    ▪ Do you ever write one document aimed at multiple audiences? If yes, how do you handle this problem?

2. Write two different paragraphs about a topic that you know thoroughly in your professional field. Write the first to a person with your level of knowledge. Write the second to a person who knows little about the topic. After you have completed these two paragraphs, make notes on the writing decisions you made to accommodate the knowledge level of each audience. Be prepared to discuss your notes with classmates on the day you hand in your paragraphs. Your topic may describe a concept, an evaluating method, a device, or a process. Below are some suggestions; if none applies to your field, choose your own topic or ask your instructor for suggestions.

Using a Web search engine

A machining process used in wood

Finding an address on the Internet

The MHz rating of a computer chip

Cranking amps of a battery

The dots-per-inch feature of a laser printer

Process for welding magnesium

A pH meter

The food pyramid

The relation of calories to grams

Registering for a class

Antilock brakes

Planning decisions for a desktop-published brochure

Just-in-time manufacturing

3. Form groups of three or four. If possible, the people in each group should have the same major or professional interest. Decide on a short process (four to ten steps) that you want to describe to others. As a group, analyze the audience knowledge and then write the description.

Alternate: After writing the memo, plan and write the same description for an audience with different characteristics than your first audience.

▪ WEB EXERCISE

Analyze a Web site to determine how the authors of the site "envision" their readers. What have they assumed about the readers in terms of knowledge and needs, role and community attitudes? Write an analytical report to your classmates or coworkers in which you explain strategies they should adopt as they develop their Web sites.

■ WORKS CITED

Coney, Mary. "Technical Communication Theory: An Overview." *Foundations for Teaching Technical Communication: Theory, Practice, and Program Design.* Ed. Katherine Staples and Cezar Ornatowski. Greenwich, CT: Ablex, 1997. 1–16.

Driskill, Linda. "Understanding the Writing Context in Organizations." *Writing in the Business Professions.* Ed. Myra Kogen. Urbana, IL: NCTE, 1989. 125–145.

Fielden, John S. "What Do You Mean You Don't Like My Style?" *Harvard Business Review* 60 (1982): 128–138.

Huckin, Thomas. "A Cognitive Approach to Readability." *New Essays in Technical and Scientific Communication: Research, Theory and Practice.* Ed. Paul V. Anderson, R. John Brockman, and Carolyn Miller. Farmingdale, NY: Baywood, 1983. 90–108.

Kostelnick, Charles. "The Rhetoric of Text Design in Professional Communication." *The Technical Writing Teacher* 17.3 (1990): 189–203.

Magolan, Todd. Personal memo, 15 March 1991. Used by permission.

Odell, Lee, Dixie Goswami, Ann Herrington, and Doris Quick. "Studying Writing in Non-Academic Settings." *New Essays in Technical and Scientific Communication: Research, Theory, and Practice.* Ed. Paul V. Anderson, R. John Brockman, and Carolyn Miller. Farmingdale, NY: Baywood, 1983. 17–40.

Selzer, Jack. "Composing Processes for Technical Discourse." *Technical Writing: Theory and Practice.* Ed. Bertie E. Fearing and W. Keats Sparrow. NY: MLA, 1989. 43–50.

Shriver, Karen. *Dynamics in Document Design: Creating Texts for Readers.* NY: Wiley, 1997.

Stern, Judith, and Robert Littieri. *QuickTime and Moviemaker Pro for Windows and Macintosh.* NY: Peachpit, 1998. 146.

Focus on CREDIBILITY

When you deliver information, a key ingredient of your message is your credibility. I will tend to accept your message if I feel you are a credible person in the situation. Credibility grows out of competence and method.

Competence is control of appropriate elements. If you act like a competent person, you will be credible. The items discussed in this text will all improve your credibility—attention to formatting, to organization, to spelling and grammar, and to the audience's needs. Competence is also shown by tone. You will not seem credible if you sound informal when you should sound formal or facetious when you should sound serious.

Method includes the acts you have taken in the project. Simply put, audiences will view you as credible—and your message as believable—if they feel you have "acted correctly" in the situation. If I can be sure that you have worked through the project in the "right way," I will be much more likely to accept your requests or conclusions. If you have talked to the right people, followed the right procedures, applied the correct definitions, and read the right articles, I will be inclined to accept your results. For instance, if you tell me that package design A is unacceptable because it failed the Mullen burst test—an industrywide standard method of applying pressure to a corrugated box until it splits—I will believe you, because you arrived at the conclusion the right way.

In all the information memos and reports you write, you should try to explain your methodology to your reader. The IMRD report provides a specific section for methodology, and in other types of reports you should try to present the methodology somewhere, often in the introduction, as explained in this chapter. Sometimes one sentence is all you need: "To find these budget figures I interviewed our budget analyst." Sometimes you need to supply several sentences in a paragraph that you might call "background." However you handle it, be sure to include methodology in both your planning (what did I do to find this information?) and in your writing (be sure to add a reference or a lengthier section).

3 The Technical Writing Process

Chapter 3
IN A NUTSHELL

You have to plan, draft, and edit your document, either by yourself or in a group.

Plan by establishing your relationship with your audience. You want them to accept what you tell them. They have to accept you as credible—because they know "who you are" or because you have performed the "right action" to familiarize yourself with the topic.

Draft by carrying out your plan. Find your best production method. Some people write a draft quickly, focusing on "getting it out," whereas others write a draft slowly, focusing on producing one good sentence after another. Keep basic strategies—for instance, the "top-down" method of first announcing the topic and then filling in the details—in mind as you write. If the writing causes you to see a new, better way to present the material, change.

Finish by making the document consistent. Look for surface problems, such as spelling, grammar, and punctuation. Make sure all the presentation elements—heads, captions, margins—are the same.

Work in a group by expanding your methodology. For groups, add into your planning a method to handle group dynamics—set up a schedule, assign responsibilities, and, most important, select a method for resolving differences.

Like all processes, document production proceeds in stages. This chapter explains each of these stages and introduces you to writing as a member of a group, a practice common in industry and business.

AN OVERVIEW OF THE PROCESS

The goal of the writing process is to generate a clear, effective document that allows an audience to act. Experienced writers achieve this goal by performing activities in three stages:

- *Prewriting Stage:* Plan by discovering and collecting all the relevant information about the communication situation and deciding what steps to follow.
- *Writing Stage*: Draft and revise by selecting and arranging all the elements in the document.
- *Postwriting Stage:* Finish by editing the document into final form.

Figure 3.1, a flow chart of this process (adapted from Goswami et al. 38), indicates that the process is both linear and recursive. The heavy black arrows indicate the linear sequence: first plan, then write, then edit. This path is the standard logical process that most people try to use in any project. The light arrows, however, indicate the recursive nature of this process—you must be ready to return to a previous stage or temporarily advance to a subsequent stage to generate a clear document.

PLANNING YOUR DOCUMENT

During the planning stage, you answer a set of questions concerning your audience, your message, your document's format, and the time available for the project. The answers to these questions will give you important information about your audience and a general idea of the document you should present.

Depending on the situation, planning can be brief or lengthy. For a short memo, the planning session could result in simply a few mental notes that guide the composition. For a lengthy proposal or manual, the planning sessions could yield a written document that specifies the audience and explains the way they will use the planned document, a detailed style sheet for format, and a realistic production schedule.

Regardless of the amount of time spent on this step, planning is a key activity in writing any document. Better writing results from better planning (Flower; Dorff and Duin).

To plan effectively, you should consider the audience and the goal (see Chapter 2), determine constraints, choose an effective strategy, and develop a production schedule.

FIGURE 3.1
The Technical Writing Process

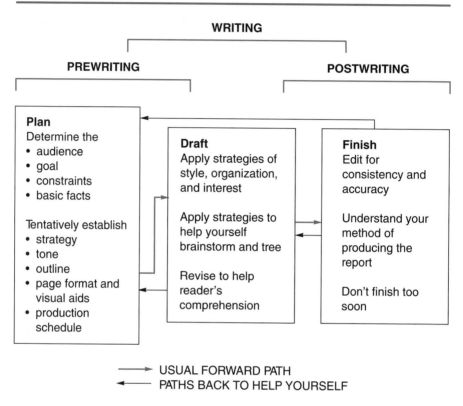

What Constraints Affect This Situation?

Constraints are factors that affect your production of the document. These constraints include time, length, budget, method of production, method of distribution, and place of use (Goswami et al.).

■ *Time* is the number of hours or weeks until the date the document is due.

■ *Length* is the number of pages in the final document.

■ The *budget* specifies the amount of money available to produce the document. A negligible concern in most brief documents (one to three pages), the budget can greatly influence a large, complex document. For instance, a plastic spiral binding could increase costs slightly, but a glued "professional" binding could be prohibitively expensive.

■ *Method of production* is the type of equipment used to compose the document. If you plan to use two word processors, one in a public lab and one at home, both must run the same software so that you can use your disk in either system.

■ *Method of distribution* is the manner in which the document is delivered to the reader. If it is to be mailed, for instance, it must fit into an envelope of a certain size.

■ *Place of use* is the physical surroundings in which the audience reads the document. Many manuals are used in confined—even dirty—spaces that could require smaller paper sizes and bindings that can withstand heavy use.

Choose an Effective Strategy

Strategy is a plan to achieve a goal. Strategy is your "creative concept"— the way you present the material so that your reader can easily grasp it and act. Essentially, in your writing, you must create a path that gives the reader easy access to your meaning. Part of strategy is your overall organization. For instance, as Figure 3.2 (p. 51) shows, you should arrange your material hierarchically (emphasizing structure) or as a list (emphasizing details). Another part of strategy involves the way you "carry out" the message. You could use one example all the way through your document (as Chapter 2 did in constantly referring back to the Magolan memo), or you could use a different example for each concept. Strategy also involves the visual logic you will use. (That aspect is discussed in "Develop a Style Sheet," later in this section.)

Should You Use a Genre? A common starting point is to decide whether or not to use a *genre* (set of instructions, proposal, standard trip report, or meeting agenda) that the reader understands and expects. A genre is a standardized way to present information. For instance, in instructions, lists of necessary materials appear in the introduction, and the steps appear in the body in sequential order. In the chapters that follow genre is referred to as *usual form*.

If no genre exists, you can use other methods. You might develop a central metaphor ("computer storage is like a giant file cabinet") that the reader understands. Or you could use a common rhetorical sequence: for instance, definition followed by example and analogy.

Another approach is to establish an organizational progression, such as most vital to least important or top to bottom. To treat the components of a computer system from most to least important, you might start with the central processing unit and end with the electrical cord. To discuss it from top to bottom, you might start with the screen and end with the keyboard.

Develop a Style Sheet. A *style sheet* describes your page format, specifying how you will present each item of format. A style sheet keeps your format—your visual logic—consistent, a key factor for helping readers grasp the overall structure and find the relevant details of your message.

The basic format decisions are

- ■ Width of margins
- ■ Appearance of heads
- ■ Treatment of visual aids and lists
- ■ Position of page numbers
- ■ Selection of type face (or font)

Most sophisticated word processing programs (Microsoft Word® and WordPerfect®, for instance) allow you to set these formats before you begin. Chapter 7 contains more details about formatting. See Figure 7.17 for a sample style sheet.

An Example of Developing a Style Sheet.   Let's return again to the memo on pages 25–26 to see how the author developed a style sheet. He used headings to make the three sections of the report easy to locate, and he used numbering to set off each item. His lists use the "hanging indent" method, the second line starting under the first word of the first line. The visual aid is set at the left margin with the caption above it.

Develop a Production Schedule

A *production schedule* is a chronological list of the activities required to generate the document and the time they will consume. Your goal is to have a realistic schedule for the time available and the complexity of the document. You need to answer these questions: How much time do I have? Who is involved in producing the document?

How Much Time Do I Have?   You have from the present to the deadline—1 hour, 2 weeks, 4 months, or whatever. Determine the end point and then work backward, considering how long it will take to perform each activity. How long will it take to print the final document? How much time must you allot to the revision and review stage? How long will it take to draft the document? How much time do you need to discover the gist of your document?

A major problem with time management is "finishing too soon." Many people bring hidden time agendas to projects. They decide at the beginning that they have only so many hours or days to devote to a particular project. When that time is up, they must be finished. They do not want to hear any suggestions for change, even though these suggestions are often useful and, if acted upon, could produce a much better document. Another time management problem often occurs in research projects. A fascinated researcher continually insists on reading "just one more" article or book, consuming valuable time. When he or she begins to write the report, there is not enough time left to do the topic justice. The result is a bad report.

As your ability to generate good documents increases, you will get better at estimating the time it will take to finish a writing project. You will also develop a willingness to change the document as much as necessary to get it right. Developing these two skills is a sure sign that you are maturing as a writer. The worksheet on page 58 provides a useful editing checklist.

Also consider the time it will take to produce the final document. Who will type it? What kind of system will you use? typewriter? word processor? professional typesetter and printer? E-mail? How well do you know the system? The less familiar you are with your production tools, the more time you are likely to spend.

For a short document, a type you have created before, the answers are obvious. But for long, complex documents, these questions are critical. The creation of such a document is far easier if you answer these questions realistically and accurately in the planning stage.

Who Is Involved in Producing the Document?   The number of people involved in the procedure varies from one (you) to many, especially if there is a review process. If only you are involved, you need to consider only your own work habits as you schedule time to work through the document. If many people are involved—such as reviewers for technical accuracy, legality, and internal consistency—you will have to schedule deadlines for them to receive and return your document.

An Example of Scheduling.   To produce the site-visit memo was an easy task for Todd. Because he had noted all the facts and had drawn a rough sketch while on the site, he could see that he could produce the memo in less than an hour on his word processor. He also knew that drawing would require another half-hour at most. No one else had to review the document, so Todd scheduled an hour of time and easily completed the document.

■ WORKSHEET FOR PLANNING

Answer the following questions:

❑ *What is true of my audience?*
   a. Who will read this document?
   b. Why do they need the document?
   c. What will they do with it or because of it?
   d. How much do they know about the topic?

    e. Do the readers know and trust you?

    f. What is the reader's personal history with the topic?

    g. What expectations exist for this kind of document's appearance or structure?

    h. Will other people read this document? What do they need to know?

    i. What tone do they expect? Should I use personal pronouns and active voice?

❏ *What is true of me?*

    a. Why should the reader trust me?

    b. Why am I credible? because of my role? because of my actions? Do I need to tell the reader that role or those actions?

    c. What authority do I feel I have? Do I believe that I have the right to speak expertly and be taken seriously?

    d. What should I sound like? How formal or informal should I make myself appear?

❏ *What is my goal in this writing situation?*

    a. What basic message do I want to tell my audience?

    b. Why do I need to convey that message? to inform? to instruct? to persuade?

❏ *What constraints affect this situation?*

    a. How much time do I have?

    b. How long should the document be?

    c. Is budget an issue? If so, how much money is available? Can I produce the document for that amount?

    d. How will I produce the document? Do I really understand the potential problems with that process? (For example, will the library printers be working that day?)

    e. Is distributing the document an issue? If so, do I understand the process?

    f. Where will the reader read the document? Does that affect the way I create the document?

❏ *What are the basic facts?*

    a. What do I already know?

    b. Could a visual aid clarify essential information?

    c. Where can I read more?

    d. With whom can I discuss the matter further?

    e. Where can I observe actions that will reveal facts?

❑ *What is an effective strategy?*
   a. What identity should I establish? How do I do that?
   b. What starting point should I choose?
   c. Should I choose a standard genre (set of instructions, technical report)?
   d. Should I follow one example throughout the document or should I use many examples?
   e. Should I develop a central metaphor?
   f. Should I use definition followed by example and analogy?
   g. Which organizational principle (such as top to bottom) is best?

❑ *What format should I use?*
   a. What margins, heads, and fonts do I want?
   b. How can I write a style sheet?

❑ *What is my production schedule?*
   a. Which tasks will I finish first?
   b. How long will it take to complete each task?

■ EXERCISES

1. Following the format of the on-site review (pp. 25–26), write a one-page plan for one of the following situations. Your instructor may ask you to form groups of three. In each situation, assume that you have completed the research; that is, the plan is for the document, not the entire project.
    a. Recommend a change in the flow of work in a situation. For example, change the steps in manufacturing a finished part or in moving the part from receiving to point of sale.
    b. Think of a situation at your workplace or at your college that you want changed. Write the plan for a document proposing that change.
    c. You have discovered a new opportunity for manufacturing or retail at your workplace. Plan a report to obtain permission to use this opportunity.
    d. You have been assigned to teach coworkers or fellow students how to create a simple Web page. Plan the set of instructions you will write. Your goal is to enable your audience to create a page with four or five paragraphs, heads, one hyperlink to another document, and one visual (optional).

2. In groups of three, critique the plans you wrote in Exercise 1. Your goal is to evaluate whether a writer could use the plan to create a

document. Your instructor will ask for oral reports in which your group explains helpful and nonhelpful elements of plans.

DRAFTING AND FINISHING YOUR DOCUMENT

Drafting is often part of planning because, as you write, you discover more about the topic and how to present it. You may suddenly think of new ideas or new ways to present your examples. In the finishing stage you produce a consistent, accurate document. This section explains strategies for these stages. Or you may discover an entirely new way to organize and approach the whole topic, and so you discard much of your tentative plan.

Choose Devices to Help Your Reader

Researchers (Huckin; Duin; Slater) have developed some specific guidelines to help you create the kind of interactive document your reader needs. For more detailed information on these topics, see Chapters 4 and 9.

1. For an audience with little prior knowledge about a topic, use the familiar to explain the unfamiliar. Provide examples, operational definitions, analogies, and illustrations. These devices invite your reader to become imaginatively involved with the topic and make it interesting.

2. For readers familiar with a topic, don't belabor the basics. Use accepted terminology.

3. For all readers, do the following:

   ■ State your purpose explicitly. Researchers have found that most readers want a broad, general statement that helps them comprehend the details.

   ■ Make the topic of each section and paragraph clear. Use heads. Put topic sentences at the beginning of paragraphs. This method is called "top-down," and is very effective. Notice how the author of the Bafflegab memo handles this (pp. 87–88).

   ■ Use the same terminology throughout. Do not confuse the reader by changing names. If you call it *baud* the first time, don't switch to *bps* later.

   ■ Choose a structuring method that achieves your goal. If you want your readers to remember main ideas, structure your document hierarchically; if you want them to remember details, use a list format. Figure 3.2 shows the same section of a report arranged as a hierarchy and as a list. Writers typically combine both methods to structure an entire document or smaller units such as paragraphs. The list provides the details that fill out the hierarchy.

FIGURE 3.2
Hierarchical and List Formats

Hierarchy	List
Site A has two basic problems.	Site A has these problems.
Terrain	Water drains into the basement
Water in the basement	Hills block solar heating
Hills block solar heating	Roof leaks
Disrepair	Windows are broken
Roof leaks	Air conditioning system is broken
Windows are broken	
Air conditioning system is broken	

- Write clear sentences. You should try to write shorter sentences (under 25 words), rely on the active voice, employ parallelism, and use words the reader understands.

- Make your writing interesting (Duin; Slater). Use devices that help readers "picture" the topic. Include helpful comparisons, common examples, brief scenarios, and narratives. Include any graphics that might help, such as photographs, drawings, tables, or graphs.

Use Context-Setting Introductions

Your introduction should supply an overall framework so that the reader can grasp the details that later explain and develop it. You can use an introduction to orient readers in one of three ways: to define terms, to tell what caused you to write, and to explain the document's purpose.

Define Terms.   You can include definitions of key terms and concepts, especially if you are describing a machine or a process.

> A closed-loop process is a system that uses feedback to control the movement of hydraulic actuators. The four stages of this process are: position sensing, error detecting, controlling the flow rate, and moving the actuator.

Tell What Caused You to Write.   Although you know why you are writing, the reader often does not. To orient the reader to your topic, mention the reason you are writing. This method works well in memos and business letters.

In response to your request at the June 21 action group meeting, I have written a brief description of the closed-loop process. The process has four stages: position sensing, error detecting, controlling the flow rate, and moving the actuator.

State the Purpose of the Document. The purpose of the document refers to what the document will accomplish for the reader.

This memo defines the basic concepts related to the closed-loop system used in the tanks that we manufacture. Those terms are: position sensing, error detecting, controlling the flow rate, and moving the actuator.

Place Important Material at the Top

Placing important material at the top—the beginning of a section or a paragraph—emphasizes its importance. This strategy gives readers the context so that they know what to look for as they read further. Put statements of significance, definitions, and key terms at the beginning.

The following two sentences, taken from the beginning of a paragraph, illustrate how a writer used a statement of significance followed by a list of key terms.

A bill of materials (BOM) is an essential part of every MRP plan. For each product, the BOM lists each assembly, subassembly, nut, and bolt.

The next two sentences, also from the beginning of a paragraph, illustrate how a writer used a definition followed by a list of key terms.

The assets of a business are the economic resources that it uses. These resources include cash, accounts receivable, equipment, building, land, supplies, and merchandise held for sale.

Use Preview Lists

Preview lists contain the key words to be used in the document. They also give a sense of the document's organization. You can use lists in any writing situation. Lists have various formats. The basic list has three components: an introductory sentence that ends in a "control word," a colon, and a series of items. The *control word* (*parts* in the sample that follows) names the items in the list and is followed by a colon. The series of items is the list itself (italicized in this sample).

A test package includes three parts: *test plans, test specifications,* and *tests.*

A more informal variation of the basic list has no colon, and the control word is the subject of the sentence. The list itself still comes at the end of the sentence.

> The three parts of a test package are *test plans, test specifications,* and *tests.*

Lists can appear either horizontally or vertically. In a horizontal list, the items follow the introductory sentence as part of the text. In a vertical list, the items appear in a column, which gives them more emphasis.

> A test package includes three parts:
>
> ■ Test plans
> ■ Test specifications
> ■ Tests

Use Repetition and Sequencing

Repetition means restating key subject words or phrases from the preview list; *sequencing* means placing the key words in the same order in the text as in the list. The author of the following paragraph first lists the three key terms—*test plans, test specifications,* and *tests.* She repeats them at the start of each sentence in the same sequence as in the list.

> A test package includes test plans, test specifications, and tests. Test plans specify cases that technicians must test. Test specifications are the algorithmic description of the tests. The tests are programs that the technicians can run.

Use Structural Parallelism

Structural parallelism means that each section of a document follows the same organizational pattern. Readers react positively once they realize the "logic" of the structure you are presenting. The following paragraphs have the same structure: first a definition, then a list of terms, then the definitions of the terms.

> ### TEST EXECUTION
>
> #### CUTTING PHASE
>
> The cutting phase is the process of cutting the aluminum stock to length. The aluminum stock comes to the cutoff saw in 10-foot lengths and the saw cuts off 6-inch lengths.

MILLING PHASE

The milling phase is the process of shaving off excess aluminum from the stock. The stock comes to the milling machine from the cutoff saw in exact lengths. The milling machine shaves the stock down to exact height and width specifications of 5 inches.

DRILLING/THREADING PHASE

The drilling/threading phase has two steps: drilling and threading.

The drilling phase is the process of boring holes into the aluminum stock in specified positions. After the stock comes from milling, the drilling machine bores a hole in each of the four sides, creating tunnels. These tunnels will serve as passageways for oil to flow through the valve.

The threading phase is the process of putting threads into the tunnels. After a tool change to enable threading, the drilling machine cuts threads into the tunnels. The threads allow valve inlets and outlets to be screwed into the finished stock.

■ WORKSHEET FOR DRAFTING

❑ *Choose strategies that help your readers.*
   a. For unspecialized readers, use comparison, example, and brief narrative to make the unfamiliar familiar.
   b. For specialized readers, do not overexplain.
   c. For all readers:
      State your purpose.
      Make topic sentences and headings clear.
      Use consistent terminology.
      Organize material hierarchically to emphasize main ideas.
      Use a list format to emphasize details.
      Employ the active voice and parallelism.
      Note: If these strategies inhibit your flow of ideas, ignore them in the first draft and use them later.

❑ *Be sure your introductory material accomplishes one of these three purposes:*

   ■ Defines terms.

   ■ Tells why you are writing.

   ■ States the purpose of the document.

❑ *Use preview lists as appropriate in the body.*

❑ *Repeat key words from the preview list in the body.*

❑ *Use structural parallelism to develop the paragraphs in the body.*

■ EXERCISES

3. Using the plan that you constructed in Exercise 1 (p. 49), draft the document.

4. Revise the following paragraph. Use the strategies listed in the Worksheet for Drafting (p. 54) under "Choose strategies." The new paragraph should contain sections on reasons for writing and on format. Revise individual sentences as well.

> Proposals are commonly used in the field of retail management. These recommendations are written in a standard format which has a number of company parts that we often use. These are stating the problem, a section often used first in the proposal. Another one is providing a solution, of course, to the problem which you had. You write a proposal if you want to knock out a wall in your department. You also write a recommendation if you want to suggest a solution that a new department be added to your store. Another section of the proposal is the explanation of the end results. You could also write a proposal if in the situation you wanted to implement a new merchandise layout. A major topic involved with writing proposals is any major physical change throughout the store. A proposal can be structured so as to enable implementation of any major physical changes to the upper management level, who would be the audience for which the proposal is intended.

Editing

Editing means developing a consistent, accurate text. In this stage, you change the document until it is right. You are looking for surface, consistency problems. You check spelling, punctuation, basic grammar, format of the page, and accuracy of facts. You make the text agree with various rules of presentation. When you edit, ask: Is this correct? Is this consistent? In general, you edit by constructing checklists.

Constructing checklists of typical problems is a helpful strategy. The key is to work on only one type of problem at a time. For example, first read for apostrophes, then for heading consistency, then for spelling errors, then for consistency in format, and so forth. Typical areas to review include paragraph indicators (indented? space above?); heads (every one of each level treated the same?); figure captions (all treated the same?); and punctuation (for instance, the handling of dashes).

The following paragraphs demonstrate the types of decisions that you make when you edit. The goal is to correct errors in spelling, punctuation, grammar, and consistency of presentation. Version 1 is the original; Version 2 is edited.

VERSION 1

TECHNICAL REPORTS

The detailed technical report to upper management will be submitted at the end of the project. It must explain;

1. the purpose of the machine,
2. its operation,
3. and the operation of its sub systems.
4. Assembly methods will also be presented.

It will also include all design calculations for loads, stresses, velocities, and accelerations. Justification for the choice of materials of subsystems. An example might be; the rationale for using plastic rather than steel and using a mechanical linkage as compared to a hydraulic circuit. The report also details the cost of material and parts.

Unclear topic sentence

Misused semicolon

List elements are inconsistent

Vertical list misemphasizes content

Sentence fragment

"An" indicates one example, but two appear

VERSION 2

TECHNICAL REPORTS

The technical report to upper management, submitted at the end of the project, contains several sections. The report explains

1. the machine's purpose and operation.
2. the operation of its subsystems and methods to assemble it.

It also includes all design calculations for loads, stresses, velocities, and accelerations, as well as justification for the choice of materials in subsystems. Examples of this justification include the rationale for using plastic rather than steel and a comparison between a mechanical linkage and a hydraulic circuit. The report also details the cost of material and parts.

Clear topic sentence

List consistent

Two examples suggested

Complete sentence

Producing the Document

Producing a document involves the physical completion—the typing or printing—of the final document. This stage takes energy and time. Failure to plan enough time for physical completion and its inevitable problems will certainly cause frustration. Many people have discovered the difficulties that can plague this stage when their hard drive crashes or their printer fails. Although physical completion is usually a minor fac-

TIP: Editing with a Word Processor

As you work to achieve the consistency that is the goal of the finishing stage, you can use style aids.

Style aids are word processing features that highlight errors in standard usage. The two most common are spell checkers and grammar checkers (Krull).

A spell checker indicates any words in your document that are not in its dictionary. If you have made a typo, such as typing *wtih*, the checker highlights the word and allows you to retype it. Most spell checkers have an autocorrect feature. Once you engage it (check your program's instructions), it will automatically change every mistake, such as *teh* to *the*. However, these programs have problems. If your typo happens to be another word—such as *fist* for *first*—the program does not highlight it. Also, if you misuse a word—such as *to* instead of *too*—the program does not detect the error.

Grammar checkers indicate many stylistic problems, not just faulty grammar. Checkers detect such problems as subject-verb disagreement, fragments, and comma splices. Checkers also can detect features of your writing. For instance, the checker might highlight all the forms of *to be* in your paper, thus pointing out all the places where you may have used the passive voice. Checkers can also highlight words that could be interpreted as sexist or racist, that are overused, or that are easily confused. Thus the checker will highlight every *your* and *you're,* but you must decide whether you have used the correct form.

Follow these guidelines:

- Use your spell checker.
- Set your spell checker to "AutoCorrect."
- Use your grammar checker for your key problems. (If you have trouble with fragments or passive voice, set the checker to find only those items.)

tor in brief papers, in longer documents it often takes more time than the drafting stage.

■ WORKSHEET FOR EDITING

❑ *Make a checklist of possible problems.*
   a. Head format (does each level look the same?)
   b. Typographical items (for example, are all dashes formed the same way?)
   c. Handling of lists
   d. Handling of the beginning of paragraphs (for example, are they all indented five spaces?)
   e. References to figures
   f. Spelling
   g. Grammar
   h. Consistent word use

■ EXERCISES

5. Produce the final version of Exercise 1 (p. 49): the change in work flow, the situation change, the new opportunity, or the creation of a Web page. Then write a memo in which you (1) describe the process you used, step by step, and (2) evaluate the strength of your process.

6. Edit the following sections for consistency. Correct errors in spelling and grammar, as well as such details of presentation as indentation, capitalization, and treatment of heads.

    For whom will I write?

    For quick correspondence, memos will be sent to entry level employees, co-workers, Immediate Supervisors and, occasionally, to chief executives. Proposals will be sent to potential clients in hopes of attracting their business. Response request forms are to be sent out following the Preposals in order to obtain a response regarding the proposal.

    When I Will Write:

    Memos will be written on a daily basis. Proposals and response request letters will be written on demand—once or twice a week.

    Importance of Writing

    Memos are crucial for effective inter-office communication. Proposals are the key for attrcating business to the organiztion—with successful proposals come revenue. The Response Request Forms are important in communication because they complete the process begun by the proposal. Because of all these forms are written, good writing is the core of good communion.

Importance to promotion—

Since writing is tangible, it is easily alleviated. Hence, the quality of writing is the primary source for promotional evaluation.

LONGER DOCUMENTS

I would be required to write a longer document if a proposal is excepted by a client. Once a proposal is excepted, I will be required to write longer documents -- workbooks, reasearch reports, and needs analysis evaluations.

Workbooks which consist of guidelines for a workshop and appropriate information on the subject.

RESEARCH REPORTS--a closer and more detailed look at a particular topic or organization

Needs Analysis Elevations. These are documents we use in order to determine the needs of the organization and to assist in setting up a workshop

---

7. Edit this paragraph for effective structure.

Additional Writing

Additional types of writing that may be encountered by a software developer include quality tips memos, trip reports, and development proposals. Other types of proposals are infrequently submitted since there are no moving parts or assembly lines in software development. In addition, since hardware is so expensive, changes in hardware are generally management directed. Consequently, proposals for a change in machinery are also rarely submitted. These types of suggestions and requests are generally incorporated into weekly status reports. Development proposals rise from recognizing the need for a software tool to do work more efficiently. These proposals are directed at management in areas that could utilize this tool. It describes the need for the tool and the advantages using it. The quality tips memos are usually for the department and are a summary of a quality roundtable. Trip reports contain an overview of the conference materials and the points that the attender found most interesting. It also makes the conference literature available to interested parties.

---

8. Analyze and revise the following paragraph. Create several paragraphs, and revise sentences to position the important words first.

The problem solving process is started by the counselor and client working together to define the problem. The goal of defining the problem is getting the client to apply the problem in concrete and measurable terms. The client may have several problems, so the counselor should allow the client to speak on the problem he or she may want to talk about first. The client usually speaks about smaller problems first until the client feels comfortable with the counselor. Determining the desired goal of the client is the second step in the process. The main point of determining the desired goal of the client is making sure the client and counselor feel the patient's goal is realistic. A bad example of this would be "I don't want to be lonely anymore," but a measurable example that would be realistic is getting the client to spend two hours a day socializing with other people. A realistic goal is considered to be one in which the client can reach without overcoming huge obstacles. The next step is for the counselor to discover the client's present behavior. The goal of this step is for the counselor to rationalize where the client is in relation to the problem. The present behavior of the client is what they are currently doing in concrete terms. Following the previous example, the lonely client could state, "I spend about a half hour a week with other people outside of working." Working out systematic steps between the present behavior and the goal is the final step in the problem solving process. The object is for the counselor to break the process into small parts so the client can work toward their goal and to give the client concrete, real work. Making schedules is a common formality clients use to follow their goals. Counselors are to be supportive and give feedback when the client is not working toward the goal. Feedback would be pointing out to the client that he or she is procrastinating. The client is always open to redefine their goals and the counselor is to stay open and to renegotiate the process.

---

9. Create a brief top-down document. Choose a topic that you can easily break into parts (e.g., computer memory includes RAM and ROM). Use a preview list, structural parallelism, and key words in dominant positions. Use a highlighter or some other method to indicate the devices you used to achieve the top-down structure.

---

10. Exchange documents with a classmate, rewrite that document, and then compare results and report to the class.

---

11. From any document that explains technical information to lay readers, photocopy a page that illustrates several of the organization strategies explained on pages 50–54. In groups of three or four, read one another's photocopies to identify and discuss the strategies; list them in order of how frequently they occur. Give an oral report of your findings to the class or, as a group, prepare a one-page memo of your findings for your instructor. In either case, base your report on the list you construct and use specific examples.

---

12. Your instructor will divide you into groups of three or four. Each member interviews three or four people on a relevant topic in your community. (Are you getting a good education at this college? Does the school district meet your children's needs?) Combine the results into a report to the relevant administrator or official, using one visual aid.

    First, as a group, create a memo report in which you answer the questions in the Group Drafting and Revising and Group Editing Worksheets (pp. 54, 58). Then give each member of your group and your instructor a copy, conduct the interviews, and create the final report. Your instructor will provide you with more details about constraints. After you hand in the report, be prepared to give an oral report describing the process you used and evaluating the strengths and weaknesses of the process.

13. In groups of three or four, develop the document you planned in Exercise 1 (p. 49). Plan the entire project, from collecting data and assessing audiences to producing a finished, formatted report. First, create a memo report in which you complete the Worksheet for Planning (pp. 47–49) and for Drafting (p. 54). Give each member of your group and your instructor a copy. Then produce the report. Your instructor will provide you with more detailed comments about constraints.

■ WRITING ASSIGNMENTS

1. Assume that you have discovered a problem with a machine, process, or form that your company uses. Describe the problem in a memo to your supervisor. She will take your memo to a committee that will review it and decide what action to take. Before you write the description, do the following:

   ■ Write your instructor a memo that contains your plan, that is, the answers to all the planning questions about your document. Include a schedule for each stage of your process.

   ■ Hand in your plan with your description of the problem.

   Here are some suggestions for a problem item. Feel free to use others.

oscilloscope	deposit slip for a bank
oxyacetylene torch	application form for an internship
condenser/enlarger	
photoelectric sensing device	black-and-white plotter
speed drive system for a conveyor	tool control software
	bid form

layout of a facility (a computer lab, a small manufacturing facility)

instruction screen of a database

plastic wrap to cover a product

method of admitting patients

method of deciding when to order

desktop publishing program, an older version

method for testing X (you pick the topic)

tamper-evident cap to a pill bottle

compliance with an **OSHA** (Occupational Safety and Health Administration) or a **DOT** (United States Department of Transportation) regulation

method for inspecting X (you pick the topic)

disposal of styrofoam drinking cups

logging on to your local network

2. Interview three people who write as part of their academic or professional work to discover what writing process they use. They should be a student whose major is the same as yours, a faculty member in your major department, and a working professional in your field. Prepare questions about each phase of their writing process. Show them the model of the process (Figure 3.1), and ask whether it reflects the process they go through. Then prepare a one- to two-page memo to your classmates summarizing the results of your interviews.

3. Your instructor will assign you to groups of three or four on the basis of your major or professional interest. As a group, perform Writing Assignment 2. Each person in the group should interview different people. Your goal is to produce a two-page memo synthesizing the results of your interviews. Follow the steps presented in the group writing section of this chapter. In addition to the memo, your teacher may ask you to hand in a diary of your group activities.

4. Write a one- to two-page paper in which you describe the process you use to write papers. Include a "process model" diagram of your process. Then, as part of a group, produce a second paper in which your group describes either the "optimal" process or "two competing models."

■ WEB EXERCISE

Explain the "strategy" of a Web site that you investigate. Establish the ways in which the authors develop a starting point, a presentation "map," and an identity. Write an analytical report to your classmates or coworkers in which you explain strategies they should adopt as they develop their Web sites.

■ WORKS CITED

Dorff, Diane Lee, and Ann Hill Duin. "Applying a Cognitive Model to Document Cycling." *The Technical Writing Teacher* 16.3 (1989): 234–249.

Duin, Ann Hill. "How People Read: Implications for Writers." *The Technical Writing Teacher* 15.3 (1988): 185–193.

Flower, Linda. "Rhetorical Problem Solving: Cognition and Professional Writing." *Writing in the Business Professions.* Ed. Myra Kogen. Urbana, IL: NCTE, 1989. 3–36.

Goswami, Dixie, Janice C. Redish, Daniel B. Felker, and Alan Siegel. *Writing in the Professions: A Course Guide and Instructional Materials for an Advanced Composition Course.* Washington, DC: American Institute for Research, 1981.

Huckin, Thomas. "A Cognitive Approach to Readability." *New Essays in Technical and Scientific Communication: Research, Theory, Practice.* Ed. Paul V. Anderson, R. John Brockman, and Carolyn R. Miller. Farmingdale, NY: Baywood, 1983. 90–108.

Krull, Robert. "Using Electronic Writing Aids." *Word Processing for Technical Writers.* Ed. Robert Krull. Amityville, NY: Baywood, 1988. 61–71.

Slater, Wayne H. "Current Theory and Research on What Constitutes Readable Expository Text." *The Technical Writing Teacher* 15.3 (1988): 195–206.

Focus on GROUPS

Once they are in business and industry, many college graduates discover that they must cowrite their documents. Often a committee or a project team with three or more people must produce a final report on their activities (Debs). Unless team members coordinate their activities, the give and take of a group project can cause hurt feelings, frustration, and an inferior report. The best way to generate an effective document is to follow a clear writing process. For each of the writing stages, not only must you perform the activities required to produce the document, you must also facilitate the group's activities.

Before you begin planning about the topic, you must:

- select a leader
- understand effective collaboration
- develop a method to resolve differences
- plan the group's activities
- choose a strategy for drafting and revising
- choose a strategy for editing
- choose a strategy for producing the document

Select a Leader

The leader is not necessarily the best writer or the person most informed about the topic. Probably the best leader is the best "people person," the one who can smooth over the inevitable personality clashes, or the best manager, the one who can best conceptualize the stages of the project. Good leadership is an important ingredient in a group's success (Debs).

Understand Effective Collaboration

Group members must understand how to collaborate effectively. Two effective methods are goal sharing and deferring consensus (Burnett).

Goal sharing means that individuals cooperate to achieve goals. As any individual strives to achieve a goal, he or she must simultaneously try to help someone else achieve a goal. Thus, if two members want to use different visual aids, the person whose visual is used should see that the other person's point is included in the document. This key idea eliminates the divisiveness that occurs when people see each issue competitively, so that someone wins and someone loses.

Deferring consensus means that members agree to consider alternatives and voice explicit disagreements. Groups should deliberately defer arriving at a consensus in order to explore issues. This process initially takes more time, but in the end it gives each member "ownership" of the project and document.

According to one expert, group success is greatly helped by the "ability to plan and negotiate through difficulties; failures may be caused by a group's inability to resolve conflict and to reach consensus" (Debs 481).

Develop a Method to Resolve Differences

Resolving differences is an inevitable part of group activity. Your group should develop a reasonable, clear method for doing so. Usually the group votes, reaches a consensus, or accepts expert opinion. Voting is fast but potentially divisive. People who lose votes often lose interest in the project. Reaching a consensus is slow but affirmative. If you can thrash through your differences without alienating one another, you will maintain interest and energy in the project. Accepting expert opinion is often, but not always, an easy way to resolve differences. If one member who has closely studied citation methods says that the group should use a certain format, that decision is easy to accept. Unfortunately, another group member may disagree. In that case, your group will need to use one of the other methods to establish harmony.

Plan the Group's Activities

Your group must also develop guidelines to manage activities and to clarify assignments and deadlines.

To *manage activities,* the group must make a work plan that clarifies each person's assignments and deadlines. Members should use a calendar to set the final due date and to discuss reasonable time frames for each stage in the process. The group should put everything in writing and should schedule regular meetings. At the meetings, members will make many decisions; for example, they will create a style sheet for head and citation format. Write up these decisions and distribute them to all members. Make—and insist on—progress reports. Help one another with problems. Tell other group members how and when they can find you.

To *clarify assignments and deadlines,* answer the following questions:

- What is the exact purpose of this document?
- Must any sections be completed before others can be started?
- What is each person's research and writing assignment?
- What is the deadline for each section?
- What is the style sheet for the document?

Each member should clearly understand the audience, the intended effect on the audience, any constraints, and the basic points that the document raises. This sense of overall purpose enables members to write individual sections without getting off on tangents (McTeague).

■ WORKSHEET FOR GROUP PLANNING

❏ *What considerations are necessary if this is a group planning situation?*
a. Who will be the leader?
b. How will we resolve differences?
c. What are the deadlines and assignments?
d. Who will keep track of decisions at meetings?
e. Who will write progress reports to the supervisor?

Choose a Strategy for Drafting and Revising

To make the document read "in one voice," one person often writes it, especially if it is short. A problem with this method is that the writer gets his or her ego involved and may feel "used" or "put upon," especially if another member suggests major revisions. The group must decide which method to use, considering the strengths, weaknesses, and personalities of the group members.

Once drafting begins, groups should review each other's work. Generally, early reviews focus on large matters of content and organization. Reviewers should determine whether all the planned sections are present, whether each section contains enough detail, and whether the sections achieve their purpose for the readers. At this stage, the group needs to resolve the kinds of differences that occur if, for instance, one person reports that the company landfilled 50,000 square yards of polystyrene and another says it was 5 tons. Later reviews typically focus on surface-level problems of spelling, grammar, and inconsistencies in using the style sheet.

■ WORSHEET FOR GROUP DRAFTING AND REVISING

❏ *Ask and answer planning questions.*

    a. What is the sequence of sections?

    b. Must any sections be completed before others can be started?

    c. What is each person's writing assignment?

    d. Does everyone understand the style sheet?

    e. What is the deadline for each section?

❏ *Select a method of drafting.*

    a. Will everyone write a section?

    b. Will one person write the entire draft?

Choose a Strategy for Editing

Groups can edit in several ways. They can edit as a group, or they can designate an editor. If they edit as a group, they can pass the sections around for comment, or they can meet to discuss the sections. However, this method is cumbersome. Groups often "overdiscuss" smaller editorial points and lose sight of larger issues. If the group designates one editor, that person can usually produce a consistent document and should bring it back to the group for review. The basic questions that the group must decide about editing include:

■ Who will suggest changes in drafts? one person? an editor? the group?

■ Will members meet as a group to edit?

■ Who will decide whether to accept changes?

In this phase, the conflict-resolving mechanism is critical. Accepting suggested changes is difficult for some people, especially if they are insecure about their writing.

Choose a Strategy for Producing the Document

The group must designate one member to oversee the final draft. Someone must collect the drafts, oversee the typing, and produce a final draft. In addition, if the document is a long, formal report, someone must write the introduction and attend to such matters as preparing the table of contents, the bibliography, and the visual aids. These tasks take time and require close attention to detail.

Questions for the group to consider at this stage include:

- Who will write the introduction?
- Who will put together the table of contents?
- Who will edit all the citations and the bibliography?
- Who will prepare the final version of the visual aids?
- Who will oversee production of the final document?

The group writing process challenges your skills as a writer and as a team member. Good planning helps you produce a successful report and have a pleasant experience. As you work with the group, it is important to remember that people's feelings are easily hurt when their writing is criticized. As one student said, "Get some tact."

■ WORKSHEET FOR GROUP EDITING

❏ *Select a method of editing.*
  a. Will the members meet as a group to edit?
  b. Who will determine that all sections are present?
  c. Who will determine that the content is complete and accurate?
  d. Who will check for conflicting details?
  e. Who will check for consistent use of the style sheet?
  f. Who will check spelling, grammar, punctuation, etc.?
  g. Oversee the production process.
     Who will write the introduction?
     Who will put together the table of contents?
     Who will edit the citations and bibliography?
     Who will prepare the final versions of the visual aids?
     Who will direct production of the final document?

Note: Each project generates its own particular editing checklist. Formulate yours on the basis of the actual needs of the document.

Works Cited

Burnett, Rebecca E. "Substantive Conflict in a Cooperative Context: A Way to Improve the Collaborative Planning of a Workplace Document." *Technical Communication* 38.4 (1991): 532–539.

Debs, Mary Beth. "Recent Research on Collaborative Writing in Industry." *Technical Communication* 38.4 (1991): 476–484.

McTeague, Michael. "How to Write Effective Reports and Proposals." *Training and Development Journal* (Nov. 1988): 51–53.

4 Technical Writing Style

CHAPTER CONTENTS

Chapter 4
IN A NUTSHELL

You need to develop strategies to use as you write and revise documents. Mastering just a few key strategies makes your ideas seem clearer to your audience and causes them to trust you.

The basic principles are

- Write in the active voice.
- Use parallelism.
- Write 12-to-25-word sentences.
- Use *there are* sparingly.
- Change tone by changing word choice.

The first four principles are common writing advice. The last principle helps create an identity that is appropriate for the situation.

When you draft and edit, it is helpful if you have developed a repertoire of strategies to guide the choices you have to make. Having a sense of effective ways to present sentences, paragraphs, and tone helps you produce a document that your readers find clear and easy to grasp. The basic concept is to arrange material top-down: put the most important idea at the beginning (the "top"), and follow with the explanatory details (the "down").

As you revise drafts, look for language that might cause confusion, making your writing harder to understand. The key is to learn to recognize these constructions as "flags," indicators that the spot needs to be evaluated. For instance, whenever you write a *there are* or whenever you repeat a word, decide whether to change the sentence. The following sections help you develop an awareness of many constructions that cause imprecise, difficult-to-read sentences. Although you may produce some of these constructions in your early drafts, learn to identify and change them. For more information, review Appendix A, which outlines basic problems in sentence structure.

WRITE CLEAR SENTENCES FOR YOUR READER

Following these guidelines for composing sentences will make your writing clear:

- Place the sentence's main idea first.
- Use normal word order.
- Use the active voice.
- Employ parallelism.
- Write sentences of 12 to 25 words.
- Use *there are* sparingly.
- Avoid nominalizations.
- Avoid strings of choppy sentences.
- Avoid wordiness.
- Avoid redundant phrases.
- Avoid noun clusters.
- Use *you* correctly.
- Avoid sexist language.

Place the Main Idea First

To put the main idea first (at the "top") is a key principle for writing sentences that are easy to understand. Place the sentence's main idea—its subject—first. The subject makes the rest of the sentence accessible. Readers relate subjects to their own ideas (their schema) and thus orient themselves. After readers know the topic, they are able to interact with the complexities you develop.

Note the difference between the following two sentences. In the first, the main idea, "two types of professional writing," comes near the end. The sentence is difficult to understand. In the second, the main idea is stated first, making the rest of the sentence easier to understand.

The writing of manufacturing processes, which explain the sequence of a part's production, and design specifications, which detail the materials needed to produce an object, are two types of professional writing I will do.	Main idea is last
Two types of professional writing that I will do are writing manufacturing processes, which explain the sequence of a part's production, and design specifications, which detail the materials needed to produce an object.	Main idea is first

Use Normal Word Order

The normal word order in English is subject-verb-object. This order makes reading easier because it reveals the topic first and then develops the idea. It also usually produces the clearest, most concise sentences.

Normal	The ASTM definition describes the process by which polymers break down.
Inverted	Polymers break down in a process described by the ASTM definition.

Use the Active Voice

The active voice emphasizes the performer of the action rather than the receiver. The active voice helps readers grasp ideas easily because it adheres to the subject-verb-object pattern and puts the performer of the action first. When the subject acts, the verb is in the active voice ("I wrote the memo"). When the subject is acted upon, the verb is in the passive voice ("The memo was written by me").

Change Passive to Active. To change a verb from the passive to the active voice, follow these guidelines:

■ Move the person acting out of a prepositional phrase.

Passive	The memo was sent *by the manager.*
Active	*The manager* sent the memo.

■ Supply a subject (a person or an agent).

Passive	This method was ruled out.
Active	*The staff* ruled out this method.
Active	*I* ruled out this method.

■ Substitute an active verb for a passive one.

Passive	The heated water *is sent* into the chamber.
Active	The heated water *flows* into the chamber.

Use the Passive If It Is Accurate. The passive voice is sometimes more accurate; for instance, it is properly used to show that a situation is typical or usual or to avoid an accusation.

Typical situation needs no agent	Robots are used in repetitive activities.
Active verb requires an unnecessary agent (companies)	Companies use robots in repetitive activities.
Active accuses	You violated the ethics code by doing that.
Passive avoids accusing	The ethics code was violated by that act.

The passive voice can also be used to emphasize a certain word.

Use passive to emphasize *milk samples*	Milk samples are preserved by the additive.
Use active to emphasize *additive*	The additive preserves the milk samples.

Employ Parallelism

Using parallelism means to use similar structure for similar elements. Careful writers use parallel structure for *coordinate elements,* elements with equal value in a sentence. Coordinate elements are connected by coordinating conjunctions (*and, but, or, nor, for, yet, so*) or are words, phrases, or clauses that appear in a series. In the following sentence, the italicized words make up a series.

> Technical writers create *memos, proposals, and manuals.*

If coordinate elements in a sentence are not treated in the same way, the sentence is awkward and confusing.

Faulty	Managers guarantee *that they will replace the old system* and *to consider the new proposal.*
Parallel	Managers guarantee *that they will replace the old system* and *that they will consider the new proposal.*
Faulty	Typical writing situations include *proposals, the sending of electronic mail,* and *how to update the system.*
Parallel	Typical writing situations include *editing proposals, sending electronic mail,* and *updating the system.*

Write Sentences of 12 to 25 Words

An easy-to-read sentence is 12 to 25 words long. Shorter and longer sentences are weaker because they become too simple or too complicated. However, this is only a rule of thumb. Longer sentences, especially those exhibiting parallel construction, can be easy to grasp. The first of the following sentences is harder to understand not just because it is long, but also because it ignores the dictum of putting the main idea first. The revision is easier to read because the sentences are shorter and the main idea is introduced immediately.

The problem is the efficiency policy, which has measures that emphasize producing as many parts as possible, for instance, 450 per hour, compared to a predetermined standard, usually measured by the machine's capacity, say, 500, for a rating of 90%.	One sentence, 40 words long
The problem is the efficiency policy, which calls for as many parts as possible compared to a predetermined standard. If a machine produces 450 per hour and if its capacity is 500 per hour, it has a rating of 90%.	Two sentences, 19 and 21 words long

Use *There Are* Sparingly

Overuse of the indefinite phrase *there are* and its many related forms (*there is, there will be,* and so on) weakens sentences by "burying" the subject in the middle of the sentence. Most sentences are more effective if the subject is placed first.

Ineffective	*There is* a change in efficiency policy that could increase our profits.
Effective	Our profits will increase if we change our efficiency policy.

Use *there are* for emphasis or to avoid the verb exist.

Weak	Three standard methods exist.
Stronger	There are three standard methods.

Avoid Nominalizations

Avoid using too many nominalizations, verbs turned into nouns by adding a suffix such as *-ion, -ity, -ment,* or *-ness.* Nominalizations weaken sentences by presenting the action as a static noun rather than as an active verb. These sentences often eliminate a sense of agent, thus making the idea harder for a reader to grasp. Express the true action in your sentences with strong verbs. Almost all computer style checkers flag nominalizations.

Static	The training policy for most personnel will have the requirement of the completion of an initial one-week seminar.
Active	The training policy will require most personnel to complete a one-week seminar.
Static	There will be costs for the installation of this machine in the vicinity of $10,000.
Active	We can install this machine for about $10,000. The machine will cost $10,000 to install.

■ EXERCISES

Passive Sentences.   Make the following passive sentences active.

1.   When all work is completed, turn the blueprint machine off.

2. The drawing of objects and entities is more quickly accomplished on the computer tablet functions.

3. When the display has been noted and is no longer needed, press the R/S button to proceed with the program.

4. Tests are specified in the military's purchasing documents for the pouched meals; they include 27 dimensional checks on pouches.

5. Recently it was determined that the purchase of a personal computer was needed.

6. Revise the passive voice sentences in this paragraph.

> The base is the main part of the Cheese Cutting Board which all other parts come to. Rough lumber is cropped to 30" lengths and checked for knots, splits, etc. One face and one edge are jointed. Board is surfaced to 3/4" thickness. Inspected randomly to check thickness. Ripped to 6 1/8" width. One end is squared and then crosscut to final length 9 1/2". Inspected 100% on length and better top is marked. 5/16" diameter hole drilled 3 1/2" deep. Drill position and depth are checked randomly. 1/4" and 3/8" dados are cut. Dado is inspected randomly. All surfaces are sanded and 100% inspected.

Parallel Structure. Revise the following sentences to make their coordinate elements parallel.

1. It serves the purpose of pulling the sheet off the coil and to straighten or guide the sheet through the rest of the machine.

2. The two main functions of the tractor are supplying the necessary power to pull the load and to provide steering to guide the vehicle.

3. The seven steps in selling are (1) opening, (2) present merchandise, (3) handling, (4) to complete the sale, (5) suggesting, (6) record made of the sale, (7) finalize sale.

4. The plan would consist of how the system is used, how to use the system, and every little detail of information about the system.

5. The features that favor the Johnson receiver include more durability, better noise reduction, and it is more efficient.

6. Write a sentence in which you give three reasons why a particular Web search engine is your favorite. Alternate: Your instructor will provide topics other than Web search engines.

7. Create a paragraph in which your sentence from Exercise 6 is the topic sentence. Write each body sentence using active voice and parallelism.

Use of *There Are*.　Eliminate *there are,* or any related form, from the following sentences.

1. There are six basic requirements that blister material must fulfill.

---

2. There is a reverse beeper on this model, which sounds while the truck is backing.

---

3. With more shops being installed, there should be more traffic generated.

---

4. There are claims made by both companies that their computers are easy to learn and easy to use.

---

5. There is a necessity to satisfy customers for a business success to occur.

Nominalization.　Correct the nominalizations in the following sentences.

1. Writing skills cause enhancement of promotion possibilities.

---

2. For a successful business, the satisfaction of the customer's needs at a profit must be done by the company.

---

3. A comparison of specification sheets was the first step I took.

---

4. The process we use to accomplish these objectives is through the concise description of limitations, the investigation of alternatives, and the establishment of communication channels.

---

5. Avoidance of tooling costs is accomplished if you pick a stock size.

---

6. Write a paragraph about a concept you know well. Use as many nominalizations, *there are*'s, and passive voice combinations as you can. Then rewrite it eliminating all those constructions.

Avoid Strings of Choppy Sentences

A string of short sentences results in choppiness. Because each idea appears as an independent sentence, the effect of such a string is to de-emphasize all the ideas because they are all treated equally. To avoid this, combine and subordinate ideas so that only the important ones are expressed as main clauses.

Choppy	Both models offer safety belts. Both models have counterbalancing. Each one has a horn. Each one has lights. One offers wing-sided seats. These seats enhance safety.
Clear	Both models offer safety belts, counterbalancing, a horn, and lights. Only one offers wing-sided safety belts, which enhance safety.

Avoid Wordiness

Generally, ideas are most effective when they are expressed concisely. Try to prune excess wording by eliminating redundancy and all unnecessary intensifiers (such as *very*), repetition, subordinate clauses, and prepositional phrases. Although readers react positively to the repetition of key words in topic positions, they often react negatively to needless repetition. In the "lead weight" example, notice that one sentence ends and the next begins with exactly the same words. This construction is almost always a good one to rewrite.

Unnecessary subordinate clause	Two important concepts *that go along with this field* are inventory control and marketing.
Revised	Two important concepts *in this field* are inventory control and marketing.
Redundant intensifiers plus unnecessary subordinate clause	It is made of *very* thin glass *that is milky white in color.*
Revised	It is made of thin, milky white glass.
Redundant	The tuning handle is a metal protrusion that can be easily grasped *hold of by the hand* to turn the gears.
Revised	The tuning handle is a metal protrusion that can be easily grasped to turn the gears.
Unnecessary repetition plus overuse of prepositions	The lead weight arms sit on each side of the specimen holder and *can be broken down into two parts. The two parts* of the arms are the abrading discs and the weights.
Revised	The lead weight arms, located on each side of the specimen holder, have two parts: the abrading discs and the weights.

Avoid Redundant Phrases

Here is a list of some common redundancies. A better way to express the idea follows each.

Redundant Phrase	*More Concise Word or Phrase*
due to the fact that	because
employed the use of	used
basic fundamentals	fundamentals
completely eliminate	eliminate
alternative choices	alternatives
actual experience	experience
connected together	connected
final result	result
prove conclusively	prove
in as few words as possible	concisely

Avoid Noun Clusters

Noun clusters are three or more nouns joined in a phrase. They crop up everywhere in technical writing and usually make reading difficult. Try to break them up.

Noun cluster	Allowing *individual input variance* of *data process entry* will result in higher morale in the keyboarders.
Revised	We will have higher morale if we allow the keyboarders to enter data at their own rate.

Use *You* Correctly

Do not use *you* in formal reports (although writers often use *you* in informal reports). Use *you* to mean "the reader"; it should not mean "I," or a very informal substitute for "the" or "a" (e.g., "This is your basic hammer.").

Incorrect as "I"	I knew when I took the training course that *you* must experience the problems firsthand.
Correct	I knew when I took the training course that I needed to experience the problems firsthand.
Incorrect for "the"	From looking at Table 2, you can see that with an increase in the concentration of the plasticizer, your oxygen permeability goes up and your tensile strength drops.
Correct	You can see that increasing the concentration of the plasticizer increases the permeability and decreases the tensile strength.

Avoid Sexist Language

Language is considered sexist when the word choice suggests only one sex even though both are intended. Careful writers rewrite sentences to avoid usages that are insensitive and, in most cases, inaccurate. Several strategies can help you write smooth, nonsexist sentences. Avoid such clumsy phrases as *he/she* and *s/he*. Although an occasional *he or she* is acceptable, too many of them make a passage hard to read.

Sexist	The clerk must make sure that *he* punches in.
Use an infinitive	The clerk must make sure *to punch* in.
Use the plural	The clerks must make sure that *they* punch in.
Use the plural to refer to "plural sense" singulars	Everyone will bring their special dish to the company potluck.

In the last example, *their,* which is plural, refers to *everyone,* which is singular but has a plural sense.

■ EXERCISES

Choppiness.   Eliminate the choppiness in the following sentences.

1.   The impellers are jam free. They pivot on a turntable. Their name implies their shape. It is like blades of a rotor.

2.   The computer is an Iconglow. It is 4 years old. It does not have sufficient RAM. No new programs will run on it.

3.   On-line registration is frustrating. It should make it faster to register. The words on the screen are not self-explanatory. Screen notices say things like "illegal command." Retracing a path to a screen is difficult.

Wordiness.   Revise the following sentences, removing unnecessary words.

1.   The need to keep our recharging capacity to its maximum is necessary.

2.   When preparing the fabric, it is wise to clean and treat the fabric, depending on the type of fabric, in the very same manner as the finished garment would be cleaned, to remove this residue.

3.   The plate is supported again by a thick wire that extends down into a connecting pin in the base, and the exact position of the pin is the pin next to the notch in the base.

Use of *You*.   Correct the use of *you* in the following sentences.

1.   The operator of the grain spout can maneuver it to deliver grain anywhere in the barge hold. Your spout adjustments compensate for
changes in your water level.

2.   In the microwave the aluminum heats up the oil and pops the popcorn. This process is where you get your increase in efficiency because
you are using the heat to pop the popcorn.

Sexist Language.   Correct the sexist language in the following sentences.

1.   Each manager will direct his division's budget.

2.   Every secretary will hand in her timecard on Friday.

3.   If he understands the process, the machinist can improve production.

4.   Each supervisor will present his/her budget to his/her vice-president at
a meeting that s/he schedules.

5.   We must inform each employee that she must fill out a W-4 form.

WRITE CLEAR PARAGRAPHS FOR YOUR READER

A paragraph consists of a topic sentence followed by several sentences of
explanation. The *topic sentence* expresses the paragraph's central idea, and
the remaining sentences develop, explain, and support the central idea.
This top-down arrangement enables readers to grasp the ideas in paragraphs more quickly (Slater).

Put the Topic Sentence First

Putting the topic sentence first, at the top of the paragraph, gives your paragraphs the direct, straightforward style most report readers prefer (Slater).
Consider this example:

> Assembly drawings are drawings that portray and   Topic sentence
> explain the completely fabricated final product. Assem-
> blies are drawn on a large sheet of paper. They generally   Supporting details
> have two or three views that convey all the information
> the reader needs about the part. The assembly also ex-
> plains different parts of the drawing through the bill of
> materials, a listing of all the different parts that make up
> the entire piece. It gives the costs, quantity, and descrip-
> tion of each part. The assembly drawings, then, provide a
> basic overview of the entire product.

Structure Paragraphs Coherently

In a paragraph that exhibits coherent structure, each sentence amplifies the point of the topic sentence. You can indicate coherence by repeating terms, by placing key terms in the dominant position, by indicating class or membership, and by using transitions (Mulcahy). You can also arrange sentences by level.

Repeat Terms. Repeat terms to emphasize them. In the following example, *path* is repeated in the second sentence to provide further details. Note that *path* was the new idea in sentence 1 but is the old idea in sentence 2.

> Because fluid doesn't compress, its only path is between the gears and the housing. This path is least resistant—it allows the fluid to flow in that direction easily.

Use the Dominant Position. Placing terms in the dominant position means to repeat a key term as the subject, or main idea, of a sentence. As a result, readers return to the same topic and find it developed in another way. In the following short paragraph, *contrast* is the dominant term, and it is always in a dominant position at the beginning of the sentence.

> Contrast is one of the most important concepts in black-and-white print-making. Soft contrast—just a range of grays—is used to portray a calm effect, such as a fluffy kitten. Hard contrast, on the other hand, creates sharp blacks and bright whites. It is used for dramatic effects, such as striking portraits.

Maintain Class or Membership Relationships. To indicate class or membership relationships, use words that show that the subsequent sentences are subparts of the topic sentence. In the following sentences, *store management* and *merchandising* are members of the class *career paths.*

> Retailing has two career paths. Store management involves working in the store itself. Merchandising involves working in the buying office.

Provide Transitions. Using transitions means connecting sentences by using words that signal a sequence or a pattern. Common examples include:

Sequence	first . . . second . . . then . . . next . . .
Addition	and also furthermore
Contrast	but however

Cause and effect   thus
                   so
                   therefore
                   hence

Arrange Sentences by Level.   You can also develop coherence by the way you place sentences in a paragraph. In almost all technical paragraphs, each sentence has a level. The first level is that of the topic sentence. The second level consists of sentences that support or explain the topic sentence. The third level consists of sentences that develop one of the second-level ideas. Four sentences, then, could have several different relationships. For instance, the last three could all expand the idea in the first:

   1 First level
      2 Second level
      3 Second level
      4 Second level

Or sentences 3 and 4 could expand on sentence 2, which in turn expands on sentence 1:

   1 First level
      2 Second level
         3 Third level
         4 Third level

Putting the topic idea in the first sentence makes it possible for readers to get the gist of your document by skimming over the first sentences.

   As you write, evaluate the level of each sentence. Decide whether the idea in the sentence is level 2, a subdivision of the topic, or level 3, which provides details about a subdivision. Consider this example:

> (1) To develop an MRP program, our only investment will be two IBM printers. (2) One will be accessed by the line foreman for planning and controlling production orders. (3) The second printer will be used by the marketing and sales staff for customer orders. (4) This printer must be able to produce various fonts. (5) The two printers will cost $1,000 each, plus a setup fee of $500, totaling $2,500.

The sentences of this paragraph have the following structure:

> (1) To develop an MRP program, our only investment will be two IBM printers.

(2) One will be accessed by the line foreman for planning and controlling production orders.

(2) The second printer will be used by the marketing and sales staff for customer orders.

(3) This printer must be able to produce various fonts.

(2) The two printers will cost $1,000 each, plus a setup fee of $500, totaling $2,500.

CHOOSE A TONE FOR THE READER

The strategies discussed thus far in this chapter produce clear, effective documents. Using them makes your documents easy to read. These strategies, however, assume that the reader and the writer are unemotional cogs in an information-dispensing system. It is as though reader and writer were computers and the document were the modem. One computer emotionlessly activates the modem and sends out bits of information. The other, activated, receives and stores that information.

In fact, situations are not so predictable. The tone, or emotional attitude implied by the word choice, can communicate almost as much as the content of a message (Fielden). To communicate effectively, you must learn to control tone. Let's consider four possible tones:

- Forceful
- Passive
- Personal
- Impersonal

The *forceful* tone implies that the writer is in control of the situation or that the situation is positive. It is appropriate when the writer addresses subordinates or when the writer's goal is to express confidence. To write forcefully,

- Use the active voice.
- Use the subject-verb-object structure.
- Do not use "weasel words" (*possibly, maybe, perhaps*).
- Use imperatives.
- Clearly indicate that you are the responsible agent.

I have decided to implement your suggestion to form quality circles in our plant. This proposal has great merit. You have demonstrated that we

can raise morale and increase the bottom line. Make an appointment to
see me in order to set up the basic planning.

The *passive* tone implies that the reader has more power than the
writer or that the situation is negative. It is appropriate when the writer
addresses a superior or when the writer's goal is to neutralize a potentially
negative reaction. To make the tone passive,

- Avoid imperatives.
- Use the passive voice.
- Use "weasel words."
- Use longer sentences.
- Do not explicitly take responsibility.

The suggestion to form quality circles has not been accepted. The discussion of morale and bottom-line benefits could possibly have other results
than those indicated. Because this decision could affect the planning
cycle, a meeting will be scheduled soon in order to hold a discussion on
this matter.

Compare this to a forceful presentation:

We reject your quality circles proposal. Your conclusions about morale
and benefits are wrong. Neither morale nor benefits will increase as
much as you predict. Make an appointment to see me if you want.

The *personal* tone implies that reader and writer are equal. It is appropriate to use when you want to express respect for the reader. To make a
style personal,

- Use the active voice.
- Use first names.
- Use personal pronouns.
- Use short sentences.
- Use contractions.
- Direct questions at the reader.

Jack, thanks for that suggestion about quality circles. It's great. We all like
the way it will raise morale and increase our bottom line. I'd like to see
you soon on this. Would you make an appointment to see me?

This tone is also appropriate for delivering a negative message when both
parties are equal.

Jack, thanks for the suggestion about quality circles, but we just can't do it right now. I agree with your point about morale, but I think you've missed an important figure for the bottom-line argument. Fred pointed out the error. I know this is a disappointment for you. Could we get together to discuss what to do next?

The *impersonal* tone implies that the writer is not important or that the situation is neutral. Use this tone when you want to downplay personalities in the situation. To make the tone impersonal:

- Do not use names, especially first names.
- Do not use personal pronouns.
- Use the passive voice.
- Use longer sentences.

A decision to implement a quality circles proposal has been made. This project should increase both employee morale and the profits of the company. The following people will attend a meeting on Monday at 4:00 P.M. to discuss implementation of this proposal: Jim Jones, Jill Smith, and Ed Johnson.

■ WORKSHEET FOR STYLE

❏ *Use the top-down principle as your basic strategy.*

❏ *Find sentences that contain passive voice. Change passive to active.*

❏ *Look for sentences shorter than 12 or longer than 25 words. Either combine them or break them up.*

❏ *Check each sentence for coordinate elements. If they are not parallel, make them so.*

❏ *Use the old/new principle. Does the main idea come first in your sentences?*

❏ *Does each paragraph have a clear topic sentence?*

❏ *Check paragraph coherence by reviewing for*
  a. Repetition of terms.
  b. Placement of key terms in a dominant position.
  c. Class or membership relationships.
  d. Transitions.

❑ *Evaluate the sentence levels of each paragraph. Revise sentences that do not clearly fit into a level.*

❑ *Read carefully for instances of the following potential problems:*

- ▪ Nominalizations
- ▪ Sexist language
- ▪ Too frequent use of *there are*

- ▪ Choppiness
- ▪ Incorrect use of *you*
- ▪ Wordiness

❑ *Sentences.* Look for four types of phrasing. Change the phrasing as suggested here or as determined by the needs of your audience and the situation.

- ▪ The word *this*. Usually you can eliminate it (and change the sentence that is left slightly), or else you should add a noun directly behind it. ("By increasing the revenue, this will cause more profit" becomes "Increasing the revenue will cause more profit.")

- ▪ The words *am, is, are, was, were, be,* and *been*. If these are followed by a past tense (*was written*) the sentence is passive. Try to change the verb to an active sense (*wrote*).

- ▪ Lists of things or series of activities. Put all such items, whether of nouns, adjectives, or verb forms, in the same grammatical form (*to purchase, to assemble, and to erect*—not *to purchase, assembling, and to erect*). This strategy will do more to clarify your writing than any other style tip.

- ▪ The phrases *there are* and *there is*. You can almost always eliminate these phrases and a *that* which appears later in the sentence. ("There are four benefits that you will find" becomes "You will find four benefits.")

EXAMPLE

The example that follows on pages 87–88 exemplifies many of the devices explained in this chapter.

▪ EXERCISES

1. In class, analyze Example 4.1 in order to determine how the sentence strategies make the piece easily accessible for its intended audience.

EXAMPLE 4.1
Sample Well-Organized Document

A LAYMAN'S GUIDE TO NETWORK BAFFLEGAB (A GLOSSARY)

The world of local area networks, like any other field that is still young enough to be dominated by technologists, is full of baffling vocabulary. Not to worry. It wasn't so long ago that terms like "mainframe," "micro-processor," and "PBX" were equally mysterious. What follows will help you get up to speed in this technology and may even serve to impress your teenager (no mean trick these days).

The essential element in any network is the physical medium through which signals are transmitted. In local area networks, media are gener-ally of three sorts: twisted pair, fiber optics, and coaxial cable. **Twisted pair** is the medium used for conventional telephone systems. Each path comprises two thin copper wires twisted together to form a single strand. **Fiber optics** is a new technology that uses pulses of light transmit-ted through a thin strand of glass, instead of pulses of electrical current transmitted through copper. Light waves can carry much more informa-tion than wires. **Coax cable** has been around for decades as the principal medium for transmitting TV signals over relatively short distances. If you have cable TV service at home, you know what this looks like.

The amount of information that can pass through a given medium in a given amount of time—its capacity—is described as its **bandwidth**. This is usually measured in bits per second (bps) and given in magnitudes of thousands of bps (Kbps, or kilobits) or millions of bps (Mbps, or mega-bits). Of the three media described in the preceding paragraph, twisted pair has the lowest bandwidth, optical fibers the greatest.

When coax cable is used, there are two transmission modes possible: baseband and broadband. In **baseband** transmission, the signals are im-posed directly onto the medium, and the entire bandwidth of the cable is used for a single high-capacity channel. In the **broadband** mode, the cable's bandwidth is divided into a number of high-capacity channels en-abling several transmissions to occur in parallel. Your cable TV service at home is a broadband system, which is why you can tape one program while viewing another at the same time.

Dividing bandwidth into a number of channels is accomplished through a process called **multiplexing**. There are two techniques: frequency division multiplexing (FDM) and time division multiplexing (TDM). In **frequency division**, the bandwidth is split into several parallel paths defined by bands of wave frequencies that are usually measured in millions of cycles per second (abbreviated as MHz). Look at the FM radio dial to see how this form of multiplexing is used to divide a single radio beam into several "stations." In **time division**, the entire bandwidth is used for every signal, but individual channels get into a queue, and each one has an allotted time slot to insert its signal into the sequence. The

EXAMPLE 4.1
(continued)

sequence is very short and is repeated very rapidly. It's like several lanes of traffic merging in an orderly fashion into a single high-speed tunnel.

When several communicating devices share a single channel (such as a group of terminals, each of which needs to access a computer only occasionally), there needs to be an access method which acts as the traffic cop. Two such major methods are "polling" and "random access." In local area networks, these are implemented, respectively, by techniques called token-passing and CSMA/CD. **Token-passing** requires each device to wait its turn for a chance to use the channel. It knows when its turn comes because the network passes it a "token" in the form of a go-ahead signal. When it's through with the channel, the token is passed to the next device in a pre-determined order. **CSMA/CD (Carrier Sense Multiple Access with Collision Detect)** is a more random method, but one which generally yields higher utilization of the channel. It requires each device to constantly "listen" to the channel and jump on any time no other device is using it. If two devices jump on at exactly the same time (a collision), they both back off and retry. It's really an automated party line with "politeness" programmed into it.

Most networks you've dealt with (such as AT&T's long distance telephone system) simply provide a transmission path and leave the rest to you. There are other kinds of data networks, however, that start with "raw" transmission capacity and offer other things along with it, such as speed matching, error detection, and protocol conversion. By adding these valuable functions to straightforward transmission, they have become known as value added networks (VANs). GTE's Telenet is one example of a nationwide VAN. ContelNet is an example of a local area network with VAN characteristics. (Finney 28)

2. Review the sentences of the following paper. Focus on passive voice, ineffective use of pronouns, and long sentences.

In your request to be informed on the process to develop a formal cost estimate, I have broken up the steps as follows: request from manager, research, develop plan, review plan, finalize plan, contact contractors, write estimate, return to manager. These steps are not set in stone, but are a very good outline to follow.

A manager will contact an engineer and request a cost estimate on a certain project which he/she would like to have done. A manager needs this cost estimate in order to forward a written request with the cost of the project on it. The request goes through a series of channels to receive the necessary signatures to get the approval for the project. At any time the project can be rejected.

The engineer will research any projects, files, or drawings, which are related to the requested project in order to gain any useful information. This will hopefully inform them of any special circumstances that must be considered, and give them an idea of where to start with the project. Types of drawings, which should be checked are: HVAC, Electrical, Plumbing, Sprinkler Protection, and Floor Plans.

The engineer develops the necessary drawings, which are needed to carry out the project. These drawings are used first to demonstrate what it is he/she wishes to do to the manager requesting the project, and then they are used by the contractors to perform the work. The goal is to always keep the project as similar as possible to the original request; however, safety, convenience, cost, and many other factors may require the engineer to alter the original request.

The engineer will then set up a meeting with the individual requesting the project and anyone else who may be affected by the project, and simply review what is going to happen. This is necessary to iron out any of the wrinkles that may exist and properly inform the necessary people of what may happen if the project is approved. The more people involved the better.

The engineer will gather all the information, which was generated during the review and attempt to create a final revision. These drawings and specifications are what will be used to give to the contractors. They will develop their bids from these drawings. Therefore, they need to be complete and accurate.

The engineer will contact the various contractors with which the company typically does business, and ask them to come in and see what needs to be done. At this time the engineer gives the contractor the drawings and explains to them what he/she is looking to do. It is important that all contractors have a clear idea of what is needed to be done in order to get an accurate bid on the project. When all bids are in, the engineer selects the contractor to go with, and uses their bids for the cost estimate.

The engineer writes a proposal which summarizes what is to be done and for how much. This is done to illustrate to upper management what will be done if they approve this project. They try to write it so everyone understands, but at the same time they do not include every detail involved. The numbers are basically what everyone is concerned about.

When finished writing the most accurate and acceptable proposal possible, it is returned to the manager who requested it. At this point you no longer have any further responsibility, unless the project is approved.

---

3. Rewrite two paragraphs of Example 4.1 in order to relate to a different audience. Keep the content the same, but change the sentence strategies and the tone.

---

4. Analyze Example 9.3 on p. 222 to determine the sentence strategies and tone used for the intended audience.

---

5. Rewrite part or all of Example 9.3 to apply to a different audience.

---

6. Compare strategies in Examples 9.3 and 4.1. Write a brief memo in which you give examples that illustrate how sentence tone creates a definition of an intended audience. Alternative: In groups of 3 or 4, compare Examples 9.3 and 4.1. Rewrite one of them for a different audience. Read your new memo to the class, who will identify the audience and strategies you used.

---

7. Revise the following paragraphs so that the sentences focus on the Simulation Modeling Engineer as an actor.

I am writing in response to your request for an explanation of our Simulation Modeling Process. I have tailored our process over the last fifteen years to meet the needs of our simulation modeling. This memo gives an overview of our Simulation Modeling Process. Our process consists of the following phases: Formulating the Problem, Building the Model, Acquiring the Data, Translating the Model, and Validating the Results.

Formulating the Problem involves defining the problem to be studied. The Simulation Model Engineer (SME) must accurately identify the system problem before the model building process continues to the next phase. The steps in problem formulation include: determining the objectives, and identifying the assumptions and decision variables. The objectives may be very specific or much more vague. By identifying the assumptions and decision variables, the SME determines which part of the total system to model and which parts are assumed to be unimportant or irrelevant. After problem formulation, the modeling can begin.

The process of abstraction of the system into mathematical-logical relationships with the problem formulation is the Model Building Phase. The assumptions and decision variables are used to mathematically determine the system responses. Also, the desired performance measures and design alternatives are evaluated. The system being modeled is broken down into events. For each event, relevant activities are identified. The basic model of the system is now an abstraction of the "real" system.

The Data Acquisition Phase involves the identification and collection of data. This phase is often the most time consuming and critical. If the data collected is not valid, the simulation will produce results that are not valid. The data to be acquired is determined by the decision variables and assumptions. All organizations collect large quantities of data for day to day management and for accounting purposes. To collect data for simulation, the SME's need cooperation of management in order to gain knowledge and access to the information sources. When the existing data sources are inadequate, a special data-collection exercise is required or the data is estimated.

Once the simulation logic has been determined, it must be represented as a computer program. The Model Translation Phase involves translating the model for computer processing. There are numerous simulation programming languages for this task. The advantages of using a simulation programming language is that it imposes structure on the model. However, an alternative is to use a general purpose programming language such as Pascal. Our Simulation Models use this alternative because it allows the SME greater flexibility and creativity. The model is implemented by an SME into a large computer program and thoroughly tested to verify the intended execution.

The results of the simulation program must be validated. The Validation Phase involves establishing that a desired accuracy or correspondence exists between the simulation model and the real system. This phase often uses statistical analysis to analyze the simulation output and draw inferences. The important question the SME asks is "Did we build the right simulation model?" If the answer is "no," then the SME usually must return to the Formulating the Problem Phase.

8. Write a memo in which you reject an employee's solution to a problem. Give several reasons, including at least one key item that she or he overlooked.

9. In groups of three or four, review the memos you wrote in Exercise 8 for appropriate (or inappropriate) tone. Select the most (or least) effective one and explain to the class why you chose it.

▦ WRITING ASSIGNMENTS

1. You are a respected expert in your field. Your friend, an editor of a popular (not scholarly) magazine, has asked you to write an article describing basic terms employed in a newly developing area in your field. Write a two- or three-page article, using Example 4.1 (pp. 87–88) as a guide.

2. Write a learning report for the writing assignment you just completed. See Chapter 5, Assignment 7, page 123, for details of the assignment.

■ WEB EXERCISE

Investigate any Web site to analyze the style and organization devices used in the site. Use the principles discussed in this chapter: Are the sentences written differently from what they might be if they were in a print document? What devices are used to make organization obvious? Write an analytical report (see Chapter 12) to alert your classmates or coworkers to changes they should make as they develop their Web sites.

■ WORKS CITED

Fielden, John S. "What Do You Mean You Don't Like My Style?" *Harvard Business Review* 60 (1982): 128–138.

Finney, Paul R. "A Layman's Guide to Network Bafflegab (A Glossary)." *Management Technology* July 1983: 28.

Mulcahy, Patricia. "Writing Reader-Based Instructions: Strategies to Build Coherence." *The Technical Writing Teacher* 15.3 (1988): 234–243.

Slater, Wayne H. "Current Theory and Research on What Constitutes Readable Expository Text." *The Technical Writing Teacher* 15.3 (1988): 195–206.

Focus on BIAS IN LANGUAGE

Current theory has made clear just how much language and language labels affect our feelings. Biased language always turns into biased attitudes and actions that perpetuate demeaning attitudes and assumptions. It is not hard to write in an unbiased way if you apply a few basic rules. The American Psychological Association (APA) publication manual suggests that the most basic rule focuses on exclusion. A sentence that makes someone feel excluded from a group needs to be revised. It's rather like hearing yourself discussed while you are in the room. That feeling is often uncomfortable, and you should not write sentences that give that feeling to others. The APA manual (46–60, based heavily on Maggio) offers several guidelines.

Describe People at the Appropriate Level of Specificity

This guideline helps whenever you have to describe people. Technical writing has always encouraged precise description of technical objects. You should apply the same principle to the people who use and are affected by those objects. So, when referring to a group of humans of both sexes, say "men and women," not just "men."

Be Sensitive to Labels

Call people what they want to be called. However, be aware that these preferences change over time. In the 1960s, one segment of the American population preferred to be called "black"; in the 1990s, that preference changed to "African-American."

Basically, do not write about people as if they were objects—"the complainers," "the strikers." Try instead to put the person first—"people who complain," "people who are striking." Because this can get cumbersome, you can begin by using a precise description and after that use a shortened form as long as it is not offensive. The issue of what is offensive is a difficult question. How do you know that "elderly" is offensive but "older" is not? There is no easy answer. Ask members of that group. Listen to the words that national TV news applies to members of the group.

Acknowledge Participation

This guideline asks you to treat people as action initiators, not as the recipients of action. In particular, it suggests using the active voice to talk about people who are involved in large mass activities. So say,

"The secretaries completed the survey," not "The secretaries were given the survey."

Avoid Ambiguity in Sex Identity or Sex Role

This guideline deals with the widespread use of masculine words, especially *he*, when referring to all people. This usage has been changing for some time but still causes much discussion and controversy. The basic rule is to be specific. If the referent of the word is male, use *he*; if female, use *she*; if generic, use *he or she* or, more informally, *they*.

Choose Correct Terms to Indicate Sex Orientation

Currently the preferred terms are *lesbians* and *gay men, straight women* and *straight men*. The terms *homosexual* and *heterosexual* could refer to men or women or just men, so their use is not encouraged.

Use the Preferred Designations of Racial Groups

The preferred designations change and sometimes are not agreed upon even by members of the designated group. Be sensitive to the wishes of the group you are serving. At times, *Hispanic* is not a good choice because individuals might prefer *Latino*, *Chicano*, or even a word related to a specific country, like *Mexican*. Similar issues arise when you discuss Americans of African, Asian, and Arabic heritage. If you don't know, ask.

Do Not Use Language That Equates a Person with His or Her Condition

"Disability" refers to an attribute of a person. Say, "person with diabetes" to focus in a neutral way on the attribute; do not say, "diabetic," which equates the person with the condition.

Choose Specific Age Designations

Use *boy* and *girl* for people up to 18; use *man* and *woman* for people over 18. Prefer *older* to *elderly*.

Works Cited

American Psychological Association. *Publication Manual.* 4th ed. Washington DC: APA, 1994.

Maggio, R. *The Bias-Free Word Finder: A Dictionary of Nondiscriminatory Language.* Boston: Beacon, 1991.

The rise of a true global economy means that more people than ever before must know something about international communication. Large multinational corporations have divisions, even headquarters, in many countries. Small manufacturing and service corporations, which once dealt only with customers within a 100-mile radius, now find themselves doing business with international customers, few of whom speak and write English.

Although the goal of all communication is to use words and forms that enable the receiver to grasp your meaning (Beamer, "Learning"), in intercultural communication you need to give special consideration to cultural factors as well as to actual word choice. Cultural factors include your ability to look at social behavior from another culture's point of view, the thinking patterns of the other person's culture, the role of the individual in the other person's culture, the culture's view of direct and indirect messages, and writing conventions (Beamer, "Teaching"; Martin and Chancey).

Points of View

Your ability to look at the meaning of behavior from a point of view other than your own is crucial to good communication. The associations commonly made by one culture about some objects, symbols, words, and ideas are not the same as those made by another culture for the same items—and, remember, the differences do not indicate that one group is superior to the other. For example, in China the color red is associated with joy and festivity; in the West, red can mean "stop," "financial loss," or "revolution." In the United States, *janitor* means a person who maintains a building and is often associated with sweeping floors. But in Australia that same job is called a *caretaker*—a word that in the United States means someone who maintains the health of another person (Gatenby and McLaren).

Thinking Patterns

Much of U.S. thought focuses around cause-effect patterns and problem solving—identifying the causes of perceived effects and suggesting methods to alter the causes. In other cultures, however, a more common thought pattern is "web thinking." In Chinese tradition, for instance, everything exists not alone but in a relationship to many other things, so that every item is seen as part of an ever-larger web, but the web is as important as the individual fact. These thinking patterns become part of the way people structure sentences. In American English one says, "I go to lunch every day," but in Chinese one says, "Every day to lunch I go."

View of Messages

The individual is often perceived differently in a group dominated by web thinking, and web and group ideas can greatly affect the tone and form of communication. In the United States, influenced by a long history of individualism, many people feel that if they can just get their message through to the right person, action will follow. In other cultures, representatives of a group do not expect that same kind of personal autonomy or ease of identification from their readers.

In the United States we teach that the direct method is best: State the main point right away and then support it with the facts. In some other cultures, that approach is unusual, even shocking. Although in the United States a writer would simply state in a memo that he or she needs a meeting, in a web culture like China's, that request would come near the end of the letter only after a context for the meeting had been established.

Even when writing for readers for whom English is the main language, you should remember that there is more than one English. American English is the first language of most of the readers of this book. But Australian, New Zealand, Canadian, British, Indian, Irish, and many "post-colonial" (e.g., Kenyan, Malaysian) Englishes exist. Different words are valid for the same thing (*janitor* versus *caretaker; lead* versus *leader*), and the spelling is often different (*behavior* versus *behaviour*).

Writing Conventions

Conventions of writing differ. In the United States we address envelopes with the name of the recipient on the top line and the city, state, zip code, and country, if necessary, at the bottom. In Russia it is the reverse; the recipient's name appears at the bottom.

How can you provide text for international readers, text that enables them to understand and to act?

- You need to actively think about the other culture's perspective and adapt to it. To find out their perspective you must study their culture or, when possible, ask representatives of that culture for advice.

- Simplify your sentences and minimize or avoid idioms, slang, jargon, and colloquial language.

- Choose words that have a clear meaning or whose use in the sentence makes their meaning clear.

- Simplify your use of verbs, adjectives, and noun phrases (three-word phrases such as "technical enhancement implementation" are nearly impossible to translate).

- Find models of the way the other culture typically handles the particular kind of writing situation and follow that model.

- Remember that models reflect basic ways of thinking that may be foreign to you.

- Use the World Wide Web. Check sites like Getting Through Customs at www.getcustoms.com.

- Read self-help texts like *Kiss, Bow or Shake Hands: How to Do Business in Sixty Countries* or Dun & Bradstreet's *Guide to Doing Business Around the World* (Morrison and Conaway).

Works Cited

Beamer, Linda. "Learning Intercultural Communication Competence." *Journal of Business Communication* 29.3 (1992): 285–303.

Beamer, Linda. "Teaching English Business Writing to Chinese-Speaking Business Students." *Bulletin of the Association for Business Communication* LVII.1 (March 1994): 12–18.

Gatenby, Beverly, and Margaret C. McLaren. "A Comment and a Challenge." *Journal of Business Communication* 29.3 (1992): 305–307.

Martin, Jeanette S., and Lillian H. Chancey. "Determination of Content for a Collegiate Course in Intercultural Business Communication by Three Delphi Panels." *Journal of Business Communication* 29.3 (1992): 267–284.

Morrison, Terri, and Wayne A. Conaway. "Your Cultural IQ." *American Way* (Mar. 15, 1997): 140.

Technical Writing Techniques

5 Researching

Chapter 5
IN A NUTSHELL

When you conduct research, you are
finding the relevant facts about the
subject. Two strategies are *asking
questions* and *using keywords.*

Ask questions.   Start with predictable primary level *questions:* How
much does it cost? What are its
parts? What is the basic concept you
need to know? The trick, however, is
to ask secondary-level questions that
help you establish relationships. Secondary questions include cause (Why
does it do this? Why does it cost this
much?) and comparison/contrast
(How is this like that? Why did it act
differently this time?).

Use keywords.   Type in *keywords,*
following search rules, to search all
library databases and Web databases. The two basic skills are
knowing how to use this database's
"search rules" and knowing which
words to use.

Spend time learning the database
"search rules." Typing in one word is
easy, but how do you handle combinations—either phrases (municipal
waste disposal) or strings (packaging, corrugated, fluting)? All search
engines use logical connectors—
and, but, not, or—in some fashion.
"Recycle" *and* "plastic" narrows the
results to those that contain both
terms; "recycle" *or* "plastic" broad-
ens the results to all those that contain just one of the two terms.

Finding which *words* to use is a
matter of educated guesses and observation. "Packaging" is too broad
(that is, it will give you too many
"hits"—so many results that you
cannot use them), so use "corrugated"; "fluting" (the wavy material
in the middle of corrugated cardboard) will yield narrower results.

People research everything from how high above the floor to position a computer screen to how feasible it is to build a manufacturing plant. This chapter discusses the purpose of research, explores the essential activity of questioning, and suggests practical methods of finding information.

THE PURPOSE OF RESEARCH

The purpose of research is to find out about a particular subject that has significance for you. Your subject can be broad and general, such as recycling specialty plastics, or narrow and specific, such as purchasing a new photocopier for your office. The significance is the importance of the subject to you or your community. Will the new method of recycling plastics make a profit for the company? Will that new photocopier make the office run more smoothly?

Generally, the goal of research is to solve or eliminate a problem (Why does the photocopier break down?) or to answer a question (What differences are there in photocopier technologies?). You can use two strategies: talking to people and searching through printed information. To find out about the photocopier, for instance, you would talk to various users to discover features that they need, and you could read sales material that explained those features and reviews that evaluated performance.

QUESTIONING—THE BASIC SKILL OF RESEARCHING

Asking questions is fundamental to research. The answers are the facts you need. This section explains how to discover and formulate questions that will "open up" a topic, providing you with the essential information you and your readers need.

How to Discover Questions

To learn about any topic—such as which photocopier to buy for the office— ask questions. Formulate questions that will help you investigate the situation effectively and that will provide a basis for a report. For instance, the question "In what ways does our staff use the photocopier?" will not only produce important data but will also be the basis for a section on "usage patterns" in a report. Several strategies for discovering helpful questions are to ask basic questions, ask questions about significance, consult the right sources, and interact flexibly.

Ask Basic Questions.   Basic questions lead you to the essential information about your topic. They include

- What are the appropriate terms and their definitions?
- What mechanisms are involved?

■ What materials are involved?

■ What processes are involved?

Ask Questions About Significance.   Questions about significance help you "get the big picture" and grasp the context of your topic. They include

■ Who needs it and why?

■ How is it related to other items?

■ How is it related to current systems?

■ What is its end goal?

■ How do parts and processes contribute to the end goal?

■ What controversies exist?

■ What alternatives exist?

■ What are the implications of those alternatives?

■ What costs are involved?

Consult the Right Sources.   The right sources are the people or the printed information that has the facts you need.

People who are involved in the situation can answer your basic questions and your questions about significance. They can give you basic facts and identify their needs. The basic facts about photocopying machines can come from engineers, experienced users, or salespeople. Information about needs comes from people who use the product. They expect a photocopier to perform certain functions, and they know the conditions that make performing those functions possible.

Printed information also answers basic questions and questions of significance, often more thoroughly than people. It can be hard copy, or words printed on paper, and on-line copy, or words available electronically. Printed information includes everything from sales brochures to encyclopedias to bulletin board discussions. For the photocopier, sales literature would give you prices, features, and specifications; review articles would evaluate performance; and bulletin boards could give you testimony of users.

Interact Flexibly.   To ask questions productively, be flexible. Although people have the information you need, you must elicit it. Sometimes questions produce a useful answer, sometimes not. If you ask, "Which feature of the photocopier is most important to you?" the respondent might say, "Its speed," which is a broad answer. To narrow the answer, try an "echo technique" question, in which you repeat the key word of the answer: "Speed?" On the other hand, if you ask, "Is the ability to collate pages important to you?" The respondent might say, "No, I seldom use that, but I often copy on both sides of a sheet of paper." That answer opens two lines of questioning for you. Why is collating not important? Why is back-to-back copying important? How frequently do you do it? for what type of job?

You can also use questions to decide what material to read. If your question is "How does this model compare to others?" an article that would obviously interest you is "A Comparison of Photocopiers." Carefully formulating your questions makes your reading more efficient. Read actively, searching for particular facts that answer your questions (Spivey and King).

While reading, take notes, constantly reviewing the answers and information you have obtained. You will find patterns in the material or gaps in your knowledge. If three articles present similar evaluations of the photocopiers, you have a pattern on which to base a decision.

How to Formulate Questions

Essentially researchers ask two kinds of questions: closed and open (Stewart and Cash). You can use both types for interviewing and reading.

A closed question generates a specific, often restricted answer. Technically it allows only certain predetermined answers.

> Closed question   How many times a week do you use the copier?

An open question allows a longer, more involved answer.

> Open question   Why do you use red ink in the copier?

In general, ask closed questions first to get basic, specific information. Then ask open questions to probe the subtleties of the topic.

COLLECTING INFORMATION FROM PEOPLE

You collect information, or find answers to your questions, in a number of ways. You can interview, survey, observe, test, and read. This section explains the first four approaches. Collecting published information, especially in a library, is treated in a later section.

Interviewing

One effective way to acquire information is to conduct an information interview (Stewart and Cash). Your goal is to discover the appropriate facts from a person who knows them. To conduct an effective interview, you must prepare carefully, maintain a professional attitude, probe, and record.

Prepare Carefully. To prepare carefully, inform yourself beforehand about your topic. Read background material, and list several questions you think will produce helpful answers.

If you are going to ask about photocopiers, read about them before you interview anyone so that you will understand the significance of your answers. Listing specific questions will help you focus on the issue and discourage you and the respondent from digressing. To generate the list, brainstorm questions based on the basic and significance questions we have suggested. A specific issue to focus on could be photocopier problems: How exactly does the photocopier malfunction? Has that happened before? How often?

Maintain a Professional Attitude. Schedule an appointment for the interview, explaining why you need to find out what the respondent knows. Make sure she or he knows that the answers you seek are important. Most people are happy to answer questions for people who treat their answers seriously.

Be Willing to Probe. Most people know more than they say in their initial answers, so you must be able to get at the material that's left unsaid. Four common probing strategies are as follows:

■ Ask open-ended questions.
■ Use the echo technique.
■ Reformulate.
■ Ask for a process description.

The basic probing strategy is to ask an *open-ended* question and then develop the answer through the echo technique or reformulation. The *echo technique* is repeating significant words. If an interviewee says, "Red really messes up a print run," you respond with "Messes up?" This technique almost always prompts a longer, more specific answer. *Reformulation* means repeating in your own words what the interviewee just said. The standard phrase is "I seem to hear you saying. . . ." If your reformulation is accurate, your interviewee will agree; if it is wrong, he or she will usually point out where. *Asking for a process description* produces many facts because people tend to organize details around narrative. As the interviewee describes, step by step, how he or she uses the machine, you will find many points where you'll need to ask probing questions.

Record the Answers. As you receive answers, write them down in a form you can use later. Put the questions on an 8½ × 11 sheet of paper, leaving enough room to record answers. Record the answers legibly; avoid listing terms and abbreviations. Ask people to repeat if you didn't get the whole answer written down. After a session, review your notes to clarify them so they will be meaningful later and to discover any unclear points about which you must ask more questions.

Surveying

To survey people is to ask them to supply written answers to your questions. You use a survey to receive answers from many people, more than you could possibly interview in the time you have allotted to the project. Surveys help you determine basic facts or conditions and assess the significance or importance of facts. They have three elements: a context-setting introduction, closed or open questions, and a form that enables you to tabulate all the answers easily.

A context-setting introduction explains (1) why you chose this person for your survey; (2) what your goal is in collecting this information; and (3) how you will use the information. The questions may be either closed or open. The answers to closed questions are easier to tabulate, but the answers to open questions can give you more insight. A good general rule is to avoid questions that require the respondent to research past records or to depend heavily on memory.

The form you use is the key to any survey. It must be well designed (Warwick and Lininger). Your goal is both to make it look easy to read (so that people will be willing to respond) and to make it easy to tabulate (so you can tally the answers quickly). For instance, if all the answers appear at the right margin of a page, you can easily transfer them to another page. Here is a sample survey.

SURVEY

In the past two weeks, we have had many complaints about how difficult the new photocopier is to operate. In order to reduce frustration, we plan to develop a brief manual and to hold training sessions. To help us choose the most effective topics, please take a moment to fill in the attached survey. Please return it to Peter Arc, 150 M Nutrition Building, by Friday, January 30. Thanks.	Context-setting introduction
How often do you use the copier?	Closed question

once a week   ____

once every 2–3 days   ____

once a day   ____

several times a day   ____

Do you use any of these functions?			Closed question
	Yes	No	
2-sided copying	____	____	
overlay copying	____	____	
2-page copying	____	____	

Do you know how to do the following?			Closed question
	Yes	No	
select the proper paper key	____	____	
fill an empty paper tray	____	____	
get the number of copies you want	____	____	
lay the paper on the glass with the correct orientation	____	____	

Please describe your problems when you use the
machine. Use the back of this sheet if you need more
space.   Open question

Are you available at any of the following times during   Open question
the week of 2/20–2/25 for a training session? Give first
and second preferences.

M ____   8–10 ____

W ____   1–3 ____

Th ____   3–5 ____

How much notice do you need so that you can attend a   Closed question
training session?

1 day ____

1 week ____

Observing and Testing

In both observing and testing, you are in effect carrying out a questioning strategy. You are interacting with the machine or process yourself.

Observing.   Observing is watching intently. You place yourself in the situation to observe and record your observations. When you observe to collect information, you do so with the same questions in mind as when you interview: What are the basic facts? What is their significance?

To discover more about problems with the office photocopier, you could simply watch people use the machine. You would notice where people stand, where they place their originals, how carefully they follow the instructions, which buttons they push, how they read the signals sent by the control panel, and so on. If you discover that all steps move along easily except reading the control panel, you may have found a possible source of the complaints. By observation—looking in a specific way for facts and their significance—you might find the data you need to solve the office problem.

Testing. To test is to compare items in terms of some criterion or set of criteria. Testing, which is at the heart of many scientific and technical disciplines, is much broader and more complex than this discussion of it. Nevertheless, simple testing is often a useful method of collecting information. Before you begin a test, you must decide what type of information you are seeking. In other words, what questions should the test answer?

In the case of deciding which photocopier to buy, the questions should reflect the users' concerns. They become your criteria, the standards you will use to evaluate the two machines. Typical questions might be

- Which one produces 100 copies faster?
- Which one makes clearer back-to-back copies?
- Which one generates the least heat?

After determining suitable questions, you have people use both machines and then record their answers to your questions. To record the answers, you need a recording form much like the one used for surveys.

COLLECTING PUBLISHED INFORMATION

This section discusses the basic techniques for gathering published information. As with all writing projects, you must plan carefully. You must develop a search strategy, search helpful sources, and record your findings.

Develop a Search Strategy

With its thousands of books and periodicals, the library can be an overwhelming place. The problem is to locate the relatively small number of sources that you actually need. To do so, develop a "search strategy" ("Tracking Information") by determining your audience, generating questions, predicting probable sources, and searching for "keys."

Determine Your Audience. As in any writing situation, determine your audience and their needs. Are you writing for specialists or nonspecialists?

Do they already understand the concepts in the report? Will they use your report for reference or background information, or will they act on your findings? Experts expect to see information from standard sources. Thus quoting from a specialized encyclopedia is more credible than using a popular one, and mentioning articles from technical journals is more credible than citing material from the popular press. However, in some areas, particularly computing but also in subjects like photography, monthly magazines are often the best source of technical information. For computers, *Macworld, PC World,* and *SUN Expert* are excellent sources for technical decisions. Nonspecialists may not know standard sources, but they expect you to have consulted them.

Generate Questions. Generate questions about the topic and its subtopics. These questions fall into the same general categories as those for interviews: What are the basic facts? What is their significance? They include

- What is it made of?
- How is it made?
- Who uses it?
- Where is it used?
- What is its history?
- Do experts disagree about any of these questions?
- Who makes it?
- What are its effects?
- How is it regulated?

Such questions help you focus your research, enabling you to select source materials and to categorize information as you collect it.

Predict Probable Sources. All concepts have a growth pattern, from new and unusual to established and respected. Throughout the pattern they are discussed in predictable—but very different—types of sources. New and unusual information is available only from a few people, probably in the form of letters, conversations, E-mail, answers to LISTSERV queries, and personal websites. More established information appears in conference proceedings and technical journal articles. Established information appears in textbooks, encyclopedias, and general periodicals and newspapers ("Tracking Information").

If you understand this growth pattern, you can predict where to look. Two helpful ways to use the pattern are by age and by technical level. Use the following guidelines to help you find relevant material quickly:

■ *Consider the age of the information.* If your topic demands information less than a year old, consult periodicals, government documents, annual reviews, and on-line databases. Write letters, call individuals, ask on a LISTSERV, or search the Web (see "Focus on Web Searching"). If your topic requires older, standard information, consult bibliographies, annual reviews, yearbooks, encyclopedias, almanacs, and textbooks.

■ *Consider the technical level of the information.* If you need information at a high technical level, use technical journals, interviews with professionals, and specialized encyclopedias or handbooks. On the job, also use technical reports from the company's technical information department. If you need general information, use popular magazines and newspapers. Books can provide both technical and general information.

Search for "Keys."   A helpful concept to guide your searching is the "key," an item that writers constantly repeat. Look for keywords and key documents.

■ *Find keywords.* Keywords are the specific words or phrases that all writers in a particular field use to discuss a topic. For instance, if you start to read about the Internet, you will quickly find the terms *navigation* and *hyperlink* in many sources. Watch for terms like these, and master their definitions. If you need more information on a term, look in specialized encyclopedias, the card catalog, periodical indexes, abstracts, and databases. Keywords can also lead you to other useful terms through cross-references and indexes.

■ *Watch for key documents.* As you collect articles, review their bibliographies. Some works will be cited repeatedly. These documents— whether articles, books, or technical reports—are *key documents.* If you were searching for information about the World Wide Web, you would quickly discover that three or four books are the "bibles" of the Web. Obviously, you should find and review those books. Key documents contain discussions that experts agree are basic to understanding the topic. To research efficiently, read these documents as soon as you become aware of them.

Search Helpful Sources

To locate ideas and material, you can use encyclopedias, electronic catalogs, and electronic databases.

Read Encyclopedias in Your Field.   Start with encyclopedias because they provide basic frameworks for research topics. Encyclopedias give background information and often bibliographies that list sources of more specific and detailed data. They also define standard terms and a topic's subdivisions. Learning those terms and subdivisions enables you to use indexes and databases more efficiently.

Become familiar with your field's specialized encyclopedias. Of the many available, a few are *Encyclopedia of Electronics, Encyclopedia of Computer Science and Engineering,* and *Encyclopedia of Management.*

Search the Electronic Catalog.   The electronic catalog is your most efficient information-gathering aid. You can easily find information by subject, author, title, keyword, or call number. Many systems allow you to search periodical indexes. All of them allow you to print out an instant bibliography.

Because several major systems and many local variations exist, no textbook can give you all the information you need to search electronically. Take the time to learn how to use your local system. Each system differs, so take the time to learn them. Do several practice searches to find the capabilities of the system and the "paths," or sequences of commands, you must follow to produce useful bibliographies. This section focuses on a few items available in a typical catalog and offers information on keywords, the basis for finding material electronically.

The Typical Catalog.   The typical catalog presents you with screens for individual items, bibliographies of related items, and categories of searching. An individual item screen appears in Figure 5.1. This screen describes the book in detail: its authors, printing information, call number, and, very importantly, the subject keywords that can be used to locate it. If you use those words as keywords in the database, you will find even more books on this subject.

A bibliography screen appears in Figure 5.2 on page 112. This screen lists the first 8 of 282 books contained in the library under the subject heading "Internet." Note, however, that the books' topics are not all the same; the term *Internet* is too broad to create a focused list. A researcher would have to use Boolean logic (Internet and corporation) to narrow the 282 items down to a group on the same topic.

Obviously, these systems can generate a working bibliography almost instantly on any subject. Categories of searching include by subject, title, keyword, author, date, and call number. Use the method that agrees with what you know. For instance, if you know the author—perhaps she has written a key document, and you want to find what else she has written—use the author method. If you know little about the topic, start with a subject search.

Keywords.   By now you can see that the "trick" to using an electronic system is the effective use of *keywords,* any word for which the system will

FIGURE 5.1
General Information Screen
Source: Reprinted with permission of the University of Wisconsin at Stout.

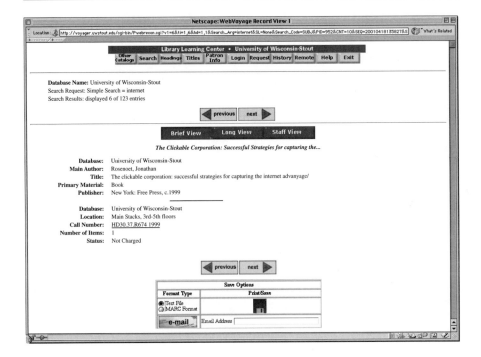

conduct a search. Figure 5.3 on page 113 shows that, if you want to search for all the items that have *Internet* in their title, enter your keyword ("internet") in the locator box and select "subject" in the *Search in:* pull-down menu. An effective initial strategy is to use the keyword category, which searches for the word anywhere on the individual item screen. If the word appears, for instance, in the item's title, subject heading, or abstract, the system includes the item in the bibliography.

To find keywords, you can use the *Library of Congress Subject Headings* (LCSH) or your own common sense. Because most of the systems are keyed to Library of Congress headings, you can use the two-volume *Library of Congress Subject Headings* to find your headings. All electronic card catalog systems use these words to classify their material. Figure 5.4 on page 113 is an example of a subject heading listing. The boldface word (**Internet**) is used in the catalog. If you enter it into the computer, the system responds with a list of books on that subject. Various symbols can also help you; for example, *BT* means "broader term," and *RT* means "restricted term."

If the LCSH books are not available, brainstorm and use the system's rules. Brainstorm a list of general words that apply to your topic—internet,

FIGURE 5.2
Subject Bibliography Screen
Source: Reprinted with permission of the University of Wisconsin at Stout.

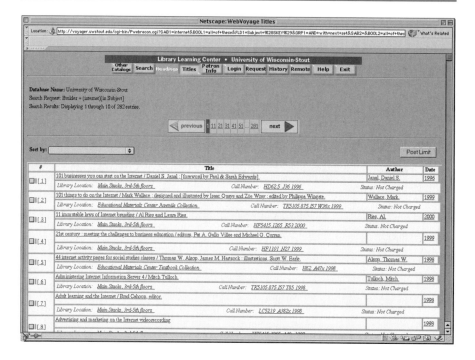

web, hypermedia, cyberspace, URL, domain. This method, however, might turn up hundreds or thousands of titles—too many to use. To limit the size of your bibliography, you can combine terms by using Boolean "logical operators" such as *and, not,* and *or.* Notice, in Figure 5.3, that you can enter a new keyword in each locator box, choose an appropriate Boolean operator, and choose a different category for every *Search in:* choice. In effect, then, you can mix types of searching, such as author and subject.

Search On-line Databases.   On-line databases are as efficient as the electronic catalog in generating resources for your topic. If you access the database correctly (by using the correct keyword), it produces a list of the relevant articles on a particular subject—essentially a customized bibliography.

Databases are particularly helpful for obtaining current information; sometimes entries are available within a day of when they appear in print, or even before. Most university and corporate libraries provide their patrons with many databases for free. If your library offers databases such as Ebscohost, use them.

FIGURE 5.3
Search by Subject
Source: Reprinted with permission of the University of Wisconsin at Stout.

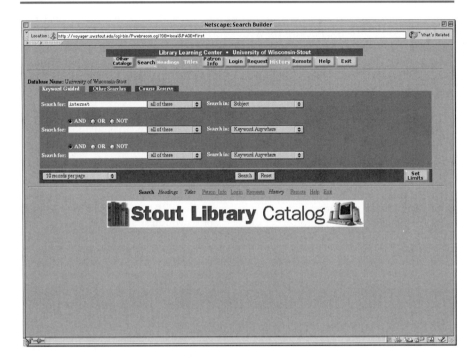

FIGURE 5.4
Sample Subject Heading Entry
Source: Reprinted with permission from the Academic Index™. ©1998 Information
Access Company.

Internet (Computer network)
   (May Subd Geog)
      [TK5105.875.I57]
     UF   DARPA Internet (Computer network)
     BT   Wide area networks (Computer
          networks)
     RT   World Wide Web (Information
          retrieval system)
     NT   Gopher servers
          WAIS (Information retrieval systems)

To search a database effectively, you must choose your keywords carefully. Just as in the computerized catalog, if you pick a common term, like *manufacturing* or *packaging* or *retail,* the database might tell you it has found 10,000 items. To narrow the choices, combine descriptors. For example, if you combine *packaging* with such descriptors as *plastic* and *microwavable,* the computer searchs for titles that contain those three words and generates a much smaller list of perhaps 10 to 50 items. Figure 5.5 shows a list of 25,000 articles generated for the keyword *Internet.* Obviously, this search would have to be narrowed (by using Refine Search, the button at the top middle). Figure 5.6 shows an item entry, giving all the relevant information. Notice especially the subject line. These words are keywords. Type them into the locator to find articles close in topic to the one described. Also notice the abstract, which you can use to decide whether or

FIGURE 5.5
Generated List of Articles
Source: Reprinted with permission of the University of Wisconsin at Stout.

not to find the full text of the article. (Most systems will let you retrieve full text articles, an invaluable aid as you collect information for your report.)

Databases provide information on almost every topic. One vendor, Ebscohost, offers many indexes, including Applied Science and Technology, ERIC, Hoover's Company Profiles, and Health Service Plus. Contact your library for a list of the services available to you.

Record Your Findings

As you proceed with your search strategy, record your findings. Construct a bibliography, take notes, consider using visual aids, and decide whether to quote or paraphrase important information.

Make Bibliography Cards. List potential sources of information on separate 3-by-5-inch cards. These bibliography cards should contain the name of the author, the title of the article or book, and facts about the book or article's publication (Figure 5.7). Record this information in the form that you will use in your bibliography. Also record the call number and any

FIGURE 5.6
On-Line Bibliographic Entry with Abstract
Source: Reprinted with permission of the University of Wisconsin at Stout.

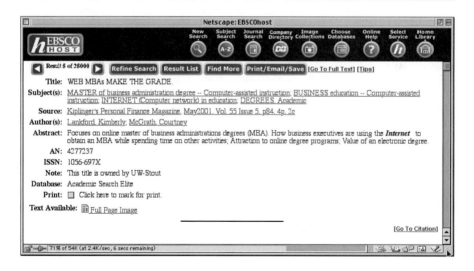

FIGURE 5.7
Bibliography Card

```
  ( 20 )


                    Negrino, Tom

                    "Protect Your E-Mail"

                    Macworld July 2000: 72–77
```

special information about the source (for instance, that you used a micro-fiche version). Such information will help you relocate the source later.

Take Notes.   As you read, take notes and put these ideas on cards as well (Figure 5.8). On each card, write the topic, the name of the author, and the page number from which you are recording information. Then write down a single idea you got from that source. Each card should contain notes on a single subject and from a single source, no more. This practice greatly simplifies arranging your notes when you finally organize the report.

Make Visual Aids. Visual aids always boost reader comprehension. You either find them in your research and or create them yourself. If a key source has a visual aid that clarifies your topic, use it, citing it as explained in Appendix B (pp. 561–588). As you read, however, be creative and construct your own visual aids. Use flow charts to show processes, tables to give numerical data, and drawings to explain machines—whatever will help you (and ultimately your readers) grasp the topic.

Quoting and Paraphrasing. It is essential in writing research reports to know how and when to quote and paraphrase. *Quoting* is using another writer's words verbatim. Use a quote when the exact words of the author clearly support an assertion you have made or when they contain a precise statement of information needed for your report. Copy the exact wording of

FIGURE 5.8
Note Card

> ⟨20⟩
>
> Definitions
>
> linking = "ability to call one
> program from another program"
>
> embed = "ability to put a piece of
> data into a foreign program"
>
> (96)

- Definitions.
- Comments about significance.
- Important statistics.

Paraphrasing means conveying the meaning of the passage in your own words. Learning to paraphrase is tricky. You cannot just change a few words and then claim that your passage is not "the exact words" of the author. To paraphrase, you must express the message in your own original language. Write paraphrases when you want to

- Outline processes or describe machines.
- Give illustrative examples.
- Explain causes, effects, or significance.

The rest of this section explains some basic rules for quoting and paraphrasing. Complete rules for documenting sources appear in Appendix B. Consider this excerpt from *Thriving on Chaos*, by Tom Peters.

> Studies show that each day, like it or not, is marked by thousands of symbolic acts. Your personal note on a memo will be copied by hundreds and deciphered by thousands before nightfall. Your seemingly minor personnel decision will be debated in every outpost of the company, within minutes of your "secretly" making it. Your candid conversation with a

salesperson during a customer call you made together flashes through the grapevine. Your inadvertent decision to park in a different slot this morning is causing reverberations of 5.9 on the Richter scale: "What's it mean?" You are spewing forth signals by the thousand, to thousands, each day. This is a plain fact. Whether or not you approach this inevitable set of signals opportunistically is up to you. But never doubt that you will send them—or that others will make a pattern from them, no matter what you do. What this pattern will suggest to those others, however, can be influenced dramatically. Grab hold of these opportunities. You are a rich, daily pattern to others. You must manage it in today's environment, when the conventional systems (such as policy proclamations and strategic planning) are overwhelmed by the pace of change and proving to be wholly inadequate. Only proactive management of the torrent of signaling activities can create the pace of implementation necessary for business survival. (508)

To quote, place quotation marks before and after the exact words of the author. You generally precede the quotation with a brief introductory phrase.

> According to Tom Peters, "Your seemingly minor personnel decision will be debated in every outpost of the company, within minutes of your 'secretly' making it" (508).

Note that the quotation marks around *secretly* are single, not double, because they occur within a quotation.

If you want to delete part of a quotation from the middle of a sentence, use ellipsis dots (. . .).

> Peters points out that "Your seemingly minor personnel decision will be debated . . . within minutes of your 'secretly' making it" (508).

If you want to insert your own words into a quotation, use brackets.

> Peters feels that "What this pattern [of sending significant signals] will suggest to those others, however, can be influenced dramatically" (508).

To paraphrase, rewrite the passage using your own words. Be sure to indicate in your text the source of your idea: the author and the page number on which the idea is found in the original.

> According to Peters, a creative manager realizes that he or she constantly sends symbolic messages that, amazingly enough, are actually watched closely by other members in the organization. No minor act escapes. Everything you do is interpreted, no matter how minor you think it is. Even parking in a different spot will cause people to talk about the

meaning of that move. Although this situation could be merely annoying, in fact, it is a real opportunity to affect the direction of the company. Overwhelmed by paper and pronouncements, employees ignore or simply do not notice the directives. Because the small acts are not unnoticed and not ignored, they are precisely the forum to use to cause change. The person who realizes and uses the potential of this channel is the true creative manager. A good manager, realizing the inadequacy of such conventional methods of managing change as strategic planning, can actively control the messages to ensure the business's survival. (508)

Remember, when you quote or paraphrase, that you have ethical obligations both to the original author and to the report reader.

1. When in doubt about whether an idea is yours or an author's, give credit to the author.
2. Do not quote or paraphrase in a way that misrepresents the original author's meaning.
3. Avoid stringing one quote after another, which makes the passage hard to read.

▪ WORKSHEET FOR RESEARCH PLANNING

❏ *Name the basic problem that you perceive or a question that you want answered.*

❏ *Determine your audience. Why are they interested in this topic?*

❏ *Think through the implications of the topic. For instance, could the introduction of E-mail (the topic) change gender attitudes in the corporation (implication)?*

❏ *List three questions about the topic that you feel must be answered.*

❏ *List three or four search words that describe your topic.*

❏ *Determine how you find information about this topic. Do you need to read? interview? survey? perform some combination of the three?*

❏ *List the steps you will follow to find the information. Include a time line on which you estimate how many hours or days you need for each step.*

❏ *Name people to interview or survey, outline a test, or list potential sources (technical or nontechnical) of printed information.*

> ❏ *Select a form on which to record the information you discover. If you use interviews or surveys, create this form carefully so that you can later collate answers easily.*

▪ EXERCISES

1. Develop a research plan and implement it.
   a. Create a list of five to eight questions about a topic you want to research. For each question, indicate the kind of resource you need (book, recent article) and a probable search source (*Applied Science and Technology Index, Engineering Index,* library electronic catalog). Explain your list to a group of two or three. Ask for their evaluation, changing your plan as they suggest.
   b. Based on the list you created in Exercise 1a, create a list of five to ten keywords. In groups of two or three, evaluate the words. Try to delete half of them and replace them with better ones.
   c. Select a database (e.g., Compendex) or a Web search engine (e.g., Alta Vista).
   d. Go on to Writing Assignment 3.

2. Conduct a subject search of your library's computerized catalog. Start with a general term (*Internet*) and then, using the system's capabilities, limit the search in at least three different ways (e.g., Internet not E-mail, Internet and manufacturing engineering, Internet or World Wide Web). Print out the bibliography from each search. Write a description of the process you used to derive the bibliographies, and evaluate the effectiveness of your methods.
   Alternate: Write a memo to your classmates on at least two tips that will make their use of the catalog easier.

3. Select a topic of interest. Generate a list of three to five questions about the topic. Read a relevant article in one standard reference source. Based on the article, answer at least one of your questions and pose at least two more questions about the topic.

4. Write a memo in which you analyze and evaluate an index or abstracting service. Use a service from your field of interest, or ask your instructor to assign one. Explain which periodicals and subjects the service lists. Discuss whether it is easy to use. For instance, does it have a cross-reference system? Can a reader find keywords easily?

Explain at what level of knowledge the abstracts are aimed. beginner? expert? The audience for your report is other class members.

5. Write a memo in which you analyze and evaluate a reference book in your field of interest. Explain its arrangement, sections, and intended audience. Is it aimed at a lay or a technical audience? Is it introductory or advanced? Can you use it easily? Your audience is other class members.

6. Form groups of three. One person is the interviewer, one the interviewee, and one the recorder. Your goal is to evaluate an interview. The interviewer asks open and closed questions to discover basic facts about a technological topic that the interviewee knows well. The recorder keeps track of the types of questions, the answers, and the effectiveness of each question in generating a useful answer. Present an oral report that explains and evaluates your process. Did open questions work better? Did the echo technique work?

7. Use Example 9.1 (p. 219) and the information provided in the excerpts of Appendix B, Exercise 4 (p. 581), to create a brief research report on pixels. Your audience is people who are just beginning to use color in documents.

■ WRITING ASSIGNMENTS

1. Write a short research report explaining a recent innovation in your area of interest. Your goal is to recommend whether your company should become committed to this innovation. Consult at least six recent sources. Use quotations, paraphrases, and one of the citation formats explained in Appendix B (pp. 561–588). Organize your material into sections that give the reader a good sense of the dimensions of the topic. The kinds of information you might present include

   ■ Problems in the development of the innovation and potential solutions.
   ■ Issues debated in the topic area.
   ■ Effects of the innovation on your field or on the industry in general.
   ■ Methods of implementing the innovation.

   Your instructor might require that you form groups to research and write this report. If so, he or she will give you a more detailed schedule, but you must formulate questions, research sources of information, and write the report. Use the guidelines for group work outlined in Chapter 3.

2. You (or your group, if your instructor so designates) are assigned to purchase a word processing package for your campus computer lab (or your company network). Research three actual programs and recommend one. Investigate your situation carefully. Talk to users, discover the capabilities of the current computers (RAM, etc.), discover their ability to support this new program (training), and investigate cost and site licenses. Read several reviews.

3. Following one of the documentation formats, write a brief research paper in which you complete the process you began in Exercise 1.

   a. In your chosen database or Web search engine, use your search words and combinations of them to generate a bibliography.

   b. Read two to five articles that will answer one of your questions.

   Alternate: Write a brief report in which you explain the questions you asked, the method you used, and the results you achieved.

4. Divide into groups of three or four. Construct a three- or four-item questionnaire to give to your classmates. Write an introduction, use open and closed questions, and tabulate the answers. At a later class period, give an oral report on the results. Use easy topics, such as demographic inquiries (size of each class member's native city, year in college, length of employment) or inquiries into their knowledge of some common area in a field chosen by the group (such as using search engines on the Web).

5. Interview four people in a workplace to determine their attitude toward a technology (FAX, phone system, photocopying). Present to an administrator a memo recommending a course of action based on the responses. One likely topic is the need for training.

6. Write the report your instructor assigns.

   a. Describe your actions, the number of items and type of information, the value of the entries.

   b. Answer the question in several paragraphs. See Appendix B for listing sources.

   c. Describe your database or search engine. Explain why you selected it; whether it was easy to use; whether it was helpful.

   d. Describe your article. Summarize it and explain how it relates to your topic.

   e. List two questions that you can research further as a result of reading your article.

7. After you have completed your writing assignment, write a learning report, a memo to your instructor. Explain, using details from your work, what new things you have learned or old things confirmed. Use some or all of this list of topics: writing to accommodate an audience, presenting your identity, selecting a strategy, organizing, formatting, creating and using visual aids, using an appropriate style, developing a sense of what is "good enough" for any of the previous topics. In addition, explain why you are proud of your recent work, and tell what aspect of writing you want to work on for the next assignment.

■ WEB EXERCISE

Decide on a topic relevant to your career area. Using the Web, find three full-text professional articles that previously appeared in print and three documents that have appeared only on a Web site. Usually, access through a major university library will achieve the first goal; access to a corporate site will usually achieve the second goal.

Do either of the following, whichever your instructor designates:

a. In an analytical report (see Chapter 12) compare the credibility and the usability of the information in the two types of sources.

b. Write a research paper in which you develop a thesis you have generated as a result of reading the material you collected.

■ WORKS CITED

Library of Congress. *Library of Congress Subject Headings.* 20th ed. 4 vols. Washington, DC: Library of Congress, 1997.

Peters, Tom. *Thriving on Chaos: Handbook for a Management Revolution.* NY: Harper, 1987.

Spivey, Nancy Nelson, and James R. King. "Readers as Writers Composing from Sources." *Reading Research Quarterly* Winter 1989: 7–26.

Stewart, Charles J., and William B. Cash, Jr. *Interviewing Principles and Practices.* 8th ed. Boston: McGraw, 1997.

"Tracking Information." *INSR* 33. Menomonie, WI: University of Wisconsin–Stout Library Learning Center, January 2000.

Warwick, Donald P., and Charles A. Lininger. *The Sample Survey: Theory and Practice.* NY: McGraw, 1975.

Focus on WEB SEARCHING

The World Wide Web (usually just called "the Web") contains stunning amounts of information, so much that, curiously, the problem is to find something you can use. The key is to know how to search effectively.

Search the Web as you would any other database. Choose a search engine, a software program (like Yahoo or Alta Vista) whose purpose is to search a database for instances of the word you ask it to look for. Type keywords into the appropriate box on the search engine's "search page." Review the resulting list of sites, or hits, that contain the word you looked for. The list is the problem—you can get a list that tells you there are a million sites. Which ones to look at? Unfortunately, there is no standard answer. You will have to go through a certain amount of trial and error to find which search engine and which method produces the best results for you.

You can help yourself by understanding how the search engines work, by developing strategies for finding sites, and by learning how to use keywords (Seiter; "Searching").

How Search Engines Work

Search engines are not all the same. Find out how various search engines work. Invesitgate these characteristics:

- Engines look for word or phrases, but they do not all look in the same place. Various engines search for the word in just one of the following: the URL (e.g., *http://www.college.edu/ communication/textbook.html*), the abstract, the keywords that the Web site creator sent to the search engine database, the title, and the full text (all the words in the site). (See "Use a search engine," p. 125.)

- All search engines have Advanced, or Custom, or Power options—the terms vary—that tell you how to limit the number of hits you receive. (See "Using Keywords and Boolean Logic," pp. 125–126.)

Strategies for Finding Sites

Several strategies can help you locate appropriate sites:

- *Surf.* You can find information by surfing, simply starting at one site and clicking on a hyperlink and then on another until you find something interesting.

- *Locate hub sites.* Because a hub site lists many other sites that have a similar interest, finding one is often a way to shorten your search. Hub sites exist for every topic. You can find them for writing centers, for dietetics, for packaging. The problem is that there is no directory of these. Often you can find them in "Web Columns" that appear in many magazines and newspapers. You can often find them by accident, perhaps by surfing out from the first site listed in a search result.

- *Use a search engine.* Search engines usually search just their database. Common search engines include Lycos, Alta Vista, Infoseek, Excite, and Yahoo. Each of these engines searches by a different technique (Alta Vista searches full text; Lycos searches abstracts). Each engine reports a list with a relevancy factor, the database's "guess" of which sites will give the best information. Evaluate the effectiveness of this characteristic; it can be very helpful or misleading. Take the time to perform a comparative search—try the same keyword or phrase in three search engines and compare the results.

- *Use a megasearch engine.* Megasearch engines search a number of databases simultaneously. Common megasearch engines are Metacrawler, Google, and Sherlock. However, these engines do not allow very sophisticated advanced searching.

Using Keywords and Boolean Logic

Most search engines allow you to join keywords with Boolean connectors—*and, or,* and *not.* The engine then reports results that conform to the restrictions that the connectors cause.

The basic guidelines are

- *Choose specific keywords.* Be willing to try synonyms. For example, if *plastic* gives an impossibly long list, try *polymer* or *monomer.*

- *Understand how to use Boolean terms.* Read the instructions in the custom search or help sections of the search engine. Alta Vista, for instance, has an excellent help section.

– *And* (sometimes you have to type + and sometimes AND; it depends) asks the engine to report only sites that contain all the terms. Generally because *and* narrows a search, eliminating many sites, it is an excellent strategy.

– *Or* causes the engine to list any site that contains the term. Entering the words *French and wine* generates a list of just those sites that deal with French wine. *French or wine* generates a much larger list that includes everything that deals with either France or wine.

– *Not* excludes specific terms. Entering *French and wine not burgundy* generates a list that contains information about the other kinds of French wine.

■ Be willing to experiment with various strings of keywords.

Works Cited

"Searching the World Wide Web." Online. Available at *http://www.uwstout. edu/lib/srchwshp.html*. August 4, 1997.

Seiter, Charles. "Better, Faster Web Searching." *Macworld.* December 1996: 159–162.

6 Summarizing

CHAPTER CONTENTS

Chapter 6
IN A NUTSHELL

Summaries tell readers the main points of an article or report. Readers may use summaries to decide whether to read the entire article or report, to get the gist of the article or report without reading it, or to preview the material before reading it.

Your goal is to write the main point of the article in one sentence. Then briefly list the topics or divisions of the article, or explain each of the support points in the same order as they appear in the article, or create a minipaper in which you rearrange the way the parts are presented in order to give a helpful sense of the point of the paper. Be brief (usually one paragraph to one page) and give your readers enough detail so that they can carry out their goal (to get the gist).

I n a world awash in information, the ability to construct and present concise, short versions of long documents is not only helpful but essential. *Summarizing,* or *abstracting*—the terms are nearly synonymous—is fundamental to technical writing. You will often summarize your own documents, as well as those written by others. This chapter explains those skills.

SUMMARIZING

This section defines summaries and abstracts, explains the various audiences that use them, and presents the skills you need in order to write them.

Definitions of Summaries and Abstracts

Both summaries and abstracts are short restatements of another document (Vaughan). A *summary* restates major findings, conclusions, and support data found in a document. Summaries, which accompany many types of reports, are aimed at readers within an organization, typically executives (a common term for this type of writing is *executive summary*). They appear at the beginning of the report, before the body. An *abstract* is generally a short version of a journal article. Abstracts appear in two places: with the article in the periodical and as an independent unit provided by abstracting services for professionals in the field. Abstracts are either indicative or informative. *Indicative abstracts* list the document's topics; *informative abstracts* present short versions of the document's qualitative and quantitative information. An abstract usually mentions the document's purpose, scope, methodologies, results, and conclusion (ANSI).

Audiences for Summaries and Abstracts

Summaries and abstracts serve similar functions, allowing readers to discover the gist of the report or article without reading the entire document, to determine whether the report or article is relevant to their needs, or to get an overview before focusing on the details.

Readers use summaries to review a short version of a longer document when they don't have the time or the need to read the longer document. Readers use abstracts to keep up with current developments in the field and to review literature relevant to a research project. After reading the abstract, the reader can decide whether to read the entire article.

Planning Summaries

To plan for an abstract or a summary, you need to understand basic summarizing strategies, two methods of organizing a summary or abstract, and certain details of form.

Use Basic Summarizing Strategies.   To summarize effectively, perform two separate activities.

1.   Read to find the main terms and concepts.
2.   Decide how much detail to include.

In reading to find the main idea, look for various elements:

■ What are the main divisions of the document?
■ What are the key statements?
■ Which sentence expresses the overall purpose of the document?
■ Which sentences tell the main ideas of each paragraph?
■ What details support the main ideas?
■ What are the key terms? Which words are repeated or emphasized?

Consider the underlining in the article on pages 130–133. Note how the summarizer has underlined key sentences and terms. With practice, you will become confident of your ability to find the major divisions, main points, and main support in a document.

To decide how much detail to include, consider your audience's needs. The general rule is to be as complete as your readers require. If they need just a description of the contents, name only the main sections. (See "Descriptive Abstract," p. 133.) If they need to understand the underlying ideas, provide details (see pp. 133–135).

Choose an Organization.   The two main strategies for organizing a summary are proportional reduction, and main point followed by support.

Proportional reduction refers to the idea that each part in the summary should be proportionally equal to the corresponding part in the original. Suppose the original has four sections, three of which are the same length and one of which is much longer. Your summary of this piece should have the same proportions: three shorter sections of about the same length and a fourth, longer section. You can make the overall summary shorter or longer, depending on how much detail you report for each section, but still maintain the same proportions.

Main point followed by support means you should write a clear topic sentence that repeats the central thesis of the document. This topic sentence could be the purpose of the report or its main findings, conclusions, or recommendations (see pp. 134–135). This method is generally harder to write, but it is often more effective for readers because you can slant the summary to meet the reader's needs (ANSI).

Use the Usual Form.   Summaries generally have the following characteristics:

- Length of 250 words to 1 page (Abstracts that will be reprinted must stay brief, about 250–300 words. Summaries can be longer; a 200-page report might need 2 to 5 pages for a clear, inclusive summary.)
- Verbs in the active voice and present tense
- A clear reference to the document (Abstracts always include a complete bibliographic entry. Generally report summaries contain the title of the report either in the first sentence or in the title.)
- No terms, abbreviations, or symbols unfamiliar to the reader (Do not define terms in a summary unless definition was the main point of the document. Notice the unexplained technical terms in "Summary Emphasizing Major Idea," pp. 134–135.)
- No evaluative comments such as "In findings related tangentially at best to the facts she presents . . ." (Report the contents of the document without bias.)
- Main points first (The first sentence usually gives the purpose of the report or the main findings; support follows.)

Writing Summaries

Read the following article. Then review the abstract and the two types of summaries on pages 134–135. Because the article is rather difficult for nonexperts, the summary can increase your ability to comprehend the article. Many harried managers might prefer the summary to the article. To save space, the figures, which are fairly technical, are not reproduced here.

EUROPEAN SHIPPING PLATFORMS

DEVELOPING A DOMESTIC SOURCE

When the French subsidiary of a major U.S. fruit juice processor requested that shipments of finished product be made on Europallets, some interesting and complicated packaging aspects had to be addressed. The request was made in an effort to expedite distribution in the expanding French market and in preparation for entry into the single European market that will replace the common market.

PROJECT OBJECTIVE

The subsidiary, based in Paris, was receiving containerized shipments of both refrigerated and dry juice products loaded on standard 48" × 40" GMA pallets and shipped through the Port of Miami. Upon arrival at the French Port of Le Havre, the containers were being off-loaded and hauled approximately 145 kilometers to a distribution center where the product was transferred to 800 mm × 1200 Europallets for shipment to the actual customer. In some cases this meant backtracking toward the coast and, as is true in most cases when additional handling is involved, there was an above-normal amount of damaged product.

DOMESTIC VS. EUROPEAN

It was first thought that the request for product shipments on European style pallets, or Europallets, would not be a very difficult packaging change to make, especially for a company that was ready to make direct shipments to customers in Canada and England. Both countries have tight control over the supply and quality of pallets entering their pallet float. What was quickly discovered was that not only were the block style European pallets not being produced in the U.S., but quantities of used Europallets used to ship European goods to the U.S. were also unavailable. Shipping on slip sheets for transfer to Europallets upon arrival in Europe had to be ruled out due to unavailability of push-pull equipment at most of the customers' locations.

The decision was made to explore producing the pallets locally. A sample pallet was obtained from France in an effort to determine the feasibility of manufacturing European-type pallets in the U.S. on a commercial basis. The European pallet is described as an 800 × 200 millimeters nine-post block pallet, double-face, nonreversible flush construction, whereas a standard GMA pallet measures 48 inches × 40 inches or 1219 × 1016 millimeters, has three stringers rather than nine blocks, and is double-face, nonreversible, flush construction. It became readily apparent that this stringer versus block construction difference in the way the pallet types are built would be a dictating factor on the cost of Europallets if they were to be manufactured domestically. As to be expected, no U.S. pallet manufacturers had automated pallet production equipment capable of building block type pallets.

REGULATORY OBSTACLES

In addition to the lack of automated pallet manufacturing equipment in the U.S., it was discovered that the manufacturers of Europallets were required to be licensed by the PEP and that only railroad companies that were members of the PEP could issue a license to a pallet producer.

To further complicate matters, in an effort to control pallet quality and prevent inferior pallets from entering the pallet float from Eastern Bloc Nations, no licenses were being issued to non-European countries. This obstacle was overcome by entering into an agreement with a pallet rental company who was already operating in Europe and held a manufacturing license. Under the agreement, pallets woud be produced in the U.S. by a domestic pallet manufacturer under the license of the European pool maker. The juice producer would ship its product into France on the new Europallets. As the juice products were off-loaded from the pallets, the pallets would enter the French Pallet Float as property of the French licensee, with the juice producer paying an issue, delivery, and transfer fee in addition to daily pallet rent for the time the juice products were actually on the rental pallets, the only condition being that the U.S.-produced pallets meet the PEP standards for quality.

PALLET TESTING

A pallet manufacturer with plants in several Southern States was contracted to build the initial supply of Europallets that would be used in the qualifying shipping and construction tests.

The pallets were loaded by hand, using pallet platforms developed with the juice producer's standard case sizes and then stretch-wrapped using a portable stretch wrapper. The product was loaded into sea/land containers and transported to Miami for loading aboard a container vessel for the 12-day voyage to the Port of Le Havre. Upon arrival at the juice producer's Paris distribution center, the product was offloaded from the test pallets and transported to the TNO Industrial Research Center at Delph, Holland.

The object of the initial test was to obtain some comparative data on pallets made from southern yellow pine by utilizing three of the tests specified in the ISO (International Standards Organization) series of pallet tests, ISO 8611.

The three tests performed are as follows:

- Racked across stringers (boards) 800 span (Figure 1)
- Racked across deck board 1200 span (Figure 2)
- Corner drop test (Figure 3)

TEST RESULTS

The U.S.-manufactured pallets exceeded the quality requirements of the European-based pallet rental company. [Note: Figures 1–3, too large to reproduce here, show the following results. 1. Racked across stringers 800 span—the ISO-allowed deflection is 16.25 mm; the average deflection of the tested unit was 12.76 mm. 2. Racked across board 1200 span—the ISO-allowed deflection is 26.25 mm; the average deflection of the tested unit was 16.39 mm. 3. Corner drop test—the allowed change in draft is 4%; the tested pallet changed 3.06%.]

INPLANT HANDLING ISSUES

Numerous difficulties were encountered at the juice processor's Florida Production Plant when the test Europallets were entered into the production system. Due to the Europallets' shorter length, 800 millimeters compared to the GMA pallet's 1200+ millimeters, the Europallets would not fit properly into the magazines of the palletizers.

Discussions with the palletizer manufacturer disclosed that only the newest of the various models in use at the processor's plant could be modified to accommodate the Europallet configuration. In addition, the cost of the equipment modifications was almost equal to total replacement of the palletizers.

The bottom design of the Europallet was not compatible with existing conveyor configurations, nor did the Europallet design lend itself to storage in gravity feed type storage racks.

When placed in the gravity racks, the Europallets had a tendency to break off the lead bottom board and the lead board's three supporting blocks upon contact with the rack's braking mechanism.

The short length of the Europallet proved to be a problem for lift trucks equipped with the standard-length (42-inch) forks, normally used for handling GMA pallets, as the forks protruded out the back of the Europallet and had a tendency to damage the second pallet in the row when the first pallet was lifted. This disadvantage can be corrected by changing to 30-inch forks prior to handling the Europallets, although changing the fork length back and forth was time consuming.

The biggest downside found using the Europallets in a high-volume materials handling equipment was that the Europallet design proved to be quite fragile compared to the GMA pallet and the nine-block UK (United Kingdom) pallets normally used by the juice processor.

IN CONCLUSION

The European shipping platform project proved that direct shipments of juice products to consumers in Europe was economically and physically possible and provided a new packaging material source that will allow other American companies easier access to a potentially unlimited European market. However, due to the high capital cost of palletizing capable of utilizing European style pallets and the in-plant handling issues, coupled with the small customer base capable of receiving entire container load product order, product shipments unitized on Europallets are not being made on a regular basis at this time.

DESCRIPTIVE ABSTRACT

Cartwright, Mark A. (1993). European shipping platforms: Developing a domestic source. *IoPP Technical Journal* *11*(1):20–24.

Bibliographic information

This article reports the results of a project to build European-style pallets in the U.S. Topics include producing the pallets in the U.S., resolving regulatory problems, test procedures and results, and in-plant handling issues.

List of article's contents

SUMMARY USING PROPORTIONAL REDUCTION

Cartwright, Mark A. (1993). European shipping platforms: Developing a domestic source. *IoPP Technical Journal 11*(1):20–24.

A major U.S. fruit juice processor successfully constructed and shipped Europallets. The old method of shipping caused abnormal product damage because the product was shipped on GMA pallets (48″ × 40″) and transferred to Europallets (800 mm × 1200 mm). Because European pallets were not available in any form, the processor contracted with an American company to provide them. The pallets' block construction (nine-post, double-face, non-reversible flush) caused cost problems because of the re-tooling necessary. Only European manufacturers can receive licenses to use Europallets, so the U.S. company agreed to produce the pallets in the United States under the license of a French company. Pallets were shipped to Europe, then tested. Standard ISO tests (8611) prove that the U.S. pallets exceeded European quality requirements. Major in-plant issues included improper fit into maga-zines of palletizers, cost of equipment modifications, breakage caused by the lead bottom board, short length, and fragility. The project is economically and physically successful but the cost, in-plant issues, and small customer base prevent regular production.	Purpose Part 1 Part 2 Part 3 Part 4 Part 5

SUMMARY EMPHASIZING MAJOR IDEA

Cartwright, Mark A. (1993). European shipping platforms: Developing a domestic source. *IoPP Technical Journal 11*(1):20–24.

Despite large obstacles, a major U.S. fruit juice processor has concluded that using U.S.-built Europallets for Euro-pean shipment is economically and physically possible. Built for a French subsidiary, the American-produced Europallets (800 mm × 1200 mm, nine-block, double-face, nonreversible, flush construction) surpassed Euro-pean (PEP) quality standards in ISO 8611 tests (across 800 span—average deflection of 12.76 versus 16.25 mm allowed; across 1200 span—average deflection of 16.39 versus 26.25 mm allowed; corner drop—3.06% drop change versus 4% allowed). Problems overcome include production, licensing, and handling. No automated equipment was available to build the pallets in the U.S.; modifications to existing machines cost the same as purchasing new ones. Since licenses to allow entry into	Purpose Situation Test results Each problem followed by a solution

Europe are not granted to non-European manufacturers, the processor had to contract with a licensed French company, who took possession of the pallets and rented them back to the American company. Tested in Delph, Holland, at TNO Industrial Research Center, the pallets met all requirements. The shorter length Europallets did not fit into the magazines of palletizers, which had to be modified at considerable cost. The bottom design of the Europallet caused the lead board and its blocks to break off in existing conveyor configurations. Lift trucks needed to use 30-inch (rather than 42-inch) forks; the changeover was time consuming. Despite the success of the project, the small customer base currently prevents regular unitized shipments.

■ WORKSHEET FOR SUMMARIZING

❑ *Read over the article or report you intend to summarize.*

❑ *Determine your audience for this summary.*
How much do they know about the topic?

❑ *How will your audience use this summary? (Experts want names of people and companies, and they understand common jargon in the field; nonexperts don't.)*
Do they want an overview? Are they trying to "keep up"? Will they use it instead of reading the entire document? Will they make a decision on the basis of its contents?

❑ *Mark all keywords and phrases.*

❑ *Arrange all the words and phrases into groups or clusters.*

❑ *Write a sentence stating the main point you want to convey.*

❑ *List the groups or clusters you have created in the order in which you will present them.*

EXAMPLES

Both of the following professional abstracts clearly indicate the contents and main points of their respective articles. Readers can determine the main point of each article, even if they do not have the knowledge background to evaluate the specifics.

EXAMPLE 6.1
Professional Abstract

A high-brightness, high-yield cheminmechanical pulp was obtained from *Eucalyptus globulus* using low-environmental-impact chemical reagents. The pulping chemicals were nitric acid and sodium hydroxide, and the bleaching chemical was hydrogen peroxide. Chips were impregnated for 24 h in nitric acid, cooked under variable conditions, washed, impregnated with soda for 24 h, cooked again, rewashed, defibrated, refined, screened, and finally bleached under variable conditions. Under the optimal pulping conditions identified in this study, pulp strenth was not especially high (tensile strength 2.04 km, tea strength 3.9 mN·m^2/g), but the ease of bleaching and final pulp brightness were impressive enough (light-scattering coefficient 49.3 m^{2}kg, brightness 81.3% Elrepho) to warrant further research.

EXAMPLE 6.2
Professional Abstract

From Johnson-Eilola, Johndan. "Relocating the Value of Work: Technical Communication in a Post-Industrial Age," *Technical Communication Quarterly* 5.3 (Summer 1996): 245. Reprinted by permission of the author and the Association of Teachers of Technical Writing.

This article analyzes the location of "value" in technical communication contexts, arguing that current models of technical communication embrace an outdated, self-deprecating, industrial approach subordinating information to concrete technological products. By rethinking technical communication in terms of Reich's "symbolic-analytic work," technical communicators and educators can move into a post-industrial model of work that prioritizes information and communication, with benefits to both technical communicators and users.

■ EXERCISES

1. Rewrite the major idea summary (pp. 134–135) to emphasize the processes involved in the pallet report.

2. Write an abstract for the report in Example 12.1 found in Chapter 12, pages 306–308.

3. Write a one-paragraph summary of Example 4.1 in Chapter 4 (pp. 87–88). Make the summary a proportional reduction of the original. Keep the points in the same order as in the original.

4. Photocopy a short (two- to four-page) article in your field (or an article your instructor supplies).
   a. Decide who your audience is and the type of information they need from the article (details of test results? details of methodology? broad implications?).
   b. Create a major idea summary.
   c. Optional: Create a proportional reduction summary.

5. Evaluate this summary to decide its type and effectiveness. Rewrite it if necessary.

   Regulatory obstacles prevented a successful introduction of Europallets into an American juice processor's product line. This manufacturer had a subsidiary in France who wanted the U.S. firm to send the finished juice product to Europe on Europallets. However, the U.S. firm could not send the pallets because they were not licensed by the PEP. The U.S. firm entered into an agreement with a French firm. In effect, the U.S. firm sold the pallets to the French firm so that the pallets would enter the French Pallet Float as property of the French licensee. The French firm paid the various fees and rent required by the PEP. After this arrangement was made, the U.S. firm had to build the pallets, which were smaller than standard U.S. pallets. The pallets were often broken by gravity racks and forklifts. The high capital cost of palletizing, due to these rules, caused the U.S. firm to not make product shipments using Europallets on a regular basis at this time.

6. Analyze Example 6.1 (p. 136) for type and strengths.

7. Analyze Example 6.2 (p. 137) for type and strengths.

8. Write a learning report for the assignment you just completed. See Chapter 5, Writing Assignment 7, page 123, for details of the assignment.

■ WEB EXERCISE

Select an innovative technology in your field (biodegradable plastics, digital television, micromachines). Find a Web site that contains an article or report on the technology. Write a descriptive abstract and a proportional reduction abstract of the document for a nontechnical audience.

■ WORKS CITED

American National Standards Institute (ANSI). *American National Standard for Writing Abstracts* (Z39.14-1979). NY: ANSI, 1979.

Cartwright, Mark A. "European Shipping Platforms: Developing a Domestic Source." *IoPP Technical Journal* 11(1) (1993): 20–24.

Vaughan, David K. "Abstracts and Summaries: Some Clarifying Distinctions." *The Technical Writing Teacher* 18.2 (1991): 132–141.

7 Designing Pages

Chapter 7
IN A NUTSHELL

Design is the *visual arrangement* of your page. The key idea is to establish a *visual logic*—the same kind of information always looks the same way and appears in the same place (page numbers are italicized in the upper right corner, for instance). The two key concepts in format are *heads* and *chunks*.

Visual logic. Visual logic establishes your credibility, because you demonstrate that you know enough about the topic and about communicating to be consistent. Visual logic helps your audience to see the "big picture" of your topic, and as a result they grasp your point more quickly.

Heads and chunks. *Heads* are words or phrases that tell the content of the next section. Heads should inform and attract attention—use a phrase or ask a question; avoid cryptic, one-word heads.

Heads have levels—one or two are most common; more than four is rare. The levels should look different and make their contents helpful for readers. Most audiences normally expect that bigger and closer to the left symbolize higher levels than smaller and indented. However, when centered heads are present, by tradition, they always indicate the highest level.

Chunks are any pieces of text surrounded by white space. Typically, readers find a topic presented in several smaller chunks easier to grasp than one longer chunk.

Chunks should relate to organization. For instance, you can indent a chunk, thus indicating that the topic in that chunk is subordinate to the one above it—as often happens in lists.

Technical writing is presentational, communicating in part by visually engaging readers. Clearly designed pages clarify organization and increase readability. Desktop publishing programs such as Quark®, Pagemaker®, and all advanced word processing programs now give writers design capabilities. With these programs, writers can lay out documents that present their message clearly and help the reader find and understand information quickly (Southard; Kostelnick; Kramer and Bernhardt). To help readers grasp the visual logic of the format, trusting it to guide them through the document, writers should design for readers, learn the elements of page design, use basic design guidelines, and develop a style sheet.

DESIGN FOR READERS

As in all other aspects of technical communication, affecting the reader positively is your most important goal in page design.

According to Karen Shriver, an expert in document design, the real task of a writer is to make the audience feel that "someone has taken the time to speak clearly, knowledgeably, and honestly to them" (204). One effective way to accomplish this task is through design. Writers can use design to set the mode of a document (formal or informal), reveal the document's structure, affect the way readers navigate the document, and reveal what is important (250).

If writers take the time to plan each document around the reader's needs, using design to reveal mood, structure, navigation and importance, they will make a favorable impression on the reader. That favorable impression, as much as the words in the sentences, will help effectively convey the message of the document.

According to Shriver (387–388), some effective general guidelines for solving design problems are

- Specify the intended audience.
- Provide overviews.
- Use a consistent approach to all design features.
- Focus on readers' needs in the situation.
- Use text features to reveal the document's structure for the reader.

LEARN THE ELEMENTS OF PAGE DESIGN

This section explains terms that are basic to page design and gives some general guidelines for their use. The basic elements of page design are page parts, white space, text features, and heads.

Page Parts

The basic page parts are subdivisions of a page that give readers structural information. These parts are the live area, headers (also called "running heads"), footers (also called "running feet"), and page numbers (see Figure 7.1).

The *live area* is the part of the page that lies inside the margins. Word processors create live areas by default; they automatically give each page a set of margins, often 1 inch on all four edges. A one-column text has one unit of live area. A two-column text has two live areas. *Headers,* which appear at the top of pages, describe the content of the page or chapter. Major information such as chapter titles usually appears in headers. Usually, documents use only headers. *Footers,* which appear at the bottom of pages, also describe the contents of the page or chapter. Footers generally add only minor information, such as the contents of a page.

A *page number* appears on each page, usually in one of the three positions shown in Figure 7.1. Place page numbers in the same position throughout the document. (The number 1 may or may not appear on page 1.)

White Space

White space (see Figure 7.2 on page 144) is any area of the page that does not contain text or visuals. White space groups the text into *chunks,* visual organizational units. Too much white space makes items appear disconnected from surrounding items. Too little white space causes items to appear crowded and jumbled (Sadowski; Shriver). White space includes the four margins, indentations, and leading.

Margins indicate the boundaries of the text. The left margin is usually 1.5 inches, especially if the document will be bound. The other three margins are usually at least 1 inch. The bottom margin is often much larger because text does not fill the page.

Indentations (see Figure 7.2) indicate that a new item or subject begins (a paragraph indentation) or that it is subordinate (an indented list). Five spaces, or ½ inch, are standard increments of indentation. *Leading* (which rhymes with *heading*) determines the space between lines of text. Leading is measured in points; a point equals $\frac{1}{72}$ of an inch. For easy reading, leading size is always larger than font size (discussed below).

Text Features

Text features are characteristics of the words and lines of print (see Figure 7.3 on page 145). They include fonts (typefaces), type size, rules, columns, justification, and highlighters.

The *font,* or *typeface,* is the style of type. Fonts have "personality"—some seem frivolous, some interesting, and some serious and "workaday." Some typefaces frequently used in reports and letters are Times, Helvetica,

FIGURE 7.1
Basic Page Parts

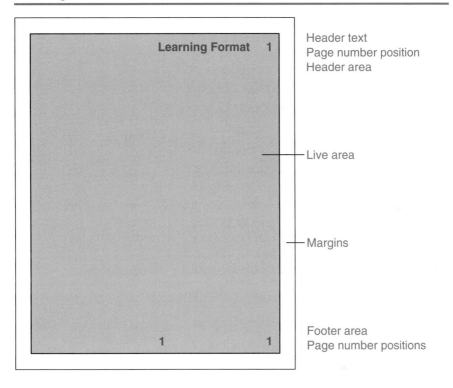

and Palatino, all of which appear "average" or "usual," the normal way to deliver information.

This is Times.

This is Helvetica.

This is Palatino.

Typefaces belong to one of two major groups (see Figure 7.3): serif and sans serif. The letters in *serif* faces have extenders at the ends of their straight lines. *Sans serif* faces do not. Serif faces give a classical, more formal impression, whereas sans serif faces appear more modern and informal. There is evidence that serif faces are easier to read.

Serif   Technical writing makes the world go around.

Sans serif   Technical writing makes the world go around.

Practice with fonts. Find one that "feels appropriate."

FIGURE 7.2
White Space

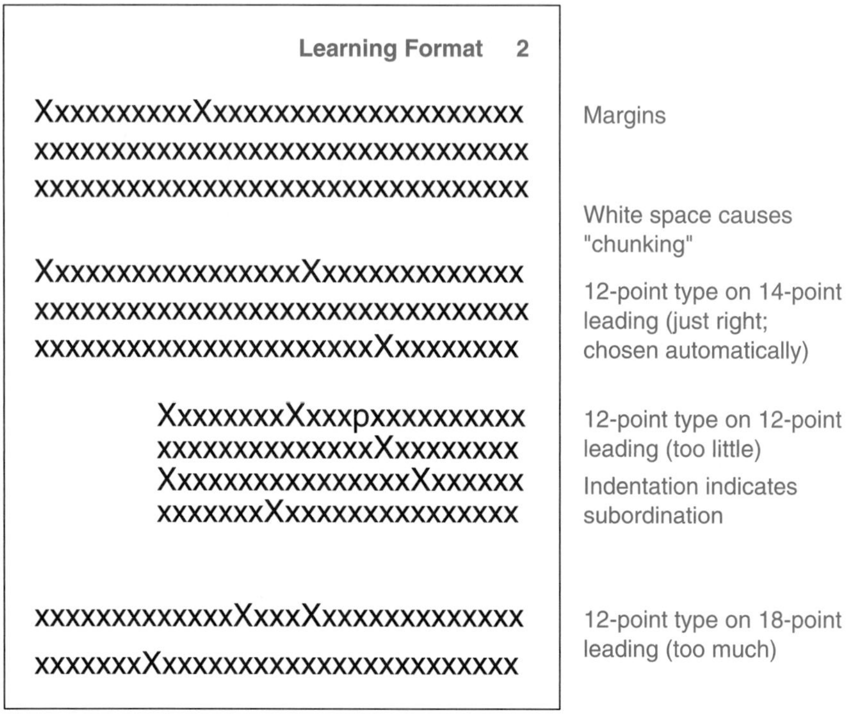

Learning Format 2	
XxxxxxxxxxXxxxxxxxxxxxxxxxxxxxx	Margins
xxxxxxxxxxxxxxxxxxxxxxxxxxxxxxxx	
xxxxxxxxxxxxxxxxxxxxxxxxxxxxxxxx	
	White space causes "chunking"
XxxxxxxxxxxxxxxxXxxxxxxxxxxxxx	12-point type on 14-point leading (just right; chosen automatically)
xxxxxxxxxxxxxxxxxxxxxxxxxxxxxxxx	
xxxxxxxxxxxxxxxxxxxxxxxXxxxxxxxx	
XxxxxxxxXxxxpxxxxxxxxxx	12-point type on 12-point leading (too little)
xxxxxxxxxxxxxxXxxxxxxxx	
XxxxxxxxxxxxxxxXxxxxxx	Indentation indicates subordination
xxxxxxxXxxxxxxxxxxxxxx	
xxxxxxxxxxxxxxXxxxXxxxxxxxxxxxx	12-point type on 18-point leading (too much)
xxxxxxxXxxxxxxxxxxxxxxxxxxxxxxx	

- Use the same font for text and heads.
- If you must use two fonts, put the text in a serif font and the heads in a sans serif font.
- Avoid "show" fonts (like Chicago or San Francisco) in reports.

Type size is the height of the letters. Size is measured in points; 1 point equals ½₂ of an inch. Common text sizes are 9, 10, and 12 points. Common heading sizes are 14, 18, and 24 points. Type size affects the number of characters in a line; the larger the point size, the fewer characters in a line.

18-POINT type allows this many characters.

9-POINT type allows many more characters in a line of the same length, causing a different sense of width. (Felker et al.)

As Figure 7.3 shows, type size affects the appearance, length, and readability of your document.

FIGURE 7.3
Text Features

Learning Format   3

18-Point Helvetica

One column

Rule

This paragraph appears in 12-point Palatino, a *serif* font. The paragraph is "ragged right," which means I turned off the "right-justification" command in my word processor. It is set in 12-point type because it is extremely easy to read.

Italics highlight
Serif font

Ragged right margin

This paragraph appears in 9-point Helvetica, a **sans serif** font. The paragraph is right-justified. The right margin appears as a straight line. Research and practice vary on right-justifying. Research suggests not to.
• *Time* magazine does not justify.
• The *New Yorker* does.
Long paragraphs of Helvetica are not comfortable to read.

Bold highlight
Sans serif font

Right-justified

Vertical list highlight

▪ Use 10- or 12-point type in your documents. Most magazines use 10-point, but 12-point is often used in reports.

▪ Relate your type size to your column line length, explained below.

Rules are lines that are often used to separate elements on pages. Usually they set off headers and footers or visual aids, but they can also be used as design elements. Do not use rules thicker than 2 points; a *hairline* (or ½-point) rule is a good choice. The thicker the rule, the more it draws the reader's eye. A thicker rule causes a thinner rule to appear subordinate. In general, thick rules appear above words and thin rules appear below.

Columns are vertical lines of type; a normal typed page has one wide column. Many word processing programs allow multiple columns (12 or more); in practice, however, reports seldom require more than 2 columns. In general, use a single column for reports. To achieve a "modern" design, consider using a 2- or 2½-inch left margin. In other cases, two columns are especially useful for reports and manuals if you plan to include several graphics. For various column widths, see Examples 7.1 and 7.2, pages 160–161.

Column width affects *line length,* the number of characters that will fit into one line of type. Line length affects readability (Felker; Shriver). If the lines are too long, readers must concentrate hard as they travel along a line and then painstakingly locate the correct next line back at the left margin. If the lines are too short, readers become aware of shifting back more frequently than normal. Short lines also cause too much hyphenation.

Typographers use three rules of thumb (White) to choose a line length and a type size.

- ◼ Use one and a half alphabets (39 characters) or 8 words per line.
- ◼ Use 60 to 70 characters per line (common in books).
- ◼ Use 10 words of average length (about 50 characters).

Unfortunately, no rule exists for all situations. You must experiment with each situation. In general, increase readability by adding more leading to lines that contain more characters (White).

Justification (see Figure 7.3) means aligning the first or last letters of the lines of a column. Documents are almost always "left-justified": the first letter of each line starts at the left margin. Right-justified means that all the letters that end lines are aligned at the right margin. Avoid right-justified margins if your software achieves right justification by inserting too many spaces between words or by hyphenating excessively. Research shows that "ragged-right" text reads more easily than right-justified text (Felker).

Highlighters emphasize text by making it look different from the surrounding text. The highlighters are

boldface

underlining

italics

ALL CAPITALS

vertical lists

Here are basic highlighting guidelines:

- ◼ Highlight, but not too much.
- ◼ Boldface and underlining are the most effective highlighters of words or phrases. Use boldface with laser printers, underlining with typewriters.
- ◼ Use italics and all capitals to highlight individual words; because they are harder to read, do not use them to highlight one or more lines. Italics, frequently used in this chapter, is a quiet emphasizer. If all the *italicized* words were **boldfaced,** the pages would appear **cluttered.**

- Use vertical lists to emphasize the items in a series.
- Use numbers or bullets to emphasize where each item starts.
- Use computer trick devices rarely. These gimmicks include shadow lettering, outline lettering, and reverse type (white characters on black rectangles).

Notice the difference in these two versions of the same sentence.

Not highlighted   The major units of the company are manufacturing, sales, and development.

Highlighted   The **major** units of the company are

- manufacturing
- sales
- development

System of Heads

The head system imposed on a document shows its contents and organization. A *head* is a word or phrase that indicates the contents of the following section or subsection (see Figure 7.4). Heads appear in *levels*. Level 1 heads indicate the major divisions of a document. Level 2 heads indicate subdivisions of the major divisions. Most documents contain one or two levels of heads. Here are four basic guidelines for developing a system of heads:

1. Make each level look different to express your visual logic. Use boldfacing or underlining and different print sizes. For instance, if you capitalize all the words in level 1, capitalize only the first letter of words in level 2 (see Figure 7.4, p. 148).
2. Make higher levels more prominent than lower levels (see Figures 7.5–7.6, pp. 149–150). Phrases in all capital letters ("all caps") are more prominent than phrases with only the first letters capitalized.
   - Larger is more prominent than smaller. A 14-point head indicates a higher level than a 10-point head.
   - Left is more prominent than indented.
   - The center of the page is the highest position, but use it only if you have three or more levels.
   - Boldface print is more prominent than nonboldface print. Use italics for heads only if you boldface them.
3. Make the wording parallel within each level. Use all noun phrases, all questions, or all *-ing* words.

FIGURE 7.4
Three Levels of Boldface Open Heads

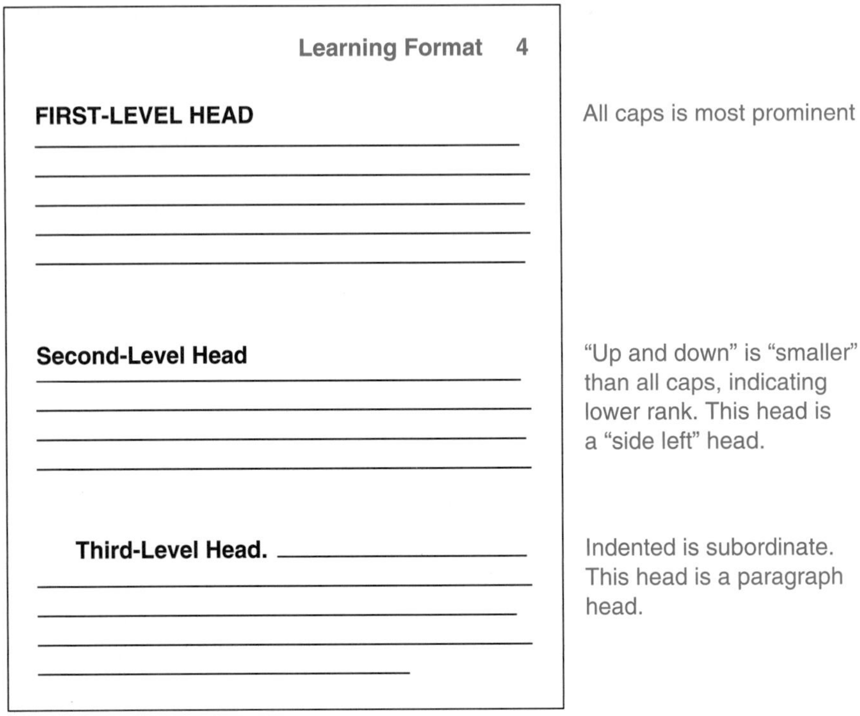

Learning Format 4	
FIRST-LEVEL HEAD	All caps is most prominent
Second-Level Head	"Up and down" is "smaller" than all caps, indicating lower rank. This head is a "side left" head.
Third-Level Head. ――――――	Indented is subordinate. This head is a paragraph head.

4. Use wording specific to your content, not generic wording. For instance, use *Factors in Total Cost* rather than *Cost,* or use a question such as *What Factors Affect Total Cost?*

Indicating Two Levels of Heads.   Most documents need only one or two levels of heads (see Figure 7.5). Most writers use a *side left* head as the level 1 head and a *paragraph* head as the level 2 head. For a side left head, place the head at the left margin, leave white space above and below, use no punctuation after, and boldface it. For a paragraph head, place the head at the start of the paragraph, indent five spaces, and follow it by a period.

Compare the use of paragraph heads in Figures 7.4 and 7.5. Notice that the same style (paragraph head) can indicate different levels, depending on the total number of levels (two or three). In Figure 7.4 the paragraph heads are level 3, but in Figure 7.5 they are level 2.

Indicating More Than Two Levels of Heads.   The key here is to be consistent. Figures 7.5 to 7.7 indicate common ways to arrange heads. Head systems can be *open* or *numbered;* both can indicate up to four or five levels of heads. In Figures 7.5 and 7.6, note which letters are capitalized, how much space is left above and below, and whether punctuation follows.

The numbered system, often used in more technical or more complex material, indicates level by a number before the head. Each succeeding level uses more numbers. The first level is 1.0, 2.0, etc. The second level is 1.1, 1.2; the third level 1.1.1, 1.1.2. (see Figure 7.7, p. 151).

USE BASIC DESIGN GUIDELINES

Properly designed pages guide readers through a document and enable them to grasp main points and subpoints quickly. The key to page design is to develop a visual logic by treating each element obviously and consistently (Xerox). Readers will quickly grasp that all 14-point bold words are level 1 heads indicating a new major topic or that bullets signal a list. Once you establish your system, do not change it. The following guidelines (established by researchers and practitioners) will help you:

1. Use larger-to-smaller orientation (see Figure 7.8). Readers react to size, looking at larger items first (Sadowski). Put more important

FIGURE 7.5
Two Levels of Heads

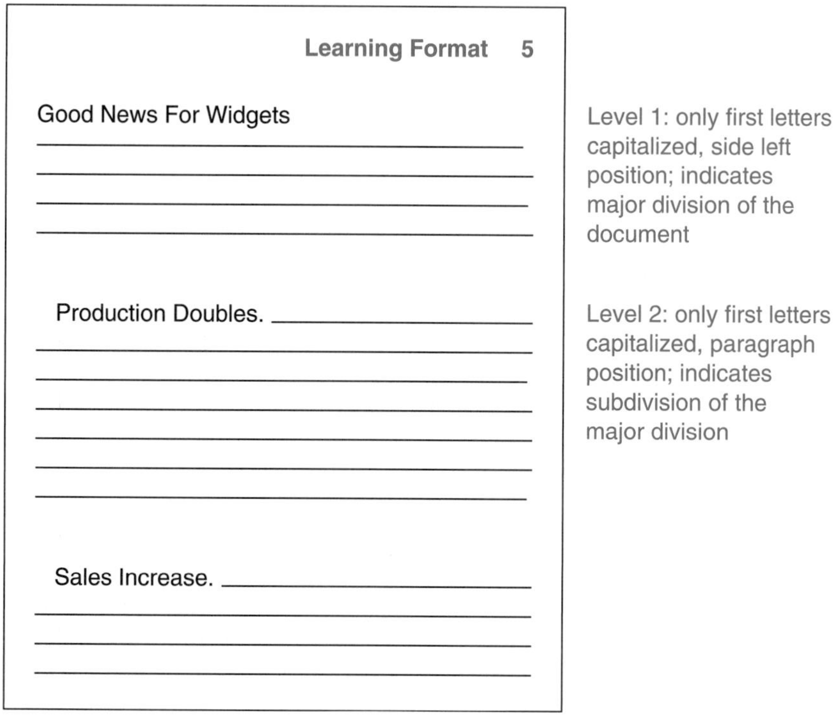

Learning Format   5

Good News For Widgets
_____
_____
_____
_____

Level 1: only first letters capitalized, side left position; indicates major division of the document

Production Doubles. _____
_____
_____
_____
_____
_____

Level 2: only first letters capitalized, paragraph position; indicates subdivision of the major division

Sales Increase. _____
_____
_____
_____

FIGURE 7.6
Four Levels of Boldface Open Heads

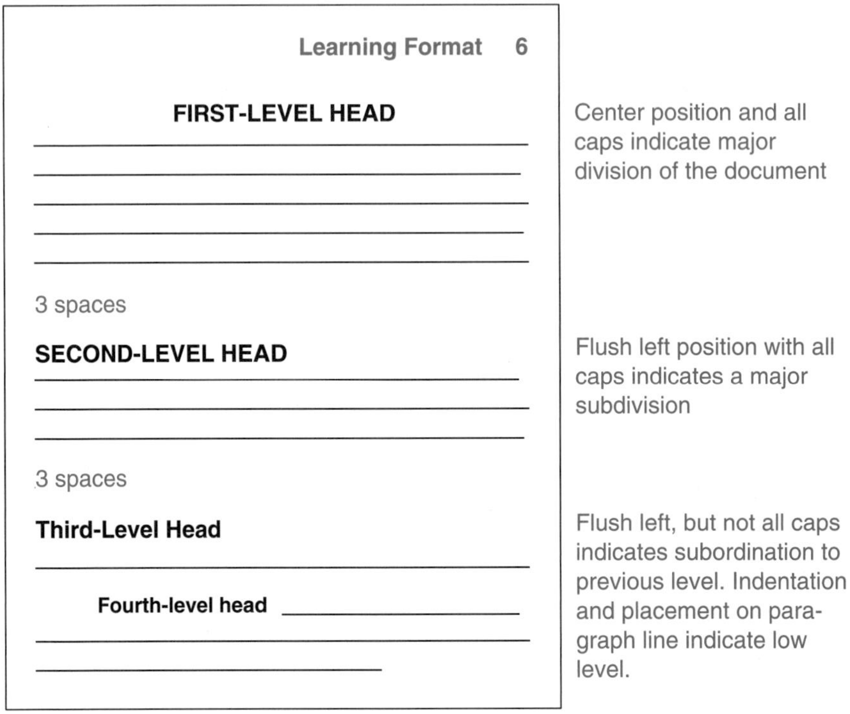

Learning Format   6

FIRST-LEVEL HEAD

———————————————————————
————————————————————
—————————————————————
—————————————————————
—————————————————————

3 spaces

SECOND-LEVEL HEAD

—————————————————————
—————————————————————
——————————————————

3 spaces

Third-Level Head

—————————————————————

Fourth-level head ——————————
—————————————————————
————————————————

Center position and all caps indicate major division of the document

Flush left position with all caps indicates a major subdivision

Flush left, but not all caps indicates subordination to previous level. Indentation and placement on paragraph line indicate low level.

material (such as heads) in larger text type. *Note:* Emphasizing causes a similar effect. Boldfaced 12-point type seems larger than normal (or roman) 12-point type.

2. Use left-to-right orientation to lead your readers through the text (Rubens). Place larger heads or key visuals to the left and text to the right to draw readers into your message (see Figure 7.9, p. 152 and Example 7.1, p. 160). In Example 7.1, the large left margin gives a "modern" look, now often used in reports.

3. Chunk white space to group items into visually coherent units for the reader (Cook and Kellogg). See Figure 7.10 (p. 153).

4. Queue your text. To queue text is to use many format elements to indicate hierarchy. Figure 7.11 (p. 153), which uses only white space to set off each item of text, indicates that three items are equal and one is subordinate; they all look the same. In Figure 7.12 (p. 154), the items of text have been organized from most to least important, shown by

FIGURE 7.7
Four Levels of Numbered Heads

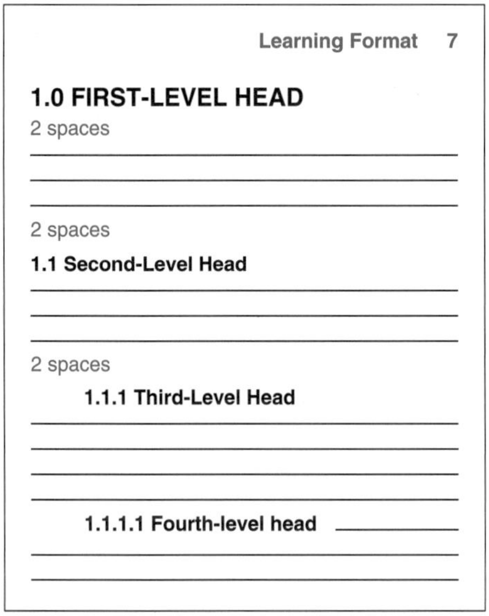

Learning Format   7

1.0 FIRST-LEVEL HEAD
2 spaces
_____
_____

2 spaces
1.1 Second-Level Head
_____
_____

2 spaces
    1.1.1 Third-Level Head
_____
_____
_____

    1.1.1.1 Fourth-level head _____
_____
_____

FIGURE 7.8
Larger-to-Smaller Orientation

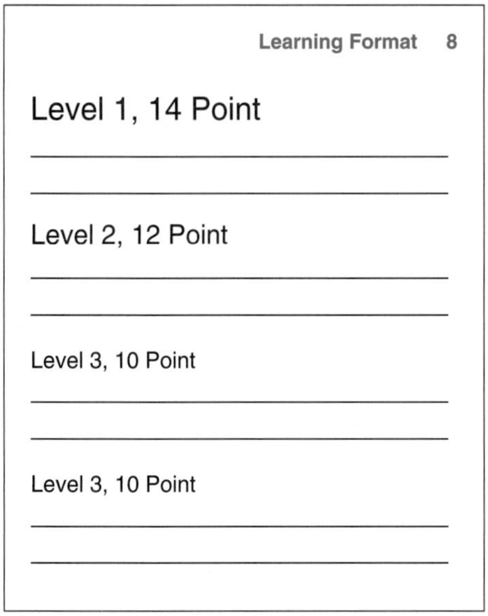

Learning Format   8

Level 1, 14 Point
_____
_____

Level 2, 12 Point
_____
_____

Level 3, 10 Point
_____
_____

Level 3, 10 Point
_____
_____

FIGURE 7.9
Left-to-Right Orientation

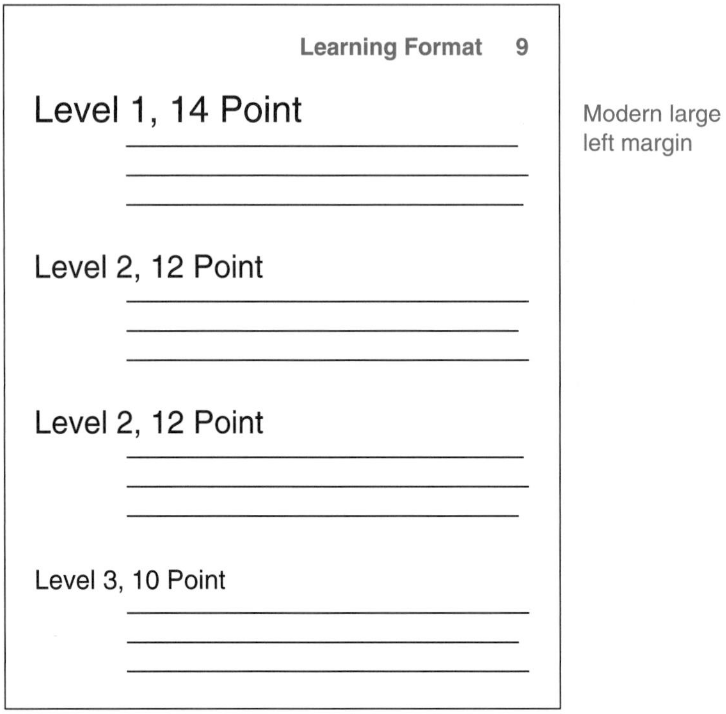

> Learning Format   9
>
> ## Level 1, 14 Point
>
> _____
> _____
> _____
>
> Modern large
> left margin
>
> ## Level 2, 12 Point
>
> _____
> _____
> _____
>
> ## Level 2, 12 Point
>
> _____
> _____
> _____
>
> ## Level 3, 10 Point
>
> _____
> _____
> _____

the head system, indentation, bullets, white space, header, and rules
(Watzman).

5. Use visual aids and vary the sizes and densities of white space, visuals,
   rules, and highlighters (Figure 7.13, p. 155).

6. Place visuals so that they move the reader's attention from left to right
   (Rubens; Xerox). In a two-column format (see Figure 7.14b, c, p. 155),
   you can place the visual to the left and the text to the right, or vice
   versa, depending on which you want to emphasize. Whatever you do,
   always "anchor" visuals by having one edge relate to a text margin
   (Sadowski). Figure 7.15 (p. 156) compares inattentive and attentive
   use of relating to margins.

7. In a multiple-page document, "hang" items from the top margin. In
   other words, keep a consistent distance from the top margin to the top
   of the first element on the page (whether head, text, or visual) (Cook
   and Kellogg). See Figure 7.16 (p. 157).

FIGURE 7.10
Chunked White Space

Random white space   Chunked white space

FIGURE 7.11
White Space Causes Subordination

Learning Format 11

FIGURE 7.12
Queued Text

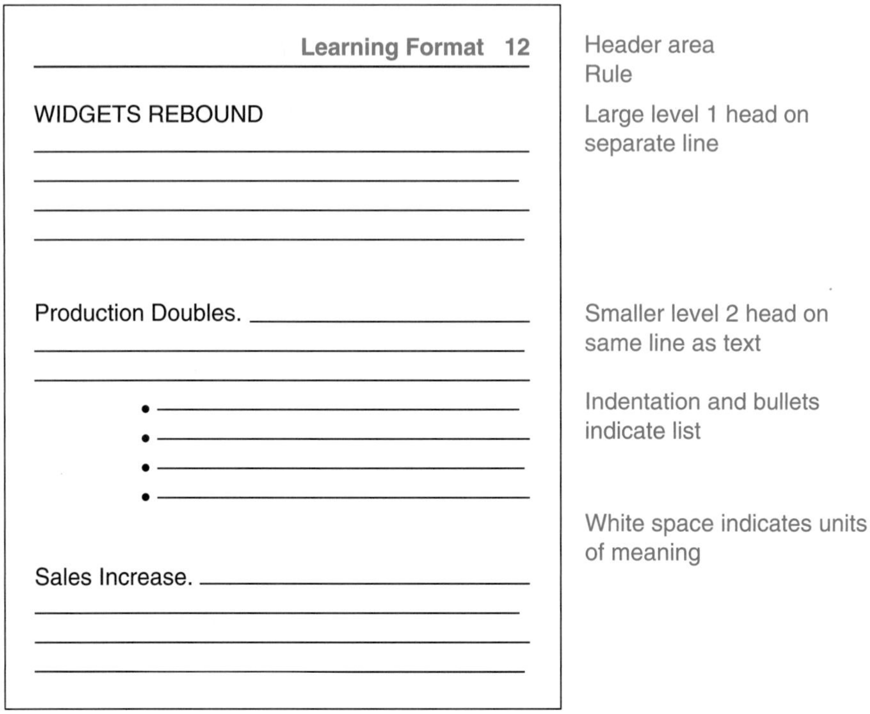

Learning Format 12	Header area
	Rule
WIDGETS REBOUND	Large level 1 head on separate line
Production Doubles. _____	Smaller level 2 head on same line as text
• _____	Indentation and bullets indicate list
• _____	
• _____	
• _____	
	White space indicates units of meaning
Sales Increase. _____	

DEVELOP A STYLE SHEET

A style sheet is a list of specifications for each element of format. You develop this list as part of your planning process. For brief documents you may not need to write it out, but you do need to think it through. Longer documents or group projects require a written or electronic style sheet. For instance, for a two-page memo, the style sheet would be quite short.

- Margins: 1-inch margin on all four sides
- Line treatment: no right justification
- Spacing within text: single-space within paragraphs, double-space between paragraphs
- Heads: heads flush left and boldfaced, triple-space above heads and double-space below
- Footers: page numbers at bottom center

FIGURE 7.13
Mixed-Mode Page

GOOD NEWS FOR WIDGETS	Level 1 head
	Rule
	Rule
Production Doubles	Level 2 head
	Text
	Rule
Sales Increase	Level 2 head
(bulleted list)	Bulleted indented list
(visual box)	Visual aid

FIGURE 7.14
Placement of Visuals

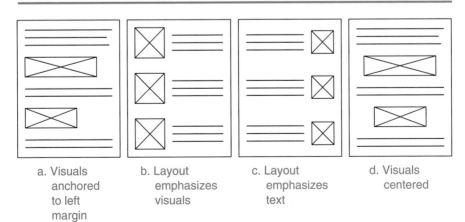

a. Visuals anchored to left margin

b. Layout emphasizes visuals

c. Layout emphasizes text

d. Visuals centered

FIGURE 7.15
Ineffective Versus Effective Use of Edges

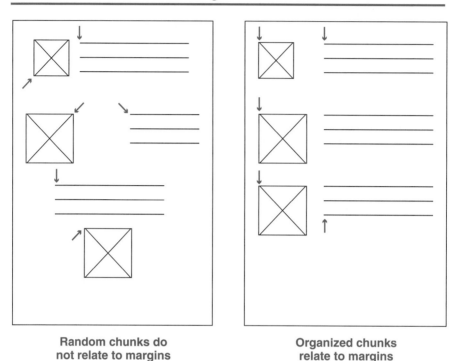

<table>
<tr><td style="text-align:center">Random chunks do
not relate to margins</td><td style="text-align:center">Organized chunks
relate to margins</td></tr>
</table>

For a more complicated document, you need to make a much more detailed style sheet. In addition to margins, justification, and paragraph spacing, you need to include specifications for

■ A multilevel system of heads.
■ Page numbers.
■ Rules for page top and bottom.
■ Rules to offset visuals.
■ Captions for visuals.
■ Headers and footers—for instance, whether the chapter title is placed in the top (header) or bottom (footer) margins.
■ Lists.

Figure 7.17 (p. 158) shows a common way to handle style sheets. Instead of writing out the rules in a list, you make a template that both explains and illustrates the rules. (For more on planning style sheets, see Chapter 17, "Format the Pages," pp. 454–457.)

The electronic style sheet is a particularly useful development. Many word processing and desktop publishing programs allow you to define specifications for each style element, such as captions and levels of heads. Suppose you want all level 1 heads to be Helvetica, 18-point, bold, flush left, and you want all figure captions to be Palatino, 8-point, italic. The style feature allows you to enter these commands into the electronic style sheet for the document. You can then direct the program to apply the style to any set of words.

Usually you can also make global changes with an electronic style sheet. If you decide to change all level 1 heads to Palatino, 16-point, bold, flush left, you need only make the change in the style sheet, and the program will change all the instances in the document.

FIGURE 7.16
Items Hanging from Top Margin

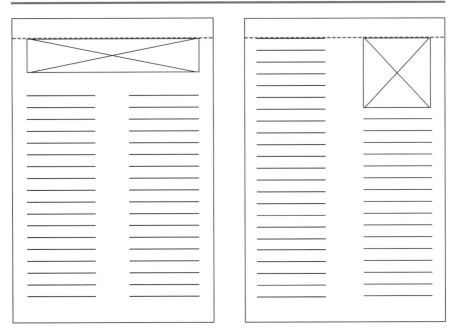

Hang items from the same top margin

FIGURE 7.17
Sample Template

CHAPTER HEADER
_____

HEAD LEVEL 1

Introductory level 1 text is not indented. Double-space between head and text. Text at all levels is not right-justified. Triple-space above level 2 heads.

Head Level 2
Introductory level 2 text is not indented. Skip no space between text and head. Subsequent paragraphs are indented 5 spaces, single space text.

    Head Level 3. Third level head is indented 5 spaces. Text is placed at left margin. Double space above level 3 head.

    To make a list:
- use a colon
- use bullets, but no end punctuation
- skip 2 spaces to the right and start the second line under the first letter of the first line

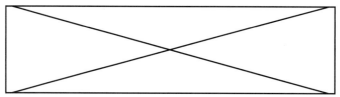

Fig 1. *Italicize caption at left edge*

■ WORKSHEET FOR A STYLE SHEET

❏ *Select margins.*

❏ *Decide how many levels of heads you will need.*

❏ *Select a style for each level.*

❏ *Select a location and format for your page numbers.*

❏ *Determine the number of columns and the amount of space between them.*

❏ *Choose a typeface, type size, and leading for the text.*

❏ *Place appropriate information in the header or footer area.*

❏ *Establish a method for handling vertical lists.*
Determine how far you will indent the first line. Use a bullet, number, letter, or some other character at the beginning of each item. Determine how many spaces will follow the initial character. Determine where the second and subsequent lines will start.

❏ *Choose a method for distinguishing visuals from the text.*
Will you enclose them in a box or use a rule above and below? Where will you place visuals within the text? How will you present captions?

EXAMPLES

Examples 7.1 and 7.2 present the same report section in two different formats, each the result of a different style sheet.

EXAMPLE 7.1
Two-Column Design

DISCUSSION

High-Protein Diets

Introduction

The goal of this search was to determine if the Internet was a valuable source of information regarding high protein diets. To define my information as usable, it must meet three criteria.

The three criteria are as follows: the information must be no older than 1997, the sites must be found to be credible sites, and it must take no longer than 10 minutes to find information pertinent to the topic on each site.

Findings

I used the Dogpile search engine to find my sites on high-protein diets. The keywords I used were *protein, high protein,* and *fad diets*. These key words led me to the sites listed below (Table 1).

As seen in Table 1, most of the sites fit the criteria. Using Dogpile to search for nutrition information yielded mixed results of commercial and professional sites. The Internet provided a vast amount of information regarding high-protein diets.

In my results I determined that the information from the Web site *cyberdiet.com* was credible even though it was a commercial site. The Tufts University Nutrition Navigator, a well-known, credible Web site that evaluates nutrition Web sites, recommended Cyberdiet and gave it a score of 24 out of 25.

Conclusion

The credibility and recency of the information did not all meet the criteria. Because of this, I conclude that the Internet does have valuable information regarding high-protein diets, but that the Web user must use caution and be critical in determining the validity of each Web site.

Table 1. Standards of High-Protein Diet Search

	Less Than 10 Min.?	Recency (>1997)	Credibility
Cyberdiet.com "High Protein, Low Carbohydrate Diet"	Yes	1999 Yes	Yes
Heartinfo.org "The Reincarnation of the High Protein Diet"	Yes	1997 Yes	Yes-Professional
more.com "Information on High Protein Diets"	Yes	——	No-Commercial
Prevention.com "A Day in the Zone"	Yes	1995 No	No-Consumer
Eatright.org (ADA) "In the News: High-Protein/Low Carbohydrate Diets"	Yes	1998 Yes	Yes-Professional

EXAMPLE 7.2
One-Column Design

DISCUSSION

High-Protein Diets

Introduction. The goal of this search was to determine if the Internet was a valuable source of information regarding high protein diets. To define my information as usable, it must meet three criteria.

The three criteria are as follows: the information must be no older than 1997, the sites must be found to be credible sites, and it must take no longer than 10 minutes to find information pertinent to the topic on each site.

Findings. I used the Dogpile search engine to find my sites on high-protein diets. The keywords I used were *protein, high protein,* and *fad diets*. These key words led me to the sites listed below (Table 1).

Table 1. Standards of High-Protein Diet Search

	Less Than 10 Min.?	Recency (>1997)	Credibility
Cyberdiet.com "High Protein, Low Carbohydrate Diet"	Yes	1999 Yes	Yes
Heartinfo.org "The Reincarnation of the High Protein Diet"	Yes	1997 Yes	Yes-Professional
more.com "Information on High Protein Diets"	Yes	———	No-Commercial
Prevention.com "A Day in the Zone"	Yes	1995 No	No-Consumer
Eatright.org (ADA) "In the News: High-Protein/Low Carbohydrate Diets"	Yes	1998 Yes	Yes-Professional

As seen in Table 1, most of the sites fit the criteria. Using Dogpile to search for nutrition information yielded mixed results of commercial and professional sites. The Internet provided a vast amount of information regarding high-protein diets.

In my results I determined that the information from the Web site *cyberdiet.com* was credible even though it was a commercial site. The Tufts University Nutrition Navigator, a well-known, credible Web site that evaluates nutrition Web sites, recommended Cyberdiet and gave it a score of 24 out of 25.

Conclusion. The credibility and recency of the information did not all meet the criteria. Because of this, I conclude that the Internet does have valuable information regarding high-protein diets, but that the Web user must use caution and be critical in determining the validity of each Web site.

■ EXERCISES

1. For a nonexpert audience, write a three- to five-paragraph description of a machine or process you know well. Your goal is to give the audience a general familiarity with the topic. Create two versions. In version 1, use only chunked text. In version 2, use at least two levels of heads, a bulleted list, and a visual aid. Alternate: Using the same instructions, create a description for an expert audience.

2. Write a paragraph that briefly describes a room in which you work. Create and hand in at least two versions with different designs (more if your instructor requires). Alter the size of the type, the font, and the treatment of the right margin. For instance, produce one in a 12-point sans serif font, right-justified format, and another in a 10-point serif font, ragged-right format. Label each version clearly with a head. Write a brief memo explaining which one you like the best.

3. Create a style sheet and template for any of the examples in Examples 7.1 and 7.2.

4. In groups of three or four, analyze Examples 7.1 and 7.2. Decide which one you prefer, and explain your decision in a group memo to the class.

5. Use principles of queueing and mixing to revise the following paragraph. Also eliminate unnecessary information.

    Capabilities of System. The new system will need to provide every capability that the current system does. I spoke with Dr. Franklin Pierce about this new system. Dr. Pierce has a vast amount of experience with Pascal (the old system is written in it) and in Ada (the new system is to be written in it). He also developed many software systems, including NASA's weather tracking system. After looking at the code for the current system, Dr. Pierce assured me that every feature in the old system can be mapped to a feature written in Ada. He also said that using Ada will allow us *multiple versions* of the program by using a capability of Ada to determine what type of computer is used for the menu. Furthermore, he said that using Ada will allow us to *improve the performance* of some of the capabilities, such as allowing the clock to continually be updated instead of stopping while another function is being performed and then being updated after that function has been completed. Thus, the first criterion could be met.

6. Rearrange the following layout so that it is more pleasing. Write a memo that explains why you made your changes.

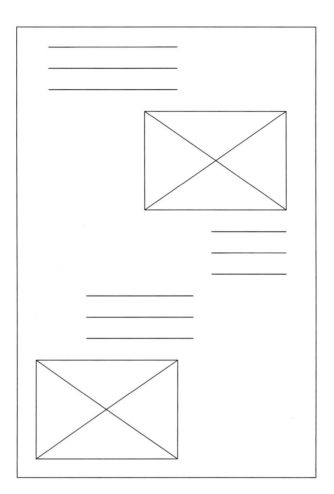

7. Create a layout for the following instructions and visual aids. Develop a style sheet to submit to your instructor before you redo the text. Use a desktop publishing program if you can.

Morning Startup for the Hell Color Scanner

This set of instructions will enable you to start up the Hell color scanner located in the Graphic Communications building. This procedure must be done every morning before 8:00 A.M. These instructions must be done in the order in which they are presented.

Right Power Panel
See Figure 1.

- Press the DAY button ON.
- Press the SCANNING DIRECTION button so the arrow is pointing left.

FIG. 1

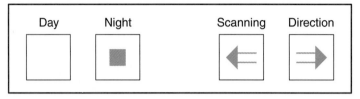

Right Side of Scanner

■ See Figure 2. Press the LASER button ON. The green THERMOSTAT light will blink when up to temperature. Press the DEFINITION button to NORMAL. Turn the TEST switch to TEST. Turn the MEASURE 6 switch to MEASURE 6.

FIG. 2

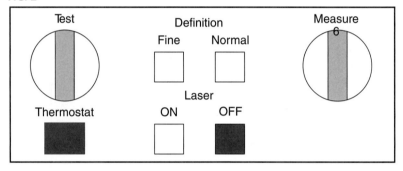

■ LEFT POWER PANEL
  See Figure 3.

1. Press SCREEN RULING to the 44 (110 line) button.

2. Load program tape in the tape reader located on the table just to the left of the left power panel. You must feed the tape under the tension bar.

3. Press READ IN READY button ON.

4. Press TAPE START button ON.

5. You must let the tape run completely through the tape reader until the tape is finished.

FIG. 3

Screen Lines/Inch						Read in Ready ON	Tape Start ON
85	110	133	150	17	200		
34	44	54	6	70	80		

Main Control Panel
(See Figure 4.) Turn COLOR SEPARATION switch to the YELLOW position.

Take CROPPING PIN out of the D3 row and place it in the bottom row. Press SCANLIGHT SOURCE button to TRANS. Press SCANLIGHT SOURCE button to the ON position. Press the START button. Let the drums come up to speed for 10 seconds. Press the STOP button.

You are now ready to begin setting up the scanner for exposing film.

FIG. 4

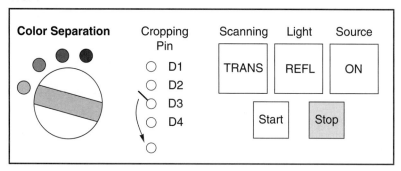

8. In groups of two, create a design for the following text, which recommends that a student center purchase a particular sound board. Your instructor will assign some groups to design for skimming, others for searching, and others for receptive reading. Be prepared to present an oral report explaining your format decisions.

> This is a recommendation on whether to purchase a Goober sound board or a Deco sound board for the Technical Services Crew at the Student Center. Over the past few years, we have rented a sound board when bands or other large speaking groups come to the Student Center. The rental costs run from $200 to $500, and now that money has been allocated to buy a sound board, we should seriously consider purchasing one. The use we will get out of the board will make it pay for itself in two or three years. This memo will detail my recommendation as to which board to purchase.
>
> I recommend we purchase the Goober XS-2000 24-channel sound board. Greg Newman, the Tech Crew Chief, and I have compared the Goober XS-2000 to the Deco TXS-260 24-channel board in audio magazines and by talking to people who have used the Goober board and the Deco board. We found the Goober to be an overall better board. We have also experienced using both boards on many occasions and have liked the Goober board better. We compared the boards in terms of these criteria: features, reliability/experience, and cost.

The first criterion is the features. This is the most important factor in deciding which sound board to purchase. We are looking for a sound board that provides 24 channels in and 8 lines out. The lines out are used for sound effects and equalization. The more "outs" you have, the better the sound will be. This is what the Goober XS-2000 has: 24 channels in and 8 lines out. The Deco TXS-260 has 24 channels in and only 6 lines out. We find it necessary to have 8 lines out because we want to offer bands the best-quality sound possible.

Reliability is another important factor. Goober and Deco are both reputable companies that make good sound boards, but when it comes down to operating at maximum efficiency, we feel the Goober board can offer us better reliability. I had the opportunity to speak with Will Hodges of Southern Thunder Sound, a sound rental company from which we have rented sound boards. He said that most bands that come in to rent his equipment rent the Goober boards because they are easier to work with and don't break down as often as the Deco boards. Mr. Hodges's opinion lends further credibility to my recommendation that we purchase the Goober board.

Greg and I have had experience working with both boards. Once when we rented a Deco board, a loud buzzing sound began to be emitted from the speakers halfway through the concert. We did everything we could, but the buzzing continued throughout the concert. On the occasions when we have worked with a Goober board, it has operated without any problems.

The cost is the last criterion. We have allocated an amount of $3500 to purchase a sound board. The Deco TXS-260 is $2800 with a two-year limited warranty. The Goober XS-2000 is $3600 with a five-year limited warranty. We have dealt with this Goober dealer before, and she said she would throw in a 100-foot 24-channel snake (a $700 value) free and would knock $300 off the total price—a $4300 value for $3300. A $1000 savings. Although the Deco board is less expensive, we should spend the extra $500 for a better board with a longer warranty, greater reliability, and a free 100-foot snake.

9. Use the following information to create a poster on your desktop system or word processor.
   a. The campus "golden oldies" club will hold a workshop for interested potential members on Wednesday, November 4, 2005, from 6:30 to 8:30 P.M. at the main stage in the University Student Center. No prior experience is necessary.
   b. The local Digital Photo Club will hold a benefit auction for the area United Way Food Pantry on Sunday, May, 8, at 1:00 P.M. at the local fairgrounds. Admission is $10.00. The event will consist of photos for sale and workshops on buying digital cameras and creating digital photos.

10. Create a poster for an event that interests you.

■ WRITING ASSIGNMENTS

1. In one page of text (just paragraphs), describe an opportunity for your firm, and ask for permission to explore it. Your instructor will help you select a topic. Your audience is a committee that has resources to take advantage of the opportunity. Use a visual aid if possible. Then use the design guidelines in this chapter to develop the same text into an appropriate document for the committee. In groups of three or four, review the documents to see whether the format conveys the message. Report to the class your conclusion about why the best one worked.

2. Write a learning report for the assignment you just completed. See Chapter 5, Writing Assignment 7, page 123, for details of the assignment.

■ WEB EXERCISES

1. Analyze two Web screens in order to explain to a beginner audience how to lay out a screen—where to place titles, how large to make them, etc. To give your advice from a range of examples, use a home page/ index screen and an "information" screen from "deeper" in the site ("deeper" means following a particular path through several links, e.g., About Us/Our Products/Cameras/FX20MicroZoom/Technical Spec).

2. Analyze the color scheme in a Web site. Use a major corporation like AT&T or Sun Micro. Write a memo to your classmates that explains how the site uses color to make its message clear.

■ WORKS CITED

Cook, Marshall, and Blake R. Kellogg. *The Brochure: How to Write and Design It.* Madison, WI: privately printed, 1980.

Felker, Daniel B., Frances Pickering, Veda R. Charrow, V. Melissa Holland, and Janice C. Redish. *Guidelines for Document Designers.* Washington, DC: American Institutes for Research, 1981.

Kostelnick, Charles. "Supra-Textual Design: The Visual Rhetoric of Whole Documents." *Technical Communication Quarterly* 5.1 (1995): 9–33.

Kramer, Robert, and Stephen A. Bernhardt. "Teaching Text Design." *Technical Communication Quarterly* 5.1 (1995): 35–60.

Rubens, Phillip M. "A Reader's View of Text and Graphics: Implications for Transactional Text." *Journal of Technical Writing and Communication* 16 (1986): 73–86.

Sadowski, Mary A. "Elements of Composition." *Technical Communication* 34 (1987): 29–30.

Shriver, Karen A. *Dynamics in Document Design: Creating Texts for Readers.* NY: Wiley, 1997.

Southard, Sherry. "Practical Considerations in Formatting Manuals." *Technical Communication* 35.3 (1988): 173–178.

Watzman, Suzanne. "Principles of Effective Communication Design: A Tutorial." *Proceedings of the International Technical Communication Conference.* Washington, DC: Society for Technical Communication, 1988. 128–129.

White, Jan V. *Graphic Design for the Electronic Age.* NY: Watson-Guptill, 1988.

Xerox Publishing Standards: A Manual of Style and Design. NY: Xerox Press, 1988.

Focus on COLOR

People like color. They prefer color TVs, color newspapers, colorful ads, colorful Web screens. Cheaper technology that allows individuals to add color to documents has opened a new world for communicators. Now anyone can produce a multiple-color document. Working effectively with color means knowing

- How color relationships cause effects.
- How color can be used in documents.

Effects Produced by Color Relationships

When colors are placed next to each other, their relationships cause many effects. The concepts of the color wheel and value illustrate how color affects visibility. Various hues cause emotional and associational reactions.

The Color Wheel and Visibility. The key concept is the color wheel, which provides a way to see how colors relate to one another. Figure 1 shows the six basic "rainbow" colors, from which all colors can be made.

FIGURE 1.
The Basic Color Wheel

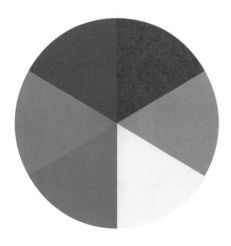

The colors that are across from one another are called complementary (e.g., red and green), those that touch are called adjacent (e.g., red and orange or violet), and those that are two apart are called contrasting (e.g., red and yellow, red and blue, orange and green, orange and violet). The relationships are shown in Figures 2 through 4. Each of the relationships affects visibility.

Maximum visibility. Figure 2 shows that sets of complementary colors cause high contrast or maximum visibility. This relationship strongly calls attention to itself. Notice, however, that the colors tend to "dance." Most people find them harsh and can view them for only a short time.

FIGURE 2.
Complementary Colors

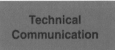

Minimum visibility. Figure 3 shows that sets of adjacent colors cause low contrast or minimal visibility. These relationships tend to have a relaxing, pleasing effect. The colors, however, tend to blend in with each other, making it difficult to distinguish the object from the background.

FIGURE 3.
Adjacent Colors

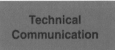

Pleasing visibility. Figure 4 shows that sets of contrasting colors cause medium contrast or pleasing visibility. These relationships have strong contrast, but they do not dance. Most people find them bold and vivid.

FIGURE 4.
Contrasting Colors

Value Affects Visibility of Individual Hues.   In addition to having relationships with other colors, any color has relationships with itself. So a basic color, like blue, is called a *hue*.

However, you can mix white or black with the hue and so create a value—a *tint* (a hue and white) or a *shade* (a hue and black). Figure 5 shows blue as a hue in the center, but as a tint to the left and a shade to the right. The more white you add, the lighter the tint; the more black, the darker the shade.

FIGURE 5.
Tint, Hue, Shade

Reduce harsh contrast by changing value. Understanding value allows you to affect the impact of color relationships. Although complementary colors of equal value are quite jarring, as shown in Figure 2, notice how the jarring decreases when the background color changes value either as a tint (Figure 6) or a shade (Figure 7).

FIGURE 6.
Tinted Background

FIGURE 7.
Shaded Background

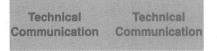

Increase visibility by using innate value. Colors have innate value. In other words, the basic hue of some colors is perceived as brighter than the basic hue of others. The brightest basic hue is yellow and the darkest is violet (see Figure 8). The brighter hues are more difficult to read (because they do not contrast as well with white, the color of most pages) than the darker ones.

FIGURE 8.
Innate Values

Colors and emotions. As shown in Figure 9, colors are divided into warm (red, orange, yellow) and cool (green, blue, violet). Warm colors appear to most people to be soft, cozy, linked to passions, celebrations, and excitement. Cool colors appear to most people as harder, icier, linked to rational, serious, reliable decorum.

FIGURE 9a.
Warm Colors

Technical Communication	Technical Communication	Technical Communication

FIGURE 9b.
Cool Colors

Technical Communication	**Technical Communication**	**Technical Communication**

Colors and associations. Colors also have traditional associations, usually a positive and a negative one. In most Western cultures, red is passion and danger, green is fertile but rotted, white is pure but icy, yellow is caution but wealth. So, for example, warning signs seldom appear in white or green, but mostly in red or sometimes yellow. Of course, these color associations are "culture specific"; they apply only to Western cultures. White, for instance, is associated with death in Japan and mourning in India; green is a holy color in Moslem countries, one that should be used very cautiously; and green or orange could be potent political statements in Ireland.

How Color Can Be Used in Documents

Color has four important functions in documents. Use color to

- Make text stand out.
- Target information.
- Indicate organization.
- Indicate the point in a visual aid.

Use Color to Make Text Stand Out.   As Figures 2 through 7 illustrate, one common use of color is to make text clearly visible, or legible. Legibility is a matter of contrast. If the text contrasts with its background, it will be legible. Two principles are helpful.

- The best contrast is black type on a white background.
- Colored type appears to recede from the reader. Higher values (yellow) appear farther away and less legible than lower values (blue).

Color alone will not cause individual words to stand out in black text. To make colored text stand out from black text, you must also change its size. Figures 10 and 11 show that colored words do not

FIGURE 10.
Minimal Emphasis via Size

| It is a well-known fact that technical communication is the best of all possible subjects to study. |

FIGURE 11.
Minimal Emphasis via Color

| It is a well-known fact that technical communication is the best of all possible subjects to study. |

173

stand out from the text, but Figure 12 shows that colored words made larger do. Figure 13 shows that words will stand out if the color contrasts with the color of the surrounding text.

FIGURE 12.
Emphasis via Size and Color

It is a well-known fact that **technical communication** is the best of all possible subjects to study.

FIGURE 13.
Emphasis via Contrast

It is a well-known fact that technical communication is the best of all possible subjects to study.

Use Color to Target Information.   Color focuses attention. It does this so strongly that color creates "information targets." In other words, people see color before they see anything else. As a consequence, you should follow these guidelines:

- Use color to draw attention to "independent focus" text—types of text that readers must focus on independently of other types.
- Make each type of text look different from the other types. Use different value (tint or shade, not hue) and different areas or shape to cause the difference.

Common examples of independent focus texts are

- Warnings.
- Hints.
- Cross references.
- Material the reader should type.
- Sidebars.

Figure 14 shows a page that has each of these items. Notice that the difference is achieved by differences in value, shape, and location.

FIGURE 14.
Examples of Independent-Focus Text

Getting Started on Web Research

Create questions, select a search engine, and start. The password is gogetter.

sidebar/hint

cross reference

1. Select a topic.
2. Create questions about the topic. (See Chapter 5 for a memory jog.)
3. Select sources that are likely to provide answers to those questions.
4. Use those sources. Remember to keep track of
   a. Exactly where you have been (e.g., the exact http address of the documents you download)
   b. The titles and authors of the material you use
   c. The keywords you have used and an evaluation of their effectiveness
5. To gain access to the network
   a. Turn on your computer
   b. Double-click on the Webscape icon
   c. Enter this password at the $prompt:

reader types this ———— gogetter <r>.

Use Color to Indicate Organization. Color creates a visual logic. Readers quickly realize that color indicates a function. The intensity of the indicating is increased when color is combined with shape and area.

You can use color to indicate different levels in your document's hierarchy. Common functions that color can indicate are

- Marginal material.
- Running information—in headers and footers, or in the head system.

Figure 15 shows a page that has each of these items. Notice that the difference is achieved by differences in value, shape and location.

FIGURE 15.
Examples of Color Function

header   The Creative Concept   1

level 1 head

Finding Your Gist Through Analogy

Here you will present a lot of report text. This text is very important, and readers should focus on this. After all it is the main point of what they have to read, and you have spent a lot of time researching all the information and figuring out what it means and how you can present it to the readers so that they feel comfortable with it.

level 2 head

Note: If you want to add notes in the margin, you could try them in some value other than the one the heads are in. Notice the different shade and thinner shape of this text.

marginal comment

The Passenger Train Analogy.   You have finally found the gist of the material and have a wonderful creative concept—a fine metaphor that you have discovered only after trying six or seven of them. The one you are about to use is the Passenger Train analogy. You will explain creating Web sites to your readers by leading them through the train and pointing out where they have their regular seats, where they can go to sit to enjoy an unrestricted view of the countryside in the observation car, where their sleeping berth is, and most important of all where the dining car is.

You will also have a "before section" in which you explain how to decide which train to take, how to buy a ticket, and how to use the station effectively.

The Rejected Analogies.   You know now that you have decided against the menu metaphor in which the Web creators would be simply pulling things off the page and more or less plopping them onto their plate and the thunderstorm analogy in which they would build and swirl for a long time, perhaps with the surrounding area very still until finally they unleashed their Web site in a fury of lightning and thunder.

Use Color to Indicate the Point of a Visual Aid. Use color in visual aids to draw readers' attention to specific items. For instance,

- To highlight a single line in a table.
- To highlight the data line in a line graph.
- To focus attention on a particular bar or set of bars in a bar graph.
- To differentiate callouts and leaders from the actual visual.

TABLE 1
Frequency of Analogies Used in Technical Articles

	Train	Thunderstorm	Food Menu
Packaging	30	40	30
Hospitality	20	15	65
Automotive	10	75	15

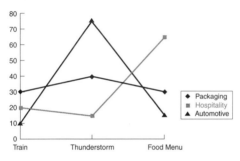

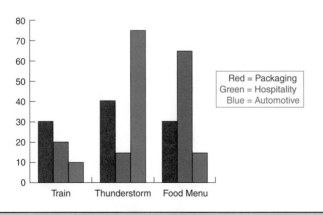

Be aware that many of the graphics programs provide you with color but that the color is not chosen to make this visual aid make more sense.

Summary Guidelines for Using Color

Follow these basic guidelines in your handling of color in your documents:

- Be consistent. For each type of item, use the same hue, value, shape, and location.
- Correctly use contrast. Follow the color wheel to select combinations of colors that create high visibility. Remember that black and white create the highest contrast. Colored text must change size to contrast with surrounding black text.
- Correctly use feeling and association. Use warm colors for action items, especially warnings. Use cool colors for reflection items.
- Generally use only one hue with varying tints and shades. Use two or more colors after you have practiced with color and have had your creations critiqued by readers and users.
- Help color-blind readers by using different brightnesses of the same color. Remember that location on the page will help color-blind readers also. (Even if they cannot "read" the red, they will know it is a marginal comment because of where it is located.)

Works Consulted

The Basics of Color Design. Cupertino, CA: Apple, 1992.

Horton, William. "Overcoming Chromophobia: A Guide to the Confident and Appropriate Use of Color." *IEEE Transactions of Professional Communication* 34.3 (1991): 160–171.

Jones, Scott L. "A Guide to Using Color Effectively in Business Communication." *Business Communication Quarterly* 60.2 (1997): 76–88.

Keyes, Elizabeth. "Typography, Color, and Information Structure." *Technical Communication* 40.4 (1993): 638–654.

Mazur, Beth. "Coming to Grips with WWW Color." *Intercom* 44.2 (1997): 4–6.

White, Jan. *Color for the Electronic Age.* NY: Watson-Guptill, 1990.

8 Using Visual Aids

CHAPTER CONTENTS

Chapter 8
IN A NUTSHELL

Visual aids help readers by summarizing data and by showing patterns.

Common Types of Visual Aids

Tables have rows and columns of figures. Place the items to compare (corporate sales regions) down the left side and the ways to compare them (by monthly sales) along the top. The data fill in all the appropriate spaces.

Line graphs illustrate a trend. Place the items to compare along the bottom axis (days of the week) and the pattern to illustrate (the price of the stock) along the left axis. The line shows the fluctuation.

Bar graphs illustrate a moment in time. Place the items to compare along the bottom axis (four cities) and the terms to compare (population figures) along the left axis. The bars show the difference immediately.

Illustrations, either photos or drawings, show a sequence or a pattern—the correct orientation for inserting a disk into a computer for example.

Guidelines for Using Visual Aids

- Develop a *visual logic*—place visuals in the same position on the page, make them about the same size, treat captions and rules (black lines) the same way. Be consistent.
- Create neat visuals to enhance your clarity and credibility.
- Tell readers what to notice and explain pertinent aspects, such as the source or significance of the data.
- Present visual aids below or next to the appropriate text.

Visual aids are an essential part of technical writing. Graphics programs for personal computers allow writers to create and refine visual aids within reports. Many of the bar graphs, line graphs, and pie charts shown in this chapter are computer generated. This chapter presents an overview of visual aids. It explains general information on using, creating, and discussing visual aids, as well as specific information on all the common types of visual aids.

THE USES OF VISUAL AIDS

Visual aids have a simple purpose. According to noted theorist Edward Tufte, visual aids "reveal data" (13). This key concept controls all other considerations in using visual aids. You will communicate effectively if your visual aids "draw the reader's attention to the sense and substance of the data, not to something else" (91). Technical writers use visual aids for four purposes:

- To summarize data
- To give readers an opportunity to explore data
- To provide a different entry point into the discussion
- To engage reader expectations

To summarize data means to present information in concise form. Figure 8.1, a graph of a stock's price for one week, presents the day-end price of the stock for each day. A reader can tell at a glance how the stock fared on any day that week.

To give readers an opportunity to explore data means to allow them to investigate on their own. Readers can focus on any aspects that are relevant to their needs. For instance, they might focus on the fact that the stock rose at the beginning and again at the end of the week, or that the one-day rebound on Friday equaled the two-day climb on Monday and Tuesday.

To provide a different entry point into the discussion means to orient readers to the topic even before they begin to read the text. Studying the graph of a stock's price could introduce the reader to the concept of price fluctuation or could provide a framework of dollar ranges and fluctuation patterns.

To engage reader expectations is to cause readers to develop questions about the topic. Simply glancing at the line that traces the stock's fluctuation in price would immediately raise questions about causes, market trends, and even the timeliness of buying or selling.

FIGURE 8.1
Graph That Summarizes and Engages

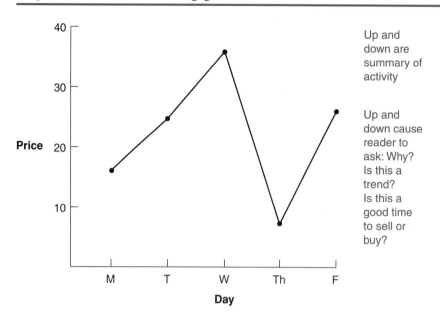

CREATING AND DISCUSSING VISUAL AIDS

How to Create Visual Aids

The best way to create a visual aid is to follow the basic communication process: plan, draft, and finish.

Plan the Visual Aid Carefully.   Make the visual aid an opportunity both to present your data and to engage your readers. Your overall goal is to help your readers as they research for the information they need and help them to make sense of it once they find it (Shriver). Consider your audience's knowledge and what they will do with the information. Are they experts who need to make a decision? Consider your goal in presenting the information. Is it to summarize data? to offer an opportunity to explore data? to provide a visual entry point to the discussion? to engage reader expectations? Your visual aid should have just one main point. Take into account the fact that graphs have an emotional impact. For example, in graphs about income, lines that slope up to the right cause pleased reactions, whereas those that slope down cause anxiety. Consider also any constraints on your process. How much time do you need to make a clear visual aid? Consider the layout of the visual aid. In tables, which items should be in rows and which in columns? In graphs, which items should appear on the horizontal axis and which on the vertical?

Draft the Visual Aid Just as You Draft Text.   Revise until you produce the version that presents the data most effectively. For graphs, select wording, tick marks, and data line characteristics (solid, broken, dots). For tables, select column and row heads, enter the data, create a format for the caption and any rules, and add necessary notes. For charts and illustrations, select symbols, overall dimensions, a font for words, and a width for rules. Reread the visual aid to find and change unclear elements, in either content or form.

Finish by Making the Visual Aid Pleasant to View.   Treat all items consistently. Reduce clutter as much as possible by eliminating unnecessary lines and words.

How to Discuss Visual Aids

Carefully guide the reader's attention to the aspect of the visual aid you want to discuss. Your goal is to enrich the reader's understanding of the topic (Shriver). For instance, you could choose to explain elementary, intermediate, or overall information (Killingsworth and Gilbertson). *Elementary* information is one fact: on Wednesday, the stock's price rose. *Intermediate* information is a trend in one category: as the week progressed, the stock price fluctuated. *Overall* information is a trend that relates several categories: after the price dropped, investors rushed to buy at a "low."

In addition, you must explain background, methodology, and significance. *Background* includes who ordered or conducted the study of the stock, their reasons for doing so, and the problem they wanted to investigate. *Methodology* is how the data were collected. *Significance* is the impact of the data for some other concern—for instance, investor confidence. See pages 184–185 and 186–191 for examples of discussions.

How to Reference Visual Aids

Refer to the visual aid by number. If it is several pages away, include the page number in your reference. You can make the references textual or parenthetical.

Textual Reference.   A *textual* reference is simply a statement in the text itself, often a subordinate clause, that calls attention to the visual aid.

> . . . as seen in Table 1 (p. 10).
>
> If you look at Figure 4, . . .
>
> The data in Table 1 show . . .

Parenthetical Reference.   A *parenthetical* reference names the visual aid in parentheses in the sentence. A complete reference is used more in reports, and an abbreviated reference in sets of instructions. In reports, use *see* and spell out *Table*. Although *Figure* or *Fig.* are both used, *Figure* is preferable in formal writing.

> The profits for the second quarter (see Figure 1) are . . .
>
> A cost analysis reveals that we must reconsider our plans for purchasing new printers (see Table 1).

In instructions, you do not need to use *see*, and you may refer to figures as *Fig.*

> Insert the disk into slot A (Figure 1).
>
> Set the CPM readout (Figure 2) before you go on to the next step.

Do not capitalize *see* unless the parenthetical reference stands alone as a separate sentence. In that case, also place the period inside the parentheses.

> All of these data were described above. (See Tables 1 and 2.)

Guidelines for Effective Visual Aids

The following five guidelines (Felker et al.; MacDonald-Ross; Shriver) will help you develop effective visual aids. Later sections of the chapter explain which types of visual aids to use and when to use them.

1. Develop visual aids as you plan a document. Because they are so effective, you should put their power to work as early as possible in your project. Many authors construct visuals first and then start to write.
2. As you draft, make sure each visual aid conveys only one point. If you include too many data, readers cannot grasp the meaning easily. (Note, however, that tables often make several points successfully.)
3. Position visual aids within the draft at logical and convenient places, generally in the middle of the discussion or after it.
4. Revise to reduce clutter. Eliminate all words, lines, and design features (such as the needless inclusion of three dimensions) that do not convey data.
5. Construct high-quality visual aids, using clear lines, words, numbers, and organization. Research shows that the quality of the finished visual aid is the most important factor in its effectiveness (Felker et al.; MacDonald-Ross).

USING TABLES

A table is a collection of information expressed in numbers or words and presented in columns and rows. It shows the data that result from the interaction of an independent and a dependent variable. An *independent variable* is the topic itself. The *dependent variable* is the type of information you discover about the topic (White, *Graphic*). In a table of weather conditions, the independent variable, or topic, is the months. The dependent variables are the factors that describe weather in any month: average temperature, average precipitation, and whatever else you might want to compare. The data—and the point of the table—are the facts that appear for each month.

Parts and Guidelines

Tables have conventional parts: a caption that contains the number and title, rules, column heads, data, and notes, as shown in Figure 8.2.The following guidelines will help you use these parts correctly (based in part on *Publication*).

1. Number tables consecutively throughout a report with arabic numerals in the order of their appearance. Put the number and title above the table. Use the "double-number" method (e.g., "Table 6.3") only in long reports that contain chapters.

2. Use the table title to identify the main point of the table. Write brief but informative titles. Do not place punctuation after the title.

3. Use horizontal rules to separate parts of the table. Place a rule above and below the column heads and below the last row of data. Seldom use vertical rules to separate columns; use white space instead. If the report is more informal, use fewer or no rules.

4. Use a *spanner* head to characterize the column headings below it. Spanners eliminate repetition in column heads.

5. Arrange the data into columns and rows. Put the topics you want to compare (the independent variables) down the left side of the table in the *stub* column. Put the factors of comparison (the dependent variables) across the top in the column headings. Remember that columns are easier to compare than rows.

6. Place explanatory comments below the bottom rule. Introduce these comments with the word *Note*. Use specific notes to clarify portions of a table. Indicate them by raised (superscript) lower-case letters within the table and at the beginning of each note.

7. Cite the *source* of the data unless the data were obviously collected for the paper. List the sources you used, whether primary or secondary.

FIGURE 8.2
Elements of a Table

TABLE 1. Winter Weather Conditions in Minnesota								Number Title
	Average Temp (°F)		Record Temp (°F)		Average Snow (in.)[a]	Record Snow (in.)		Spanners
Month	High	Low	High	Low		High	Low	Column Heads
January	20	3	59	−41	9.0	46	0.0	Data
February	25	9	64	−40	7.7	26	Tr	
March	38	23	83	−32	9.6	40	.02	

Rule

[a]Snowfall data began in 1859.

Note: February includes calculations based on 28 and 29 days.

Source: Based on 1997 *Minnesota Weatherguide Calendar.* Eds. Bruce Watson and Jim Gilbert. Minneapolis: WCCO, 1996.

Notes

When to Use a Table

Because tables present the results of research in complete detail, they generally contain a large amount of information. For this reason, professional and expert audiences grasp tables more quickly than do nonexperts. When your audience knows the topic well, use tables to do the following (Felker et al.):

■ To present all the numerical data so that the audience can see the context of the relationships you point out

■ To compare many numbers or features (and eliminate the need for lengthy prose explanations)

In the text, you should add any explanation that the audience needs to understand the data in the table.

A Sample Table and Text.   Table 1 in the following example appeared in a recommendation report. Although the data are clear, the numbers do not give enough background to explain the differences in cost. The explanatory text provides this background; it tells what features come with the base price and explains the figures in the two middle rows.

Purchase Cost

The Deutz Z291 has a base price of $150,000 (see Table 1).   Background
Deutz also offers a 5% discount ($7,500) if we purchase
before June 1. At this price the Deutz Z291 comes fully   Explanation
assembled, ready for use. The price does not include two
tractor trucks and trailers that would be required to trans-
port the conveying system and generators to run the
equipment. However, we have no need to purchase these
trucks and trailers because we have two trucks and trailers available. The final cost of the Deutz Z291 is $142,500.

   The Pioneer 7000A has a base price of $120,000 (see   Background
Table 1). The Pioneer 7000A comes fully assembled and
ready for use. The price includes mounting it on a flat   Explanation
bed truck. When the Pioneer 7000A is mounted, it
requires no additional trucks or trailers for transportation. The Pioneer 7000A also comes with 50 feet of
pumping hose. However, we feel that some of our
projects will require 100 feet of hose. The additional
pumping hose costs $5,000, boosting the total cost of
the Pioneer 7000A to $125,000.

TABLE 1
A Comparison of Purchase Costs

Cost	Deutz Z291	Pioneer 7000A
Base price	$150,000	$120,000
Discount	7,500	0
Additional cost	0	5,000
Final cost	142,500	125,000

USING LINE GRAPHS

A *line graph* shows the relationship of two variables by a line connecting points inside an X (horizontal) and a Y (vertical) axis. These graphs usu-ally show trends over time, such as profits or losses from year to year. The line connects the points, and its ups and downs illustrate the changes—often dramatically. On the horizontal axis, plot the indepen-dent variable, the topic whose effects you are recording, such as months of a year. On the vertical axis, record the values of the dependent vari-able, the factor that changes when the independent variable changes, such as sales. The line represents the record of change—the fluctuation in sales (see Figure 8.3).

FIGURE 8.3
Dependent and Independent Variables

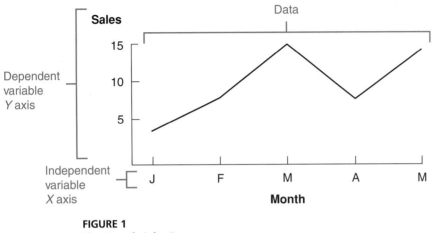

FIGURE 1
Five-Month Sales Data

Parts and Guidelines

Line graphs have conventional parts: a caption that contains the number and title (with a source note when necessary), axis rules, tick marks and tick identifiers, axis labels, a data line, and a legend. These parts are illustrated in Figure 8.4. The following guidelines will help you treat these parts correctly.

1. Number figures consecutively throughout the report, using arabic numerals. Use double-numbering (e.g., "Figure 6.6") only if you have numbered chapters.
2. Use a brief, clear title to specify the content of the graph. Do not punctuate after the title.
3. Put the caption below the figure. (Many computer programs automatically place the caption above the figure. This method is acceptable, especially for informal reports. Choose one placement or the other and use it consistently throughout the document.)
4. Place the independent variable on the horizontal axis; place the dependent variable on the vertical axis.
5. Space tick marks equally along the axis rule. Use varying thicknesses to indicate subordination. (Note that in Figure 8.4 the 15 and 25 tick marks are smaller than the 20 and 30 marks.)

FIGURE 8.4
Elements of a Line Graph

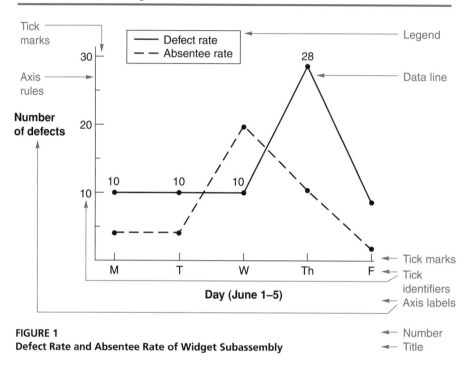

FIGURE 1
Defect Rate and Absentee Rate of Widget Subassembly
◄── Number
◄── Title

6. Provide clear axis labels. In general, spell out words and write out numbers from left to right. Use abbreviations only if they are common.

7. Present a data line with definite marks that indicate the intersection of the two axes (such as the dot in Figure 8.4 where Monday meets 10). Add explanatory numbers or words inside the graph.

8. If the graph has two or more lines, make them visually distinct and identify them with labels or in a legend, or key.

When to Use a Line Graph

Line graphs depict trends or relationships. They clarify data that would be difficult to grasp quickly in a table. Research shows that expert readers grasp line graphs more easily than nonexperts (Felker). Use a line graph

▪ To show that a trend exists (see Figure 8.3).

▪ To show that a relationship exists, say, of pollutant penetration to filter size.

■ To give an overview or general conclusion, rather than fine points.

■ To initiate or supplement a discussion of cause or significance (Figure 8.3 alerts readers to ask why April is unusual).

Add explanatory text that helps the audience grasp the implications of the graph.

The following line graphs are taken from a report (Makki and Durance) on one enzyme's ability to prevent spoilage in beer. The enzyme is lysozyme, a natural food preservative found in egg whites. The cause of the spoilage is two bacteria, *L. brevis* and *P. damnosus*. Figure 4 reports on two tests on *L. brevis*; Figure 5 reports on one test on *P. damnosus*.

The paragraph describing the figures uses a number of strategies that are effective in relating graphs to readers. Notice that as you read the text and review the graphs, you can grasp the point even if you know nothing about microbiology. The basic strategies are

■ Provide a topic sentence that announces the main point of the paper: "Viability . . . is shown."

■ Indicate what to notice: "*L. brevis* initially decreased" but "by Day 9 . . . was almost identical."

■ Phrase conclusions: "Although the levels of lysozyme did not prevent growth of *L. brevis,* they did delay growth."

■ Relate to research context: "Similar conclusions were made by Bottazzi et al. (1978). . . ."

Viability of *L. brevis* and *P. damnosus* in beer containing lysozyme is shown in Figures 4 and 5. *L. brevis* initially decreased in number in bottles containing 10 and 50 ppm lysozyme (Figure 4a). But by Day 9, the survival in bottles with 10 ppm lysozyme was almost identical to that observed in bottles with no lysozyme, with counts reaching 10^6 CFU/ml. The counts in the bottles with 50 ppm lysozyme remained at the Day 3 level (10^3 CFU/ml) throughout the rest of the experiment. Although 10 ppm lysozyme did not have much inhibitory effect on *L. brevis,* 50 ppm seemed to exert some degree of inhibition. The results of a second trial (Figure 4b) suggested that even 50 ppm lysozyme cannot always inhibit *L. brevis.* After a sharp initial drop in the survival curve, the CFU/ml counts in the bottles with 50 ppm lysozyme recovered after Day 12, reaching even higher levels than in control bottles in the following days. Although the levels of lysozyme did not prevent growth of *L. brevis,* they did delay growth. Similar conclusions were made by Bottazzi et al. (1978) who studied the effect of lysozyme of thermophilic lactic acid bacteria in milk. They found that *L. helviticus* in milk was inhibited by greater than 50 ppm lysozyme. As for the results obtained with *P. damnosus* (Figure 5), there was little difference between the survival trend observed in the bottles with 10 ppm and 50 ppm lysozyme although both treatment levels reduced the growth of *P. damnosus* in beer. A more complete investigation of the effects of lysozyme on the beer spoilage bacteria used in this study would require the use of a wider range of lysozyme concentrations and a higher upper limit. (643–644)

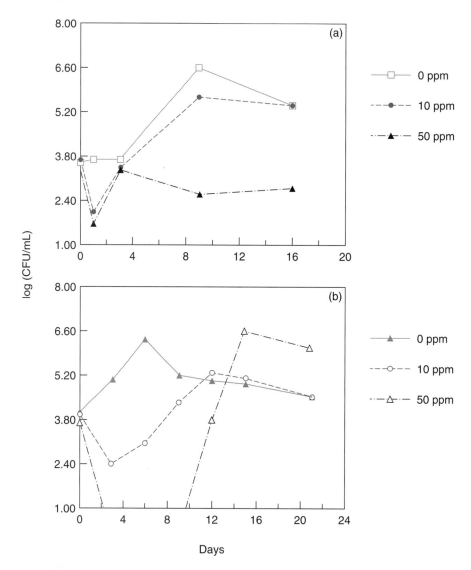

FIGURE 4
Survival of *Lactobacillus brevis* B-12 in unpasteurized beer in the presence of lysozyme: (a) first trial; (b) second trial. [Makki, F. and T. D. Durance, "Thermal Inactivation of Lysozyme as Influenced by pH, Sucrose and Sodium Chloride and Inactivation and Preservative Effect in Beer" from *Food Research International* 29, 7 (October 1996): 635–645. Reprinted with permission.]

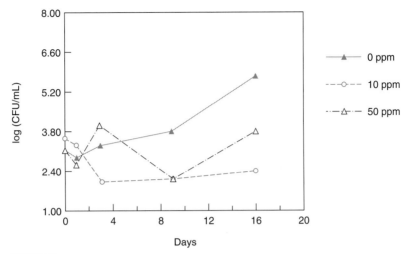

FIGURE 5
Survival of *Pediococcus damnosus* B-130 in unpasteurized beer in the presence of lysozyme. [Makki, F. and T. D. Durance, "Thermal Inactivation of Lysozyme as Influenced by pH, Sucrose and Sodium Chloride and Inactivation and Preservative Effect in Beer" from *Food Research International* 29, 7 (October 1996): 635–645. Reprinted with permission.]

USING BAR GRAPHS

A *bar graph* uses rectangles to indicate the relative size of several variables. Bar graphs contrast variables or show magnitude. They can be either horizontal or vertical. Horizontal bar graphs compare similar units, such as the populations of three cities. Vertical bar graphs (often called *column graphs*) are better for showing discrete values over time, such as profits or production at certain intervals.

In bar graphs the independent variable is named along the base line (see Figure 8.5). The dependent variable runs parallel to the bars. The bars show the data. In a graph comparing the defect rates of three manufacturing lines, the lines are the independent variable and are named along the base line. The defect rate is the dependent variable, labeled above the line parallel to the bars. The bars represent the data on defects.

Parts and Guidelines

Bar graphs have conventional parts: a caption that contains the number and title (with source line when necessary), axis rules, tick marks and tick identifiers, axis labels, the bars, and the legend (see Figure 8.6). The following guidelines (based on Tufte) will help you treat these parts effectively. (These guidelines are for vertical bar graphs; rearrange them for horizontal bar graphs.)

1. As with other visual aids, provide an arabic numeral and a title that names the contents of the graph. This caption material appears

FIGURE 8.5
Dependent and Independent Variables

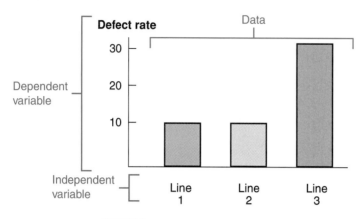

FIGURE 1
Defect Rates of Manufacturing Lines

FIGURE 8.6
Elements of a Bar Graph

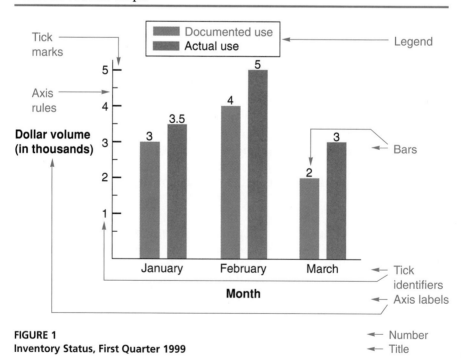

FIGURE 1
Inventory Status, First Quarter 1999

below the figure in formal reports but is often found above in informal reports.

2. Place the names of the items you are comparing (the independent variable) on the horizontal axis; place the units of comparison (the dependent variable) on the vertical axis.

3. Space tick marks equally along the axis rule. Use varying thicknesses to indicate subordination.

4. Provide clear axis labels. Spell out words and write out numbers.

5. Make the spaces between the bars one-half the width of the bars. (You may have to override the default in your computer program.)

6. Use a legend or callouts to identify the meaning of the bars' markings.

7. Avoid elaborate cross hatching and striping, which create a hard-to-read "op art" effect.

8. Use explanatory phrases at the end of bars or next to them.

9. Subdivide bars to show additional comparisons (see Figure 8.7).

When to Use a Bar Graph

Bar graphs compare the relative sizes of discrete items, usually at the same point in time. Like line graphs, they clarify data that would be difficult to

FIGURE 8.7
Column Graph with Shading

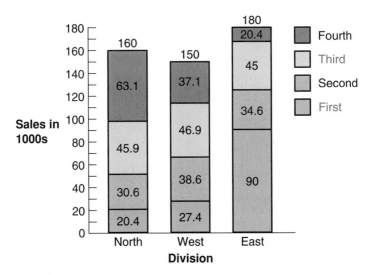

FIGURE 1
Quarterly Sales of the Three Divisions

extract from a table or a lengthy prose paragraph. Nonexpert readers find bar graphs easier to grasp than tables. Use a bar graph

- ▨ To compare sizes.
- ▨ To give an overview or a general conclusion.
- ▨ To initiate or supplement a discussion of cause or significance. (For example, the bar graph of the defect rates of three widget lines [Figure 8.5, p. 192] prompts a reader to ask why the rate was high on line 3.)

Use accompanying text to help readers grasp the implications of the graph.

USING PIE CHARTS

A *pie chart* uses segments of a circle to indicate percentages of a total. The whole circle represents 100 percent, the segments of the circle represent each item's percentage of the total, and the callouts identify the segments in the graph. Data words or symbols provide detailed information.

Parts and Guidelines

Like other graphs, pie charts have conventional elements: a caption, the circle, the segments ("pie slices"), and callouts (see Figure 8.8). The following

FIGURE 8.8
Elements of a Pie Chart

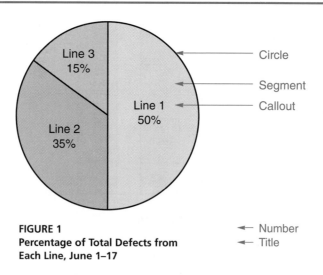

FIGURE 1
Percentage of Total Defects from
Each Line, June 1–17

guidelines (based in part on *Publication*) will help you treat these parts effectively.

1. The caption may appear above or below the chart. Use arabic numerals and a title that names the contents of the graph. Informal charts often have only a title.
2. Start at "12 o'clock," and run the segments in sequence, clockwise, from largest to smallest. (Sometimes you cannot satisfy all these requirements. If you are comparing the grades in a chemistry class, the A segment is usually smaller than the C segment. However, you would logically start the A segment at 12 o'clock.)
3. Identify segments with callouts or legends. *Callouts* are phrases that name each segment (see Figure 8.8). Use callouts if space permits, and arrange them around the circumference of the circle. A *legend* is a small sample of each segment's markings plus a brief identifying phrase, as shown in Figure 8.9. Cluster all the legend items in one area of the visual.
4. In general, place percentage figures inside the segments.
5. For emphasis, shade important segments, or present only a few important segments rather than the whole circle.
6. In general, divide pie charts into no more than five segments. Readers have difficulty differentiating the sizes of small segments. Also, a chart with many segments, and thus many callouts, looks chaotic.

When to Use a Pie Chart

Pie charts work best to compare magnitudes that differ widely (see Figure 8.9). Because pie chart segments are not very precise, most people cannot distinguish between close values, such as 17 percent and 20 percent. Nonexpert audiences find pie charts easier to use than tables (Felker). Use pie charts

- To compare components to one another.
- To compare components to the whole.
- To show gross differences, not fine distinctions.

THREE PRINCIPLES FOR MANIPULATING GRAPHS

Jan White, in his book *Using Charts and Graphs,* illustrates three ways in which you can affect the perception of graphic data. Your goal is to present the graph in such a way that it reports the data honestly.

1. Changing the width of the units on the *X* axis alters the viewer's emotional perception of the data. The graphs in Figure 8.10 plot exactly the same data.

FIGURE 8.9
Pie Chart with Legend

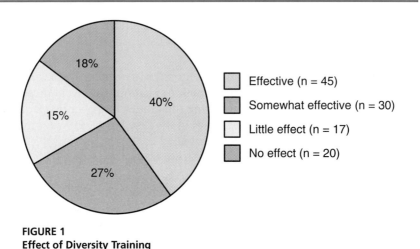

Effective (n = 45)

Somewhat effective (n = 30)

Little effect (n = 17)

No effect (n = 20)

FIGURE 1
Effect of Diversity Training

FIGURE 8.10
Three Graphs That Plot the Same Data
Source: Jan White, *Using Charts and Graphs* (NY: Bowker, 1984). Reprinted by permission of
R. R. Bowker.

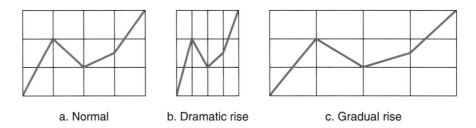

a. Normal   b. Dramatic rise   c. Gradual rise

2. The nearer a highlighted feature appears, the more impact it has on one's consciousness. The pie charts in Figure 8.11 report the same data. Note that the wedge on the left appears largest and that the wedge on the right is forced into the viewer's consciousness. The middle wedge appears unimportant because it is far away.

3. Darker elements seem more important than lighter elements (Figure 8.12).

USING CHARTS

Chart is the catchall name for many kinds of visual aids. Charts represent the organization of something: either something dynamic, such as a

FIGURE 8.11
Three Pie Charts That Plot the Same Data
Source: Jan White, *Using Charts and Graphs* (NY: Bowker, 1984). Reprinted by permission of R. R. Bowker.

FIGURE 8.12
Three Bar Graphs That Plot the Same Data

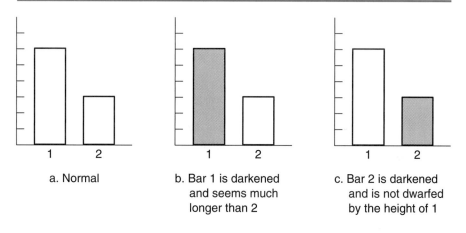

process, or something static, such as a corporation. They include such varied types as troubleshooting tables, schematics of electrical systems, diagrams of the sequences of an operation, flow charts, decision charts, and layouts. Use the same techniques to title and number these as you use for graphs. (Some software companies, including Microsoft, use *chart* to mean *graph,* and you will find these terms used interchangeably.)

Troubleshooting Tables

Troubleshooting tables in manuals identify a problem and give its probable cause and cure. Place the problem at the left and the appropriate action at the right. You can also add a column for causes (see Figure 8.13). Almost all manuals include these tables.

FIGURE 8.13
Troubleshooting Table
Source: Jill Adkins, *Rotary Piston Filler: Eight Head* (Menomonie, WI: MRM/Elgin, 1985).
Reprinted by permission of MRM/Elgin.

TABLE 1
Troubleshooting Table

You Notice	This May Mean	Caused by	You Should
Containers do not center with nozzle	Infeed Starwheel is out of time	Misadjustment or loose mounting bolts	Readjust & retighten
	Machine speed is too fast	Speed not reset during change-over	Reset speed (see "Speed Adjust," p. 5)
	Wrong change parts being used		Install correct change parts (see "Change Parts Data Sheet," p. 27)
Machine vibrates	Lack of maintenance	Tight roller chains (chains that drive the conveyor) or the two chains on the end of the Spiral Screw Feed	Loosen chains
		Roller chains running dry	Lubricate chains
		Cross beam bearing dry	Lubricate (see Figure 5–148)

Flow Charts

Flow charts show a time sequence or a decision sequence. Arrows indicate the direction of the action, and symbols represent steps or particular points in the action (see Figure 8.14). In many cases, especially in computer programming, the symbols have special shapes for certain activities. For instance, a rectangle signals an action to perform and an oval signals the first or last action. Use a flow chart to help readers grasp a process.

Decision Charts

A *decision chart* (or *decision tree*) is a flow chart that uses graphics to explain whether or not to perform a certain action in a certain situation. At each point, the reader must decide yes or no and then follow the appropriate path until the final goal is reached (see Figure 8.15).

FIGURE 8.14
Flow Chart

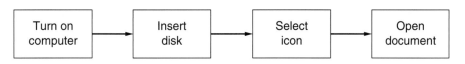

FIGURE 8.15
Decision Chart

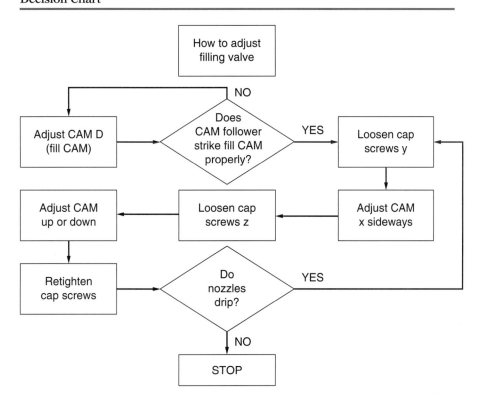

Gantt Charts

A *Gantt chart* (named after its inventor) represents the schedule of a project. Along the horizontal axis are units of time; along the vertical axis are subprocesses of the total project (see Figure 8.16). The lines indicate the starting and stopping points of each subprocess.

Layouts

A *layout* is a map of an area seen from the top. As Figure 8.17 shows, layouts can easily show before and after arrangements. Draw simple lines,

FIGURE 8.16
Gantt Chart

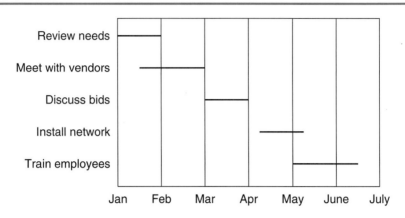

FIGURE 8.17
Sample Layout

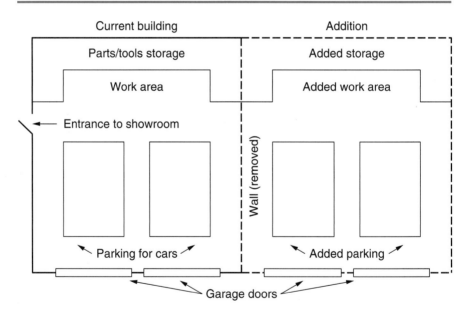

and use callouts and arrows precisely. Callouts may appear inside the figure.

USING ILLUSTRATIONS

Illustrations, usually photographs or drawings of objects, are often used in sets of instructions and manuals.

Guidelines

There are two basic guidelines for using illustrations.

1. Use high-quality illustrations. Make sure they are clear, large enough to be effective, and set off by plenty of white space.
2. Keep the illustrations as simple as possible. Show only items essential to your discussion.

   Use an illustration (Felker)

   ▪ To help explain points in the text.
   ▪ To help readers remember a topic.
   ▪ To avoid lengthy discussions. (A picture of a complex part is generally more helpful than a lengthy description.)
   ▪ To "give the reader permission." (A visual of a computer screen duplicates what is obviously visible before the user, but gives the user permission to believe his or her perception. It reassures the reader.)

Photographs

A good photograph offers several advantages: it is memorable and easy to refer to; it duplicates the item discussed (so audiences can be sure they are looking at what is intended); and it shows the relationships among various parts. The disadvantages are that it reduces a three-dimensional reality to two dimensions and that it shows everything, thus emphasizing nothing. Use photographs to provide a general introduction or to orient a reader to the object (Killingsworth and Gilbertson). In manuals, for instance, writers often present a photograph of the object on the first page. Figure 8.18 shows a skillfully "cropped" photograph. The original contained much more visual information, but the designer blocked out a great deal of it, simplifying it so it makes only one point.

Drawings

Drawings, whether made by computer or by hand, can clearly represent an item and its relationship to other items. Use drawings to eliminate unnecessary details so that your reader can focus on what is important. Two commonly used types of drawings are the exploded view and the detail drawing.

Exploded View.   As the term implies, an *exploded view* shows the parts disconnected but arranged in the order in which they fit together (see Figure 8.19). Use exploded drawings to show the internal parts of a small and intricate object or to explain how it is assembled. Manuals and sets of instructions often use exploded drawings with named or numbered parts.

Detail Drawings. *Detail drawings* are renditions of particular parts or assemblies. Drawings have two common uses in manuals and sets of instructions.

- They function much as an uncluttered, well-focused, cropped photograph, showing just the items that the writer wishes.
- They show cross-sections; that is, they can cut the entire assembled object in half, both exterior and interior. (In technical terms, the object is cut at right angles to its axis.) A cross-sectional view shows the size and the relationship of all the parts. Two views of the same object—front and side views, for example—are often juxtaposed to give the reader an additional perspective on the object (see Figure 8.20).

▪ WORKSHEET FOR VISUAL AIDS

❑ *Name the audience for the visual aid.*

❑ *What should your visual aid do?*
Summarize data? present an opportunity to explore data? provide a visual entry point? engage expectations?

❑ *Choose a format: Where will you place the caption—above or below?*

❑ *Decide on a way to treat this visual's conventional parts. Follow the guideline lists in this chapter.*

❑ *Create a draft of the visual aid. Review it to determine whether you have treated its parts consistently.*

FIGURE 8.18
Cropped Photograph
Source: Rotary Piston Files by Jill Adkins. Reprinted by permission of MRM/Elgin.

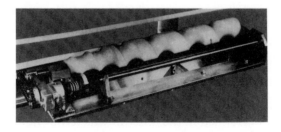

FIGURE 8.19
Exploded View
Source: John R. Mancosky, *Manual Controls: Independent Study Workbook.* Used by permission of Microswitch and John R. Mancosky.

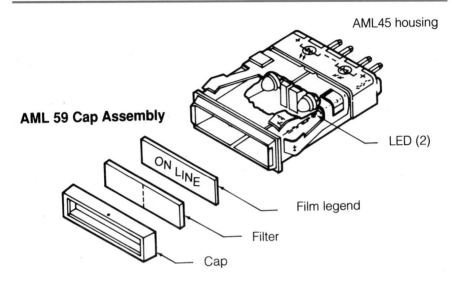

AML45 housing

AML 59 Cap Assembly

LED (2)

ON LINE

Film legend

Filter

Cap

FIGURE 8.20
Detail Drawing

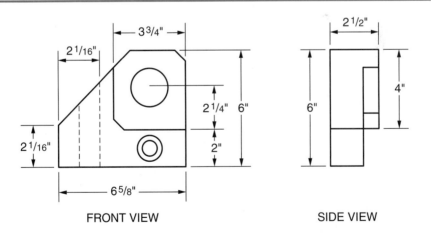

FRONT VIEW

SIDE VIEW

❑ *Eliminate unnecessary clutter.*

❑ *How large will the visual aid be? Do you have room for it in your document?*

❑ *How much time do you have? Will you be able to construct a high-quality visual in that time?*

❑ *Select a method for referring to the visual in your text.*

▇ EXERCISES

1. Collect data from the entire class on an easy-to-research topic, such as type of major, year in school, years with the company (e.g., 1, 2, 3–5, 6–10, 10+), or population of home town or birthplace (e.g., 100K+, 50–100K, 5–50K). Collect data from the entire class. Then create two visual aids: a bar graph and a pie chart. Make them as neat and complete as possible, including captions and callouts. Write a brief memo that states a conclusion you can read by looking at the visual or that tells an audience what to notice in the visual.

    Alternates: (1) Create the visuals in groups of three to four. (2) Create the visuals on a computer. (3) Write a memo explaining the process you used to create the visuals. (4) Write an IMRD (see Chapter 12) to explain your project.

2. Use one of the visuals created in Exercise 1 as the basis for a brief story for the student newspaper or company newsletter, explaining the interesting diversity of your technical writing class.

3. Use a line graph to portray a trend (e.g., sales, absentees, accepted suggestions, defect rate) to a supervisor. Write a brief note in which you name the trend, indicate its significance, and offer your idea of its cause.

4. Use the following data to create a table (Jaehn). Monthly from July to December, the following machines had the following percentages of rejection for mechanical quality defects: #41 — 4.0, 3.1, 3.9, 4.3, 3.5, 3.2; #42 — 3.0, 3.3, 2.4, 3.2, 3.7, 3.1; #43 — 3.4, 3.7, 4.1, 4.5, 4.4, 4.8. Include averages for each month and for each machine. Additional: Write a memo to a supervisor explaining the importance of the trend you see in the data.

5. If you have access to a computer graphics program, make three different graphs of the data in Exercise 4. In a brief paragraph, explain the type of reader and the situation for which each graph would be appropriate.

6. Divide the class into three sections. Have individuals in each section convert the numbers in either of the following paragraphs into visual aids. Section 1 should make a line graph, section 2 a bar graph, and section 3 a pie chart. Have one person from each section put that group's visual on the board. Discuss their effectiveness. Here are the figures:

   Respondents to a survey were asked whether they would pay more for a tamper-evident package. 8.2% said they would pay up to $.15 more; 25.8% were unwilling to pay more; 51.6% would pay $.05 more; and 14.4% would pay $.10 more.

   Industrial designers report that they use various tools to reduce the time they spend on design. Those tools are faster computers (57%), 3D solid modeling (32%), 2D CAD software (26%), Computerized FEA (24%), Rapid Prototyping (15%), other (3%). (Based on Colucci)

7. Convert the following paragraph into a table. Then rewrite the paragraph for your manager, proposing that the company start a recycling program. Refer to specific parts of the table in your paragraph. Alternate: Recommend that the company not start a recycling program. Refer to specific parts of the table.

   The company can recycle 100 pounds of aluminum per week. The current rate for aluminum is 25¢ per pound. This rate would earn the company $25.00 per week and $1200.00 per year. The company can also recycle 200 pounds of paper per week. The current rate for paper is 5¢ per pound. Recycling paper would earn the company $10.00 per week and $520.00 per year. The total earnings from recycling is $1820.00 per year.

8. Divide into groups of three or four, by major if possible. Select a process you are familiar with from your major or from your campus life. Possibilities include constructing a balance sheet, leveling a tripod, focusing a microscope, constructing an isometric projection, threading a film projector, finding a periodical in the library, and making a business plan. As a group, construct a flow chart of the process. For the next class meeting, each person should write a paragraph explaining the process by referring to the chart. Compare paragraphs within your group; then discuss the results with the class.

9. Read over the next four paragraphs from a report. Then construct a visual aid that supports the writer's conclusion.

    The pipe cutter must be small enough so it can be transported in our truck. The Grip-Tite model takes up 2 cubic feet, and it comes with a stand so that it can be folded out when in use and then folded up when not in use. The Mentzer model takes up 5 cubic feet and doesn't come with a stand.

    The pipe cutter must be able to run off 110-volt electricity. Because 220-volt electricity is not easily accessible on the job site, 110-volt must be used. The Grip-Tite model is capable of running off 220-volt, 110-volt, and DC current. The Mentzer cutter is capable only of running off 220-volt.

    The cutter should be able to switch threaders to accommodate ⅜" pipe up to 3" pipe. The Grip-Tite model has two threaders. One can be adjusted from ¼" up to 2", and the other can be adjusted from 2" up to 3". The Mentzer model has only one threader that threads ¾" pipe.

    The cost of the pipe cutter should not exceed $2000. The Grip-Tite model costs $1750, whereas the Mentzer model costs $2250.

10. Discuss the differences between these two table designs. Which one is more effective? Why? Alternate: Create your own table for these data.

TABLE 1
Comparison of Three Trucks

Brand	Purchase Price	3-Year Maintenance Cost	Warranty	Warranty
Big Guy	$11,999	$ 700	2 years	24,000 miles
Friend	13,200	1,000	3 years	30,000 miles
Haul	13,700	850	5 years	50,000 miles

TABLE 1
Comparison of Three Trucks

Brand	Purchase Price in Dollars	3-Year Maintenance Cost	Warranty	
			Years	Miles
Big Guy	$11,999	$ 700	2	24K
Friend	13,200	1,000	3	30K
Haul	13,700	850	5	50K

11. Redo this table and the paragraph that explains it.

I have estimated construction costs at a price of $50.00 per square foot as quoted by Lamb and Associates Construction Company (see Table 3). This will include construction of perimeter walls, carpeting, decor, and lighting. The cost of this will be $37,500.

TABLE 3
Renovation Costs

Construction:			$37,500.00
carpeting	15,000		
decor	8,000		
lighting	6,000		
perimeter walls	8,500		
Loose Fixtures:			
#5021 (7 ball Chrome)	15 @ $ 5.95 each	$ 89.25	
#4596 (4 straight arm)	4 @ $78.00 each	312.00	
#4597 (2 straight 2 slant)	3 @ $81.00 each	243.00	
			$644.25
			$38,144.25
Personnel:			
2 full-time stock men 2/8 hour days @ $4.50/hr.			144.00
Total Renovation Costs:			$38,288.25

■ WRITING ASSIGNMENTS

1. Write a report to your manager to alert him or her to a problem you have discovered. Include a visual aid whose data represent the problem (such as a line graph that shows a "suspect" defect rate).

2. Divide into groups of three. From some external source, acquire data on some general topic such as population, budget, production, or volume of sales. Sources could be your Chamber of Commerce, a government agency, an office in your college, or your corporation's personnel office. As a group, decide on a significant trend that the data show. Write a memo to the appropriate authority, informing him or her of this trend and suggesting its significance. Use a visual aid to convey your point.

3. As a class, agree on a situation in which you will present information to alert someone to a trend or problem. Then divide into several groups. Each group should select one of the four reasons for using a visual aid (p. 180). Write a memo and create the visual aid that illustrates the reason your group chose it (e.g., to provide a different entry

point). Make copies for each of the other groups. When you are finished, circulate your reports and discuss them.

4.   Use a flow chart and an accompanying memo to explain a problem with a process—for example, a bottleneck or a step where a document must go to two places simultaneously. Your instructor may ask you to go on to Writing Assignment 5.

5.   Use Writing Assignment 4 as a basis to suggest a solution to a problem. Create a new flow chart that illustrates how your solution solves the problem. Discuss the solution in a memo to your manager requesting permission to put it into effect.

6.   Write a learning report for the writing assignment you just completed. See Chapter 5, Writing Assignment 7, page 123, for details of the assignment.

■ WEB EXERCISE

Write a memo or an IMRD (see Chapter 12) to your classmates in which you analyze the use of visual aids in Web sites. Your goal is to give hints on how to incorporate visuals effectively into their Web documents. Do the visual aids exemplify one of the four uses of visual aids explained in this chapter? Explain why the visual aid is effective in the Web document.

■ WORKS CITED

Adkins, Jill. *Rotary Piston Filler: Eight Head.* Menomonie, WI: MRM/Elgin, 1985.

Colucci, D. "How to Design in Warp Speed." *Design News* (1996): 64–76.

Felker, Daniel B., Francis Pickering, Veda R. Charrow, V. Melissa Holland, and James C. Redish. *Guidelines for Document Designers.* Washington, DC: American Institutes for Research, 1981. This volume was used extensively in the preparation of this chapter.

Jaehn, Alfred H. "Al." "How to Effectively Communicate with Data Tables." *Tappi Journal* 70 (1987): 183–184.

Killingsworth, M. Jimmie, and Michael Gilbertson. "How Can Text and Graphics Be Integrated Effectively?" *Solving Problems in Technical Writing.* Ed. Lynn Beene and Peter White. NY: Oxford, 1988. 130–149.

MacDonald-Ross, M. "Graphics in Texts." *Review of Research in Education.* Vol. 5. Ed. L. S. Shulman. Itasca, IL: F. E. Peacock, 1978.

Makki, F., and T. D. Durance. "Thermal Inactivation of Lysozyme as Influenced by pH, Sucrose and Sodium Chloride and Inactivation and Preservative Effect in Beer." *Food Research International* 29.7 (October 1996): 635–645.

Mancosky, John R. *Manual Controls: Independent Study Workbook.* Freeport, IL: Microswitch, 1991.

Publication Manual of the American Psychological Association. 4th ed. Washington, DC: APA, 1994.

Shriver, Karen A. *Dynamics in Document Design: Creating Texts for Readers.* NY: Wiley, 1997.

Tufte, Edward R. *The Visual Display of Quantitative Information.* Cheshire, CT: Graphics Press, 1983.

White, Jan. *Graphic Design for the Electronic Age.* NY: Watson Guptil, 1988.

White, Jan. *Using Charts and Graphs.* NY: Bowker, 1984.

9 Defining

Chapter 9
IN A NUTSHELL

Definitions orient readers. Definitions help readers place new concepts in context. Definitions explain new terms and concepts to readers. The traditional way to define is to put the term in a class and then explain how it is different from other members of the class:

"A camera is a device (the class) for taking photographs (the difference)."

Often, however, writers use an extended definition because the reader needs to understand the concept, not just the term. In an extended definition, use one or more strategies to make the term familiar to your audience; for example, compare or contrast, use a common example, explain cause and effect, or add a visual aid.

The following paragraph explains cause (within 300 light-years), uses a common example (spherical ball), and a comparison (mothballs):

"In other places in the sky, thousands or hundreds of thousands of stars of a common origin may be located within 300 light-years or so, forming a huge spherical ball. These groupings are called globular clusters. In the northern sky, the globular cluster M13 in the constellation Hercules is the easiest to see. A globular cluster may look like a hazy mothball to the naked eye or when viewed through a small telescope; larger telescopes are necessary to see individual stars in this type of cluster . . ." (Menzel and Pasachoff, p. 116).

210

Providing definitions—giving the precise meanings of terms—is an important strategy in presenting new concepts. Definitions help readers relate new material to ideas they already hold. They take readers from the familiar to the new. This chapter explains formal definitions, informal definitions, and extended definitions. It also provides advice on planning definitions.

CREATING FORMAL DEFINITIONS

A *formal definition* is one sentence that contains three parts: the term that needs defining, the class to which the item belongs, and the differentiation of that item from all other members of its class. Here are some examples (Raup et al.; Shipman):

> Slate is a compact, fine-grained metamorphic rock formed from such rocks as shale and volcanic ash.
>
> A cirque is a steep-walled, amphitheaterlike hollow carved by a glacier at the head of a valley.
>
> A camera is a light-tight box that holds a piece of film so an image can fall on it.

Classify the Term

To define a term, you first place it in a class, the large group to which the term belongs. A class can be either broad or narrow. For instance, a pen can be classed as a "thing" or as a "writing instrument." A carburetor can be a "part" or a "mixing chamber." The narrower the class, the more meaning conveyed, and the less that needs to be said in the differentiation. The class, however, must be broad enough to be included in the reader's knowledge base. For the definition to be effective, readers must be able to relate it to something they know.

Differentiate the Term

To *differentiate* the term, explain those characteristics that belong only to it and not to the other members of the class. If the differentiation applies to more than one member of the class, the definition is imprecise. For instance, if a writer says, "*Evaporation* is the process of water disappearing from a certain area," the definition is too broad; water can disappear for many reasons, not just from evaporation. The differentiation must explain the characteristics of evaporation that make it unlike any other process: the change of a substance from a liquid to a vapor.

Here are four common methods for differentiating a term:

- Name its essential properties: the characteristic features possessed by all individuals of this type.
- Explain what it does.
- If the term is an object, describe what it is made of and what it looks like.
- If the term is a process, explain how to make or do it.

In the following examples, note that the classification is often deleted. In many cases, it would be a broad statement such as ". . . is a machine."

NAME THE ESSENTIAL PROPERTIES

Engineering is the application of scientific principles to practical ends, such as the design, construction, and operation of efficient and economical structures, equipment, and systems.

Capital equipment is the large, expensive equipment you use to do your job (Caernarven-Smith).

EXPLAIN WHAT IT DOES

AutoLAYER is an AutoCAD layer management utility. It allows users to save layer groups and their properties from a current drawing ("AutoCAD").

DESCRIBE WHAT IT LOOKS LIKE

The stem, or gooseneck, as it is sometimes called, is a curved or angled piece of aluminum or chrom-moly tubing, one end of which holds the handlebars, the other end of which fits inside the headset (Cutherbertson).

A well-focused photograph is a print of a negative in which all lines demarking contrast are sharp.

DESCRIBE WHAT IT IS MADE OF

Concrete is made of sand, gravel, water, gypsum, and, its key ingredient, portland cement (Henkenius).

The varnish oil is pure linseed oil, pressed from flax seed, oxidized by heating, with no additives (Becksvoort).

EXPLAIN HOW TO MAKE OR DO IT

Simple staining is [a process of] coloring bacteria by applying a stain—methylene blue—to a fixed smear.

Avoid Circular Definitions

Do not use circular definitions, which repeat the word being defined or a term derived from it. You will not help a reader understand *capacitance* if you use the word *capacitor* in the differentiation. Noncrucial words, such as *writing* in the term *technical writing,* may, of course, be repeated.

CREATING INFORMAL DEFINITIONS

For specialized or technical terms that your readers will not know, you can provide an informal definition. Two common informal definitions are operational definitions and synonyms.

Operational Definitions

An *operational definition* gives the meaning of an abstract word for one particular time and place. Scientists and managers use operational definitions to give measurable meanings to abstractions. The operational definition "creates a test for discriminating in one particular circumstance" (Fahnestock and Secor 84). For instance, to determine whether a marketing program is a success, managers need to define success. If their operational definition of success is "to increase sales by 10 percent" and if the increase occurs, the program is successful. In this sense, the operational definition is an agreed-upon criterion. If everyone agrees, the definition facilitates the discussion and evaluation of a topic.

Synonyms

A *synonym* is a word that means the same as another word. It is effective as a definition only when it is better known than the term being defined. People are more familiar with *cardboard* than with *f-flute corrugated,* the technical term that has the same meaning. If your audience knows less about the topic than you do, use common words to clarify technical terms.

When using synonyms, put the common word or the technical term in parentheses or set it off with dashes, as in the following examples. Writers often highlight the term that they are defining (Raup et al.).

Parentheses   Most of the rock consists of *calcium carbonate* (limestone).

The fossil algae (stromatolites) take many forms.

Dash	Mount Oberlin and many other pyramidal peaks—*matter-horns*—owe their distinctive form to the erosive action of glaciers on two or more sides of the peak.
End of the sentence	The Altyn Formation was deposited in a shallow, warm sea, an environment indicated by the presence of fossil algae called stromatolites.

DEVELOPING EXTENDED DEFINITIONS

Extended definitions are expanded explanations of the term being defined. After reading a formal definition, a less knowledgeable reader often needs more explanation to understand the term completely. Eight methods for extending definitions follow.

Explain the Derivation

To explain the *derivation* of a term is to explain its origin. One way is to show how it is a combination of other words. *Technology,* for example, derives from the Greek words *techne,* meaning "an art or a skill," and *logia,* meaning "a science or study." Thus the literal meaning of the word *technology* is the study of an art or skill (Ramanathan). Another is to spell out acronyms. *ASCII* is an acronym for *A*merican *S*tandard *C*ode for *I*nformation *I*nterchange.

Explicate Terms

In this context, to *explicate* means to define difficult words contained in the formal definition. Many readers would need definitions of terms such as *metamorphic* in the formal definitions on page 211. When explicating, you can often provide an informal definition rather than another formal one. Note that "lose their leaves" defines *deciduous* in the following example.

> In northern climates, deciduous trees—trees that lose their leaves in the autumn—are perfect for maximizing winter daylight ("Planning").

Use an Example

An example gives readers something concrete to help them understand a term. In the following paragraph, a formal definition of *laminated-strand lumber* is amplified by an extended example:

> Laminated-strand lumber, or LSL, is a relatively new prod-   Definition
> uct on the market, constructed from ½ × 1 × 12-in.
> strands of wood that are bonded with a polyurethane

adhesive. LSL is available in 1¼-in. and 3½-in thickness, with varying depths up to 16 in. and lengths to 35 ft. This product is used for shorter door and window headers, rim joists for floor construction, and as a core stock for flush doors with a veneer overlay. In traditional solid-wood framing techniques, a carpenter builds headers on site from nominal 2-in. stock and plywood, a slow and inefficient task. When using headers of solid LSL, the material can be ordered precut to specified length or can be cut to size on the job site. In either case, there can be a substantial savings in labor cost. (Barrett 66)

Example
Common terms

Example

Use an Analogy

An *analogy* points out a similarity between otherwise dissimilar things. If something is unknown to readers, it helps if you compare it to something they do know. Here is an analogy that compares electricity to golf balls.

An electric current travels with lightning speed—20,000 miles per second along a copper wire—but individual electrons do not: they amble along at less than an inch per second. The current streaks through the wire because the electrons jostle each other all the way. The phenomenon can best be understood by imagining a pipe completely filled with golf balls. If an additional ball is pushed in at one end of the pipe, a ball will pop out almost instantly at the other end. Similarly, when a distant power plant forces electrons into one end of a wire, other electrons almost immediately come out at the other end—to light a lamp, perhaps, or start the coffee. (*How Things* 125)

Comparison to
pipe of golf balls
Golf ball
references
continue

Compare and Contrast

A *comparison-contrast* definition shows both the similarities of and the differences between similar objects or processes. An example is comparing water flowing through a pipe to electricity flowing through a wire. Like other methods of extending a definition, the comparison-contrast method takes advantage of something the readers know to explain something they do not know. Comparing and contrasting a *semiconductor* with a *conductor* of electricity works only if the reader knows what a conductor is.

Here is an extended definition that compares and contrasts two types of color laser printers.

Wax-head elements always heat to the same tempera-   First term
ture, transferring a pixel of wax that's always the same
density and size. By dithering pixels of different primary   Details of first
colors, these printers create the illusion of many colors in term
an image. Wax heads create sharply defined pixels that   Set up contrast
overlap only enough that no image-degrading gaps form.
       Dye-head elements heat to many temperatures—the   Second term
hotter the element, the greater the density of dye it trans-
fers. Dye heads print primary colors one on top of another   Details of second
to create a full color spectrum. Dye pixels have wide, soft   term provide
edges and are darker in the center. Dye printers overlap   contrast
the edges of pixels to compensate for this. (Heid 109)

Explain Cause and Effect

Some concepts are so elusive that they must be defined in terms of their causes and effects. In the following example, the writer describes the causes and effects of pressure in order to extend the formal definition.

A valve actuator is a device that allows the hydraulic sys-   Definition
tem's pressure to regulate the flow of the system. As oil   Cause-effect
enters the inlet port of this actuator, a pressure builds up.
When this pressure exceeds the preset value, the rod ex-   Cause-effect
tends. A cam, which is mounted on the rod, is the por-
tion of the actuator that delivers the work. It then comes
in contact with the desired valve to be opened or closed.   Effect
(See Figure 1.)

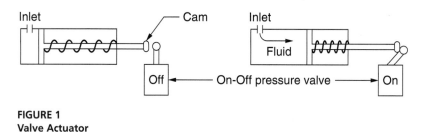

FIGURE 1
Valve Actuator

Use a Visual Aid

Drawings and diagrams can reinforce definitions. The preceding definition of an actuator is reinforced by an illustration of the actuator before and after it operates.

Analyze the Term

To *analyze* is to divide a term into its parts. Analysis helps readers understand by allowing them to grasp the definition bit by bit. For example, *elemental times,* a term used to analyze the work of a machine operator, is easier to understand when its main parts are discussed individually.

The elemental times are the objective for taking the time study in the first place. The elemental time slots on the time-study form contain the following times: overall time, average time, normal time, and standard time.	Preview
Overall time is the whole time from start to finish; it includes total times of all elements (the individual pieces studied).	Definition of part 1
Average time is the time it takes to produce or assemble each piece into a product. When the overall time is divided by the number of pieces produced, the average time per piece is obtained.	Definition of part 2
Normal time is the average time per piece multiplied by a leveling factor. This factor is just a conversion of the performance rating found by using a time-study conversion chart. This normal time represents the time required by a qualified worker, working at the normal performance level, to perform the given task.	Definition of part 3
Standard time, which is the time allowed to do a job, is obtained by adjusting the normal times according to some allowance factor.	Definition of part 4

PLANNING YOUR DEFINITION

To plan your definition, consider your audience's level of knowledge and the amount of detail they need in this situation. Either the audience does not know the term at all, or they are not sure which of several possible meanings you are using. Acronyms, for instance, must often be explained to less knowledgeable readers. Common terms such as *planning phase* may need to be defined so that readers will know what the phrase means in a particular context.

The amount of detail that you provide depends on the reader's needs. At the most basic level, defining unfamiliar words provides enough information for the reader to continue reading intelligently. Thus the definition of *file server* as a *network rest area* provides a lay reader with a general framework to grasp the basic relationship involved. However, for a reader who requires a technical orientation, you need to use a more precise formal definition.

Definitions also provide background that enables people to act in a situation. For instance, suppose a group must decide whether to continue a program. If the decision is based on the program's success, the group must first define success before it can act.

■ WORKSHEET FOR DEFINING TERMS

❏ *Name the audience for the definition.*

❏ *What do they know about the concepts on which this definition is based?*

❏ *What is your goal for your readers?*
In other words, how will they use your definition?

❏ *Select a method—one-sentence, informal, or extended.*
For one-sentence definitions, select a class and differentiation that the reader can grasp. Are both items narrow enough to be useful?
For informal definitions, select synonyms or clear operational wording that the reader knows.
For extended definitions, select a method or methods that enable the reader to grasp the new information. Is the new information based on material you can reasonably expect the reader to already know?

❏ *Select a visual aid that will enable a reader to grasp the topic.*

EXAMPLES

Examples 9.1, 9.2, and 9.3 illustrate many of the methods of defining that this chapter explains.

EXAMPLE 9.1
Model Illustrating Definitions

PHOTO INPUT: WHAT'S THE BEST WAY FOR YOU TO BRING FILM-BASED IMAGES INTO THE COMPUTER?

One thing that can be quite confusing is comparing resolution of scanners versus what's on a Photo CD or other disk-based digitized image. The problem is best understood if you think of disk-based images as already scanned images. Since they're already scanned, they have a finite size and number of "pixels" (or dots) making up the image that can be counted.

Scanners' numbers don't work that way since a scanner has to scan an image. The image can be infinitely variable in size and so will have a variable number of total pixels in the image area. Each scanner has a "dpi" or dots per inch scan that will recognize a certain number of pixels in a defined area (per square inch). As this defined area expands to include the total image area, it'll also include more total pixels, although the dpi stays the same.

Just remember that *dpi* refers strictly to an area 1 × 1-inch square—as you tell the scanner to include more 1 × 1 areas, you'll also be adding to the total number of pixels (since each 1 × 1 area has the same dpi). A small photo will have the same dpi as a large photo, but will have fewer pixels because the image area only includes so many 1 × 1-inch areas.

On a disk such as a Photo CD, the image has already been scanned to a certain size, so while there was a dpi for the scanner, it now has no relevance since the overall size has been selected. (You can change that size in image-processing software, which will change the dpi because you're changing area with the same overall number of pixels.) The total size of the image is what's important, so it's given as dimensions in pixels.

This isn't dpi, since once you start using the image, the dots or pixels per inch will change as you change the size of the image (i.e., an image with large height and width dimensions will spread out the finite pixels available for a low "dpi," while a smaller image will cram them together for a higher "dpi").

- **dpi**—dots per inch; used with a scanner to look at the resolution of the unit
- **pixels**—total number of dots per entire image; whether the image is shrunk or enlarged, the number doesn't change; when the image is shrunk, these finite number of pixels come closer together, giving a higher dpi; when the image is enlarged, these pixels spread apart, giving a lower dpi

Excerpted from "Photo Input: What's the Best Way for You to Bring Film-Based Images into the Computer?" from *PC Photo* 1.2 (July/August 1997): 66–69 by permission of *PC Photo Magazine*.

EXAMPLE 9.2
Model Illustrating Definitions

AN OVERVIEW OF SOLID MODELING

When solid modeling was first introduced it was viewed as a powerful tool but was considered unusable (Fusaro, Martinez, & Romero, 1996). Early systems required the models to be designed by means of mathematical operations. These operations, which were called Boolean operations, involved the use of algebraic formulas and calculations to construct a model piece by piece. These complex construction methods are what made the early solid modeling packages difficult to work with.

Current solid modeling packages have become much more user-friendly than these traditional versions. Most of today's solid modeling packages fall into one or more of three categories:

- Feature-based modeling
- Variational modeling
- Parametric modeling

Feature-Based Modeling

According to "Modeling" (1995) feature-based modeling is the most popular method for constructing solid models. With the feature-based method, models are constructed through the use of geometric features rather than using mathematical operations. The advantage of feature-based modeling is that it understands the designer's intentions. For example, if a cut is initially made to extend completely through a surface, and at a later date the thickness of the surface is increased, the program knows enough to automatically extend the cut. Feature-based modeling is best utilized when working with designs that involve geometric changes rather than just dimensional changes.

Variational Modeling

The variational method is more of a mathematical approach to designing a model. When a change is made to a model, the program recalculates all of the designing that has been done to that point. This method is most effective in the early stages of design because the greatest design changes occur early on. Variational modeling allows designers to create 3D models out of 2D drawings. The system does this by incorporating commands such as *extrude* and *sweep*. When the extrude command is used, it will extrude the selected feature on the 2D drawing to the specified distance. As a result, a 3D model of the extruded feature is constructed ("Modeling," 1995). For example, a two-dimensional circle can be extruded to construct a three-dimensional cylinder. The 3D illustration provides a clearer representation of what the object would look like if it was a physical model.

EXAMPLE 9.2
(continued)

Parametric Modeling

Parametric modeling is a dimension-driven modeling method. this means that rather than constructing a model based on geometric shapes, the model is created by specifying certain dimensions. With this method all of the commands that were given to construct a model are saved within the system. The reason for this is so that when a dimensional change is given, the system can update all dimensions that were affected by this initial change. Parametric modeling is best utilized when working with designs which involve dimensional changes rather than geometric changes. "For example, a circle representing a bolt hole may be constructed so it is always concentric to a circular slot. If the slot moves, so does the bolt circle" ("Modeling," 1995, p. 85). This is just one advantage to solid modeling.

Fusaro, J., Martinez, J., & Romero, G. (1996). Variational solid modeling of metal matrix composite high current power modules. *International Journal of Microcircuits and Electronic Packaging, 19,* 219–224.

Modeling, drafting, and prototypes. (1995). *Machine Design, 67,* 83–85.

EXAMPLE 9.3
Model Illustrating Definitions
Source: From Mayo Clinic Women's Health Source, September 2000.

BASIC GENETICS

You need to know the basics before you can begin to understand the complexity of gene therapy. Here's a guide.

- *Human cell.* Each of the 100 trillion cells in the human body (except blood cells) contains the entire human genome—all the genetic information needed to build a human being. This information is encoded in 6 billion base pairs, subunits of DNA. Egg and sperm cells each have half this amount of DNA.

- *DNA.* Short for deoxyribonucleic acid, the principal carrier of a cell's genetic information. It's organized into two chains that form a double helix. Units that make up these chains include four "bases"—adenine (A), thymine (T), guanine (G), and cytosine (C). These bases form interlocking pairs that can fit together in only one way: A pairs with T; G pairs with C. The organization of these base pairs provides the informational code of the DNA molecule.

- *RNA.* Short for ribonucleic acid, a single-stranded chain made by DNA that helps guide protein synthesis.

- *Cell nucleus.* Six feet of DNA are packed into 23 pairs of chromosomes. One chromosome in each pair comes from each parent inside this central structure of the cell.

- *Chromosomes.* Rod-like structures containing DNA and protein located in the cell nucleus. There are 46 chromosomes in each human cell.

- *Genes.* Genes are the biological units of heredity. They're made up of segments of DNA. Each gene acts as a blueprint for making a specific enzyme or other protein.

- *Protein.* Composed of amino acids, they're the body's workhorses—essential components of all organs and chemical activities within the body. Their function depends on their shapes, determined by the 30,000 to 50,000 genes in the cell nucleus.

EXERCISES

1. Write one-sentence definitions of four technical terms for a nonexpert reader. Alternate: Define the same four terms for an expert reader.

2. Write an extended definition of a term drawn from your major. Use one of the following methods for extending your definition: analogy, comparison-contrast, or cause and effect. Use a visual aid, if possible. If necessary, use one of the following terms:

mutual fund	serving size
cyberspace	rejection rate
hypernet	a type of testing common in your field
flat-rate pricing	
anorexia	search engine
detail drawing	keyword

3. Analyze, and redo if necessary, these definitions:

   A bibliography is a list of books.
   A manager runs the show.
   The Web is a bunch of computers hooked together.
   Software is what you use to run hardware.

4. In groups of two or three, write one-sentence formal definitions of three different objects or concepts. From that group, pick one definition and decide on any audience. For the next class, each member will write an extended definition about one page long. At the second class, in groups of three or four, compare the definitions. Then read and discuss your choices with the class.

5. Analyze either Example 9.1 or 9.2 to determine the types of definitions used and their intended audience.

6. In Example 9.2, rewrite for a different audience the section that explains the four common design flaws.

7. Provide a visual aid that clarifies one or several of the items in Example 9.2.

■ WRITING ASSIGNMENTS

1. You have been asked to provide basic background to a committee that will make a purchase decision on an object or process. Suppose, for instance, that your office wants to install a local area network. Define the basic concepts (such as *server*) that they need to know. Plan by filling out the worksheet; then draft the document. Be sure to credit any sources that you use.

2. Write a learning report for the writing assignment you just completed. See Chapter 5, Writing Assignment 7, page 123, for details of the assignment.

■ WEB EXERCISE

Write an extended definition of an effective Web site. Choose one of these categories—commercial, entertainment, professional society, university, personal, technical information.

■ WORKS CITED

"AutoCAD Layer Manager." *Building and Design Construction* July 1994: 80.

Barrett, Neal. "Engineered Lumber." *Popular Mechanics* August 1994: 64ff.

Becksvoort, Christian. "Tried and True Varnish Oil and Wood Finish." *Fine Woodworking* August 1994: 36.

Caernarven-Smith, Patricia. "Capital Equipment: How to Get It and Manage It." *Technical Communication* Second Quarter 1994: 260–268.

Cutherbertson, Tom. *Anybody's Bike Book.* Berkeley, CA: Ten Speed, 1990.

Fahnestock, Jeanne, and Marie Secor. *A Rhetoric of Argument.* NY: Random House, 1982.

Heid, Jim. "Wax and Dye Printing from One Printer." *Macworld* July 1994: 109.

Henkenius, Merle. "Pour a Concrete Sidewalk." *Popular Mechanics* August 1994: 76–80.

How Things Work in Your Home (and What to Do When They Don't). NY: Holt, 1985.

Menzel, Donald M., and Jay M. Pasachoff. *A Field Guide to the Stars.* Boston: Houghton Mifflin, 1983.

"Photo Input: What's the Best Way for You to Bring Film-Based Images into the Computer?" *PC Photo* 1.2 July/Aug. 1997: 66–69.

"Planning Guide." *Come Home Summer* 1994: 26–27.

Ramanathan, K. "The Polytrophic Components of Manufacturing Technology." *Technological Forecasting and Social Change* 46.3 (1994): 221–258.

Raup, Omer B., Robert Earhart, James Whipple, and Paul Carrara. *Geology: Along Going-to-the-Sun Road in Glacier National Park, Montana.* West Glacier, MT: Glacier Natural History Association, 1983.

Shipman, Carl. *Understanding Photography.* Tucson, AZ: H.P. Books, 1974.

10 Describing

Chapter 10
IN A NUTSHELL

Description orients readers to objects and processes. Your goal is to make the readers feel in control of the subject.

- Show readers how this subject fits into a larger context that is important to them.
- Tell them what you are going to say; write this kind of document in a top-down manner.
- Choose clear heads; write in manageable chunks; define terms sensibly; use visual aids that helpfully communicate.
- Choose a tone that enables readers to see you as a guide.

Mechanism descriptions. In the *introduction*

- Define the mechanism and tell its purpose.
- Provide an overall description.
- List the main parts.

For each *main part*

- Define the mechanism and describe it in terms of size, shape, material, location, color.
- List and describe any subparts.

Process descriptions. In the *introduction* you need to

- Tell the goal and significance of the process.
- Explain principles of operation.
- List the major sequences.

For each sequence or step

- Tell the end goal of the process.
- Describe the action in terms of qualities and quantities.

225

Description is widely used in technical writing. Many reports require that you describe something—a machine, process, or system. Sometimes you will describe in intricate detail, other times in broad outline. This chapter shows you how to describe a mechanism, an operation, and a process focused on a person in action.

PLANNING THE MECHANISM DESCRIPTION

The goal of a mechanism description is to make the readers confident that they have all the information they need about the mechanism. Obviously, you can't describe every part in minute detail, so you select various key parts and their functions. When you plan a description of a mechanism, consider the audience, select an organizational principle, choose visual aids, and follow or adopt the usual form for writing descriptions.

Consider the Audience

To make the audience feel confident, consider their knowledge level and why they need the information. Basically, the principle is to give them the physical details that they need to act. The details you choose and the amount of definition you provide reflect your understanding of their knowledge and need. Here is a brief, simple description for an audience that must make a decision about a topic easily understood by most people. The author can safely assume that length and width terms need no definition.

> The truck box size is an important factor because we frequently transport 4 ft by 8 ft sheets of wood. The box size of the Hauler at the floor is 3.5 ft by 6 ft. The box size of the X-200 at the floor is 4 ft by 8 ft. This factor means we should purchase the X-200.

Here, however, is another brief description, also the basis for a decision, directed at an audience that has a specialized technical knowledge. The writer here assumes that the audience understands terms like "dpi resolution." If the writer assumed the audience did not understand the term, he or she would have to enlarge the discussion to define all the terms.

> The ABC scanner has 50–1200 dpi resolution, 24-bit color scanning, and an optional transparency adaptor. The XYZ scanner has 400–1600 dpi resolution, 24-bit color, and an optional transparency adaptor. The higher resolution capabilities make XYZ the preferable purchase to fill our needs.

Select an Organizational Principle

You can choose from a number of organizational principles. For instance, you can describe an object from

- Left to right (or right to left).
- Top to bottom (or bottom to top).
- Outside to inside (or inside to outside).
- Most important to least important (or least important to most important).

Base this decision on your audience's need. For a general introduction, a simple sequence like top to bottom is best. For future action, say, to decide whether or not to accept a recommendation, use most to least important.

An easy way to check the effectiveness of your principle of organization is to look for *backtracking*. Your description should move steadily forward, starting with basic definitions or concepts that the audience needs to understand later statements. If your description is full of sections in which you have to stop and backtrack to define terms or concepts, your sequence is probably inappropriate.

Choose Visual Aids

Use visual aids to enhance your description of a mechanism. As the figure of a paper micrometer (p. 229) demonstrates, overviews show all the parts in relationship. Details focus readers on specific aspects. Often a visual aid of a detail can dramatically shorten a text discussion. Consider this brief discussion of a problem with broken piping joints. It would be much longer and difficult to comprehend if it were all text.

Figure 1a shows a typical cross-section view of a copper-to-copper tube joint soldered together. Notice how the solder covers up the entire opening between the two tubes. Figure 1b shows the break in the solder due to a change in temperature.

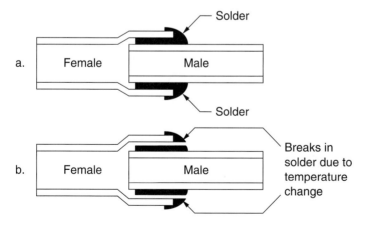

FIGURE 1
Copper-to-Copper Tube Joints

Often your visual aid focuses the text. In effect, your words describe the visual aid.

Follow the Usual Form for Descriptions

Generally, descriptions do not stand alone but are part of a larger document. However, they still have an introduction and body sections; conclusions are optional. Use conclusions only if you need to point out significance. Make the introduction brief, stating either your goal for the reader or the purpose of the mechanism. To describe a part, point out whatever is necessary about relevant physical details—size, shape, material, weight, relationship to other parts, or method of connection to other parts. If necessary, use analogies and statements of significance to help your reader understand the part.

WRITING THE MECHANISM DESCRIPTION

A stand-alone mechanism description has a brief introduction, a description of each part, and an optional conclusion.

Introduction

The introduction gives the reader a framework for understanding the mechanism. In the introduction, define the mechanism, state its purpose, present an overall description, and preview the main parts.

A paper micrometer is a small measuring instrument used to measure the thickness of a piece of paper. The micrometer, roughly twice as large as a regular stapler (see Figure 1), has four main parts: the frame, the dial, the hand lever, and the piston.	Definition and purpose Overall description Main parts

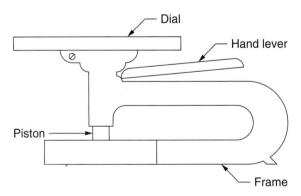

FIGURE 1
Paper Micrometer

TIP: MECHANISM DESCRIPTION

A quick way to plan a mechanism description is to use this outline:

I. Introduction
   A. Definition and Purpose
   B. Overall Description (size, weight, shape, material)
   C. Main Parts
II. Description
   A. Main Part A (definition followed by detailed description of size, shape, material, location, method of attachment)
   B. Main Part B (definition followed by overall description, and then identification of subparts)
      1. Subpart X (definition followed by detailed description of size, shape, material, location, method of attachment)
      2. Subpart Y (same as for X)
   C. Other Main Parts
   D. Etc.

Body: Description of Mechanism

The *body* of the description contains the details. Identify each main part with a heading and then describe it. In a complex description like the following one, begin the paragraph with a definition, then add details. Use structural parallelism (see p. 53, Chapter 3) for each section. If you put size first in one section, do so in all of them.

THE FRAME

The frame of the paper micrometer is a cast piece of steel that provides a surface to which all the other parts are attached. The frame, painted gray, looks like the letter C with a large flat disk on the bottom and a round calibrated dial on top. The disk is 4½ inches in diameter and resembles a flat hockey puck. The frame is 5⅛ inches high and 7½ inches long. Excluding the bottom disk, the frame is approximately 1¼ inches wide. The micrometer weighs 8 pounds.	Definitions Color Analogy Size and analogy Weight

THE DIAL

The dial shows the thickness of the paper. The dial looks like a watch dial except that it has only one moving hand. The frame around the dial is made of chrome-plated metal. A piece of glass protects the face of the dial in the same way that the glass crystal on a watch protects the face and hands. The dial, 6 inches in diameter and ⅞ inch thick, is calibrated in .001-inch marks, and the face of the dial is numbered every .010 inch. The hand is made from a thin, stiff metal rod, pointed on the end.	Definition and analogy Analogy Size Appearance

THE HAND LEVER

The hand lever, shaped like a handle on a pair of pliers, raises and lowers the piston. It is made of chrome-plated steel and attaches to the frame near the base of the dial. The hand lever is 4 inches long, ½ inch wide, and ¼ inch thick. When the hand lever is depressed, the piston moves up, and the hand on the dial rotates. When the hand lever is released and a piece of paper is positioned under the piston, the dial shows the thickness of the paper.	Analogy and definition Relationship to other parts Effect

THE PISTON

The piston moves up and down when the operator depresses and releases the hand lever. This action causes the paper's thickness to register on the dial. The piston is ⅜ inch in diameter, flat on the bottom, and made of metal without a finish. The piston slides in a hole in the frame. The piston can measure the thickness of paper up to .300 inch.	Definition Function Size Relationship to other parts

Other Patterns for Mechanism Descriptions

Two other patterns are useful for describing mechanisms: the function method and the generalized method.

The Function Method.   One common way to describe a machine is to name its main parts and then give only a brief discussion of the function of each part. The *function method* is used extensively in manuals. The following paragraph is an example of a function paragraph:

FUNCTION BUTTONS

The four function buttons, located under the liquid crystal display, work in conjunction with the function switches. The four switches are hertz (Hz), decibels (dB), continuity (c), and relative (REL).

List of subparts

    The hertz function allows you to measure the frequency of the input signal. Press the button a second time to disable. The decibel function allows you to measure the intensity of the input signal, which is valuable for measuring audio signals. It functions the same way as the hertz button.

Function and size of subpart 1

Function and size of subpart 2

    The continuity function allows you to turn on a visible bar on the display, turn on an audible continuity signal, or disable both of them. The relative function enables you to store a value as a reference value. For example, say you have a value of 1.00 volt stored; every signal that you measure with this value will have 1.00 volt subtracted from it.

Function and size of subpart 3

Function and size of subpart 4

The Generalized Method.   The *generalized method* does not focus on a part-by-part description; instead the writer conveys many facts about the machine. This method of describing is commonly found in technical journals and reports. With the generalized method, writers use the following outline (Jordan):

1. General detail
2. Physical description
3. Details of function
4. Other details

General detail consists of a definition and a basic statement of the operational principle. *Physical description* explains such items as shape, size, appearance, and characteristics (weight, hardness, chemical properties, methods of assembly or construction). *Details of function* explain these features of the mechanism:

- How it works, or its operational principle
- Its applications
- How well and how efficiently it works
- Special constraints, such as conditions in the environment
- How it is controlled
- How long it performs before it needs service

Other details include information about background, information about marketing, and general information, such as who makes it.

Here is a sample general description.

> The QMS ColorScript Laser 1000 breaks new ground: it's the first color laser printer to sell for under $10,000 (even if it is just a dollar under), and it's the first color laser printer for the desktop (if your desktop can hold a large picnic cooler that weighs 106 pounds). The ColorScript Laser 1000 uses an 8-pages-per-minute, 300-dots-per-inch print engine whose single paper tray can hold 250 sheets. (A second tray is optional.) The printer comes with 12MB of memory (expandable to 32MB), a 60MB internal hard drive that stores downloadable fonts and incoming print jobs, and 65 fonts. Built-in network ports include LocalTalk, Centronics parallel, and serial; Ethernet and Token Ring network interfaces are optional.
>
> The ColorScript Laser 1000 is about four times as complex to set up as a monochrome laser: you need to install four developer cartridges, four toner cartridges (cyan, magenta, yellow, and black), a cleaning pad, a bottle of oil (it keeps the toner from sticking to the printer's heat rollers), a photosensitive belt, and a hopper that holds waste toner. These consumables need to be replaced at varying intervals: every 3000 pages for the oil, for instance, and once a year or so for the belt.
>
> As with a monochrome laser printer, the time between toner feedings varies—pages with a lot of color or black use more toner than do pages containing very little. This contrasts with thermal-wax and dye-sublimation machines, which use the same amount of ink ribbon for each page regardless of a page's content. This, and the ColorScript Laser 1000's ability to use conventional photocopier bond paper, makes the machine's cost-per-page significantly lower than that of thermal-wax and dye-sub technologies—roughly 5 to 10 cents per color page, compared with about 60 cents for thermal-wax, and several dollars for dye-sub.
>
> How does the output look? Very good. The colors aren't as vivid as those produced by competing technologies, but they're perfectly adequate for business documents—bar charts, colored headlines, and transparencies. The printer's text quality is almost as sharp as that produced by a monochrome laser printer, and generally sharper than thermal-wax and dye-sub output. The print is also more durable than ink-jet or

thermal-wax output: it doesn't smear if it gets wet (ink-jet output sometimes does), and it's nearly indestructible: unlike the wax applied by thermal-wax machines and the ink from solid-ink printers such as Tektronix's 300i, the ColorScript Laser 1000's color toner doesn't scratch off when you paper-clip it, or flake when you fold it. The ColorScript Laser 1000 also fared well on Macworld Lab's test track, although its overall performance was half that of Tektronix's Phaser 220i, the fastest thermal-wax machine available. The printer was particularly slow in the Photoshop test. Further incentive to look elsewhere for prepress work is that the printer doesn't do as good a job with scanned images as do thermal-wax machines (such as Tektronix's Phaser 200 series) that provide enhanced halftoning options. Also, color laser technology doesn't allow for as much consistency. ("QMS" 75)

PLANNING THE PROCESS DESCRIPTION

Technical writers often describe processes such as methods of testing or evaluating, methods of installing, flow of material through a plant, the schedule for implementing a proposal, and the method for calculating depreciation. Manuals and reports contain many examples of process descriptions.

As with a mechanism description, the writer must consider the audience, select an organizational principle, choose visual aids, and follow the usual form for writing descriptions.

Consider the Audience

Your goal is to make your audience confident that they have all the information they need about the process. The knowledge level of audiences and their potential use of the document will vary. Their knowledge level can range from advanced to beginner. Uses will vary; often they use the description to make a decision. For instance, a plant engineer might propose a change in material flow in a plant because a certain step is inefficient, causing a bottleneck. To get the change approved, he or she would have to describe the old and new processes to a manager, who would use that description to decide whether to implement the new process.

Process descriptions also explain theory, thus answering the audience's need for a background understanding. The writer can describe how a sequence of actions has a cause-effect relationship, thus allowing the reader to understand where the trouble might be in a machine or what the significance of an action might be. Here is a brief process description that allows a reader to analyze his or her own leaking faucet:

When the hot- and cold-water handles of the stem faucets are turned on, the rotating stems ride upward on their threads. As they rise, the stems draw the washers away from the brass rings, called faucet seats, at the tops of the water supply lines, allowing water to flow. When both hot and cold water flow through faucets, they mix in the faucet body and run from the spout as warm water. When the handles are turned to the off position, the stems ride downward on their threads. The washers press against the faucet seats, shutting off the flow of water. (*How* 71)

Process descriptions can also present methodology, the steps a person took to complete a project or solve a problem. These statements often reassure the reader by showing that the writer has done the project the "right" way. Here is a brief methodology statement.

I started the project by sending out for price quotes on the 21 modular containers. I chose three vendors from the Phoenix area: Box Company, Johnson Packaging, and Packages R Us. I chose the first two based on their past services for the JCN-Tucson plant. I chose Packages R Us because they are the national vendor for the Modular program for the entire JCN Corporation. From these vendors I asked for two price quotes: one based on a just-in-time (JIT) inventory system, and the other based on the existing inventory system.

Select an Organizational Principle

The organizational principle for processes is *chronological:* start with the first action or step, and continue in order until the last. Also consider whether you need to use cause-effect in the arrangement. Many processes have obvious sequences of steps, but others require careful examination to determine the most logical sequence. If you were describing the fashion cycle, you could easily determine its four parts (introduction, rise, peak, and decline). If you had to describe the complex flow of material through a plant, however, you would want to base your sequence of steps on your audience's knowledge level and intended use of the description. You might treat "receiving" as just one step, or you might break it into "unloading," "sampling," and "accepting." Your decision depends on how much your audience needs to know.

Choose Visual Aids

Choose a visual aid that orients your reader to the process, either to see the entire process at a glance or to see the working of one step. If your subject is a machine in operation, visuals of the machine in different positions will clarify the process. If you are describing a process that involves people, a flow chart can quickly clarify a sequence.

Follow the Usual Form for Writing Descriptions

The process description takes the same form as the mechanism description: a brief introduction, which gives an overview, and the body, which treats each step in detail, usually one step to a section. Make the introduction brief, either a statement of your goal or the purpose of the process. Use conclusions only if you need to point out significance. In each paragraph first define the step (often in terms of its goal or end product), and then describe it. Use structural parallelism (see p. 53, Chapter 3) for each section. If you follow a definition of an end goal with a brief description of the machine and then the action in one section, do so in all sections.

Define a step's end goal or purpose, and then describe the actions that occur during that step. Point out qualities like "fast" and quantities like "60 times." Add statements of significance if you need to.

WRITING THE PROCESS DESCRIPTION

The following outline shows the usual form for a description of a process that does not involve a person. Include an introduction, a description of each step, and an optional conclusion.

Introduction

The introduction provides a context for the reader. Define the process, explain its principles of operation (if necessary), and preview the major sequences. The following introduction performs all three tasks:

Date:	March 29, 1999
To:	April Bilasky, Second Shift Floor Supervisor
From:	Brad Tanck, First Shift Floor Supervisor
Subject:	Processes involved in producing wooden puzzle in automated manufacturing cell

The following information pertains to your request for a description of the process of continuous production of wooden puzzles by an automated manufacturing cell. This memo explains that process. The wooden puzzle consists of 9 hex-shaped parts arranged in a spherical configuration when fully assembled. The automated manufacturing consists of five processes: hex-shaping the stock, cutting the stock to size, grooving the parts, deburring the parts, and finishing and packaging the parts (see Figure 1).

Background

Common examples

Preview of major sequences

Body: Description of the Operation

In the body of the paper, write one paragraph for each step of the process. Each paragraph should begin with a general statement about the end goal

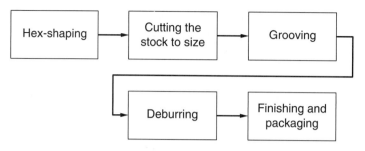

FIGURE 1
Process for Producing Wooden Puzzle Parts

or main activity. Then the remainder explains in more detail the action necessary to achieve that goal. In the following example, each paragraph starts with an overview, and all the paragraphs are constructed in the same pattern. The flow chart gives readers an overview before they begin to read.

HEX-SHAPING THE STOCK

The hex-shaping process entails running 30-inch lengths of ¾-inch-square maple stock through a set of shapers to cut the stock into a hex shape. The maple stock lengths ⟶ End goal
are hand-placed in a gravity hopper, where they drop down onto a moving conveyor system. From here, the conveyor transports the stock until it reaches a set of ⟶ Action
push rollers, one on each side of the stock. Friction from ⟶ Action
the push rollers forces the stock through a set of diamond-shaped shaper bits, which are offset at 60-degree angles to one another in order to shape the square stock into perfect hex stock. From here, the hex stock rides on a conveyor belt to the next station.

CUTTING THE STOCK TO SIZE

The purpose of cutting the stock to size is to get 9 parts, ⟶ End goal
all 3 inches in length. When the hex stock reaches the cut-to-size station, it trips a limit switch. This switch causes a stop to eject and prevents the stock from further ⟶ Action
advancing. At this point, a pneumatic circular saw is activated, which cuts a 3-inch part off the hex stock.

When this process is completed, the stop is retracted and the stock moves onward, pushing the cut-to-size part down a chute to the next station and ⟶ Action
signaling the stop in preparation for cutting another part from the stock.

TIP: PROCESS DESCRIPTION

To create a process description quickly, follow this outline:

   I. Introduction
      A. Define process
      B. Explain principles of operation or give common examples
      C. Preview main steps in the process
  II. Describe process
      A. Main Step One
          1. Define the step's goal
          2. Add necessary background material
          3. Present details of action
      B. Main steps
      C. Etc.

GROOVING THE PARTS

In order for the puzzle parts to fit together, several   End goal
different grooves must be cut into the parts at vari-
ous angles. Of the 9 parts that are processed, 3 parts
have 2 grooves in them, 3 parts have 1 groove in   Background
them, and 3 parts have 3 grooves in them.

    After the part arrives at the grooving station, it is
grasped by a set of pinch rollers. The pinch rollers   Action
feed the part into a hex-shaped aluminum collet
mounted on an x-y table. This collet is specially de-   Background
signed with 2 slots cut out of the top of it, both at
70-degree angles, and one slot cut out of its bottom   Action
at a 120-degree angle. The table moves the part and
collet through a set of 2 routers, one on top and one
on the bottom, which cut the required grooves in
the part through the slots in the collet.

    When this grooving process is completed, the   Action
pressure on the collet is released. The ram of a pneumatic cylinder pushes the part onto an outfeed
chute, where it travels to the next station.

DEBURRING THE PARTS

Deburring the parts includes removing any burrs and   End goal
shavings from the part and cleaning up its surface
before it is finished.

    When the part arrives at the deburring station, it
lands in a gravity hopper at the head of the station.   Action
The orientation of the part is changed at this time.
As the part comes through the hopper, it is handled   Action
side for side instead of end for end.

    After the part drops down onto the stationary
feed table, pressure from a small pneumatic cylinder
secures it to the back edge of the moving feed table.
At this time, a larger secondary pneumatic cylinder is
actuated. This cylinder pushes the attached moving   Action
feed table with the part through a set of abrasive
wheels, one above the part and one below it. These
wheels take the burrs off the part and clean it up for
finishing.

    At the conclusion of its stroke, the larger cylinder   Action
pauses and the smaller cylinder retracts, releasing the
part to the next station. The larger cylinder then extends
in order to deburr the next part.

FINISHING AND PACKAGING THE PARTS

The finishing and packaging process includes spraying a   End goal
lacquer finish on the part, drying the finish, and packag-

ing the puzzle parts in a sealed plastic carton. As the part drops from the deburring station, it lands on a moving conveyor system. The conveyor system's ¾-inch pins protruding from the belt keep the part from coming in contact with the belt itself. The conveyor system transports the part through a spray booth, where a lacquer finish is applied. From here the conveyor keeps moving through a drying booth, where high-intensity heat is blown on the part to dry it before packaging.	Action Background Action
Finally, the part drops off the end of the conveyor, activating a photo-electric switch, which counts the part, and a pick-and-place robot. The pick-and-place robot takes the part and places it in a plastic carton.	Action
When all 9 puzzle parts are placed in the carton, a plastic wrap is placed over the finished product and it is sealed by an electronic heat seal device.	

Conclusion

Conclusions to brief descriptions of operation are optional. At times, writers follow the description with a discussion of the advantages and disadvantages of the process or with a brief summary. If you have written a relatively brief, well-constructed description, you do not need a summary.

PLANNING THE DESCRIPTION OF A HUMAN SYSTEM

A human system is a sequence of actions in which one or more people act in specified ways. If you describe in general what happens in such a system, you have a process description. But if you tell people how to act, you have a procedure or a set of instructions. The description of the waterfall software design process in the next section describes actions that the members of the group usually take as they do this kind of work. A set of instructions, by contrast, would tell a person exactly what to do, in detail, for each step.

You plan for such a document as for a regular process description (see pp. 233–235). Like the process description shown earlier (pp. 235–238), this document contains an introduction, which defines the process and its major sequences, and the body, which describes the process in detail.

WRITING THE DESCRIPTION OF A HUMAN SYSTEM

The following outline shows the usual form for writing a description of a human system. Include an introduction and a body. The conclusion is optional.

Introduction

In the introduction, orient the reader to the process. The following introduction states the purpose of the memo, defines the process, explains why
the reader needs the information, and lists the major steps in the process.
In some situations, writers might also detail material or mechanisms necessary for performing the process.

This memo describes the waterfall software design process (see Figure 1) used by this department. Because you have worked in a department that uses an object-oriented process exclusively and are not familiar with our process, I will try to make the descriptions complete but not elementary. The four major phases of the waterfall software design process are writing software require-ments, designing, implementing, and testing.	Purpose Reader need Preview of major steps

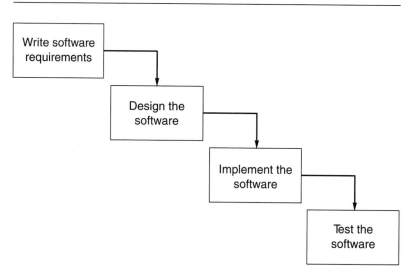

FIGURE 1
The Waterfall Design Process

Body: Sequence of a Person's Activities

In the body, describe each step in sequence. Present as much detail as necessary about the quality and quantity of the actions. Keep in mind these
two notes on style:

1. Do not overdo the imperative (command) voice. You are trying to de-
    scribe, not dictate. In this type of writing, "We determine . . ." is
    preferable to "Determine. . . ."

2. Try to name the steps. Note that step 1 in the example is named "Writing Software Requirements," a phrase that includes an action word (*writing*).

WRITING SOFTWARE REQUIREMENTS

During the requirements phase, a software specification document is written. This formal statement of the system requirements serves as a contract between the developers and the customers. The requirements phase has two major stages: analysis and specification.

During the analysis stage, the specification writer—generally a systems engineer—gathers requirements and information from the customer and also determines what is attainable. Agreements are made on system functionality to ensure that the customer is happy and that we don't promise something we can't deliver. Therefore, contact with the customer is essential.

Once the writer completes the analysis process, he or she writes a software specification. This document must state exactly what the software system will do, but it should not specify how it will be done. The customer reviews this document and may request changes. After any changes are made, the customer approves the document.

DESIGNING THE SOFTWARE

In the design phase, the developer designs a software system based on the requirement specifications and produces a software design document. This phase consists of three major steps: defining data flow, decomposing the system, and constructing an algorithm description. To define data flow, the developer identifies and defines data elements in the system. The developer constructs data flow diagrams to document the way the system handles these elements.

The developer divides the system into separate executable units called *programs,* which are further broken down into functional units. The developer then constructs a structure chart that describes the units and shows the system's hierarchy.

To construct an algorithm description, the developer uses PDL/Ada, a design language that specifies a formal structure for algorithms but also allows plain English descriptions.

After all these substeps, the developer produces the software design document by combining the data flow diagrams, the structure charts, and the PDL/Ada.

IMPLEMENTING THE SOFTWARE

The implementation phase is the actual writing of the software. The developer translates the software design into the programming language in which the system will be written. In this department we use Ada, which is closely related to PDL/Ada. The software is then compiled.

TESTING THE SOFTWARE

The testing phase verifies that each functional unit works properly and that the system meets all requirements. The tests are either functional or system. For both types of testing, the tester writes test plans describing what is to be tested, test data values, and pass/fail criteria. In this department, the developer who implemented the unit does the functional testing. The developer tests each functional unit separately to make sure it performs as stated in its design.

When the developer has tested all functional units, he or she combines them into a system. At this point, a separate department, Independent Verification and Validation, performs the system test. The members of this department check the combined program against each requirement in the specification. When they certify that the program meets all requirements, we arrange a meeting to present the software to the customer.

Conclusion (Optional)

A conclusion is optional. If you choose to include one, you might discuss a number of topics, depending on the audience's needs, including the advantages and disadvantages of the process.

■ WORKSHEET FOR DESCRIPTION

❏ *Name the audience for this description.*

❏ *Estimate the level of their knowledge about the concepts on which this description is based and about the topic itself.*

❏ *Name your goal for your readers.*
   Should readers know the parts or steps in detail or in broad outline? Should they focus on the components of each step or part, or on the effect or significance of each step or part?
   Should they focus just on the machine or process, or grasp the broader context of the topic (such as who uses it, where and how it is regulated, who makes it, and its applications and advantages)?

❏ *Select an approach.*
   What will you do first in each paragraph?
   In what sequence will you present the explanatory detail?

❏ *Plan a visual aid.*

What is your goal with the visual aid? to provide a realistic introduction? to give an overview? to be the focus of the text? to supplement the text?
Will you have one visual aid for each step or part, or will you use
just one visual and refer to it often?

❏ *Choose the type of visual aid. Use a visual that will help your reader
grasp the topic.*

❏ *Construct a rough visual now. Finish it later.*

❏ *Decide on the visual aid's size (not too large or too small) and placement (for example, after the introduction).*

❏ *Devise a style sheet. Decide how you will handle heads, margins,
paragraphing, and visual aid captions.*

❏ *To write a description of mechanisms*
Name each part.
Name each subpart.
Define each part and subpart.
List details of size, weight, method of attachment, and so forth.
Tell its function.

❏ *To write a description of processes*
Name each step.
Name each substep.
Tell its end goal.
List details of quality and quantity of the action.
Tell significance of action.

■ WORKSHEET FOR EVALUATING A DESCRIPTION

1. For each part of the report—introduction, body, visual aid—
   answer the following questions:
   ■ Is it appropriate to the goal for the audience?
   ■ Is it consistent with all the other parts and its own subparts?
   ■ Is it clear to the audience and faithful to the reality?
2. Do the visual aid and the text helpfully, actively interact with
   each other?
3. Does the report build a mental model that an audience can use
   for future action?

4. Does the writer convince you that he or she is believable? (Consider two dimensions: statement of background and method of presentation.)
5. Check these items for a process description

	Yes	No
Introduction		
■ Purpose statement is present and clear.	___	___
■ Cause of your writing is present and clear.	___	___
■ Preview of the paper is present.	___	___
■ Topic is named and defined.	___	___
■ Each item in list is an action (not a thing).	___	___
Body	**Yes**	**No**
■ Each new section has effective use of keyword.	___	___
■ Either first or second sentence defines each step (check "no" if any of the steps are not defined).	___	___
■ Any necessary background is given.	___	___
■ End result or overall goal of each step is explained.	___	___
■ Each step has enough details (specific actions, substeps, quantity and quality of actions).	___ ___	___ ___
Format	**Yes**	**No**
■ Side heads have correct format.	___	___
■ Visual aid is clearly drawn.	___	___
■ Visual aid has clear, correct caption at the bottom.	___	___
■ Visual aid has callouts.	___	___
■ Callouts are key words in text.	___	___
Style	**Yes**	**No**
■ Sentences talk about people in the third person ("The welder holds the torch," not "Hold the torch").	___	___
■ All technical and jargon terms are defined.	___	___
■ No spelling mistakes.	___	___
■ No apostrophe mistakes.	___	___
■ No comma splices and fragments.	___	___

6. Check these items for a mechanism description

	Yes	No
Introduction		
■ Purpose statement is present and clear.	___	___
■ Cause of your writing is present and clear.	___	___
■ Preview of the paper is present.	___	___
■ Topic is named and defined.	___	___
■ Each item in list is an action (not a thing).	___	___

Body	Yes	No
■ Each new section has effective use of keyword.	——	——
■ Either first or second sentence defines each step (check "no" if any of the steps are not defined).	——	——
■ Any necessary background is given.	——	——
■ End result or overall goal of each step is explained.	——	——
■ Each step has enough details (specific actions, substeps, quantity and quality of actions).	——	——
Format	Yes	No
■ Side heads have correct format.	——	——
■ Visual aid is clearly drawn.	——	——
■ Visual aid has clear, correct caption at the bottom.	——	——
■ Visual aid has callouts.	——	——
■ Callouts are key words in text.	——	——
Style	Yes	No
■ Sentences talk about people in the third person ("The welder holds the torch," not "Hold the torch").	——	——
■ All technical and jargon terms are defined.	——	——
■ No spelling mistakes.	——	——
■ No apostrophe mistakes.	——	——
■ No comma splices and fragments.	——	——

EXAMPLES

Examples 10.1 to 10.4 describe a mechanism and three processes. The mechanism description and the first process description appear as if they were parts of longer documents. The other process descriptions are memos. The form (memo or part of a longer document) depends solely on the situation.

EXAMPLE 10.1
Description of a Mechanism

SKINFOLD CALIPER

The following information explains the skinfold caliper and its individual parts. The skinfold caliper (see Figure 1) is an instrument used to measure a double layer of skin and subcutaneous fat (fat below the skin) at a specific body site. The measurement that results is an indirect estimate of body fatness or calorie stores. The instrument is approximately 10 inches long, is made of stainless steel, and is easily held in one hand. The skinfold caliper consists of the following parts: caliper jaws, press and handle, and gauge.

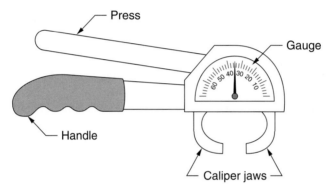

FIGURE 1
Skinfold Caliper

CALIPER JAWS

The caliper jaws consist of two curved prongs. Each prong is approximately ¼ inch long. The prongs project out from the half-moon-shaped gauge housing. They are placed over the skinfold when the measurement is taken. They clasp the portion of the skinfold to be measured.

PRESS AND HANDLE

The press is the lever that controls the caliper jaws. Engaging the press opens the caliper jaws so they can slip over the skinfold. Releasing the press closes the jaws on the skinfold, allowing the actual measurement. The press is 4.5 inches long and .5 inch thick. It is manipulated by the thumb while the fingers grip the caliper handle. The caliper handle is 6 inches long and .5 inch thick. The outside edge of the handle has three indentations, which make the caliper easier to grip.

EXAMPLE 10.1
(continued)

GAUGE

The gauge records the skinfold measurement. It is white, half-moon shaped, with 65 evenly spaced black markings and a pointer. Each marking represents 1 centimeter. The pointer projects from the middle of the straight edge of the half-moon-shaped gauge to the black markings. When the jaws tighten, the pointer swings to the marking that is the skinfold thickness.

EXAMPLE 10.2
Description of a Process

DIAGNOSING NECK PAIN

Determining the source of the pain is essential to recommend the right method of treatment and rehabilitation. Therefore a comprehensive examination is required to determine the cause of neck pain.

Your orthopaedist will take a complete history of the difficulties you are having with your neck. He or she may ask you about other illnesses, any injury that occurred to your neck and any complaints you have associated with neck pain. Previous treatment for your neck condition will also be noted.

Next, your orthopaedist will perform a physical examination. This examination may include evaluation of neck motion, neck tenderness, and the function of the nerves and muscles in your arms and legs.

X-ray studies often will be done to allow your orthopaedist to look closely at the bones in your neck. These simple diagnostic techniques often help orthopaedists to determine the cause of neck pain and to prescribe effective treatment.

Source: "Diagnosing Neck Pain." *Neck Pain.* Park Ridge, IL: American Academy of Orthopaedic Surgeons, 1989.

EXAMPLE 10.3
Description of a Process

PROCESS DESCRIPTION: IDENTIFICATION OF UNKNOWN CHEMICALS

Date: March 28, 2004
To: Auguste Dupin
From: Kris-Jilk, Lab Research Department
Subject: Identification of Unknown Chemicals

This memo is to familiarize you with one of the most common procedures done in the research laboratory at ACME Pharmaceuticals, Inc. Mr. Dupin, have you ever come across a container in your household cleaning cupboard and, because the label had fallen off, had absolutely no idea of what it was? Well, even though we in the lab do not solicit door to door for work, this whole concept of taking an unknown compound and identifying it is one of the most important aspects of our research lab. We deal almost exclusively with medicinal agents, but are often called on by the local police department to identify their seized unknown chemicals and by the hospital to work on unidentifiable agents found in blood and tissue samples. Figure 1 lists the six steps we use to identify an unknown chemical.

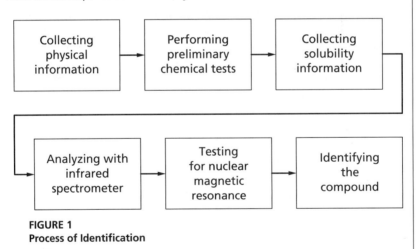

FIGURE 1
Process of Identification

COLLECTING PHYSICAL INFORMATION

Collecting physical information about an unknown compound gives general information pertaining to the overall chemical. Taking note of the physical state, color, smell, melting point, and boiling point of the compound gives you important basic information that deals with the most fundamental chemical properties of whatever it is you are working with.

EXAMPLE 10.3
(continued)

PERFORMING PRELIMINARY CHEMICAL TESTS

Running universal preliminary chemical tests on the unknown identifies what major compound classification it falls under. All organic compounds can be classified into approximately 15 different categories, and running some very basic tests helps us to place the unknown into its general category. For example, if the ignition test produces black, sooty smoke, then it is evident that the general classification of the compound is an aromatic compound.

COLLECTING SOLUBILITY INFORMATION

Collecting information on the solubility of unknown compounds identifies the properties they exhibit when they are introduced to other compounds. By observing how an unknown compound reacts with a variety of other compounds, it is possible to gain insight into some of the compound's specific chemical structure. If, for example, the unknown is soluble in water, then it is clear that it is polar.

ANALYZING WITH INFRARED SPECTROMETER

Analysis of the infrared spectrometer test shows what functional groups are attached to the carbon "backbone" of the compound. By knowing the kinds of chemicals attached to the parent chemical, it is possible to begin sketching a picture of what the unknown is. These attached chemicals are mainly responsible for how the unknown reacted in the solubility tests.

TESTING NUCLEAR MAGNETIC RESONANCE

Running the nuclear magnetic resonance test on an unknown compound gives the essential information about the parent carbon structure (this is the compound that is at the base of the molecule and is often called the *parent compound*). This test produces evidence relating to the number of carbons present, how they are bonded to one another, and how they interact with the attached hydrogens. This information is especially important because it shows what is at the core of what may be a very big structure.

IDENTIFYING THE COMPOUND

Identification of the unknown is now possible. All the information from the tests run by the researcher can be compiled, and in most cases, the unknown compound can be identified. One of the exceptions to this process is that, even with all this data, more extensive tests need to be completed before the compound is identifiable. The other exception is that the compound is common and could be identified after doing the preliminary chemical tests.

The process by which unknown compounds are identified begins by collecting very general information and continues until the information that is collected is very specific. These tests are run daily and are a vital function of the work done in the lab.

EXAMPLE 10.4
Description of a Process

Date: March 7, 2004
To: Dan Riordan
From: Steve Prickett
Subject: Processes involved in producing hydraulic valves

The purpose of this memo is to inform you of the process of producing hydraulic valves. I will explain six steps in the production phase that I oversee every day. They include: cutoff phase, milling phase, drilling and threading phase, deburring phase, assembly phase, and testing phase.

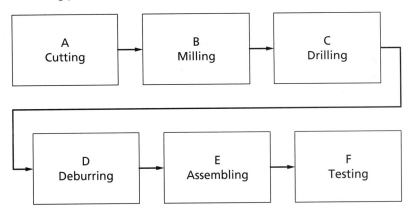

A – Cutting
B – Milling
C – Drilling
D – Deburring
E – Assembling
F – Testing

FIGURE 1
Production Process for Hydraulic Valves

CUTTING PHASE

Cutting phase (A) is the process of cutting the aluminum stock to length. The aluminum stock comes to the cutoff saw in 10-foot lengths, and the saw cuts off 6-inch lengths. The stock is then transferred to (B).

MILLING PHASE

Milling phase (B) is the process of shaving off excess aluminum from the stock. The stock comes to the milling machine from the cutoff saw in exact lengths. The milling machine shaves the stock down to exact height and width specifications of 5 inches. The stock is then transferred to (C).

EXAMPLE 10.4
(continued)

DRILLING PHASE

Drilling phase (C) is the process of boring holes into the aluminum stock in specified positions. The stock comes from the milling machine and is ready to be drilled. Holes are bored into the stock on all 4 sides connecting to each other, creating round tunnels inside the stock. These round tunnels will serve as passageways for oil to flow through the valve. Machine (C) now performs a tool change.

Threading phase (C) is the process of putting threads into the holes drilled into the block. The threads are installed so that valve inlets and outlets can be screwed in. The stock is then transferred to (D).

DEBURRING PHASE

Deburring phase (D) is the process of grinding and chiseling off any metal burrs attached to the block. The stock comes from the drilling and threading machine with little metal shavings sticking out all over. Machine (D) turns the block around and grinds and chisels all sides removing any possible burrs. The burrs must be removed, as they are dangerous and may be dislodged once the valve is in operation, thus damaging the hydraulic system. Machine (D) now performs a tool change.

Polishing phase (D) is the process of wiping the surface of the stock clean. The tunnels in the block are wiped down and blown out with forced air. The process is done to smooth and clean the surface of the tunnels of any metal dust. The stock is then transferred to (E).

ASSEMBLY PHASE

Assembly phase is the process of installing valve inlet and outlet stems. The stock comes from the polishing machine clean and ready for assembly. Inlet and outlet stems are screwed into the block; the stems have threads on both ends so that hoses can be connected to them to supply the valve with oil. The stock is then transferred to (F).

TESTING PHASE

Testing phase (F) is the process of ensuring the valves have no defects. The valves come from the assembly station ready to be tested. The valves are put on a testing machine that pressurizes the valve to see if there are any leaks or cracks that will emerge once the valve is in operation.

■ EXERCISES

1. In class, develop a brief mechanism description by brainstorming. Hand in all your work to your instructor. Your instructor may ask you to perform this activity in groups of three or four.

    ■ Brainstorm the names of parts and subparts.

    ■ Choose the most significant parts.

    ■ Arrange the parts into a logical pattern.

    ■ Name and define each part in the first sentence.

    ■ Describe each part in a paragraph.

    ■ Create a visual aid of your mechanism, complete with appropriate callouts (use keywords from the text as callouts).

2. In class, develop a mechanism description through a visual aid. Hand in all your work to your instructor. Your instructor may ask you to perform this activity in groups of three or four.

    ■ Draw a visual aid of your mechanism. Use callouts to point out key parts.

    ■ Name each part that the audience needs to understand.

    ■ Select a logical pattern for discussing the parts.

    ■ Name and define each part in a sentence.

    ■ Describe each part in a paragraph; be sure to discuss each part named in the callouts.

3. In class, develop a process description through brainstorming. Assume that you either need to demonstrate that a problem exists or need to provide cause-effect theoretical background. Hand in all your work to your instructor. Your instructor may ask you to perform this activity in groups of three or four.

    ■ Brainstorm the names of as many steps and substeps as you can.

    ■ Arrange the steps into chronological or cause-effect order.

    ■ Define the end goal of each step in one sentence.

4. In class, develop a brief process description through visual aids. Assume that your audience needs a basic understanding of the process in order to discuss it at a meeting. Hand in all your work to your instructor. Your instructor may ask you to perform this activity in groups of three or four.

■ Draw a flow chart of the process, or else a diagram of the parts interacting, as in the following diagram.

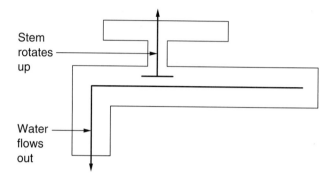

Stem
rotates
up

Water
flows
out

■ Write a brief paragraph for each step.

5. Either singly or in groups of two to four, analyze these paragraphs for consistency in presentation. Rewrite the paragraphs to eliminate passive voice. What identity does the author of this text appear to express? Do you like that? Rewrite the paragraphs to achieve a different identity.

Date: March 28, 2004
To: Dan Riordan
From: Tadd Hohlfelder
Subject: To give an overview of the Norclad case-out process

As the new supervisor it is important for you to be familiar with the Norclad case-out process. I compiled this information while reviewing the department last week.

The purpose of the process is to construct complete window units from separate clad awnings, casement, and picture assemblies. After construction, they are tagged and moved to shipping.

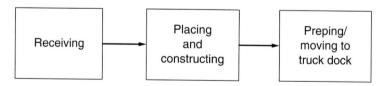

When subassemblies are received in case-out they must be checked in to be sure all are accounted for. Each of the four tables has a stack of orders which need to be built. There is not one correct method for checking in assemblies. For example, some workers check their subassemblies separately as they build them. Others choose to check them all in at the beginning of the shift.

Once they are checked in, the subassemblies for a particular order are placed on a table. All components of the unit are also placed on the table. The components are listed on the order sheet. One order might call for a 6¾-inch extension with screens and storm panes. Another may just have the standard 4⁹⁄₁₆-inch extension without other options. After correct placement, the unit can be built. We use several types and sizes of air-powered nail guns to construct our units.

After construction, the unit must be prepped and sent to shipping. We are currently using plastic strips to protect the units while shipping. The strips are placed on the facing edges of the units. Cardboard pieces are then stapled on the corners of the unit. On the work order for each unit there are three tags attached: green, white, and red. The green tag must be attached to the finished unit to identify it for shipping. The remaining tags are left on the order, which is placed in a bin on your desk upon completion. The units are loaded on racks and moved to the truck dock using either pallet jacks or fork trucks.

6. Compare these two versions of the same paragraph. Which version gives you more confidence in the writer? In groups of three or four, discuss the stylistic features that cause confidence.

A. To affix the bacteria means to "glue" them to the slide so that they are permanently mounted. Basically there are three steps. First, the lab assistant lights the Bunsen burner and grasps the slide on each end. Second, the assistant dips the loop of the sterile poker into the culture and smears the liquid onto the center of the slide. Third, the assistant passes the slide (wet side up) several times through the flame.

B. Affix the bacteria to the slide. First, the lab assistant places a sterile poker in the culture of bacteria. Then he or she places the loop on the center of the clean glass slide and smears it around in a tiny circle. The lab assistant then heat fixes the slide with the bacteria on it by passing it through the flames of the Bunsen burner two or three times.

7. Analyze the strategy of the "help" example in these two paragraphs. Do you like the way it is introduced in each section? Do you like using the same example throughout the description? Decide what kind of identity this author achieves by presenting the example as she does. Does she make you feel confident? Rewrite the paragraph so that you create a different identity for the author.

OBTAINING BACKGROUND INFORMATION

Obtaining background information means to gather information from the customers in order to get a feeling of their overall knowledge of computer software. This information is usually gathered through interviews or questionnaires. The information we get is used to design a user interface that will be easy for the customer to learn.

We can use the simple example of getting help when trying to understand that a certain function does. For example, if the customer is familiar with making the help text appear on the screen by typing "help," we design ours to work in a similar fashion.

DEFINING THE SEMANTICS

Defining the semantics of the user interface means to come up with a clear view of all the tasks the customer must do to make the system perform. When performing these tasks, two customers will, more than likely, take two different paths through the interface to obtain the same outcome. We must discuss each of these paths for each task, then create and describe them within our system.

If you refer back to the help text example, you may understand this better. If two users are looking for help on a particular topic, one may go to a help "index" to find it, and the other straight to the topic by typing in "help <subject>." Both customers will get the same result, but each did it in his or her own way.

---

8. In class (or in small groups if your instructor prefers), compare a paragraph from the memo on the waterfall design process (p. 240) with a paragraph from the ColorScript Laser process (pp. 232–233). How are the paragraphs organized? What is the function of the first sentence of each? Which paragraph seems to more effectively convey its message to the audience? Be prepared to briefly present your findings to the class.

---

9. Redo this paragraph so that your supervisor can take it to a committee that needs to know what happens in this step.

HANDLE

The handle is made from kiln dried walnut rough cut lumber 1" × 8" × 11'. Lumber is cropped to 30" lengths. Cut to 30" lengths. Jointed to get a true edge. Ripped to 1¼" widths. 1¾" sections are cropped off starting ¼" from one end leaving ¹⁄₁₆" between marks. 15 sections are turned down to ¾" diameter one end and ⅝" diameter other end. Diameter is 100% inspected and lengths are marked off. Sections are cut to 1¾" lengths. ⁵⁄₁₆" diameter hole is drilled 1¼" deep. Drill depth is inspected randomly. All surfaces are sanded and 100% inspected.

◼ WRITING ASSIGNMENTS

1. Assume that you must describe a problem with a process at your workplace. Describe the process in detail, and then explain the problem and offer a solution. Use a memo format with heads and a visual aid. As you work, you can use the worksheet in this chapter. Use Exercise 4 or 5 (above) to start your work.

---

2. Write a brief description of the steps you took to solve a problem. Assume that your audience is someone who must be assured that your solution is based on credible actions, but who does not know the terms and concepts you must use. For instance, you could explain the process you used to test an object or the process you used to select a vendor for a product your company must purchase.

---

3. Write an article for a company newsletter, describing a common process on the job. Use a visual aid. Sample topics might include the route a check follows through a bank, the billing procedure for accounts receivable, the company grievance procedure, the route a job takes through a printing plant, or the method for laminating sheets of materials together to form a package. Fill out the worksheet in this chapter. Use Exercise 4 or 5 (above) to start your work. Your article should answer the question "Have you ever wondered how we . . . ?"

---

4. Write several paragraphs to convince an audience to purchase a mechanism or to implement a process. The mechanism might be a machine, and the procedure might be a system, such as hiring new personnel. Describe the advantages that this mechanism or process offers over the mechanism or process currently in use. Fill out the worksheet in this chapter. Use a visual aid. Use Exercise 2 or 3 (above) to start your work. Choose a mechanism or process you know well, or else choose from this list (for X, substitute an actual name).

the lens system of brand X camera

the action of brand X bike gear shift

the X theory of product design

the X theory of handling employee grievances

the X retort process

how brand X air conditioner cools air

how brand X solar furnace heats a room

---

5. Expand into a several-page paper one of the brief descriptions you wrote in Exercises 1–4. Your audience is a manager who needs general background. (Alternate: your audience is a sixth-grade class.) Bring a draft of the paper to class. In groups of two to three, evaluate the draft in terms of these concerns:
   a. Does the introduction present the purpose of the mechanism process and provide a basis for your credibility?
   b. Does the introduction present a preview of the paper?
   c. Does each new section start with an effective keyword?
   d. Are the details sufficient to explain the part or step to the audience?

    e.   Is the visual aid correctly sized, clear, and clearly referred to?

    f.   Do callouts in the visual aid duplicate key terms in the text?

    g.   Is the style at a high enough quality level?

6.   Write a learning report for the writing assignment you just completed. See Chapter 5, Writing Assignment 7, page 123, for details of the assignment.

■ WEB EXERCISES

1.   Describe a Web browser home page (Netscape, Internet Explorer, one of the many search engines) as if it were a mechanism. Name and explain the function of each part of the page.

2.   Describe the process of finding some type of information (for instance, air fares or technical data relevant to your major or job focus). Name and explain the sequence of steps that a person must follow in order to find results efficiently. (Note continuation of this exercise in Chapter 11, Web Exercise 2.)

■ WORKS CITED

How Things Work in Your Home. NY: Holt, 1987.

Jordan, Michael P. *Fundamentals of Technical Description.* Malabar, FL: Robert E. Krieger, 1984.

"QMS ColorScript Laser 1000." *Macworld* July 1994: 75.

11 Sets of Instructions

Chapter 11
IN A NUTSHELL

The goal of a set of instructions is to enable readers to take charge of the situation and accomplish whatever it is that they need to do.

Introduction

- Tell the end goal of the instructions (or do that in the title).
- Define any terms they might not know; if necessary, explain the level of knowledge you expect.
- List tools they must have or conditions to be aware of.

Body Steps

- Explain one action at a time.
- Tell the readers what they need to know to do the step, including warnings, special conditions, and any "good enough" criteria that allow them to judge whether they have done the step correctly.

Format

- Use clear heads.
- Number each step.
- Provide visuals that are big enough, clear enough, and near enough (usually directly under or next to) the appropriate text.
- Use lots of white space that clearly indicates the main and the subordinate sections.
- Write the goal at the "top" of the section—so they can skip the rest if they already know how to do that.

Tone

- Be definite. Make each order explicit. If the monitor "must be placed on top of the CPU," don't say "should."
- Discover what readers feel is arbitrary by asking them in a field test.

Sets of instructions appear everywhere. Magazines and books explain how to canoe, how to prepare income taxes, and how to take effective photographs; consumer manuals explain how to assemble stereo systems, how to program VCRs, and how to make purchased items work. On the job you will write instructions for performing many processes and running machines. This chapter explains how to plan and write a useful set of instructions.

PLANNING THE SET OF INSTRUCTIONS

To plan your instructions, determine your goal, consider your audience, analyze the sequence, choose visual aids, and follow the usual form. In the following discussion, the subject is exposing Dylux paper in order to make a "proof" or "review copy" of a color print that many people will review for accuracy and effectiveness.

Determine Your Goal

Instructions enable readers to complete a project or to learn a process. *To complete a project* means to arrive at a definite end result: the reader can complete a form or assemble a toy or make a garage door open and close on command. *To learn a process* means to become proficient enough to perform the process without the set of instructions. The reader can paddle a canoe, log on to the computer, or adjust the camera. In effect, every set of instructions should become obsolete as the reader either finishes the project or learns to perform the process without the set of instructions.

Consider the Audience

When you analyze your audience, estimate their knowledge level and any physical or emotional constraints they might have.

Estimate the Audience's Knowledge Level.   The audience will be either absolute beginners who know nothing about the process or intermediates who understand the process but need a memory jog before they can function effectively.

The reader's knowledge level determines how much information you need to include. Think, for instance, about telling beginners to "turn on" a computer. They will not be able to do this because they will not know that they should look in the back for the power switch (the location on most computers). Thus you will also have to tell them where to find the switch. For an intermediate, however, all you have to say is "turn it on."

Identify Constraints.   Emotional and physical constraints may interfere with the audience's attempts to follow instructions. Many people have a good deal of anxiety about doing something for the first time. They worry that they will make mistakes and that those mistakes will cost them their labor. If they tighten the wrench too hard, will the bolt snap off? If they hit the wrong key, will they lose the entire contents of their disk? To offset this anxiety, include tips about what should take place at each step and about what to do if something else happens. Step 5 in the example "Exposing a single color (or the first color in a series)," p. 269, explains what it means when the overhead light turns off—nothing is wrong; the process is finished.

The physical constraints are usually the materials needed to perform the process, but they might also be special environmental considerations. A Phillips screw cannot be tightened with a regular screwdriver; a 3-pound hammer cannot be swung in a restricted space; in a darkroom, only a red light can shine. Physical constraints also include safety concerns. If touching a certain electrical connection can injure the reader, make that very clear. Step 1 in the example on page 269 tells readers that it doesn't make any difference how they lay the Dylux into the frame—either way achieves the same result.

Examples for Different Audiences.   To see how the audience affects the set of instructions, compare the brief version below with "Exposing a Single Color" (p. 269). The section on page 269 explains the steps in detail, assuming that the beginner audience needs detailed "hand-holding" assistance. The brief example below, designed for an "intermediate" audience, simply lists the sequence of steps to jog the reader's memory,

---

INSTRUCTIONS FOR AN INTERMEDIATE

1. Lay the Dylux and black film in the frame.
2. Select the channel and key it in. Enter.
3. Close and latch. Open after the light goes out.

Analyze the Sequence

The sequence is the chronological order of the steps involved. To analyze the sequence, determine the end goal, analyze the tasks, name and explain the tasks, and analyze any special conditions. (See the sample flow chart of an analysis in Figure 11.1.)

Determine the End Goal.   The end goal is whatever you want the reader to achieve, the "place" at which the user will arrive. This goal affects the number of steps in your sequence because different end goals will require you to provide different sets of instructions, with different sections. In the preceding example, the end goal is "The user will finish exposing a single color," and the document ends at that point. Other end goals, however, are possible. For instance, if the goal were "The user will finish exposing four colors," the sequence would obviously include more steps and sections.

Analyze the Tasks. You have two goals here: determine the sequence and name the steps. To determine the sequence, you either go backward from the end goal or perform the sequence yourself. If the end goal is to remove the exposed film, the question to ask is "What step must the user perform before removing the exposed film?" The answer is "Close and latch the frame." If you continue to go backward, the next question is "What does the user do before latching the frame?" As you answer that question, another will be suggested, and then another—until you are back at the beginning, walking into the room with the film. You can also do the process yourself; as you do it, record every act you take. Then perform the task a second time, following your written notes exactly. You will quickly find whether or not you have included all the steps.

FIGURE 11.1
Flow Chart of an Analysis

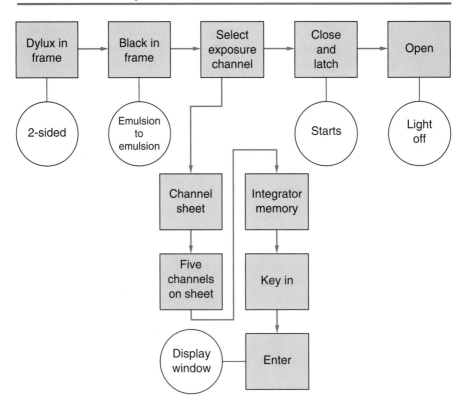

Name and Explain the Tasks. Having decided on the sequence, you name each task and explain any subtask or special information that accompanies it. The Dylux example has five subtasks under the task "Select the exposure channel," and many of the steps include explanations for the audience. For instance, step 3d (p. 269) tells the user that channel 1 is for the black exposure.

Analyze Conditions. You must also analyze any special conditions that the user must know about. For instance, step 2 explains that the films must be emulsion to emulsion. Safety considerations are very important, and safety warnings are an essential part of many instructions. *If it will hurt them or the machine, tell the audience.* Warn the user not to touch a hot bulb and to turn off the machine before working on it.

Example of Process Analysis. An easy way to conduct your analysis is to make a flow chart of the process. Put the steps in boxes and any notes in circles (see Figure 11.1).

Choose Visual Aids

Visual aids either clarify or replace the prose explanation. Figure 2 in the Dylux example *replaces* text; to describe the position of the Memory button in words would take far more than the seven words used to convey the instruction.

The figure below *clarifies* the text—and reassures the readers that their actions are correct—by showing what the screen will look like as the actions occur on a computer.

> At the TO: prompt type their NAME, not their real name but their E-mail user name, and then press enter. The SUBJ: prompt will appear. (See Figure 1.—note that you do not have to type in all capital letters, though you may.) On our system, the user name is generally the last name and the first one or two letters of the first name.

```
mail>SEND
TO: SMITHJ
SUBJ: Learning E-mail
Enter your message below
```

FIGURE 1
On-Campus E-Mail Address

Here are a few guidelines for choosing visual aids:

- Use a visual aid to orient the reader. For instance, present a drawing of a keyboard with the return key highlighted.
- Use a visual aid to show the effect of an action. For instance, show what a screen looks like *after* the user enters a command.
- Decide whether you need one or two visual aids for the entire process or one visual aid per step. Use one per step if each step is complicated. Choose a clear drawing or photograph. (To determine which one to use, see Chapter 8.)
- Place the visual aid as close as possible to the relevant discussion, usually either below the text or to the left.
- Make each visual aid large enough. Do not skimp on size.
- Clearly identify each visual aid. Beneath each one, put a caption (e.g., *Figure 1. E-mail Address* or *Fig. 1. E-mail Address*).
- Refer to each visual aid at the appropriate place in the text.
- Use *callouts*—letters or words to indicate key parts. Draw a line or arrow from each callout to the part.

Follow the Usual Form for Instructions

The usual form for a set of instructions is an introduction followed by a step-by-step body. The introduction states the purpose of the set of instructions, and the steps present all the actions in chronological order. The models at the end of this chapter illustrate these guidelines. Make a style sheet of all your decisions.

For steps and visual aids, use these guidelines:

- Place a highlighted (underlined or boldfaced) head at the beginning of each section.
- Number each step.
- Start the second and following lines of each step under the first letter of the first word in the first line.
- Use margins to indicate "relative weight"; show substeps by indenting to the right in outline style.
- Decide where you will place the visual aids. Usually place them to the left or below the text.
- Use white space above and below each step. Do not cramp the text.

For columns, the decisions are more complex. Basically you can choose one or two columns, but their arrangement can vary, and each will have different effects on the reader. Figure 11.2 presents several basic layouts

FIGURE 11.2
Different Column Arrangements for Instructions

you can choose. You can place visual aids below or to the right or left of the text. To the left and below are very common places. Generally you place to the left (text or visuals) whatever you want to emphasize.

WRITING THE SET OF INSTRUCTIONS

A clear set of instructions has an introduction and a body. After you have drafted them, you will be more confident that your instructions are clear if you field-test them.

Write an Effective Introduction

Although short introductions are the norm, you may want to include many different bits of information, depending on your analysis of the audience's knowledge level and of the demands of the process. You should always

  ▨ State the objective of the instructions for the reader.

Depending on the audience, you may also

  ▨ Define the process.
  ▨ Define important terms.
  ▨ List any necessary tools, materials, or conditions.
  ▨ Explain who needs to use the process.
  ▨ Explain where and/or when to perform the process.
  ▨ List assumptions you make about the audience's knowledge.

A SAMPLE INTRODUCTION TO A SET OF INSTRUCTIONS

In the following introduction, note that the writer states the objective ("These instructions enable you to make a single- or multicolored Dylux."), defines the topic, lists knowledge assumptions, and lists materials.

MAKING A DYLUX PROOF

INTRODUCTION

These instructions enable you to make a single- or multicolored Dylux. A Dylux proof is a single-color proof which uses different shades of blue to represent each of the process colors. A Dylux is used to check for copy content, layout, and position.	End goal Background
These instructions assume you know how to operate the integrator. Before you start, you need regular Scotch tape and films to proof.	Knowledge assumption Materials list

Write an Effective Body

The body consists of numbered steps arranged in chronological order. Construct the steps carefully, place the information in the correct order, use imperative verbs, and do not omit articles (*a, an,* and *the*) or prepositions.

Construct Steps Carefully.   To make each step clear, follow these guidelines:

- Number each step.
- State only one action per number (although the effect of the action is often included in the step).
- Explain unusual effects.
- Give important rationales.
- Refer to visual aids.
- Make suggestions for avoiding or correcting mistakes.
- Place safety cautions before the instructions.

Review the Examples on pages 276–282 to see how the writers incorporated these guidelines. An example of how to write the body follows.

SAMPLE BODY

Here is the body of the set of instructions that follows the introduction on page 266.

PREPARATION   Head for sequence

1. Turn on the exposure frame. (See Figure 1.)

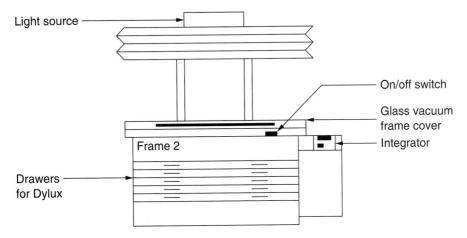

FIGURE 1
Exposure Frame

TIP: TWO STYLE TIPS FOR INSTRUCTIONS

1. Use imperative verbs.

   An imperative verb gives an order. Imperative verbs make clear that the step must be done. Notice below that "should" introduces a note of uncertainty about whether the act must be performed.

   Say

   > Turn on the exposure frame.

   Rather than

   > You should turn on the exposure frame.

2. Retain the short words.

   Use *a, an, the,* in all the usual places. Eliminating these "short words" often makes the instructions harder to grasp because it blurs the distinction between verbs, nouns, and adjectives.

   No short words

   > Using register marks on Dylux film, register film with image on Dylux.

   Short words added

   > Using the register marks on the Dylux film, register the film with the image on the Dylux.

2. Lay your films on the work counter (emulsion down; emulsion side is the dull side) in the order in which you will proof them (first film to be exposed on top, and the last film to be exposed on the bottom—usually black, yellow, magenta, cyan).

Instruction
Explanatory comment

Special condition

3. Clean both sides of the glass on the vacuum frame using the glass cleaner and cheesecloth (located on a shelf to the left of frame 2).

4. Raise the glass cover on the vacuum frame.

Action

5. Get one sheet of Dylux, large enough to hold the entire image. The Dylux paper can be found in the drawers under frame 2.

Action

EXPOSING A SINGLE COLOR (OR THE FIRST COLOR IN A SERIES)

1. Lay the Dylux in the vacuum frame. The Dylux paper is two-sided, so it does not matter which side is up.

2. Place the film to be exposed on top of the Dylux. Black is usually the first color to be exposed. Film must be emulsion down, so Dylux and film are emulsion to emulsion.

3. Select the exposure channel for the first exposure.

   a. Refer to the sheet listing the channels and what material each is set to expose. This sheet is posted above the integrator.

Note that use of substeps keeps the number of main steps small

   b. Locate the proper channel on the sheet. There should be five channels on the Dylux: one channel for each of the four process colors (black, yellow, magenta, cyan) and one for clearing.

   c. Push the **Memory** button on the integrator. (See Figure 2.)

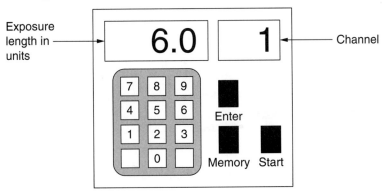

FIGURE 2
Integrator

    d. Key in the appropriate channel number on the number pad. (For example, channel 1 is for the black Dylux exposure.)

    e. Press the **Enter** button on the integrator. After you press **Enter,** the exposure time in units will appear in the top left display window.

4. Close and latch the vacuum frame.
   Note: The exposure starts when the frame is latched.

5. When the exposure is complete (when the overhead light goes out), open the vacuum frame and remove the film.
   Note: After this exposure there will be an image on   Special note
   the Dylux paper.

If You Have a Single-Color Proof

Remove the Dylux from the vacuum frame and skip to the "Clearing a Dylux" section.

Head for special condition

If You Have a Multicolor Proof

Leave the Dylux in the frame and continue with the next section, "Exposing Additional Colors."

Head for special condition

EXPOSING ADDITIONAL COLORS

The first exposure will image register marks onto the Dylux. From this point on, each film must be lined up (registered) to the register marks on the Dylux.

Introduction to subsection

1. Place the next negative film (probably yellow) over the Dylux paper. Using the register marks on the Dylux and the film, register the film with the image on the Dylux.

2. Tape the Dylux and film together.

3. Select the proper exposure channel for the color you are exposing.

4. Close and latch the vacuum frame.

5. When the exposure is complete, open the vacuum frame and remove the film, leaving the Dylux in the frame.

Repeat steps 1–5 until all colors have been exposed.

One sentence instruction avoids lengthy repetition

CLEARING A DYLUX

All main heads
emphasize action

Clearing is the final exposure. The clearing exposure is made without films. The Dylux is exposed to the light through a clearing filter, which moves into place when the clearing channel is selected.

1. After all colors have been exposed, remove the Dylux from the vacuum frame and close the vacuum frame.
2. Place the Dylux on top of the glass.
3. Select the channel for clearing a Dylux.
4. Push **Start** to clear the Dylux. (See Figure 2.)
5. Once the Dylux has been cleared, trim it according to the specifications on the job ticket.

FIELD-TESTING INSTRUCTIONS

A field test is a method of direct observation by which you can check the accuracy of your instructions. To perform a field test, ask someone who is unfamiliar with the process to follow your instructions while you watch. If you have written the instructions correctly, the reader should be able to perform the entire activity without asking any questions. When you field-test instructions, keep a record of all the places where the reader hesitates or asks you a question.

ARTICLE INSTRUCTIONS

A common method of presenting instructions is the article, which presents the steps in a more relaxed, informal manner. A sample article appears as Example 11.3. The article contains these components:

- A five-paragraph introduction that tells purpose (paragraph 1), background (paragraphs 2 and 3), and equipment needed (paragraph 4), and preview of body (paragraph 5).
- Headings that state action goals (placing Graphics).
- Explanations of actions (all the text paragraphs).
- Graphics that show what to do (all the boldface text).
- A troubleshooting paragraph.

These five components appear in all articles of this type. Writers simplify or lengthen each component based on their perception of their audience's needs.

TIP: INFORMATION ORDER IN A STEP

If your step contains more than just the action, arrange the items as action-effect. In the following example, the first sentence is the action, the second sentence is the effect.

Press **Enter** on the integrator.

After you press **Enter**, the exposure time in units will appear in the top left display window.

TIP: CAUTION

If your step contains a caution or warning, place it first, before you tell the audience the action to perform.

1. CAUTION: DO NOT LIGHT THE MATCH DIRECTLY OVER THE BUNSEN BURNER!

Light the match and slowly bring it toward the top of the Bunsen burner.

◼ WORKSHEET FOR PREPARING INSTRUCTIONS

❑ *Name the audience for these instructions.*
Estimate the amount of knowledge the audience has about the process. Are they beginners or intermediates?

❑ *What is the end goal for your readers?*

❑ *Analyze the process.*
  ◼ Construct a flow chart that moves backward from the end goal.
  ◼ Use as many boxes as you need.

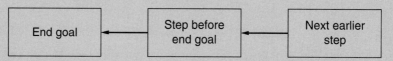

❑ *List all the conditions that must be true for the end goal to occur. (For instance, what must be true for a document to open in a word processing program? The machine is turned on, the disk is inserted, the main menu appears, and the directory appears.)*

❑ *List all the words and terms that the audience might not know.*

❑ *List all the materials that a person must have in order to carry out the process.*
  ◼ What will you tell the readers in the introduction? What will you assume about them? What do they need to know? What can they get from your instructions? How do they decide if they want to read your instructions? What will make them feel you are helpful and not just filling in lines for an assignment? How will you orient them to the situation?
  ◼ Where do the readers need a visual aid to "give them permission," or to orient them to the situation, or to show them something quickly that is easy to see but hard to describe in words?

❑ *Draw the visual aids that will help readers grasp this process. Use visuals that illustrate the action or show the effect of the action.*

❑ *How will you arrange this material on the page so that it is easy for readers to read quickly, but also to keep their place or find it again as they read?*

❑ *Construct a style sheet. Choose your head system, margins, columns, method of treating individual steps, and style for writing captions.*

❑ *Convert the topic of each box in the flow chart into an imperative instruction. Add cautions, suggestions, and substeps. Decide whether a sequence of steps should be one step with several substeps or should be treated as individual steps.*

❑ *How will you tell them each step? How—and where—will you tell them results of a step? How—and where—will you tell them background or variations in a step?*

❑ *Why should you write them a set of instructions in the first place? Why not write them a short report (IMRD) or an article? A report tells the results of a project, an article informally explains the concepts related to a project, and a set of instructions tells how to do the project.*

■ WORKSHEET FOR EVALUATING INSTRUCTIONS

❑ *Evaluate your work. Answer these questions:*
- Does the introduction tell what the instructions will enable the reader to do?
- Does the introduction contain all the necessary information on special conditions, materials, and tools?
- Is each step a single, clear action?
- Does any step need more information—result of the action, safety warning, definitions, action hints?
- Do the steps follow in a clear sequence?
- Are appropriate visual aids present? Does any step either need or not need a visual aid?
- Are the visual aids presented effectively (size, caption, position on page)?
- Does the page layout help the reader?

EXAMPLES

The three examples that follow exemplify varieties of sets of instructions. Notice that Examples 11.1 and 11.2 follow the conventional "numbered commands" format. Example 11.3, however, is an "instructional essay."

EXAMPLE 11.1
Instructions for a Beginner

INSTRUCTIONS: HOW TO USE THE MODEL 6050 pH METER

Introduction

This set of instructions provides a step-by-step process to accurately test the pH of any given solution using the pH Meter Model 6050. The pH meter is designed primarily to measure pH or mV (millivolts) in grounded or ungrounded solutions. This set of instructions assumes that the pH meter is plugged in and that the electrode is immersed in a two-molar solution of potassium chloride.

Materials Needed

- Beaker containing 100 ml of 7.00 pH buffer solution
- Beaker containing 100 ml of 4.00 pH buffer solution
- Thermometer
- Squeeze bottle containing distilled water
- Four squares of lint-free tissue paper

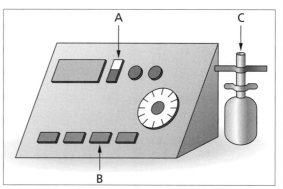

FIGURE 1
Sargent-Welch pH Meter Model 6050

How to Program the pH Meter

1. Press the button marked pH (A in Figure 1) to set the meter to pH mode.
2. Set pH sensitivity by pushing the pH sensitivity button down to .01 (B in Figure 1).
3. Gently remove the pH electrode

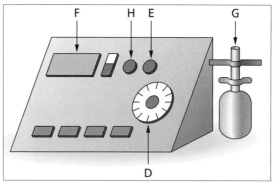

FIGURE 2
Sargent-Welch pH Meter Model 6050

EXAMPLE 11.1
(continued)

(C in Figure 1) from the plastic bottle in which it is stored, and rinse it gently with distilled water from your squeeze bottle.

4. Carefully lower the electrode into the beaker containing the pH 7.00 buffer solution.

5. Set temperature control.

   a. Using the thermometer, take the temperature of pH 7.0 buffer solution.

   b. Turn the temperature dial (D in Figure 2) to the temperature reading on the thermometer in degrees Celsius.

6. Set electrode asymmetry (intercept) by rotating the dial marked "intercept" (E in Figure 2) until the digital display (F in Figure 2) reads 7.00.

7. Raise the electrode from the 7.00 pH buffer solution, rinse gently with distilled water from your squeeze bottle, and dry tip of the electrode using lint-free tissue paper.

8. Lower the electrode (G in Figure 2) into the buffer solution of pH 4.00 to set the lower pH limit.

9. Set the response adjustment (slope) by rotating the dial marked "slope" (H in Figure 2) until the digital display reads 4.00.

10. Raise the electrode from the 4.00 pH buffer solution.

11. Rinse the electrode gently with distilled water from your squeeze bottle.

12. Dry the tip of the electrode using lint-free tissue paper.

EXAMPLE 11.2
Instructions for a Beginner

HOW TO ADD BACKGROUND SOUND TO A WEB PAGE

The process of adding background sound to a Web site will allow you to hear sound clips when your page is opened in a browser. By adding background sound to your Web page, you will add excitement to your site! Consider using background sound that enhances the information on your site and is interesting and pleasing for the listeners. There are many different sound file types that you can use. Some of these file types include MIDI, RMF, RMI, WAV, and MOD. Prior to adding sound to an HTML document, you must have a sound file and an existing HTML document saved in the same directory.

To Add Background Sound to a Web Page

1. Open Notepad by selecting **Start/Programs/Accessories/Notepad.**
2. Open an existing HTML file by selecting **File/Open** and then finding the HTML file to open.
3. Add the following code to the **BODY** section of the HTML file to add the music file **cheers.mid** to the background:

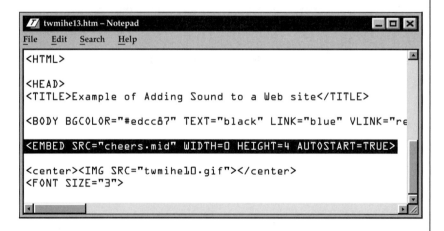

The **WIDTH** and **HEIGHT** parameters are set to small numbers so there will be no visual changes to the Web page. The **"AUTOSTART=TRUE"** statement is added so the sound will begin playing as soon as the Web page is opened in a browser.

4. Select **File/Save** to save the modified HTML document to your disk.

EXAMPLE 11.2
(continued)

To View Your Modified File in Internet Explorer

1. Double-click on the **My Computer** icon on the desktop.
2. Double-click on the 3$\frac{1}{2}$ **Floppy (A)** icon in the My Computer window.
3. Double-click on the **HTML file name** you modified to view your changes in Internet Explorer.

EXAMPLE 11.3
Instructional Essay

HOW WE DESIGNED OUR WEB PAGE, BY ANDY VOLD

Hyper Text Markup Language (HTML) is the code that makes a Web page. At first, HTML might seem like a computer code that should be left to the specialists, but actually it is quite easy to code HTML and create Web pages. In this article we will explain how we, people with no prior HTML knowledge, were able to create a Web page using the HTML code. We will explain the basics, including the codes needed to place type, graphics, and links in a page.

Our goal was to convert a "hard copy" text into an HTML document that would be readable on the Web.

Our original document file was created on a Macintosh using Microsoft Word 5.l. That file, however, contained several visual aids that we had downloaded from the Web and embedded in our Word file. We still had the original files for each graphic.

To work as HTML, the file needs to be in a .txt file format. Word 5.1 gives the users the option of saving their file in this .txt file format. But because our original document also contained graphics and because the .txt file format will not read graphics, we needed to use another program. To view graphics in a Web document, the graphics must be in one of two different file formats: .jpeg and .gif. To convert our graphics into one of these formats, we opened their original files in Adobe Photoshop and resaved them to our disk in the .jpeg file format.

Now that our text and graphics were in the appropriate file formats for HTML design, we were ready to start creating our page. To explain the process, we will show how one would start from the beginning. We did all our work in the .txt file that we had created.

GETTING STARTED

In the HTML language, almost all codes have a "start" and a "stop" form. Notice that the stop code includes a back slash:

`<html> </html>`

The `<html>` code is the first—and last—code needed and all following codes reside in between them. First we entered our title line:

`<html>`
`<title>Macintosh Screen Captures</title>`
`</html>`

EXAMPLE 11.3
(continued)

The title of our Web page resides between the title codes. These words will appear as the file title when it is viewed in a Web browser such as Netscape. Then we set the space for the contents of the actual viewed page, or the body of the page, with the body code. All body text will appear in between the two body codes.

```
<html>
<title>Macintosh Screen Captures</title>
<body>
</body>
</html>
```

To enter text, a number of different codes are needed. Every action has its own code—to change font size, to create a new paragraph, to indent, and to bold type. We chose to use the default font size so no code was needed, but we needed a code to create a new paragraph.

```
<html>
<title>Macintosh Screen Captures</title>
<body>
<p> This is where we placed our first paragraph from the .txt file.</p>
<p> This is where we placed our second paragraph from the .txt file.</p>
</body>
</html>
```

At this point, we had a Web document, so we opened it with the Netscape Web browser and viewed it as it appears on the Web. We found it easy to try new codes by writing a new line and then viewing the file in Netscape to see the change. By repeating this a few times, we felt as if we really started to understand the idea of HTML and how it works.

PLACING GRAPHICS

Now that we understood the HTML coding idea, we had to find the code to place our graphics. Many books and magazine articles are available to learn the many code options. We were able to find the code for placing graphics in a book from our campus library.

```
<img src="green.jpeg">
```

EXAMPLE 11.3
(continued)

In this line of code, the words between the quotes constitute the name of our graphics file as it resides on our disk. The Web browser will look for that file and reproduce it here. Note that the .jpeg or .gif file format is required in the file name. If we wanted to center our graphics on our page or to resize our graphics, codes are available to do so. We chose to center our graphics on the page using the following code:

```
<html>
<title>Macintosh Screen Captures</title>
<body>
<p> This is where our first paragraph would be typed.</p>
<p> This is where our second paragraph would be typed. </p>
<img src = "green.jpeg">
</body>
</html>
```

CREATING LINKS

Finally, the last item we wanted to include in our page were links. A link is simply a word or graphic that appears on the Web page. This word or graphic can be clicked on to forward the viewer to a linked page. Because our project was going to appear on our university's home page under the "student projects" page, we wanted the viewer of our page to be able to return to that page. We typed in this line:

Return to <a href="http://www.uwstout.edu/student/stntorgs. html">student projects page</a>

The link code is <a> and </a>. The code href= tells the Web browser to look for the address that follows, and the text between the quotes in the line of code is the address to the linked page. It tells the computer where to look for this link. With this code, the words "Return to student projects page" would appear on the viewed Web page. However, the words "student projects page" would appear as the link, underlined in blue. When a user clicks on the link, the file stntorgs.html appears on the screen.

Now we had all the components we wanted in our Web page. We were amazed at how easy it was for us to complete this simple project. Many more HTML codes are available. If there is something you would want on your Web page, there is an HTML code to place it.

▪ EXERCISES

1. Construct a visual aid that illustrates an action. For instance, show a jack properly positioned for changing a tire. Then write the instructions that would accompany that visual.

2. Write a set of instructions for a common activity, such as wrapping a package, tying a shoe, or programming a telephone. Choose one of the columnar formats shown in Figure 11.2 on page 265. Have a classmate try to perform the process by following your instructions. Discuss with the class the decisions you had to make to write the instructions. Consider word choice, layout, visual aids, sequence of steps, etc.

3. Make a flow chart or decision chart of a process. Choose an easy topic, such as a hobby, a campus activity, or some everyday task. In class, write the instructions that a person would need to perform the process. Depending on your instructor's preferences, you may either use your own chart or exchange charts with another student and write instructions for that student's chart.

4. Rewrite the following steps from the instructions for changing a car's oil:
   1. Get drainage pan and place it under the oil pan of the car.
   2. Grab a crescent wrench and locate the oil plug, on one side of the oil pan.
   3. Use the crescent wrench to turn the plug counterclockwise (ccw) until it comes out and oil drains out.
   4. While this is draining, grab a filter wrench and locate oil filter.
   5. Turn the oil filter counterclockwise with the filter wrench until it comes off and the oil drains into the drainage pan.

5. Rewrite the following steps from instructions for ringing up a sale:
   1. Take the piece of merchandise from the customer and read what the price tag states.
      a. Always take the lowest price on the ticket.
   2. Type the price stated on the ticket into the register.
      a. If the item costs $2.00, simply type 200, and the decimal point will automatically register.
      b. If an error has been made in the price, hit the clear button and start over with step 3.

3. Look at the price ticket again. In the upper left-hand corner there will be a classification number.

   a. The 4 stands for the classification, and the 52 refers to the subclassification.

4. Type the classification into the register.

---

6. Convert the following paragraphs into a set of instructions:

Adding background sound to a Web site will allow you to hear sound clips when your page is opened in a browser. By adding background sound to your Web page, you will add pizzazz to your site!

Just as improper use of pictures and color can be distracting in a Web site, so can the use of improper sound clips. Sound clips should enhance a Web site. They should in some way relate to the theme of your page. The sound should not be annoying to the listener. The sound clip should not be too long, and the options should not be set so the sound repeats.

There are many types of sound files available. A few of the types of files that you can use as background sound include .midi, .rmf, .rmi, .wav and .mod. I used a .midi file because they seem to take up the least amount of disk space.

I used an IBM-compatible PC with Windows 95 and software including Internet Explorer and Notepad. To hear sound from your computer, you must have a sound card installed in your computer. Also, you must have the volume of your computer turned up so it is audible. You must also have either speakers (internal or external) or headphones plugged into your computer.

Adding sound to a Web site is a very easy process. First, you must get a sound file. You may either create your own sound file or download one from the Web. I chose to download a sound file from the Web. The size of my sound file is very small (4 KB) yet it plays for longer than one minute.

Second, you need to open up an HTML file in an editor. I chose to use Notepad as my editor.

Next, you will insert the following code into your HTML file to add a background sound to your page.

<EMBED SRC = "cheers.mid" WIDTH = 0 HEIGHT = 4 AUTOSTART = TRUE>

where cheers.mid is the name of the sound file. **WIDTH** and **HEIGHT** are set to small numbers so there will be no visual changes made to the site. **"AUTOSTART = TRUE"** is used so the background sound will start as soon as the page is opened.

Finally, you can save the file to your disk. Make sure you save the HTML file in the same directory as the sound file. Otherwise, Internet Explorer will not be able to find your sound file when you open your HTML file.

Now you are ready to view your Web page in a browser. I chose to use Internet Explorer. I opened up the HTML file by clicking on **My Computer/3½ floppy (A) / filename.htm.** The background sound started up when the page was open, and there were no visual changes made to the page.

Make sure you don't have the volume of your computer muted. To check this on a IBM with Windows 95, double-click on the yellow speaker on the task bar. A **Volume Control** window should appear. Make sure none of the volume controls have the "Mute" option checked and that the volume bar is not at the minimum setting.

If you still are not hearing the Web site's sound, you may need to set an option to allow Internet Explorer to play sounds. To do this in Internet Explorer 4.0, select **View/Internet Options** from the task bar. In the **Internet Options** window that appears, scroll down to the "Play Sounds" option and make sure there is an X next to it.

7. Rewrite all of the items in Exercise 4 from the point of view of a "chatty help" columnist in a newspaper. Use paragraphs, not numbered steps.

8. Compare Example 11.2 with Example 12.2 (p. 309). In groups of three or four, discuss the differences in tone and in the presentation of the action. Report to the class which document you prefer to read and why.

9. For Writing Assignment 1 or 2, construct a flow chart of the process. Explain it to a small peer group who question you closely, causing you to explain the steps in detail. Revise the chart based on this discussion.

10. For Writing Assignment 1 or 2, create a template for your instructions, including methods for handling heads, introduction, steps, visual aids, captions, and columns. Review this template with your peer group, explaining why you have made the choices you have. Your peer group will edit the template for consistency and effectiveness.

11. For Writing Assignment 1 or 2, bring the final draft of your instructions to your peer group. Choose a person to field test. With your instructor's permission, field-test each other's instructions. Note every place where your classmate hesitates or asks a question, and revise your instructions accordingly.

12. Rewrite Example 11.3 as a numbered set of instructions.

13. Bring an article instruction to class. Computer and household magazines offer the best sources for these articles. In groups of three or

four, analyze the models and decide why the authors decided to use the article method. Depending on your instructor, either report your analysis to the class, or as a group rewrite the instructions, either with a different tone (say, as a coach) or as a numbered set.

■ WRITING ASSIGNMENTS

1. Write a set of instructions for a process you know well. Fill out the worksheet and then write the instructions. Use visual aids and design your pages effectively, using one of the columnar formats shown on page 265. Pick a process that a beginning student in your major will have to perform or choose something that you do as a hobby or at a job, such as waxing skis, developing film, ringing up a sale, or taking inventory.

2. Divide into groups of three or four. Pick a topic that everyone knows, such as checking books out of the library, applying for financial aid, reserving a meeting room, operating a microfilm reader, replacing a lost ID or driver's license, or appealing a grade. Then each team should write a set of instructions for that process. Complete the worksheet on pages 274–275. When you are finished, decide which team's set is best in terms of design, clarity of steps, and introduction.

3. Write a learning report for the writing assignment you just completed. See Chapter 5, Writing Assignment 7, page 123, for details of the assignment.

■ WEB EXERCISES

1. Give instructions to a beginner on how to create a Web page using a wizard, template, or Web-authoring tool with which you are familiar.

2. Convert the process paper that you wrote for Chapter 10, Web Exercise 2, into a set of instructions for a beginner.

Technical Writing Applications

12 Memorandums and Informal Reports

CHAPTER CONTENTS

Chapter 12
IN A NUTSHELL

Memos. A memo is any document (regardless of length) that has memo heads (Date, To, From, Subject) at the top. The subject line should relate the contents to the reader's needs.

Informal reports. Informal reports are usually short (1 to 10 pages). Their goal is to convey the message in an understandable context, from a credible person, in clear, easy-to-read text.

Informal report structure. The informal report structure is the IMRD (Introduction, Method, Results, and Discussion).

The *Introduction* explains your goal and why this situation has developed.

The *Method* outlines what you did to find out about the situation. It establishes your credibility.

The *Results* establish what you found out, the information the reader can use.

The *Discussion* describes the implications of the information. It gives the reader a new context.

Informal report strategies. Key strategies include

- Explain your purpose—what your reader will get from the report.
- Use a top-down strategy.
- Develop a clear visual logic.
- Provide the contents in an easy-to-grasp sequence and help the reader out by defining, using analogies, and explaining the significance to the person or organization.

The day-to-day operation of a company depends on memos and informal reports that circulate within and among its departments. These documents report on various problems and present information about products, methods, and equipment. The basic informal format, easy to use in nearly any situation, has been adapted to many purposes throughout industry.

This chapter explains the elements of memos, the elements of informal reports, and the types of informal reports, including analytical reports, IMRD reports, progress reports, and outline reports.

THE ELEMENTS OF MEMOS

Memos are used to report everything from results of tests to announcements of meetings. In industry you must write memos clearly and quickly. Your ability to do so tells a reader a great deal about your abilities as a problem solver and decision maker. This section explains memo headings and provides a sample memo report.

Memo Headings

The memo format consists of specific lines placed at the top of a page: *To, From, Subject,* and *Date* lines. That's all there is to it. What follows below those lines is a memo report. Usually such a report is brief—from one or two sentences to one or two pages. Theoretically there is no limit to a memo's length, but in practice such reports are seldom longer than four or five pages.

Follow these guidelines to set up a memo or memo report:

1. Fill in the blanks in the preprinted form or follow guidelines 2–5.
2. Place the To, From, and Subject lines at the left margin.
3. Place the date either to the right, without a head, or at the top of the list with a head (Date:).
4. Follow each item with a colon and the appropriate information.
5. Choose a method of capitalization and placement of colons (see examples).
6. Name the contents or main point in the subject line.
7. Place the names of those people who are to receive copies below the name of the main recipient (usually with the head cc:).
8. Sign to the right of your typed name.

MEMO FORMAT: EXAMPLE 1

February 14, 2004   Date on far right

To: E. J. Mentzer
cc: Jane Thompson   *Judy Davis*   Copy line
From: Judy Davis   Signature

Subject: Remodeling of Office Complex   Subject line—only
first letters
capitalized

MEMO FORMAT: EXAMPLE 2

DATE: February 14, 2004   Date line
TO: E. J. Mentzer   *Judy Davis*   Memo heads in
FROM: Judy Davis   all caps
Signature

SUBJECT: REMODELING OF OFFICE COMPLEX   Subject line
capitalized for
emphasis

MEMO FORMAT: EXAMPLE 3

March 29, 2004

To: E. J. Mentzer   *Judy Davis*   Memo heads
From: Judy Davis   aligned on colons

Subject: Remodeling of Office Complex

A Sample Memo Report

A memo can contain any kind of information that your audience needs.
The following memo is a recommendation based on criteria.

April 1, 2004

To: Bill Foresight
From: Carol Frank, Food Service Director
Subject: Purchase of an open-top range

Here is a preliminary recommendation on which brand of   Purpose of memo
open-top range to purchase for the Food Service Depart-   Credibility of writer
ment. After comparing the specification sheets of several   Basic conclusion
brands, I found that two brands satisfy our needs: Mon-   first
tague and Franklin, but Montague is the better choice.

     The Montague is cheaper ($499 vs. $512). It is more   Data to support
energy efficient; it has an overall rating of 103,000   conclusion
BTU/hour while the Franklin has a rating of 138,000   Four criteria: cost,
BTU/hour. The Montague has several design features not   energy efficiency,
found on the Franklin, including a 3-position rack, a re-   rating, design
features

movable oven bottom, a continuous-cleaning oven, and a
solid hot top. I will provide a detailed report next week.

THE ELEMENTS OF INFORMAL REPORTS

The informal report is used for reports that will not have wide distribution,
will not be published, and are shorter than 10 pages long (General Motors).
This kind of report follows a fairly standard form that can be adapted to
many situations, from presenting background to recommending and proposing. The form basically has two parts: an introduction and a discussion.

Introduction

Introductions orient readers to the contents of the document. You can
choose from a number of options, basing your decision on the audience's
knowledge level and community attitudes. To create an introduction, you
can do one of three things: provide the objective, provide context, or provide an expanded context.

Provide the Objective.   The basic informal introduction is a one-sentence
statement of the purpose or main point of the project or report, sometimes
of both. This type of introduction is appropriate for almost all situations
and readers.

Objective of the project	To evaluate whether the customer service counter should install an Iconglow personal computer system
Objective of the report	To report on investigation of the feasibility of installing an Iconglow personal computer system at the customer service counter

If this statement is enough for your readers, go right into the discussion. If
not, add context sections as explained below.

Provide Context.   To provide *context* for a report means to explain the situation that caused you to write the report. This type of introduction is an
excellent way to begin informal reports. It is especially helpful for readers
who are unfamiliar with the project. Include four pieces of information:
cause, credibility, purpose, and preview. Follow these guidelines:

■ Tell what caused you to write. Perhaps you are reporting on an assignment, or you may have discovered something the recipient
needs to know.

■ Explain why you are credible in the situation. You are credible because of either your actions or your position.

■ State the report's purpose. Use one clear sentence: "This report rec-ommends that customer service should install an Iconglow computer system."

■ Preview the contents. List the main heads that will follow.

Here is a sample, basic introduction.

I am responding to your recent request that I determine whether customer service should install an Iconglow computer system. In gathering this information, I inter-viewed John Broderick, the Iconglow Regional Sales Rep-resentative. He reviewed records of basic personnel activities. This report recommends that customer service install an Iconglow system. I base the recommendation on cost, space, training, and customer relations.	Cause for writing Source of credibility Purpose Preview

Special Case: Alert the Reader to a Problem.   Sometimes the easiest way to provide context is to set up a problem statement. Use one of the follow-ing methods:

■ Contrast a general truth (positive) with the problem (negative).
■ Contrast the problem (negative) with a proposed solution (positive).

In either case, point out the significance of the problem or the solution. If you cast the problem as a negative, show how it violates some expected norm. If you are proposing a solution, point out its positive effect. Here is a sample problem-solution introduction.

Processing customers at the service desk is a time-consuming process. The service representative fills out three different forms while the customer and those in line wait, annoyed. Some customers go elsewhere to shop. An Iconglow computer system would eliminate the waiting, cutting average service time from 10 minutes to 1 minute. This report recommends that we purchase the Iconglow system.	Negative problem and its significance Proposed solution Positive significance Purpose of report

Provide an Expanded Context.   To provide an expanded context, create a several-paragraph introduction. You must include a purpose or objective, and then add other sections that you might need: a summary, a back-ground, a conclusions/recommendation section, or a combination of them.

The *summary*—also called an "abstract" or sometimes "executive sum-mary"—is a one-to-one miniaturization of the discussion section. If the dis-cussion section has three parts, the summary has three statements, each giving the major point of one of the sections. After reading this section, the reader should have the gist of your report.

The *background statement* gives the reader a context by explaining the project's methodology or history. If the report has only an objective statement, this section orients the reader to the material in the report.

Writers present the *conclusions and/or recommendations* early in the report because this section contains the basic information that readers need. It can provide information that differs from the summary, but it replaces the summary.

EXAMPLES OF INTRODUCTORY OPTIONS

VERSION 1

Objective

To evaluate whether to install an Iconglow system at the customer service counter.

Conclusions and Recommendation

I recommend that we install the Iconglow System.

1. The system will pay for itself in one year.
2. The office area contains ample space for the system.
3. The system will not interfere with attending to customers.

Background

Customer service proposed installation of an Iconglow system to handle all updating functions. The system would reduce the number of employee hours required to complete these functions. The system includes two computers, a printer, programs, and cables. I reviewed personnel figures and discussed the proposal with Iconglow's sales representative.

VERSION 2

Introduction

I am responding to your recent request that I determine whether customer service should install an Iconglow computer system. In gathering this information, I interviewed John Broderick, the Iconglow Regional Sales Representative. He reviewed records of basic personnel activities. This report recommends that customer service install an Iconglow system. I base the recommendation on cost, space, training, and customer relations.

Cause for writing

Source of credibililty

Purpose
Preview

Conclusions

1. The system will pay for itself in one year.
2. The office area contains ample space for the system.
3. The system will not interfere with attending to customers.

Discussion

The discussion section contains the more detailed, full information of the report. Writers subdivide this section with heads, use visual aids, and sometimes give the discussion its own introduction and conclusion. If you write the introduction well, your reader will find no surprises, just more depth, in the introduction. Two format concerns that arise in planning the discussion section are pagination and heads.

Pagination.   Paginate informal reports either with just a page number or with header information as well. Follow these guidelines:

- If you use just page numbers, place them in the upper right corner or in the bottom center.
- If you use header information, arrange the various elements across the top of the page. Generally the page number goes to the far right and other information (report title, report number, recipient, and/or date) appears to the left.

Iconglow Recommendation   12/24/03   2

Heads.   Informal reports almost always contain heads. Usually you need only one level; the most commonly used format is the "side left." Follow these guidelines:

- Place heads at the left margin, triple-spaced above and double-spaced below. Use underline or boldface.
- Capitalize only the first letter of each main word (do not capitalize *a, an, the,* or prepositions).
- Do not punctuate after heads (unless you ask a question).
- Use a word or phrase that indicates the contents immediately following.
- At times, use a question for an effective head.

Will the New System Save Money?   Side left, boldface
                                                        Double-space

The new Iconglow system will pay for itself within 6 months. Currently employees spend 87 hours a month updating files. The new system will reduce that figure to 27, a savings of 60 hours. These 60 hours represent a payroll savings of $435.00 a month. Because the new system costs $2450, the savings alone will pay for the system in

6 months (435 $\times$ 6 = 2610). This amount of time is under the 1-year period allowed for recovery.

Triple space

Is There Enough Space for the System?

Double-space

The computers will easily fit in their allocated spaces. One computer and the printer will occupy space at the refund desk, and the other computer will sit on the customer service counter. Both areas were reorganized to accommodate the machine and allow for efficient work flow.

Will the Computers Affect Customer Relations?

The Iconglow system will allow employees to process customer complaints more quickly, reducing a 15-minute wait to seconds. This speeded-up handling of problems will eliminate customer complaints about standing in line.

TYPES OF INFORMAL REPORTS

Writers use informal reports in many situations. This section introduces you to several variations.

IMRD Reports

An IMRD (*I*ntroduction, *M*ethodology, *R*esults, *D*iscussion) report is a standard way to present information that is the result of some kind of research. This approach can present laboratory research, questionnaire results, or the results of any action whose goal is to find out about a topic and discuss the significance of what was discovered. The IMRD report causes you to tell a story about your project in a way that most readers will find satisfying. This kind of report allows you to provide new knowledge for a reader and to fit that knowledge into a bigger context. Your research project started out with some kind of question that you investigated in a certain way. You found information, and you explain that the information is important in various ways.

■ For the *introduction,* tell the question you investigated (the goal of the project) and the point of the paper. What is helpful is to give a general answer to the question. Consider these questions:

–What is the goal of this project?

–What is the goal of this report?

■ For the *methodology section,* write a process description of your actions and why you performed those actions. This section establishes your credibility. Explain such things as whom you talked to, and describe any actions you took and why. This description should allow a reader to replicate your actions. Consider these questions:

–What steps or actions did you take to achieve the goal or answer the questions? (Tell all your actions. Arrange them in sequence, if necessary.)

–Why did you perform those actions?

■ For the *results section,* tell what you discovered, usually by presenting a table or graph of the data. If a visual aid is all you need in this section, combine it with the discussion section. If you add text, tell the readers what to focus on in the results. Honesty requires that you point out material that might contradict what you expected to discover. Consider these questions:

–What are the results of each action or sequence?

–Can I present the results in one visual aid?

■ In the *discussion section,* explain the significance of what you found out. Either interpret it by relating it to some other important concept or suggest its causes or effects. Relate the results to the problem or concerns you mentioned in the introduction. If the method affects the results, tell how and suggest changes. Often you can suggest or recommend further actions at the end of this section. Consider these questions:

–Did you achieve your goal? (If you didn't, say so, and explain why.)

–What are the implications of your results? for you and your goals? for other people and their goals?

–What new questions do your results cause?

IMRD REPORT

INVESTIGATING THE INTERNET

INTRODUCTION

More and more people are turning to the Internet first as their primary source of information and ideas. Using the Internet to find information for your profession, however, is only feasible if the Web sites found are current, credible, and provide you with links to other sites. The goal of the project is to evaluate whether or not the Internet is a valuable source for finding nutrition education lesson plans.

METHODS

Using a Gateway 2000 computer, I accessed the mega-search engine, Metacrawler *(http://www.metacrawler.com)*. Metacrawler is a search engine that sends your keyword searches to 7 other search engines (Yahoo!, Alta Vista, Lycos, Excite, Infoseek, Thunderstone, and Webcrawler) and returns the top 10 hits from each of these search engines in one consolidated list. I chose Metacrawler to do my researching because I felt it was very comprehensive and it would save me time (rather than having to search each of the 7 search engines individually). Once in Metacrawler, I typed in the keywords "nutrition" and "lesson plans" together. Next, I clicked on the search option "all" so that any site containing these words together in the head, title, and/or body would be "tagged" and returned to me in the results. Finally, I began the search. I then evaluated each site that was returned by the search engine individually. I evaluated each site to see if it met my three criteria: current, credible, and provides links to at least 5 other Web sites.

RESULTS

The search described in the above section returned 30 hits. Of these 30 sites, 16 were immediately disregarded because they either had nothing to do with nutrition lesson plans or could not be opened by the server. The remaining 14 Web sites were then evaluated using the 3 criteria listed earlier. Four sites were discarded because they contained no lesson plans but only lists of links to other Web pages with lesson plans. Four more sites were discarded because they did not meet all of the desired criteria. I found that 6 of the initial 30 sites met my 3 criteria. They are listed in Table 1 below:

TABLE 1
Sites That Met All 3 Criteria

Site URL	Current?	Credible?	Number of Links to Other Pages?
http://www.kidsfood.org/	Updated, 7/31/98	Yes	40
http://www.freshstarts.com/	Published, 1998	Yes	9
http://neatsolutions.com/ index.htm	Updated, 11/29/98	Yes	23
http://www.post1.com/home/ albert_ong/lessons.htm	Updated, 4/16/98	Yes	25
http://thegateway.org/	Updated, 12/11/98	Yes	127
http://teachtech.com/k-12/ links.html	Updated, 3/98	Yes	6

DISCUSSION

The 6 sites that met all of my criteria were very impressive. The information provided in them was creative, accurate, and fun. In addition, the sites that I had to discard because they did not contain any lesson plans but links only were still a good resource that I would have used to find more Web pages with lesson plans if I were not confined to the strict boundaries specified in my research proposal. Overall, I would conclude that the Internet is a good source for nutrition education lesson plans.

Brief Analytical Reports

Brief analytical reports are very common in industry. They present conclusions about an endless array of problems that beset normal operating procedures. The following example contains a one-sentence objective, a background section, a conclusion, and a discussion ordered in terms of criteria arranged from most to least important.

DATE: April 17, 2004
TO: Helmut Schiller, Vice President of Operations
FROM: Craig Cardell, CPIM, Plant Manager
SUBJECT: Feasibility of buying a new lathe for work cell #10

This report recommends that we make a capital expenditure as we continue to implement just-in-time production.

BACKGROUND

Johnson Mfg. has been implementing JIT in work cell #10 for 12 weeks. This work cell makes the "Executive Chair," our most profitable product line. Our JIT goal is to reduce manufacturing lead times from 25 days to 5 days; our competitors already offer customers 5-day lead times.

Figure 1 shows our average manufacturing lead time for this product line since implementing JIT. Notice that lead times were reduced from 25 days to 10 days in the first five weeks. However, lead times have remained at 10 days for the past seven weeks.

John Adams is a line worker participating in the "Quality Circle," and he proposed that a new lathe be purchased for work cell #10. My recommendation is based on the following criteria: machine set-up times, machine features available, and cost.

Recommendation

I recommend that Industrial Engineering purchase a new lathe.

Discussion

Criteria were provided by people in Production Scheduling, Industrial Engineering, Manufacturing Engineering, and Accounting. Each criterion is presented in order from most to least important.

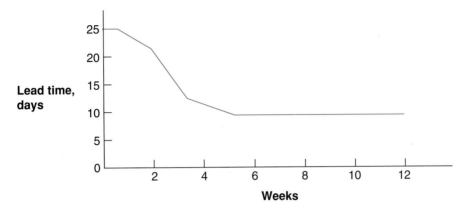

FIGURE 1
Manufacturing Lead Time Since JIT
"Executive Chair" Product Line

Machine Set-up Time

Set-up time is the total downtime that elapses when a machine has tooling changes to process different parts. When machines are grouped into
synchronous work cells, the machine with the longest set-up time is the
constraint that holds up production. Work cell #10 has three machines: a
router, a lathe, and a drill press. To be the constraint, the standard set-up
time for the lathe must be longer than the set-up times for the router
(6 minutes) and the drill press (4 minutes). Current data from the Manufacturing Engineering Department show that the lathe has average set-
up times of 19 minutes. **Proposal meets criterion.**

Machine Features

A new lathe must have two features that will reduce set-up time: adapt-
ability and flexibility. Adaptable means that the lathe can process wood
into hundreds of shapes and sizes. Our standard is that 78 different parts
can be processed, with room for additional parts when new products are
introduced. Flexibility means that the lathe's tooling is designed for quick
set-ups. Our standard is that hydraulic or pneumatic fasteners be included
rather than bolts and screws. A time-and-motion study revealed that 13 of
the 19 minutes of set-up time are the direct result of bolt and screw adjustments. Dick Hines is our Industrial Engineer, and by scanning the
Thomas Register, he noted that modern lathes are highly adaptable, often
with built-in hydraulic or pneumatic flexibility. **Proposal meets criterion.**

Total Cost

The total cost of a new lathe will include machine and installation costs.
Our standard is that the total cost of the lathe must be less than $7500.
The budget for the JIT project is $24,000: up to $10,000 for JIT training,

and $14,000 for capital equipment purchases. A quick sample of companies listed in the *Thomas Register* showed that we can find a lathe that meets our budgetary need. **Proposal meets criterion.**

Progress Reports

Progress reports inform management about the status of a project. Submitted regularly throughout the life of the project, they let the readers know whether work is progressing satisfactorily—that is, within the project's budget and time limitations. To write an effective progress report, follow the usual process. Evaluate your audience's knowledge and needs. Determine how much they know, what they expect to find in your report, and how they will use the information. Select the topics you will cover. The standard sections are the following:

- Introduction
- Work Completed
- Work Scheduled
- Problems

In the Introduction, name the project, define the time period covered by the report, and state the purpose: to inform readers about the current status of the project. In the Work Completed section, specify the time period, divide the project into major tasks, and report the appropriate details. In the Work Scheduled section, explain the work that will occur on each major task in the next time period. In the Problems section, discuss any special topics that require the reader's attention.

PROGRESS REPORT

Date: July 1, 2004
To: Mark Perry, Director of Information Systems,
         ABC Corporation
From: Jim Nord, Director of Information Systems, ABC Corporation,
         Gaithersburg, MD
Subject: Progress report on PROFS central processing unit

Here is the progress report you requested on the investigation of the PROFS CPU problem. The purpose of this memo is to outline the analysis which my staff and I have completed and alert you to any possible problems. The following memo will explain the work that has been completed to date and what needs to be done between now and the July 22 presentation date.

COMPLETED WORK

In the past few weeks my staff and I have placed top priority on this problem. We have analyzed the problem and the need for a solution by projecting future use of the system. We have calculated the capacity needed to handle the projected use and narrowed the possible solutions to two, a 4381 mg 35 or a 1234 model 600. We then calculated the necessary space requirements for each machine, and we are now in the process of analyzing all costs involved with the two solutions.

WORK TO BE COMPLETED

At this time we are waiting for the bids from vendors concerning the addition of the raised floor that would be needed for the 4381 mg 35. All costs have been calculated for the 1234 model 600, but we still must come up with an installation plan that will allow us to keep the system on line during the move. We also need to complete a plan for what will be done with the two 4381 mg 20s should we purchase the 1234 model 600. All three of these projects are well on their way to completion, and we expect no problems in meeting the July 22 deadline.

Outline Reports

An expanded outline is a common type of report, set up like a résumé, with distinct headings. This form often accompanies an oral presentation. The speaker follows the outline, explaining details at the appropriate places. Procedural specifications and retail management reports often use this form. The brevity of the form allows the writer to condense material, but of course the reader must be able to comprehend the condensed information. To write this kind of report, follow these guidelines:

- Use heads to indicate sections *and* to function as introductions.
- Present information in phrases or sentences, not paragraphs.
- Indent information (as in an outline) underneath the appropriate head.

SAMPLE OUTLINE REPORT

**FORK LIFT PURCHASE:
WEEVEL VS. HIBOY,
DECEMBER 16, 2003**

Researcher   David Zangl

Purpose   To compare the Weevel 424 and   Side heads serve
              HiBoy 1200 Fork Lifts to determine   as introductions to
              which is a better purchase.   each section

Method   Interviewed vendors, read their sales
              literature, observed each machine in
              operation. Used these criteria: Essential material
                                                        presented in
              ■ Safety   phrases and lists
              ■ Ease of repair
              ■ Cost
              ■ Load capacity
              ■ Fuel

Conclusions   Both models are nearly identical in

              ■ Safety features
              ■ Cost
              ■ Fuel efficiency

              The two are identical in load capacity.
                 The difference is ease of repairs—Weevel can sup-
              ply major parts within a week, but Hiboy can only
              guarantee within three weeks.

Recommendation   Purchase the Weevel 424 Fork Lift.

■ WORKSHEET FOR PLANNING A PROJECT

❑ *Write the question you want answered.*

❑ *Create a research plan.*
   a. List topics and keywords that might help you find information
      on your question
   b. List a method for finding about those topics. Tell which spe-
      cific acts you will undertake.
   (Explore Compendex and Ebscohost using X and Y as keywords.)
   (Talk to all employees affected by the change, using questions X
   and Y.)

❑ *Carry out your plan.*

■ WORKSHEET FOR IMRD REPORTS

❏ *Write an introduction in which you briefly describe the goal of your project and your goal in this report. Give enough information to orient a reader to your situation.*

❏ *Write the methods statement.*
   a. Name the actions that you took in enough detail so that a reader could replicate the acts if necessary.
   b. Use terms and details at a level appropriate to the reader, but necessary for the subject.
   c. Explain *why* you chose this strategy or actions.

❏ *Name the actual results of the actions. This section might be very short.*

❏ *Tell the significance of your actions.*
   a. Did you accomplish your goals?
   b. What will you do next, as a result of this project?
   c. How is this important to your classmates, in this class?

❏ *Develop a style sheet for your report.*
   a. How will you handle heads?
   b. How will you handle chunks?
   c. How will you handle page numbers?
   d. How will you handle visual aids?
   e. How will you handle the title/memo heads?

❏ *Develop an idea of how you will present yourself.*
   a. Will you write in the first person?
   b. Will you call the reader "you"?
   c. Will you write short or long sentences?
   d. Are you an expert? How do experts sound? What will you do to make yourself sound like one?
   e. *Key question:* Why should I believe you? Why are you credible?

■ WORKSHEET FOR INFORMAL REPORTS

❏ *Identify the audience.*
   Who will receive this report? How familiar are they with the topic? How will the audience use this report? What type of report does

your audience expect in this situation (lengthier prose? outline? lots of design? just gray?)?

❑ *Determine your schedule for completing the report.*

❑ *Determine how you will prove your credibility.*

❑ *Outline the discussion section. Will this section contain background? Divide the section into appropriate subsections.*

❑ *For IMRDs, outline each of the three body sections.*
Clearly distinguish methods and results.
In the discussion, relate results to the audience's concerns.

❑ *Prepare the visual aids you need.*
What function will the visuals serve for the reader? What type of visual aid will best convey your message?

❑ *Select and write the type of introduction you need*
  ■ To give the objective of the report.
  ■ To provide brief context.
  ■ To provide expanded context.

❑ *Select the combination of introductory elements you will use to give the gist of the report to the reader. Write each section.*

❑ *Prepare a style sheet for heads (one or two levels), margins, page numbers, and visual aid captions.*

■ WORKSHEET FOR EVALUATING IMRDs

Read your report or a peer's. Then answer these questions:

❑ *Introduction*
What is the goal of this project?
What is the basic question that the writer answers?

❑ *Methods*
Does the writer tell all steps or actions that he or she followed to achieve the goal or answer the question? Often there are several sequences of them.
Is it clear why the writer took those steps or actions?

❏ *Results*

Does this section present all the things that the writer found out? If there is a visual aid, does it help you grasp the results quickly?

❏ *Discussion*

Does the discussion answer the question or explain success or failure in achieving the project's goal?

What are the implications of the results? Implications mean (1) effects on various groups of people or their goals, or (2) perceptions about the system (e.g., Web search engines, Web authoring programs) discussed in the report.

What new questions do your results cause?

EXAMPLES

Examples 12.1–12.5 show four informal reports; Example 12.2 is an excerpt from a magazine article. These reports illustrate the wide range of topics that the informal report can present. Note the varied handling of the introduction and of the format of the pages. The goal in all the reports is to make the readers confident that they have the information necessary to make a decision.

EXAMPLE 12.1
IMRD Report

CRYPTOGRAPHY BY CAROLYN HAGEMANN

INTRODUCTION

The goal of this project was to find out if the Web is a feasible resource for cryptography. In particular, to answer the question "Can I find information on cryptography standards and government policies concerning encryption using the Web as a resource tool?" In the next few paragraphs, I will provide the criteria and the methods I used in trying to answer this question along with the results I found. The results will be presented in a table followed by a brief discussion.

CRITERIA

Contained in the following list are the criteria I used to establish credibility and a basis for judgment:

- Is the source reliable? By "reliable," I mean is the information from a credible source?

- Is the information up to date? By "up to date," I mean within the past year.

- Is the information hard to find? By "hard to find," I mean can I find this information in less than an hour?

- Does the Web site contain the content that I am looking for? By "content," I mean national standards, government policy, security issues, and laws.

METHODS

To search for answers to the question: "Can I find information on cryptography standards and government policies concerning encryption using the Web as resource tool?" I needed to pick a keyword. The keyword I used was "cryptography." I decided to use *webopedia.internet.com* for my search, because it is the number one on-line encyclopedia and search engine dedicated to computer technology. I typed the keyword "cryptography" into the search box and clicked on the search button. The results were as follows:

EXAMPLE 12.1
(*continued*)

RESULTS

TABLE 1
Results

HTTP Address	Credible Source	Up-to-Date	Less than an Hour	Content
http://theory.lcs.mit.edu/ ~rivest/crypto-security.html	Yes	Yes	Yes	National Security Agency, Advanced Encryption Standard
www.oecd.org/news_and_ events/release/nw97-24a.htm	Yes	Yes	Yes	Government control, OECD policy guidelines
http://csrc.ncsl.nist.gov/	Yes	Yes	Yes	Security topics, security issues
www.austinlinks/crypto/	Yes	Yes	Yes	Encryption policy, Clipper chip
http://cwis.kub.nl/~frw/ people/koops/lawsurvy.htm	Yes	Yes	Yes	International policy + U.S. import/export controls
www.epic.org/crypto	Yes	Yes	Yes	Recent developments in Congress
www.oecd.org/dist/sti/it/ secur/index.htm	Yes	Yes	Yes	Guidelines for cryptography policy

DISCUSSION

All of the above sites in my opinion more than satisfied the credibility criterion for the following reasons:

- Ronald L. Rivest is the Webster Professor of Electrical Engineering and Computer Science at MIT; also founder of RSA Data Security.

- OECD (Organization for Economic Cooperation and Development) groups 29 member countries in an organization that provides governments a setting in which to discuss, develop, and perfect economic and social policy.

- NIST (National Institute of Standards and Technology), established by Congress to assist industry in the development of technology. NIST's primary mission is to promote U.S. economic growth by working with industry to develop and apply technology, measurements and standards.

- Bert-Jaap Koops did Ph.D. research on cryptography and crime at Tilburg University and the Eindhoven University of Technology.

EXAMPLE 12.1
(continued)

- EPIC (Electronic Privacy Information Center) is a nonprofit public interest research center in Washington, D.C., established in 1994 to focus public attention on emerging civil liberties issues and to protect privacy, the First Amendment, and constitutional values.

The sites as indicated by the above table also met the three other given criteria. All the sites had publications within the last year, they could be found in much less than an hour, and the content surpassed my expectations.

Thus, the answer to the question "Can I find information on cryptography standards and government policies concerning encryption using the Web as a resource tool?" is YES!

EXAMPLE 12.2
Professional IMRD

BLOWING UP PETER THE GREAT

We took the Elicar out for a trial run, photographing a 500-ruble Czarist Russian note. All copystand photographs were made at f/11 on Kodak T-Max 400 under 75-watt flexible gooseneck floods. Exposures were in TTL, aperture-priority mode.

We were highly pleased with all results. The difference between 1:1 and 1.25:1 reproduction is evident. Using the 2.5× and 4× magnification closeup lenses ($140 per set) proved a bit tricky because lens-to-subject distance at 2.5× is only 1¼ inches while 4× shrinks even this to ⅜ inch. It's rather difficult getting illumination between lens and subject except at a fairly great angle. Few three-dimensional subjects would be suitable for such tight quarters.

However, our greatest problem photographing the 500-ruble bill at 4X was the ruble note itself. Despite my best efforts, the note wouldn't stay absolutely flat. And the most minute central billowing would cause a tiny mid-picture loss in sharpness. Of course, I could have pasted the bill down flat (but I had no intention of fouling up a 500-ruble bill). I could have used a piece of optically flat glass atop the note, but I didn't have it. Maybe present Russian notes stay flatter. Next time I'll have to try one.

In the meantime, keep in mind that zoom lenses can provide passable closeups, but not 1:1 and not without linear distortion. If closeups mean a lot to you, a true "macro" lens is needed—even if it's misnamed. And anyone needing 1.25:1, 2.5:1 and 4:1 magnification and having the proper camera lensmount can get it if they can fit their subject into a 1¼- or ⅜-inch lens-to-subject distance.

Keppler, Herbert, "SLR: Going Where No Macro Has Dared to Go Before" from *Popular Photography,* (August 1997): 18, 20, 186, 198. Reprinted with permission.

EXAMPLE 12.3
IMRD Report

IMRD: ADDING BACKGROUND SOUND TO WEB PAGES

INTRODUCTION

I set out to add background sound to a Web page. My resources included an IBM-compatible PC with Windows 98 and software that included Notepad and Internet Explorer 4.0. Computers with these resources can be found in the Main Lab of the Micheels Hall Computer Lab. Before I began, I downloaded a sound file from the Internet and had an existing HTML document to which I wanted to add the sound file. These two files were in the same directory on my disk. Some of the different sound file types that you can use include .midi, .rmf, .rmi, .wav, and .mod.

METHOD

I opened Notepad by selecting Start/Programs/Accessories/Notepad. I then opened up an existing HTML file that I wanted to add sound to by selecting File/Open and then finding the HTML file I wanted to open.

Once the file was open, I added the following code to the body section of my HTML file to add the music file, *cheers.mid,* to the background:

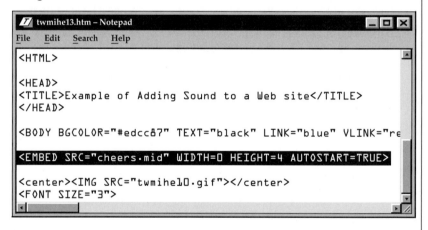

I then selected File/Save to save the modified HTML document.

Once the file was saved, I wanted to view the modified page in Internet Explorer. I did this by first double-clicking on the My Computer icon. Then I double-clicked on the 3½ Floppy (A) icon. I finally opened the file by double-clicking on the file name.

EXAMPLE 12.3
(continued)

RESULT

In the HTML code that I inserted in my file, the WIDTH and HEIGHT parameters are set to small numbers so there will be no visual changes to the Web page. AUTOSTART = TRUE is used so that the sound file will start playing as soon as the page is opened.

Once I modified and saved my HTML document in Notepad, I had a current copy of the document on my disk in the same directory as the sound file.

When I double-clicked on the My Computer icon, a list of the available drives appeared in the window.

When I double-clicked on the 3½ Floppy (A) icon, a list of the files on my disk appeared in the window.

When I double-clicked on the HTML file name that I modified, Internet Explorer opened with my HTML file and the *cheers.mid* sound file playing in the background. There were no visual changes to the Web page.

DISCUSSION

My Web page was made more interesting by following this easy process of adding music to the background.

If you are working at a computer that has a sound card, but no speakers, you can still hear the audio by plugging headphones into the computer.

EXAMPLE 12.4
Analytical Report

Date: April 29, 2004
To: Joseph King
From: Chris Lindblad
Subject: Purchase of a function generator for the control module tester

The module test area will be conducting the testing and troubleshooting of the SSD control module upon receiving the control module tester. The testing of this module will require the use of a function generator, which the test area does not currently have.

I have talked with numerous sales representatives and have discussed the purchase with other technicians in the test area. Basing my criteria on budget allowance, operating features, ease of operation, and future applications, I recommend the purchase of the Tektronix model AFG 5101 function generator.

TABLE 1
Cost of Function Generator, Options, and Accessories

Item	Tektronix AFG 5101	Philip PM 5192
Function generator	$3695	$4050
Options	350	425
Accessories	55	45
Total	4100	4520

TEKTRONIX IS WITHIN THE BUDGET

Currently the budget allows up to $6000 for the purchase of a function generator for the control module tester. As you can see from Table 1, both function generators are priced below the allowed budget. Not reflected on the total purchase price is a 10% discount the company currently receives on the purchase of electronic test equipment from Northern States Electronics Inc., the regional distributor of Tektronix Inc. With this discount included, the purchase price of the Tektronix model would drop to a total of $3690.

TEKTRONIX HAS BETTER OPERATING FEATURES

The Tektronix model AFG 5101 function generator has the ability to produce the required 10-MHz clock sine wave along with four other signal wave forms in a frequency range from .012 to 20 MHz. The Philips model

EXAMPLE 12.4
(continued)

PM 5192 function generator has the ability to produce the required clock signal and four other signal wave forms but only in the range of .1 to 20 MHz. The Tektronix model also has the feature of changeable pods, which can be quickly replaced if the unit should fail, whereas the Philips model would have to be returned to a service center for repair, which would result in downtime on the tester.

TEKTRONIX HAS BETTER OPERATIONAL SUPPORT

Both function generators are relatively easy to operate and are fully programmable. Both allow for the programming of selected wave forms, eliminating the need to lead information into the function generator before each test is run. A Tektronix representative will present a one-day training session to the module test technicians and will be available by phone for any further questions. The Philips model is accompanied by a manual and a 20-minute training video.

TEKTRONIX WILL UPGRADE EASIER

With the future module designs that will be coming into the test area and the faster speeds in which they will operate, the Tektronix model AFG 5101 has a larger operating frequency range, and the changeable pod feature will allow it to be upgraded for possible future uses. The Philips model has a lower frequency range and cannot be upgraded.

If you require any further information or documentation on my recommendation, please contact me at the module test department.

EXAMPLE 12.5
Memo Recommendation

July 17, 2004
To: Marcus Hammerle
From: John Furlano
Subject: Recommendation of tooling schedule

This letter is a followup of our discussion pertaining to the Storage Cover tooling schedule, which we discussed briefly during your visit at MPD on Thursday, June 27.

There are three main options available to expedite the pilot run date from October 21 up to the week of October 14.

1. Postpone the tool chroming until after the pilot run.

2. Postpone any major tool modifications until after the pilot run.

3. Expedite the tool building.

I believe that option 1 is the best choice. There will not be any additional costs for this option, and quality parts will still be produced for the pilot run. Option 2 may not be a reliable option because we cannot judge until after sampling what modifications may be necessary. Option 3 will carry additional cost due to overtime labor.

I am also optimistic, yet concerned, about the September 9 sample date (two samples at your facility, hand drilled and bonded, no paint). My concern is with delays through customs for shipping parts from the tool shop in Canada to the United States for assembly and back to Canada.

We are taking every step possible to stay on schedule with the Draft #3 tooling schedule, which you have a copy of. The enclosed tooling schedule (Draft #4) shows the projected pilot run date if option 1 above is employed. I welcome your comments or suggestions on any of the above issues. Thank you.

enc: tooling schedule draft #4

■ EXERCISES

1. Create an objective/summary introduction for the Iconglow report on pages 294–295.

2. Create a different introduction for the analytical report on purchasing a function generator on pages 312–313.

3. Because introductions imply a lot about the relationship of the writer to the reader, analyze the introductions of the reports in Examples 12.1–12.3 to determine what you can about the audience-writer relationship. How is that relationship affected when you change the introduction as you did in Exercise 2?

4. Write a methodology statement that explains how you recently went about solving some problem or discovered some information. When you have finished, construct a visual aid that shows the results of your actions. Compare these statements and visuals in groups of two to three.

5. Write the introduction for the material you wrote in Exercise 4.

6. Write the discussion section for the material you wrote in Exercise 4.

7. In groups of three or four, analyze the sections of the analytical report on purchasing a function generator on pages 312–313. How is the introduction related to the discussion? Do you feel that you know everything you need to know after reading the first few paragraphs? What does the discussion section add to the report?

8. In groups of three, read the introduction of each person's paper from one of the Writing Assignments below. Decide whether to maintain the current arrangement; if not, propose another.

9. Read the introduction and body of another student's paper from one of the Writing Assignments below. Does the discussion really present all the material needed to support the introduction? Are the visual aids effective? Is the format effective?

10. a. In groups of two or three, decide on a question that you will find the answer to. A good example is how to use some aspect of E-mail, the library, or the Web. Before the next class, find the answer. In class, write an IMRD that presents your answer.

I = question you wanted to answer and goal of this paper
M = relevant actions you took to find the answer
R = the actual answer
D = the implications of the answer for yourself or other people with your level of knowledge and interest

b. In groups of two or three, read each other's IMRD reports. Answer these questions:

Do you know the question that had to be answered?

Could you perform the actions or steps given to arrive at the answer?

Is the answer clear?

Is the discussion helpful or irrelevant?

---

11. In groups of two or three, compare the differences in Example 11.2 (p. 278) and Example 12.3 (p. 310). Focus on differences in tone and in presentation of the actions. Report to the class which document you prefer to read and why. What principles would affect your choice to write an IMRD or a set of instructions?

▨ WRITING ASSIGNMENTS

1. Write an informal report in which you use a table or graph to explain a problem and its solution to your manager. Select a problem from your area of professional interest—for example, a problem you solved (or saw someone else solve) on a job. Consider topics such as pilferage of towels in a hotel, difficulties in manufacturing a machine part, a sales decline in a store at a mall, difficulties with a measuring device in a lab, or problems in the shipping department of a furniture company. Use at least one visual aid.

---

2. Write an IMRD report in which you explain a topic you have investigated. The report could be a lab report or a report of any investigation. For instance, you could compare the fastest way to reproduce a paper, by scanning or retyping, or give the results of a session in which you learned something about navigating on the Internet, or present the results of an interview you conducted about any worthwhile concern at your school or business. Your instructor may combine this assignment with Writing Assignment 3.

---

3. Bring a draft of the IMRD you are writing to class. In groups of two or three, evaluate these concerns:
a. Is the basic research question clear?
b. Does the method make you feel like a professional is reporting?
c. Could you replicate the actions? Could other people?

d. Does only method—and not results—appear in the method section?
e. Is the method statement written like instructions or a process description? Which is best for this situation?
f. Are the results clear? Are they a clear answer to the original question?
g. Does every topic mentioned in the discussion section have a clear basis of fact in the methods or results section?
h. Is the significance the writer points out useful?
i. Does the visual aid help you with the methods or result section? Would it help other people?
j. Is the tone all right? Or is it too dry? too chatty? too technical?
k. Does the formatting of the report make it easy to read?

4. Rewrite the IMRD from Writing Assignment 2 from a completely different framework—for instance, a coach explaining the subject to a high school team. After you complete the new IMRD, in groups of three or four, discuss the difference "author identity" makes and create questions to tell writers how to choose an identity.

5. Convert your IMRD report from Writing Assignment 2 into an article for a newsletter.

6. Convert your IMRD report from Writing Assignment 2 into a set of instructions. After you complete the instructions, in groups of three or four, construct a list of the differences between the two, especially the method statement. Alternate: In groups of three or four, construct a set of guidelines for when to use instructions and when to use IMRD. Hand this list in to your instructor.

7. Write an outline report in which you summarize a long report. Depending on your instructor's requirements, use a report you have already written or one you are writing in this class.

8. Write a learning report for the writing assignment you just completed. See Chapter 5, Writing Assignment 7, page 123, for details of the assignment.

■ WEB EXERCISE

Write an IMRD that explains a research project on the effectiveness of a search strategy on the Web. Choose any set of three words (e.g., plastic + biodegradable + packaging). Choose any major search engine (Yahoo, Alta Vista). Using the "advanced" or "custom" search mode, type in your keywords in three sequences—plastic + biodegradable + packaging, packaging

+ plastic + biodegradable, biodegradable + packaging + plastic. Investigate the first three sites for each search. In the IMRD, explain your method and results and discuss the effectiveness of the strategy and of the search engine for this kind of topic.

Large group alternative: Divide the class into groups of four. All members of the class agree to use the same keywords, but each group will use a different search engine. After the individual searches are completed, have each group compile a report in which they present their results to the class orally, via e-mail, or on the Web.

■ WORKS CITED

General Motors. *Writing Style Guide.* Rev. ed. GM1620. By Lawrence H. Freeman and Terry R. Bacon. Warren, MI: Author, 1991.

Keppler, Herbert. "SLR: Going Where No Macro Has Dared to Go Before." *Popular Photography.* August 1997.

E-mail requires you to think a bit differently about your writing. Along with voice mail, answering machines, and faxes, E-mail is gradually creating a niche as a common method of interpersonal communication, replacing the letter and the phone call.

Several "nonstandard" characteristics of E-mail writing seem clear. When people use it, they use it often, they type messages fast, and they often make spelling and grammatical mistakes. Computer writing seems to encourage a kind of free writing, which many people find very attractive, but this same free writing can lead to "mind dumps"—long, rambling passages whose point is not clear.

Here are a few tips that will help you write effective, clear E-mail messages.

Write a Clear Subject Line. In a subject line, state content—"Response to your 7-25 budget request." Do not use vague lines like "Response." Remember that many people receive 20 or more messages a day. These messages are often displayed in a directory that lists the sender's name, the date, and the subject. Many readers choose to read or delete only on the basis of the subject line, because they can't possibly take the time to respond to so many memos. Your message will get through more easily if the subject line connects with the reader's needs.

Establish the Context. Repeat questions or key phrases. Briefly explain why you are writing, then go on with your message. If a person has sent out 20 messages the day before, he or she might not easily remember exactly what was sent to you. Offer help. Remember that you are not in a dialogue in which the other person can respond instantaneously to your statements, so avoid the temptation to use one-line speeches. For instance, don't just write one word—"NO"—but tell the person what topic you are saying no to.

Remember to Paragraph. E-mail has a kind of hypnotic quality that encourages people to write as if they were speaking. And, of course, in speech there are no obvious paragraphs. However, remember that E-mail is text that a person reads, so paragraph into manageable chunks. Use keywords at the beginning of units in order to establish the context of the following sentence or paragraph.

Signal the End. Because E-mail exists in screen after screen and because there is no obvious end to the screen progression, unlike a paper

319

where you always know when you are on the last page, signal the end. An easy way is to type your name, with or without a closing. But you could also use the words "the end" or a line of asterisks.

Avoid Mind Dumps.   The point of E-mail is to satisfy the reader's needs in a short, fast way. Do not ramble. Plan for a moment before you start to write. If you have "on-line fear," the same strange emotional response that often makes people give awkward rambling messages on the answering machine, type your message first on the word processing program that you know well, in a situation where you do not have to concern yourself with tying up phone lines. Edit in the word processor, then upload and send (again, you can see the value of knowing the capabilities of your system).

Don't Type in All Caps.   The lack of variation in letter size makes the message much harder to grasp.

Get Permission to Publish.   E-mail is the intellectual property of its creator. Do not publish an E-mail message unless the creator gives you permission.

Be Prudent.   Remember that there is little security on most systems, so decide whether you want to send a personal or sensitive message by E-mail.

Sample Message. Note the effective use of the subject line (Uses for E-mail), the salutation (Dan), and closing (Well got to go. Tim).

```
From:  IN%"71004.2799@CompuServe.COM" "Tim Riordan"
To:    IN%"driordan@UWSTOUT.EDU" "Dan Riordan"
CC:
Subj: Uses for E-mail
Dan,
    About E-mail and I don't feel very prosaic tonite.
The most important things I look for are title,
sender. Actually if they can get the whole message in
the title that is great. When I get telephone mes-
sages, I have them put the name and the number on the
title line, then I know I don't even have to open up
the message because that is all there is—a note to
call this person back.
    I want short messages at work. I really don't like
long messages—probably the best message fits on a sin-
gle screen. I don't much care about grammar, though I
admit I do a little. I send bad grammar particularly
bad capitals because I hate to capitalize.
    The effects are that you can have direct access to
people, but just like our E-mail, I can send when I
want and you can receive when you want. Also I can send
to many people at one time. And then get replies. I
think it does make people feel part of the group and
makes for a good touch even though it is indirect.
Well got to go. Tim*
```

*Used by permission of Tim Riordan.

13 Developing Web Sites

CHAPTER CONTENTS

Chapter 13
IN A NUTSHELL

Web sites and Web documents are important methods of conveying information. Creating effective Web sites requires careful planning, drafting, and testing.

To plan effectively, you need to consider your audience. Determine who they are. Of course, on the Web they could be anyone in the world, but that's too broad. A helpful way to create a sense of your audience is to define a role for them, as if they were actors in your "Web play." Are they customers? students? curiosity surfers?

In addition to considering your audience, you need to plan a flow chart and a template. The flow chart is a device that indicates how you will link your material together. For instance, if you have four files and if you want your reader to link from any one to any other one, your flow chart would look like Figure 1. Each line is a link and each box is a Web page.

Your template is a design of your site's look. It shows how you will place various kinds of information (title,

FIGURE 1
Sample Flow Chart

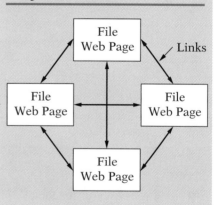

Chapter 13
IN A NUTSHELL (continued)
text, links, visuals) so that your reader can easily grasp the sense of your site.

Web sites create special concerns for writing. Good Web text is scannable (easy to find key ideas), correct (no spelling, grammar mistakes), and consistent (all items treated in a similar fashion).

Visuals must be legible, but not so large that they take up most of the screen or take a long time to load.

Web sites must be tested to make sure links work, visuals appear, and the site displays the same way in various browsers.

The Web is one of the primary means of communication today. Millions of people use it every day to find information, to purchase items, and to entertain themselves. Because it is so easy to use, the Web has changed the method of disseminating information. In the past, vital information (of whatever kind—from research data to sale items) was printed on paper (as a report or a catalog, for instance) and sent to intended audiences. Now the vital information is "posted," and the intended audience must search for it. Universities, corporations, organizations of all types, and private individuals all maintain large Web sites which make information available to viewers.

Because of this shift, technical communicators must know how to create documents that are both clear and easy to read on screen. Creating such documents requires the same general process of planning, drafting, and finishing as in creating any document, but with special considerations for the on-line situation.

This chapter covers basic Web concepts, planning, drafting, and testing Web documents. Examples show Web reports and Web instructions.

BASIC WEB CONCEPTS

Three basic concepts that will help you create effective Web sites and documents for readers are hierarchy, web structure, and reader freedom.

Hierarchy

Hierarchy is the structure of the contents of a document. All Web sites and Web documents have a hierarchy; that is, levels of information. The highest level is the *home page*, a term that can apply either to an entire site or to a document. Lower levels are called *nodes*; the paths among the nodes are the *links*.

Figure 13.1 shows three levels in the hierarchy, each giving more detail. Writing is the most general category. *Technical writing* and *fiction* are the two subcategories of writing. Reports and novels are subdivisions, respectively, of their types of writing. More levels could be added. For instance, reports could be broken down into feasibility reports and proposals.

FIGURE 13.1
Hierarchy

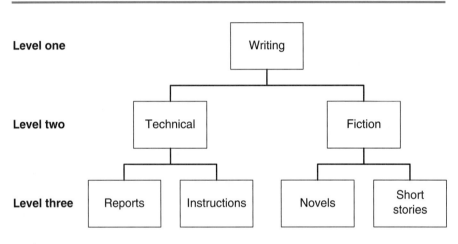

Web Structure

"Web structure" means that the document contains hyperlinks (or "links") that allow readers to structure their own reading sequence. When the reader clicks the cursor on a link, the browser opens the screen indicated by the link. This feature allows readers to move to new topics quickly and in any order. This arrangement is a radical departure in organizing strategy. The author gives the readers maximum freedom to choose the order in which they will view the site or read the document.

To see the difference between traditional and Web structures, consider these two examples. If a document has seven sections and a traditional (or "linear") structure, then a reader will progress through the sections as shown in Figure 13.2. But if the same seven sections have a Web structure, then they would look like Figure 13.3, with each line a link. Once readers arrive at the start, or home, screen, they may read the document in any order they please.

The two Web home pages in Figures 13.4 and 13.5 show two ways that authors used Web structure. Both have a lengthy report, which they want the readers to be able to read without having to scroll through various screens. Maertens (Figure 13.4) has divided the report into five linkable sections. The home page provides an index and brief abstract of each sec-

FIGURE 13.2
Linear Structure

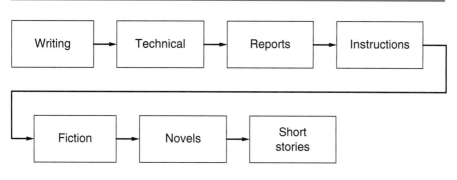

FIGURE 13.3
Web Structure

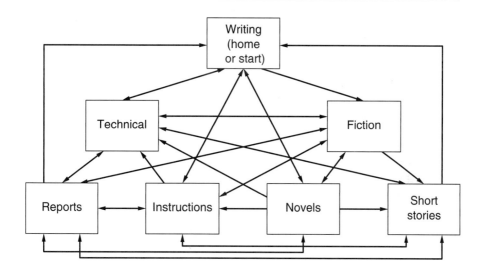

tion. The reader can choose any section and link to it. Currier (Figure 13.5) has provided "target links" which move the screen to that part of the document without scrolling.

To "think Web" is a radical departure in organizing strategy. You can give readers maximum freedom to choose in what order they read your document.

Reader Freedom

Reader freedom is the degree to which the reader of the Web site can easily select the order in which he or she will read sections of a document.

FIGURE 13.4
Linked Section Report

Tips for Making a Good Web Site

The following report contains some ideas which I feel are important to consider if one is going to produce a good web site. These are just some of the ideas I have learned through my Technical Writing class. Remember, you are free to do whatever you want, but the following ideas may be helpful in achieving your goal.

Go to

- <u>Planning is key</u>-Planning is essential in order for you to produce a good..........
- <u>Establishing a Purpose for your Web Site</u>-Before you embark on this voyage..........
- <u>Implementing Links in your Web Site</u>-In order to make your site easy to use..........
- <u>Handling visuals and text</u>-These seem to spice up your web site, but..........
- <u>Interactive Web Site</u>-People do not just want to see a web page, they want to..........

Return to

- <u>Matt Maertens Homepage</u>
- <u>Technical Writing Index Page</u>
- <u>English Department Student Projects Page</u>

Let me know what you think! e-mail me <u>maertensm@uwstout.edu</u>

Whereas hierarchy imposes control on the reader's freedom, Web structure provides freedom. The Web author must find a way to combine the two. Figures 13.6 to 13.8 demonstrate how authors can use the two concepts to affect the way readers view the document or site.

In Figure 13.6, the reader starts at the home page and can progress only to one of the two level 2 nodes, and then to one of the level 3 nodes. To arrive at *reports,* the reader must click to *technical writing* and then to *reports.* To get to *instructions* from *reports,* the reader must first go back to *technical writing.* To get to novels from reports the reader must follow the path back to writing and then click forward to novels.

Figures 13.7 and 13.8 show progressively less control by the author and more control for the reader. In the hierarchy shown in Figure 13.7, the reader can move directly from *reports* to *instructions* without clicking back to *technical writing.* In the hierarchy shown in Figure 13.8, the reader can move to any document from any other document. A reader could click from *reports* to *fiction* and then to *instructions.*

The Maertens model in Figure 13.4 appears to have a tightly controlled hierarchy, as shown in Figure 13.9. But if he would supply links between each section, then the document would have a hierarchy of little control and great reader freedom, as in Figure 13.10.

FIGURE 13.5
Target Link Strategy

How to Create a Great Web Page

HTML stands for Hyper Text Markup Language. This language allows the computer to read your document and makes it appear in web format. Once you get the hang of this computer language, the possibilities are endless. However, good quality writing and construction of your web site could determine how many people will stop and stay long enough to check out your site. The following areas are important to consider in order to create a great web site:

Before You Begin|Here Goes|Introduction|Chunks and Heads|Graphics

BEFORE YOU BEGIN
Before you start typing anything into the computer, sit down and plan out what you are going to do. Designing a web site is 90% planning and 10% actually work. Figure out the purpose of your web site. Things can get out of control fast, so knowing your boundaries is essential.

It is incredibly helpful to draw a map of your web site. When creating links, things can get confusing. Good links enable you to get in, through, and out of the document easily. Nobody likes to get trapped in a web page with no way out. Having a map of links in front of you can make linking your pages easier. You will save yourself a lot of time and hassle, if you work out what you are going to do before you do it.   **Top**

HERE GOES!
Now that you know what you are going to do, it is time to acquire the things necessary to get it done. You will need a computer, a simple word processing program, a list of html commands and what they do, and a browser. Type your information in a simple word processor, such as Simple Text, or save it in your present word processing program as a text file. You will need knowledge of HTML commands to convert your page into a language the computer can read. A browser allows you to open up your document on the web to see what it looks like.   **Top**

Introduction
An introduction is an important part of the web site. The introduction contains a lot of necessary information, such as, the reason for the site and why it would be of interest to the viewer. In the introduction, the purpose of the web site should be clearly stated. If the viewer doesn't know what the site is about or how it will benefit them, they are not going to stick around.   **Top**

FIGURE 13.5
(continued)

Chunks and Heads

People like information presented in small chunks. It is easier for them to digest. It also gives you a better chance of holding their attention. People don't have the desire or patience to read through a lot of unbroken text. It is also a good idea to use heads. They are also useful in breaking up the page. Heads inform the reader as to what each section is about, giving them the option of whether or not they want to read it.   Top

GRAPHICS

When incorporating graphics into your web page, there are several things to consider. Look out at how long it takes the graphic to load. If it takes too long, try to make the graphic smaller. If that doesn't help, you should cut it out. People don't like to wait very long for a graphic to load. Another thing to consider about graphics, is if they will appear when the document is loading or if the viewer will have to click on a graphic icon to bring up the picture. Either one is acceptable. It is up to the designer which way to go. The web can provide additional options for incorporating a graphic into you site.   Top

My Set of Instructions\How to Reply in Eudora

Nikki's Index\Technical Writing Home Page

Guidelines for Working with Web Structure

The two possibilities of rigid hierarchical organization and loose Web organization mean that the writer must choose to insert enough links to be flexible, but not so many that the reader is overwhelmed with choices.

FIGURE 13.6
Little Reader Freedom

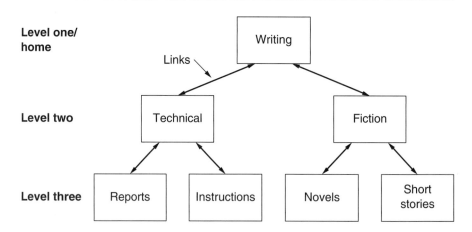

FIGURE 13.7
Moderate Freedom

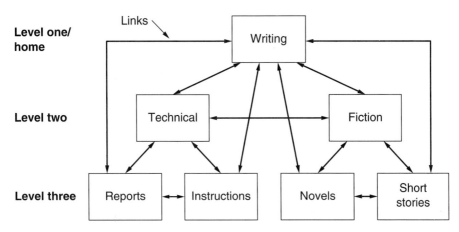

William Horton suggests that an effective strategy is to "layer" documents, "designing them so that they can serve different users for different purposes, each user getting the information needed for the task at hand" (178).

Horton suggests that each level of the hierarchy is a layer and that each layer provides more detailed information. Use this principle in these ways:

- In higher layers, put information that everyone needs. To learn about writing, everyone needs the definitions on the home page, but only a few readers need the concepts explained on the instructions page.

FIGURE 13.8
Absolute Freedom

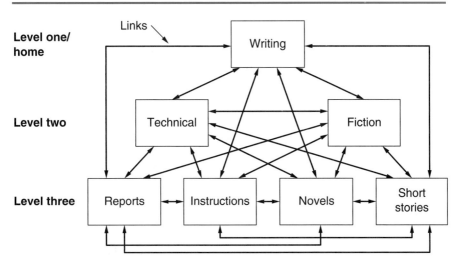

FIGURE 13.9
Controlled Hierarchy

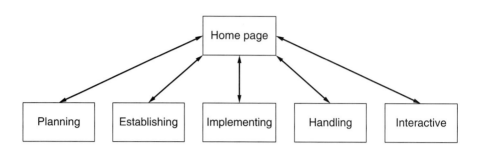

▨ Control reader's paths. Figure 13.6, for instance, indicates that readers have complete control in either of the two major categories, technical writing and fiction, but that accessing the material in the other category will require the reader to "start over." The author has assumed that readers in fiction will want to know more about that category, so it should be easy to get around in it. However, it is less likely that they would want to compare items in fiction with the items in technical writing, so the path to it is restricted.

PLANNING A WEB SITE OR WEB DOCUMENT

In the planning stage, consider these four aspects (based on Horton; December; Hunt; Wilkinson): decide your goal, analyze your audience, evaluate the questions the audience will ask, create a flow chart, and create a template.

FIGURE 13.10
Web Structure Allowing Reader Freedom

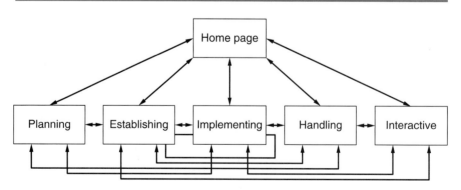

Decide Your Goal

Your site or document should have a "mission statement"—for instance, "To explain the purposes and services of the campus antique auto club." Make this statement as narrow and specific as possible. It will help you with the many other decisions that you will have to make.

Analyze Your Audience

Ask the standard questions: Who is the audience? How much do they know? What is their level of expertise? See Chapter 2 for more information on audience analysis.

Do not answer: Anyone who comes onto the Web. Such a broad answer will not allow you to make decisions. Focus these answers—they are people who are interested in antique cars, the university in general, or clubs in particular. They know a little or a lot; they will have experience or not. A Web site aimed at an audience of people who have restored antique cars is quite different from a Web site aimed at students who have some interest in old cars and wish to join a university group.

One helpful way to think about audience is to think about the site or document as a stage (Coney and Steehouder). Your audience member is a member of a cast and thus has a "role" in the site. For instance, the audience can assume the role of "antique car experts" or "students who want to join a club." Most audience members find it easy (because of their experience with TV ads) to adopt such a role if it is clear to them. If you understand the role you want your audience members to play, you will be able to make better decisions about how to present your site or document to them.

Evaluate the Questions the Audience Will Ask

Speculate on general questions: What is the purpose of the club? When does the club meet? What are the club activities? What antique cars does the club have? Can I learn about where to purchase an antique car? Can I learn how to restore an antique car? What are the bylaws of the club?

You can decide which of these questions you want to, or should, answer. Your audience decisions will help you. For instance, if you feel that only car buffs will look at the site, then there is no need to provide information on bylaws.

Create a Flow Chart of Your Site

A flow chart indicates the site's or document's nodes, their hierarchy, and the degree of freedom that the reader will have. The flow chart gives a visual map of your site, allowing you to control the creation of the links. It shows you how much control you will allow your audience, and because it is a blueprint of the site, it gives you a method to check whether you have inserted all your links. In the flow chart in Figure 13.11, the arrows indicate a link from one file to another, and the curved lines indicate escape links back to the home page from each of the files. Notice that this structure is much like the one shown in Figure 13.7 (p. 329). The reader has total control inside each section of the hierarchy, but must return at least to the second level in order to transfer to another category.

Follow these guidelines for degrees of control (Figure 13.11 illustrates all of these points):

■ Provide a link from the home page to all nodes.

■ Provide a link from the node to all subparts of the node.

■ Provide a link between nodes.

■ Provide short cut links from higher levels to key data at lower levels. Note the two lines that run from the home page to the items marked "K."

■ Provide short cut or "escape" links from all levels back to the home page. Escape links are shown by the lighter curved lines in Figure 13.11.

■ Provide enough links for multiple paths. Unless you have a compelling reason to prevent random navigation, readers should be able to read the site and the documents in it in any order. Use links to create paths that will allow this type of reader freedom.

Create a Template

Your site or document must have a consistent visual logic. Select a background color, a font (but be aware that individual users can change the font that appears on their screen), and a consistent spot to place titles, introductions, lists, return links, and E-mail links. The information on each screen will change, but the way it is presented will remain the same.

The easiest way to create a template is to make a sample page and keep a record of each of your decisions. As you make the template, include all of these items:

■ Title

■ Introductory text

■ List of nodes (actually a table of contents for the document or site)

■ Short cut links

■ Escape links

■ Color/font/size of heading

FIGURE 13.11
Full Flow Chart of a Web Site

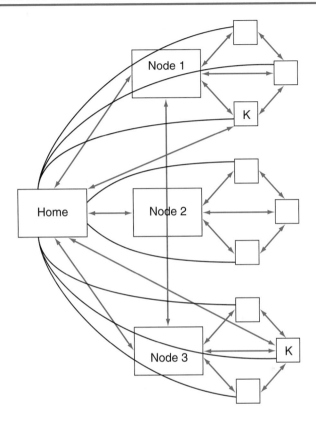

- Color/design of background
- Color/font/size of text
- Placement of blocks of similar types of text

Consider, for instance, Figures 13.12 and 13.13, pages from the Geology node of the Arches National Park Web site. Each page looks the same. Similar elements appear in the same position, color, and font. Notice all of the following:

1. Title of the section—flush left, sans serif font, rule beneath
2. Links to other nodes—left-hand column, sans serif font
3. Title of the page—flush left in right-hand column, sans serif font, black
4. Subheads—flush left in right-hand column, sans serif font, green
5. Text—block paragraphs, double-space between paragraphs, serif font

6. Short cut links—2 lines below text, sans serif font
7. Privacy/author information—3 lines at bottom left, sans serif font
8. Two-column format
9. Visually separated elements. Note that white space clearly separates the various elements of the page. Each element is said to be "grouped," a visually effective method of helping the reader grasp the information.

DRAFTING

Creating a Web site or document takes a number of drafts. Creating clear content, effective structures for reader freedom, and accessible pages seldom happens in one draft. As you create your site or document, orient your reader, write in a scannable style, establish credibility, and use visuals effectively (Spyridakis; Nielson; Williams).

Orient Your Reader

As readers surf through Web sites and documents, they lose track of where they are. This disorientation causes confusion and diminishes the ability to draw meaning from a page. Three key methods to orient the reader are shown in Figures 13.12 and 13.13:

- Provide an informative title at the top of the page.
- Provide an introductory sentence that either announces or defines the topic under discussion.
- Repeat key information at consistent spots on the page.

Write in a Scannable Style

A scannable style is one that presents information by highlighting key terms and concepts and placing them first in any sequence. Because reading from a screen is a physically difficult task, a scannable style often makes text easier to read (Nielson). A number of strategies will help you make the page scannable.

- Use chunks. Create smaller chunks; use more short paragraphs. Notice the short paragraphs in Figures 13.12 and 13.13.
- Use headings. Place heads throughout the text to help readers grasp the overall structure. Heads function as an "in-text" outline, which helps readers orient themselves (see Figure 13.12).
- Use bulleted lists. Notice the "Go To" list in Figure 1 of "Focus on HTML" (p. 358). It is much easier to read than this linear version: Go To: Planning Is Key; Establishing a Purpose for Your Web Site;

FIGURE 13.12
Arches National Park Geology Introduction Home Page

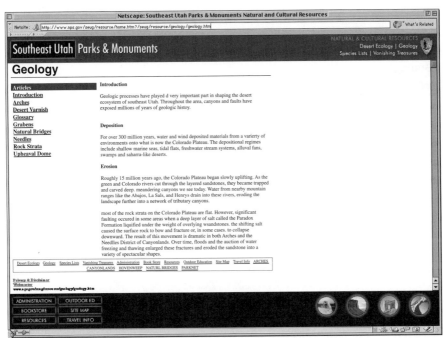

See Web page at *http://www.nps.gov/seug/resource/home.htm.*

Implementing Links in Your Web Site; Handling Visuals in Texts; Interactive Web Site.

▨ Add abstracts after the link. If the word in the link is not self-evident, add a brief description. For instance,

The steps you need to build a better telescope.   Instructions

▨ Make a link-title connection. Use a word in the link that repeats a word in the title of the section where the reader will arrive. If the link is *Planning,* the title of the page that appears should include *Planning.*

▨ Use one idea per paragraph. Notice the two paragraphs under "Erosion" in Figure 13.12. Each deals with only one idea: the creation of canyons and the creation of spectacular shapes.

▨ Use the inverted pyramid style. The term *inverted pyramid* is a synonym for top-down. Put the key idea of the paragraph first, and then give supporting detail. Notice in the "concise" example below that the first sentence gives the main idea ("prepares students") and

FIGURE 13.13
Arches National Park Desert Varnish Web Page

See Web page at *http://www.nps.gov/seug/resource/home.htm*.

the rest of the paragraph supplies details on how the program actually prepares students.

■ Use introductions that tell the purpose of the screen, especially if it is a node screen. See Figure 1 of "Focus on HTML" (p. 358) or Figures 13.12 and 13.13.

■ Write concisely. Because reading is difficult on a screen, excess wording simply compounds the difficulty. Jakob Nielson suggests that writing can be promotional (overblown, to be avoided), concise, or scannable. Writers should try for the latter two.

PROMOTIONAL

This fun program leads young scholars into the exciting world of technical communication. Scholars have the unprecedented opportunity to study multimedia in all the state-of-the-art software and hardware. They can also, in a particularly innovative aspect, develop an Applied Field which will allow them to interact with specialists in other areas. And they can, as students in many majors cannot, take a course that readies them to enter the challenging world of work.

CONCISE

This program prepares students for the exciting world of Technical Communication. The program features state-of-the-art multimedia software and hardware; Applied Fields which develop expertise in a specialty; and a professional development course which facilitates beginning a career.

SCANNABLE

Three key features of the new technical communication programs are

- State-of-the-art multimedia hardware and software.
- Applied Fields to develop specialized expertise.
- Professional development to facilitate finding a job.

Establish Credibility

Because anyone can post anything on a Web site, readers look for, and are reassured by, some proof of credibility (Spyridakis; Nielson; Coney). Some features that enhance a site's credibility are

- Information about the author, including name, E-mail address, and organizational affiliation. A Web site on effective dieting is more credible if the author is a person with an E-mail address who is an associate professor in a dietetics department at a university.
- The date that the site was posted or updated.
- A statement about privacy. Note the *Privacy & Disclaimer* link in Figure 13.12.
- No typos or spelling or grammar mistakes. These mistakes seem even more glaring on the Web. If all the world can see your material, shouldn't you care enough to get it correct?
- Links to other sites. These links show that the authors know the field. Be careful of such links because they lead viewers off your site. Careful Web authors often add a statement near an "off-site" link, telling the readers that they are about to leave the site and reminding them to use the Back button or Go menu to return. Check such links regularly to make sure that they work.
- High-quality graphics. The ability to present quality graphics shows that the writer knows how to use software and hardware, as well as that the writer wants to make a clear contact with the reader. The visual in Figure 13.13 is very clear, making the reader confident that the author has a high level of expertise.

Use Visuals Effectively

Visual aids in a Web document perform all the same functions as in a paper document (see Chapter 8). Visuals summarize data, allow readers to explore data, provide a different conceptual entry point into a report, and engage expectations. Used well, visuals enhance Web pages; but used poorly, the visuals are annoying. Visual aids must be sized correctly and interact with the text (Horton).

Correct size can be electronic or physical size or both. Electronic size is the number of kilobytes (K) that the visual uses. The larger the K, the slower the image loads. A site with several large-K (above 150K) color images will take a long time to load on a 56K modem.

Follow these guidelines to control the electronic size of your visuals:

- Use fewer visuals.
- Use a software program to compress visuals to reduce their electronic size.
- Use a "thumbnail" linked to a larger version (see Figure 13.14).

Physical size is the amount of pixels occupied on the screen. The average screen is 15 inches with 480 × 640 pixels. If the visual aid occupies most of that pixel space, there is nothing left for text (see Figure 13.15).

Learn to manipulate image size. All programs that help you produce images (such as Photoshop) allow you to alter dimensions. Often, if you

FIGURE 13.14
Use of Thumbnails

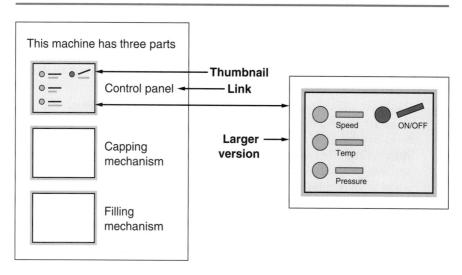

FIGURE 13.15
Effective Sizes of Visuals on Screen

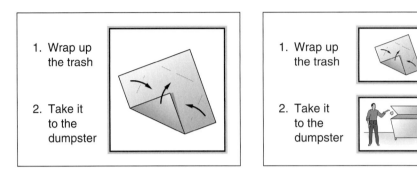

make an image smaller, you make it more illegible. If you capture the image of a screen, for instance, and then reduce it to one-fourth its original size, the text on the screen will probably be illegible. To fix this problem, Web authors "resample" the image, a process that restores legibility. Consult the help menu or manuals of programs like Photoshop or Front Page to learn how to resample.

Notice Figures 1 and 2 in "Focus on HTML" (pp. 358–359). The image of the cabin, as scanned in, originally was approximately four times as large as it is on screen. Notice in Figure 1 that the writer has sized the image by inserting *width* and *height* commands into the code.

Follow these guidelines for the best presentation of physical size:

- If the text and visual complement each other (as in a step in a set of instructions), use no more than half the screen width for the visual.
- If you reduce a visual in size, resample it.
- Use visuals on screen to clarify your message for your readers.

TESTING

Your Web document must be usable. Readers must be able to navigate the site easily and access the information they need. In order to ensure easy navigation and access, you must test your document. Either perform the test yourself or have another person do it. Testing consists of checking for basic editing, audience effectiveness, consistency, navigation, the electronic environment, and clarity.

Basic Editing

Web documents include large amounts of text that must be presented with the same exactness as text in a paper document. If the editing details are handled effectively, the credibility of the site is increased.

Check your site for stylistic elements.

▪ Spelling
▪ Fragments, run-ons, comma splices
▪ Overuse of *there are, this*
▪ Weak pronoun reference
▪ Scannable presentation, including use of the inverted pyramid style

Audience Effectiveness

Your site must put the audience into a role. Checking for audience role is highly subjective.

▪ Is it apparent what role the audience should assume, either from direct comments or from clear implications in the way the audience is addressed?
▪ Do all parts of the site help the audience assume that role?

Consistency

Readers find sites easier to navigate and access if all items are handled consistently (Pearrow). The document has many text features that should be repeated consistently in order to establish visual logic. These features include font, font size, color, placement on the screen, and treatment (bold, italics, all caps). In addition, a document has many visual features that must remain consistent in order to establish the visual logic. These features include size and placement on the screen.

Check these textual items for font, font size, color, placement on the screen, and treatment:

▪ Titles
▪ Headings
▪ Captions for figures
▪ Body text
▪ Lists
▪ Links

Check these visual items for size and placement on the screen:

▪ Clip art
▪ Photographs

■ Tables and graphs

■ Screen captures

Navigation

To check for navigation is to investigate two areas: whether all the links work and whether the path through the material makes the material accessible. To check whether all the links work is easy. Simply try each link. Make note of any that are "broken"; that is, do not lead to any document. To determine if the path through the material makes the material accessible is more subjective. An effective way to investigate accessibility is to ask questions of yourself or your tester (Pearrow):

■ Starting at the home page, can you find information X quickly?

■ From any point in the site or document can you easily return to the home page or top?

■ Does the home page give the reader an overview of the purpose and contents of the site or document?

■ Does the title of any page repeat the wording of the link that led to it?

■ At any time is the user annoyed? For instance, does a visual take a long time to open?

The Electronic Environment

The electronic environment of your site or document is the way in which it interacts with the reader's viewing equipment—modem, computer, and browser software. The basic guideline is that all your material should appear on screen quickly with the design you gave it.

Check these electronic aspects:

■ How long does the site or document take to load? Ten seconds appears to be the time readers wait before they get annoyed. Answer this question by using different access methods. Load the site over a 56K modem and over a T1 line. The differences are often large. Some programs (such as Front Page) provide a menu item that gives this information.

■ Does the browser used affect whether the features appear? The two major browsers are Internet Explorer and Netscape Communicator. In most cases, a site will appear exactly the same regardless of which browser the viewer uses. But not in all cases. For various program coding reasons, more sophisticated elements such as tables, frames, and videos, often work in one browser but not in the other. Checking a site with both browsers will ensure that readers see the items that you intended in the manner in which you intended.

If you must include features that only one browser supports, place a note to that effect in your text ("Use Internet Explorer in order to view all the features of this site.").

Clarity

The site or document must appear clearly on the screen. A viewer must be able to read all the elements.

To check for clarity, answer the following questions:

- Do all the visual aids appear? If not, edit the Web document to make sure that they do.
- Can all the text be read? Sometimes, inexperienced Web authors use color combinations that make text hard to read (black text on a blue background, yellow text on a white background). Revise the color (see "Focus on Color," pp. 169–178).
- Are the visual aids clear? If visual aids are fuzzy or illegible, edit them in a software program (such as Photoshop) that allows you to resample the image.

▪ WORKSHEET FOR PLANNING A WEB SITE OR DOCUMENT

❑ *Identify the audience and the role they will play.*
❑ *Identify questions the audience will have about the content.*
❑ *Identify probable nodes for the site or document.*
❑ *Create a flow chart that indicates hierarchy and paths.*
❑ *Plan paths that give readers the freedom they need.*
❑ *Plan features of site (both screen and text items) that will facilitate the way readers find the information that they need.*
❑ *Create a screen template that groups similar information into distinct locations, including placement of visual aids.*
❑ *Choose font and color for heads and text.*
❑ *Determine which visual aids you need to convey your information.*
❑ *Choose a neutral background (light blues are good).*
❑ *Write text in manageable chunks.*

■ WORKSHEET FOR EVALUATING A WEB SITE

Evaluation of Web Sites

Author's Name   Evaluator's Name

HOME PAGE	Yes	No
Is there a clear title?	___	___
Is there a helpful introduction that tells you the purpose and what to expect in the site?	___	___
Is the home page only one screen long?	___	___
Are the links easy to find?	___	___
Is it clear what will happen when you click a link?	___	___
Does every link work?	___	___
Is there a link to each node?	___	___
Is the page not garish?	___	___
Did the site load quickly?	___	___
DOCUMENTS		
Did the title of the document repeat the wording of the link that led to it?	___	___
Does every link work?	___	___
Do all the images load?	___	___
Are all visual elements handled consistently (size, placement, borders)?	___	___
Are all text items handled consistently (titles, heads, captions, body text, etc.)?	___	___
Is the layout consistent with other documents in the site?	___	___
Can you read the print?	___	___
Can you read the images?	___	___
Does any spot need a visual? (If yes, name it:)	___	___
Did you get "lost" navigating the document?	___	___

EXAMPLES

In this section are the report sections from the home page presented in Figure 13.4, another informational Web report, and two sets of instructions. Note that Example 13.3 contains links to many other sections that are lower in the report's hierarchy. Those sections are not reproduced here.

EXAMPLE 13.1
Report Sections from Home Page

PLANNING IS THE KEY TO SUCCESS

Much like any other project that you may tackle, creating a good Web site involves a little bit of planning. Many things have to be taken into account when you begin writing your own Web page.

The following things should be considered:

1. Appearance of your site
2. Actual size of your site
3. Links to and from your site
4. Visuals
5. Your audience
6. Web design

Go to other sections of this report:

Establishing a Purpose—Before you embark on this voyage
Implementing Links—In order to make your site easy to use . . .
Handling Visuals and Text—These seem to spice up your Web site, but . . .
Interactive Web Site—People do not just want to see a Web page, they want to . . .

ESTABLISHING A PURPOSE FOR YOUR WEB SITE

Before you decide what you are going to put up on your Web page, it is important that you define what purpose your Web site intends to serve. A lot of people have a Web page just for the sake of having one. Their home page is just kind of there for others to look at. There is no way to interact with the Web page. Web pages should have the purpose clearly stated on them, so the reader knows what they are getting into.

Go to other sections of this report:

Planning Is the Key—Planning is essential in order for you to . . .
Implementing Links—In order to make your site easy to use . . .
Handling Visuals and Text—These seem to spice up your Web site, but . . .
Interactive Web Site—People do not just want to see a Web page, they want to . . .

IMPLEMENTING LINKS INTO YOUR WEB PAGE

People need to be able to navigate their way around your Web site once they are in it. They should be able to move back, forward, and to other sites if they want to. The more links a Web page has, the more freedom the reader has to pick and choose whatever it is he or she wants to read.

EXAMPLE 13.1
(continued)

One of the biggest complaints I've heard from Web users is the fact that they often feel "trapped" inside of Web pages, with no way out except to use the "Back" key. However, one must decide carefully the number of links to include, and which ones to exclude as well.

Go to other sections of this report:

Planning Is the Key—Planning is essential in order for you to . . .
Establishing a Purpose—Before you embark on this voyage
Handling Visuals and Text—These seem to spice up your Web site, but . . .
Interactive Web Site—People do not just want to see a Web page, they want to . . .

HANDLING VISUALS AND TEXT

Much like the traditional medium of written communication, Web pages, too, benefit from visual aids. Visuals tend to catch the eye of the reader and take the place of text as well. However, when placing visuals on the Web, they must be planned just as carefully as they are when they are placed on paper. The same technical writing rules apply to visuals on the Web.

Text needs to be thought about, too. Especially on the Web, short "chunks" are necessary to keep the reader's interest. Because a computer screen seems to be smaller than what we would actually see on a regular sheet of paper, readers seemed to be turned off by large blocks of text on the Web. They are forced to keep scrolling down in order to get everything. Also, the bolding of heads and increasing their font sizes makes these items dominant over all other text, as they should be.

Go to other sections of this report:

Planning Is the Key—Planning is essential in order for you to . . .
Establishing a Purpose—Before you embark on this voyage
Implementing Links—In order to make your site easy to use . . .
Interactive Web Site—People do not just want to see a Web page, they want to . . .

INTERACTIVE WEB SITES

It is nice to have a Web page that allows readers to interact with the Web page somehow. Some examples of this may include a Web page that allows readers to E-mail the authors with questions or comments. Including your E-mail address on your Web page allows others to give you some input and constructive criticism about your Web site.

EXAMPLE 13.1
(continued)

Another way a Web page could be interactive is through links that allow you to order something or inquire about something. Many companies today have their catalogs on the Web, and people can order things directly from the Internet. It is amazing what kind of feedback you can receive, or how your sales can increase, if you make your Web site interactive.

Go to other sections of this report:

Planning Is the Key—Planning is essential in order for you to . . .
Establishing a Purpose—Before you embark on this voyage
Implementing Links—In order to make your site easy to use . . .
Handling Visuals and Text—These seem to spice up your Web site, but . . .

EXAMPLE 13.2
Informational Web Report

IMRD: RESEARCH REPORT

Introduction

With the advanced use of the electronic job-search, it is becoming difficult to ignore the increasingly important role of the on-line résumé. Since computers are becoming increasingly user-friendly, even those with relatively little computer experience are becoming familiar with this technique. One eminent problem, however, is the question of how users can get the information they need to the end they desire. This page will focus on how to translate a current résumé into one that is readily accessible for use in this type of a search. We aim to overcome the problem that there are limitless ways for an employer to request such résumés: as an attachment, as text format, as HTML, and still others limiting the characters per line to 80. A solution is a résumé done in HTML, since anyone with Web access can get it open—in most cases, if the reader is getting your E-mail, he or she also has a browser installed. The only problem that remains is that of the fonts you choose—the user may have different default fonts set. Add a line "Best read in xxx font"—is there another way?

Method

I went on to create an electronic résumé, to be either included or posted on the Web. To do this, I saved my résumé, which was previously in Word format as HTML. I inserted horizontal lines, as well as targets and anchors. Then I reopened the copy of my résumé that had been saved in Word and saved it this time in .txt format. I then changed the page layout from a contemporary design to a more standardized paragraph form.

Results

Attempt	Result
Word to HTML	When I changed my résumé from Word to HTML format, the result was that I lost much of the formatting I had done, because HTML does not support it. To force my résumé to look essentially the same, I inserted tables. Moreover, the targets and anchors were inserted to help eliminate the problem of not being able to view all of the information on the screen, as you would if the résumé was in front of you. The horizontal lines further helped to separate each section of information for the reader's understanding.
Word to text	When I changed my résumé from Word to .txt format, the result was that I lost much of the formatting I had done. In this case, I had even fewer options and ended up deciding on a different layout for my résumé altogether, simplifying it greatly. This, however, includes the issue of having 80 characters per line, as it was easy to change the page layout so that, despite any line specification, it would match.

EXAMPLE 13.2
(continued)

Discussion

Because specifications vary from employer to employer, there are limitless ways of sending a résumé electronically. Hence, there is no perfect or universal résumé—a relatively frustrating result of this process. However, it is useful at this time to have a copy of your résumé in multiple formats so that they are readily available despite the request—particularly in .txt format, as this can be attached, sent as an E-mail, and easily translated to HTML. A solution to this problem is, just as a paper résumé has standards, to have standards for the electronic résumé. This will take time and the acceptance of the résumé in this medium. The best way to be safe right now is to save your résumé as text.

EXAMPLE 13.3
Instruction Set

INSTRUCTION SET

Developing an electronic résumé is a useful technique, particularly when doing electronic job searches. It gets your credentials across to the reader, as well as allowing the freedom to move around efficiently. These instructions will lead you step by step through the process of creating an electronic résumé.

RECOMMENDATIONS

■ *It is recommended that you create your résumé before beginning this process.* Typically, résumés require a great deal of information, and the beginner will find it simpler to understand the contents of these instructions without being concerned with this information. <u>Traditional résumé sections</u>

ASSUMPTIONS

These instructions assume that the user

■ Has a basic knowledge of how to operate a personal computer.
■ Has a basic knowledge of how to operate basic features of a word processor program.
■ Has not previously created an HTML-formatted résumé.
■ Has a basic concept of a résumé.

Operational assumptions:

■ The user is currently operating in Microsoft Word.
■ The user has previously saved a copy of the résumé in Word format.

DIRECTIONS

1. Open your résumé as you would normally.
   ■ Check to assure that you have it saved in <u>Word format</u>.
2. Save your résumé as an <u>HTML document</u>.
3. As a result of the previous step, *your document will lose all formatting* that was in place in the Word document. To get the results of formatting in your new HTML document,
   a. <u>Insert a table</u>.
   b. <u>Insert horizontal lines to visually separate section bodies of the résumé</u>.

EXAMPLE 13.3
(continued)

---

4. <u>Insert a horizontal menu</u> between your name and the first section of your résumé. This menu should be horizontal, with the main sections of your résumé and index items. <u>See example</u>.

5. <u>Create internal hyperlinks</u> from each index item in the menu to the respective section body within the résumé.
   - This will let the user view the sections of your résumé that they wish to see.

6. Other formatting to enhance your résumé:
   a. <u>Horizontal menus</u> at the end of each résumé section (<u>example</u>)
      - <u>Add internal hyperlinks</u> for usability.

7. Add a Letter of Application.
   a. Save as a separate HTML document.
   b. <u>Insert a hyperlink</u> at the bottom of each page
      - So that the reader can move back and forth between your Résumé and Letter of Application.

8. Open a copy of a Web browser. Open your document and view it to assure that it is functioning properly.

9. *Your resume is now ready!* You can now
   - Send it as an attachment to anyone with a browser that can view it.
   - Contact your local Web administrator to post it on your Web site.
   - Do an electronic job search and post your résumé on their site.

EXAMPLE 13.4
Instruction Set

DOWNLOADING AND SAVING IMAGES OFF OF THE WEB

1. Open an Internet browser program like Microsoft Internet Explorer or Netscape Navigator, and "surf" the Internet until you find an image that you would like to download.

2. Using the mouse, move the pointer arrow until it is on the image that you wish to download, and click on the right mouse button. A pop-up menu will appear next to the image you have selected.

The pop-up menu that appears will let you choose several options:

Save Picture As lets you save the picture as a .gif file to your disk or the computer's hard drive.

Set as Wallpaper lets you use the picture as the "wallpaper" or background on your computer's desktop screen.

Copy lets you copy the picture into another program or document (e.g., Microsoft Word 97) using the program's edit and paste features.

Add to Favorites lets you bookmark the Web page the image is on into the "favorites" section of your Internet browser software.

Properties will tell you the name of the picture file, the address of the Web page on which it is found, the type of file the picture is (e.g., .gif), and the size of the picture file.

3. Click on Save Picture As. A Save Picture dialogue window will open that looks like this (Figure 1):

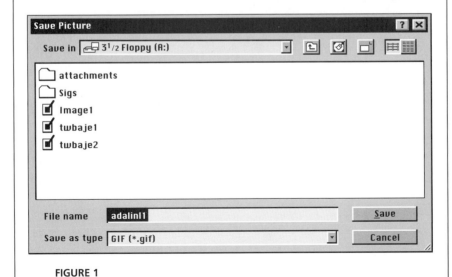

FIGURE 1

EXAMPLE 13.4
(continued)

> **Save in** allows you to choose the disk drive that you want the picture to be saved on.
>
> **File name** allows you to type in the name you wish the picture to be saved as.
>
> **Save as type** lets you choose what type of file you wish the picture to be saved as. Image or picture files are usually saved as .gif files or .jpg files. Notice that the .gif file type popped up in the "Save as type" box as a default.
>
> 4. Fill in the appropriate information in the "Save in," "File name," and "Save as type" dialogue boxes and then click Save.

■ EXERCISES

These exercises assume that they will occur in a computer lab where it is possible to project a site onto many screens or one large one. In that situation, small groups of two or three and oral reporting seem most effective. However, if individual work and written reports work better in the local situation, use that approach.

1. Create a simple Web page that includes a title, text about yourself, and at least one visual aid.

2. Using the page you created in Exercise 1, create two other versions of it. Keep the content the same, but change the design.

3. Create a series of paragraphs that presents the same information in promotional, concise, and scannable text.

4. Create or download an image. Present it on a Web page in three different sizes. In groups of two or three, discuss how you achieved the differences and the effect of the differences. Report your findings orally to the class.

5. Using the page you created in Exercise 1, make several different backgrounds. In groups of three or four, review the effeciveness of the background (Is it distracting? Does it obscure the text?), and demonstrate both a good and bad version to the class.

6. Go to any Web site. In groups of two or three, assess the role the reader is asked to assume. Orally report your findings to the class. Alternative: Write a brief analytical report in which you identify the role and present support for your conclusion.

7. Go to any Web site. In groups of two or three, assess the style of the text. Is it promotional, concise, or scannable? Present your findings orally to the class. Or, as in Exercise 6, write a brief analysis.

8. Go to any Web site. In groups of two or three, assess the use of visuals at the site. Review for clarity, length of time to load, physical placement on the site. Present an oral report to the class, or write an information analysis.

9. Go to any Web site. In groups of two or three, assess the template. Are types of information effectively grouped? Is it easy to figure out where

the links will take you? Report orally or in writing as your instructor requires.

---

10. In groups of two or three, critique any of the Examples (pp. 344–352). Judge them in terms of style, screen design, and audience role. Explain where you think the examples are strong and where they could be improved.

■ WRITING ASSIGNMENT

Create an informational Web site; if possible, load it onto the Web so that others may review it. Determine a purpose and an audience for the site. Create a home page and documents that carry out the purpose. The site should have at least three nodes. Before you create the site, fill out the planning sheet on page 342. Your instructor will place you in a "review group"; set up a schedule with the other group members so that they can review your site for effectiveness at several points in your process. To review the site, use the points in the "Testing" section above (pp. 339–342).

■ WEB EXERCISE

Review two or three Web sites of major corporations in order to determine how they use the elements of format. Review the home page, but also review pages that are several layers "in" (e.g., Our Products/Cameras/Ultra-Compacts) in the Web; typically pages further "in" look more like printed pages. Write a brief analytical or IMRD report discussing your results.

■ WORKS CITED AND CONSULTED

Brooks, Randy M. "Principles for Effective Hypermedia Design." *Technical Communication* 40.3 (August 1993): 422–428.

Coney, Mary, and Michael Steehouder. "Role Playing on the Web: Guidelines for Designing and Evaluating Personas Online." *Technical Communication* 47.3 (August 2000): 327–340.

December, John. "An Information Development Methodology for the World Wide Web." *Technical Communication* 43.4 (November 1996): 369–376.

Farkas, David K., and Jean B. Farkas. "Guidelines for Designing Web Navigation." *Technical Communication* 47.3 (August 2000): 341–358.

Gallagher, Susan. "Your First Web Page." *Intercom* 44.4 (May 1997): 13–15.

Grice, Roger A., and Lenore S. Ridgway. "Presenting Technical Information in Hypermedia Format: Benefits and Pitfalls." *Technical Communication Quarterly* 4.1 (Winter 1995): 35–46.

Horton, William. *Designing and Writing Online Documentation: Hypermedia for Self-Supporting Products.* 2nd ed. NY: Wiley, 1994.

Hunt, Kevin. "Establishing a Presence on the World Wide Web: A Rhetorical Approach." *Technical Communication* 43.4 (November 1996): 376–387.

Nielson, Jakob. "How Users Read the Web." *http://www.useit.com/alertbox/981129. html.*

Pearrow, Mark. *Web Site Usability Handbook.* Rockland, MA: Charles River Media, 2000.

Spyridakis, Jan. "Guidelines for Authoring Comprehensible Web Pages and Evaluating Their Success." *Technical Communication* 47.3 (August 2000): 359–382.

Tatters, Wes. *Teach Yourself Netscape Web Publishing in a Week.* Indianapolis: Samsnet, 1996.

Wilkinson, Theresa A. "Web Site Planning." *Intercom* 44.10 (December 1997): 14–15.

Williams, Thomas R. "Guidelines for Designing and Evaluating the Display of Information on the Web." *Technical Communications* 47.3 (August 2000): 383–396.

Focus on HTML

HTML (*H*yper*t*ext *M*arkup *L*anguage) is the invisible structure of the Web. Viewers can see a Web document because the browser (e.g., Netscape Communicator or Internet Explorer) "reads" an HTML document and displays the results on the screen. Actually, HTML is a code, a series of typed orders placed in the document. For instance, to make a word to appear boldfaced on the screen, the writer places a "start bold" () and an "end bold" () command in the HTML document:

I want you to read this book.

The browser displays the sentence

I want you to **read** this book.

HTML code exists for everything that makes a document have a particular appearance on screen. If the item appears on screen, it appears because the code told the browser to display it. Codes exist for paragraphing, fonts, font sizes, color, tables, and all other aspects of a document. Codes tell which visual aid should appear in a particular place in a document. Figures 1 and 2 show the HTML code for a simple document and the document as it displays on a browser.

The classic way to develop a site is to create material using an ASCII text editor like Notepad (DOS) or Simpletext (Mac). The method for creating it is easy.

- Open a file in one of these two programs.
- Type in certain HTML commands.
- Type in your text.

But typing in code is time consuming and susceptible to errors. If, for instance, one of the brackets (>) is omitted in the boldface code, the word will not appear as boldfaced. As a result, most Web authors use a Web authoring program that creates the code as the writer designs the Web page on screen. Many such programs exist. Some of the most frequently used are Front Page, Dreamweaver, AdobeGoLive, and Netscape Composer. Instructions on using such programs is beyond the scope of this book; however, many good instruction books are available, and all the programs have help menus and training tutorials. The best advice is to begin to practice with the programs to learn their features and to develop enough proficiency so that you can achieve the effects that you visualize.

```
<html>
<head>
<title>
Sample Display Techniques Illustrated                    browser
</title></head>                                          title
<body>
<b><h3>Sample Display Techniques Illustrated            title
</b></h3> by Dan Riordan

<p>These pages illustrate several techniques            text
for displaying information. I have illustrated
ways to use lists, the align command, the
anchor command, and escape links.

<p><b>List</b> I like to teach, especially
<ul>
<li>in groups and                                       list
<li>using technology.</ul>

<p><b>Align Center</b> My wife and I often
visit a cabin up north. Here is what the cabin          visual
looks like: <center><img src="twrida1.gif"              aid
width=100 height=167></center>

<p><b>Anchor</b> This device allows you to
"link" inside a document. I illustrate the
device by letting you read a series of
<a href="twrida5.htm">letters</a> my family's
immigrants wrote in the 1850s.
<p><b>Escape Links</b> Here are "escape links"
to sites connected to this one:
<br><b><i><small>Return to <br><a
href="http://www.uwstout.edu/english/riordan/           "escape
techwrit/techwrit.htm">Technical Writing               links"
</a>|</b>
<b><i> <a href="http//www.uwstout.edu/english/
projects.htm">English Department Student
Projects</a>|</b>
<b><i> <a href="http//www.uwstout.edu/english/
english.htm">English Department</a></p></b></i>
</small>

</body>
</html>
```

FIGURE 1
HTML Code for a Web Document

=== Sample Display Techniques Illustrated ===

Sample Display Techniques Illustrated

by Dan Riordan

These pages illustrate several techniques for displaying information. I have illustrated ways to use lists, the align command , the anchor command, and target/new window command. Explore this web to see the effects of these commands. Let's start with a :

List I like to teach, especially

- in groups and
- using technology.

I enjoy travel to anywhere. I have had great times in

- Dallas Wisconsin and
- St. Petersburg, Russia.

Align My wife and I often visit a cabin up north. Here is what the cabin looks like:

Target/New Window One feature on the inside is a large fieldstone fireplace

Anchor This device allows you to "link" inside a document. I illustrate the device by letting you read a series of letters my family's immigrants wrote in the 1850s.

Escape Links Here are the "escape links" that every web site needs:

Return to

Technical Writing| English Department Student Projects | English Department

FIGURE 2
Browser display of the Code in Figure 1

14 Formal Reports

CHAPTER CONTENTS

Chapter 14
IN A NUTSHELL

Formal format presents documents in a way that makes them seem more "official." Often the format is used with longer (10 or more pages) documents, or else in documents that establish policy, make important proposals, or present the results of significant research.

Formal format requires a title page, a table of contents, a summary, and an introduction, in that order.

The *title page* gives an overview of the report—title, author, date, report number if required, and report recipient if required. Place all these items, separated by white space, at the left margin of the page.

The *table of contents* lists all the main sections and subsections of the report and the page on which each one begins.

The *summary*—often called "executive summary" and sometimes "abstract"—presents the report in brief. The standard method is to write the summary as a "proportional reduction"; each section of the summary has the same main point and the relative length as the original section. After your readers finish the summary, they should know your conclusions and your reasons.

The *introduction* contains all the usual introduction topics but gives each of them a head—background, scope, purpose, method, and recommendations.

Formal reports are those presented in a special way to emphasize the importance of their contents. Writers often use formal reports to present recommendations or results of research. Other reasons for a formal approach are length (over 10 pages), breadth of circulation, perceived importance to the community, and company policy. Although a formal report looks very different from an informal report, the contents can be exactly the same. The difference is in the changed perception caused by the formal presentation. This chapter explains the elements of formal reports and discusses devices for the front, body, and end material.

THE ELEMENTS OF A FORMAL REPORT

To produce a formal report, the writer uses a number of elements that orient readers to the report's topics and organization. Those elements unique to the formal report are the front material and the method of presenting the body. Other elements—appendixes, reference sections, introductions, conclusions, and recommendations—are often associated with the formal report but do not necessarily make the report formal; they could also appear in an informal report.

The formal front material includes the title page, the table of contents, and the list of illustrations. Almost all formal reports contain a summary at the front, and many also have a letter of transmittal. The body is often presented in "chapters," each major section starting at the top of a new page.

Because these reports often present recommendations, they have two organizational patterns: traditional and administrative (General Motors; ANSI). The traditional pattern leads the reader through the data to the conclusion (General Motors). Thus conclusions and recommendations appear at the end of the report. The administrative pattern presents readers with the information they need to perform their role in the company, so conclusions and recommendations appear early in this report.

Traditional	*Administrative*
Title page	Title page
Table of contents	Table of contents
List of illustrations	List of illustrations
Summary or abstract	Summary or abstract
Introduction	Introduction
Discussion—Body Sections	Conclusions
Conclusions	Recommendations/Rationale
Recommendations/Rationale	Discussion—Body Sections

References	References
Appendixes	Appendixes

FRONT MATERIAL

Transmittal Correspondence

Transmittal correspondence is a memo or letter that directs the report to someone. A memo is used to transmit an internal, or in-house, report. An external, or firm-to-firm, report requires a letter. (See Chapter 19 for a sample letter.) In either form, the information remains the same. The correspondence contains

- The title of the report.
- A statement of when it was requested.
- A very general statement of the report's purpose and scope.
- An explanation of problems encountered (for example, some unavailable data).
- An acknowledgment of those who were particularly helpful in assembling the report.

SAMPLE MEMO OF TRANSMITTAL

Date:	May 1, 2003
To:	Ms. Elena Solomonova, Vice-President, Administrative Affairs
From:	Rachel A. Jacobson, Human Resources Director
Subject:	Proposal for the Spousal Employment Assistance Program

Attached is my report "Proposal for the Implementation of a Spousal Employment Assistance Program," which you requested after our March 15 meeting.   *Title of report*

Cause of writing

The report presents a solution to the problems identified by our large number of new hires. In brief, those new hires all had spouses who had to leave careers to move to Rochester. This proposal recommends initiating a spousal employment assistance program to deal with relocation problems.   *Purpose of report*

Statement of request

Compiled by the Human Resources staff, this report owes a significant debt to the employees and their spouses who agreed to be interviewed as part of its preparation.   *Praise of coworkers*

FIGURE 14.1
Title Page for a Formal Report

**PROPOSAL FOR THE IMPLEMENTATION
OF A SPOUSAL EMPLOYMENT
ASSISTANCE PROGRAM**

By
Rachel A. Jacobson
Director, Human Resources

May 1, 2003

Corporate Proposal
HRD 01-01-2003

Prepared for
Elena Solomonova
Vice-President, Administrative Affairs

Title Page

Well-done title pages (see Figure 14.1) give a quick overview of the report, while at the same time making a favorable impression on the reader. Some firms have standard title pages just as they have letterhead stationery for business letters. Here are some guidelines for writing a title page:

- Place all the elements at the left margin (ANSI). (Center all the elements if local policy insists.)
- Name the contents of the report in the title.
- Use a 2-inch left margin.
- Use either all caps or initial caps and lowercase letters; use boldface when appropriate. Do not use "glitzy" typefaces, such as outlined or cursive fonts.
- Include the writer's name and title or department, the date, the recipient's name and title or department, and a report number (if appropriate).

FIGURE 14.2
Table of Contents for an Administrative Report

Table of Contents

A table of contents lists the sections of the report and the pages on which they start (see Figure 14.2). Thus it previews the report's organization, depth, and emphasis. Readers with special interests often glance at the table of contents, examine the abstract or summary, and turn to a particular section of the report. Here are some guidelines for writing a table of contents:

■ Title the page *Table of Contents.*

■ Present the name of each section in the same wording and format as it appears in the text. If a section title is all caps in the text, place it in all caps in the table of contents.

■ Do not underline in the table of contents; the lines are so powerful that they overwhelm the words.

■ Do not use "page" or "p." before the page numbers.

■ Use only the page number on which the section starts.

■ Set margins so that page numbers align on the right.

■ Present no more than three levels of heads; two is usually best.

■ Use *leaders,* a series of dots, to connect words to page numbers.

List of Illustrations

Illustrations include both tables and figures. The list of illustrations (see Figure 14.3) gives the number, title, and page of each visual aid in the report. Here are guidelines for preparing a list of illustrations:

FIGURE 14.3
List of Illustrations for a Formal Report

LIST OF ILLUSTRATIONS

Figure 1. Schedule for Program Implementation 10
Table 1. Special Features of the Program 7
Table 2. Cost/Employee Investment Comparison 8

- Use the title *List of Illustrations* if it contains both figures and tables; list figures first, then tables.
- If the list contains only figures or only tables, call it *List of Figures* or *List of Tables*.
- List the number, title, and page of each visual aid.
- Place the list on the most convenient page. If possible, put it on the same page as the table of contents.

Summary or Abstract

A summary or abstract (or executive summary) is a miniature version of the report. (See Chapter 6 for a full discussion of summaries and abstracts.)

In the summary, present the main points and basic details of the entire report. After reading a summary, the reader should know

- The report's purpose and the problem it addresses.
- The conclusions.
- The major facts on which the conclusions are based.
- The recommendations.

Because the summary "covers" many of the functions of an introduction, recent practice has been to substitute the summary for all or most of the introductory material, placing the conclusions and recommendations last. Used often in shorter (10- to 15-page) reports, this method eliminates the sense of overrepetition that is sometimes present when a writer uses the entire array of introductory elements.

Follow these guidelines to summarize your formal report:

- Concentrate this information into as few words as possible—one page at most.

- Write the summary *after* you have written the rest of the report. (If you write it first, you might be tempted to explain background rather than summarize the contents.)
- Avoid technical terminology (most readers who depend on a summary do not have in-depth technical knowledge).

SUMMARY

This report recommends that the company implement a spousal assistance program. Swift expansion of the company has brought many new employees to us, most of whom had spouses who left professional careers. Because no assistance program exists, our employees and their spouses have found themselves involved in costly, time-consuming, and stressful situations that in several instances have affected productivity on the job.	Recommendation given first Background
A spousal assistance program will provide services that include home- and neighborhood-finding assistance, medical practitioner referrals, and employment-seeking assistance. Advantages include increased employee morale, increased job satisfaction, and greater company loyalty.	Basic conclusions Benefits
Cost is approximately $54,000/year. The major benefit is productivity of the management staff. The program will take approximately six months to implement and will require hiring one spousal employment assistance counselor.	Cost Implementation

Introduction

The introduction orients the reader to the report's organization and contents. Formal introductions help readers by describing purpose, scope, procedure, and background. Statements of purpose, scope, procedure, and background orient readers to the report's overall context.

To give readers the gist of the report right away, many writers now place the conclusions/recommendation right after the introduction. Recently, writers have begun to combine the summary and the introductory sections to cut down on repetition. Example 14.1 (pp. 375–377) illustrates this approach.

Purpose Statement. State the *purpose* in one or two sentences. Follow these guidelines:

- State the purpose clearly. Use one of two forms: "The purpose of this report is to present the results of the investigation" or "This report presents the results of my investigation."
- Use the *present* tense.

■ Name the alternatives if necessary. (In the purpose statement in the example below, the author names the problem [lack of a spousal assistance program] and the alternatives that she investigated.)

Scope Statement. A *scope statement* reveals the topics covered in a report. Follow these guidelines:

■ In feasibility and recommendation reports, name the criteria; include statements explaining the rank order and source of the criteria.

■ In other kinds of reports, identify the main sections, or topics, of the report.

■ Specify the boundaries or limits of your investigation.

Procedure Statement. The *procedure statement*—also called the *methodology statement*—names the process followed in investigating the topic of the report. This statement establishes a writer's credibility by showing that he or she took all the proper steps. For some complex projects, a methodology section appears after the introduction and replaces this statement. Follow these guidelines:

■ Explain all actions you took: the people you interviewed, the research you performed, the sources you consulted.

■ Write this statement in the *past tense.*

■ Select heads for each of the subsections. Heads help create manageable chunks, but too many of them on a page look busy. Base your decision on the importance of the statements to the audience.

Brief Problem (or Background) Statement. In this statement, which you can call either the *problem* or *background statement,* your goal is to help the readers understand—and agree with—your solution because they view the problem as you do. You also may need to provide background, especially for secondary or distant readers. Explain the origin of the problem, who initiated action on the problem, and why the writer was chosen. Follow these guidelines:

■ Give basic facts about the problem.

■ Specify the causes or origin of the problem.

■ Explain the significance of the problem (short term and long term) by showing how new facts contradict old ways.

■ Name the source of your involvement.

In the following example, the problem statement succinctly identifies the basic facts (relocating problems), the cause (out-of-state hires), the significance (decline in productivity), and the source (complaints to Human Resources). Here are the purpose, scope, procedure, and background statements of the proposal for Spousal Employment Assistance:

INTRODUCTION

Purpose

This proposal presents the results of the Human Resources Department's investigation of spousal employment assistance programs and recommends that XYZ Corp. implement such a program.

Two-part purpose: to present and to recommend

Scope

This report details the problems caused by the lack of a spousal employment assistance program. It then considers the concerns of establishing such a program here at XYZ. These concerns include a detailed description of the services offered by such an office, the resources necessary to accomplish the task, and an analysis of advantages, costs, and benefits. An implementation schedule is included.

Lists topics covered in the report

Procedure

The Human Resources Department gathered all the information for this report. We interviewed all 10 people (8 women and 2 men) hired within the past 12 months and 6 spouses (4 men and 2 women). We gathered information from professional articles on the subject. The personnel office provided all the salary and benefits figures. We also interviewed the director of a similar program operating in Arizona and a management training consultant from McCrumble University.

Enough information given to establish credibility

Problem

In the past year XYZ has expanded swiftly, and this expansion will occur throughout the near future. In the past year 10 new management positions were created and filled. Seven of these people moved here from out of state. A number of these people approached the Human Resources Department for assistance with the problems involved in relocating.

Background (cause)

Some of these problems were severe enough that some decline in productivity was noted and was also brought to the attention of Human Resources. Four of the managers left, citing stress as a major reason. That turnover further affected productivity. A spousal employment assistance office is one common way to handle such concerns and offset the potential bad effects of high turnover.

Basic facts

Source of impetus to solve problem

Possible solution

Lengthy Problem (or Background) Statements.   Some reports explain both the problem and its context in a longer statement called either *Problem* or *Background*. A *background statement* provides context for the problem and the report. In it you can often combine background and problem in one statement.

Some situations require a lengthier treatment of the context of the report. In that case, the background section replaces the brief problem statement. Often this longer statement is placed first in the introduction, but practices vary. Place it where it best helps your readers.

To write an effective background statement, follow these guidelines:

- Explain the general problem.
- Explain what has gone wrong.
- Give exact facts.
- Indicate the significance of the problem.
- Specify who is involved and in what capacity.
- Tell why you received the assignment.

BACKGROUND

Management increases have brought many new persons into the XYZ team in the past year. This increase in personnel, while reflecting an excellent trend in a difficult market, has had a marked down side. The new personnel have all experienced significant levels of stress and some slide in productivity as a result of the move. All 10 of the recent hires had spouses who left professional career positions to relocate in Rochester. These people have experienced considerable difficulty finding career opportunities in our smaller urban region, and all the families have reported a certain amount of stress related to everything from finding a home to finding dentists. Four of these managers subsequently left our employ, citing stress as the major reason to leave. These departures caused us to undertake costly, time-consuming personnel searches.

After interviews revealed the existence of such stress, the Executive Committee of Administrative Affairs discussed the issue at length and authorized Human Resources to carry out this study. The Director of Human Resources chaired a committee composed of herself, one manager who did not leave, and a specialist on budget. HR staff conducted the data gathering.

Annotations (right margin):

General problem

Data on what is wrong

Significance

Why the author received the assignment

Conclusions and Recommendations/Rationale

Writers may place these two sections at the beginning of the report or at the end. Choose the beginning if you want to give readers the main points first and if you want to give them a perspective from which to read the data in the report. Choose the end if you want to emphasize the logical flow of the report, leading up to the conclusion. In many formal reports, you present only conclusions because you are not making a recommendation.

Conclusions. The conclusions section emphasizes the report's most significant data and ideas. Base all conclusions only on material presented in the body. Follow these guidelines:

- Relate each conclusion to specific data. Don't write conclusions about material you have not discussed in text.
- Use concise, numbered conclusions.
- Keep commentary brief.
- Add inclusive page numbers to indicate where to find the discussion of the conclusions.

CONCLUSIONS

This investigation has led to the following conclusions. (The page numbers in parentheses indicate where supporting discussion may be found.)

1. The stresses experienced by the new hires are significant and are expected to continue as the company expands (6).

   Conclusions presented in same order as in text

2. Stress is not related to job difficulties but instead is related more to difficulties other family members are experiencing as a result of the relocation (6).

3. Professionals exist who are able to staff such programs (7).

4. The program will result in increased employee morale, increased job satisfaction, and greater company loyalty (9).

5. A program could begin for a cost of $54,000 (10).

6. The major benefits of the program will be increased productivity of the management staff and decreased turmoil created by frequent turnover (11).

7. A program would take six months to initiate (13).

Recommendations/Rationale.   If the conclusions are clear, the main recommendation is obvious. The main recommendation usually fulfills the purpose of the report, but do not hesitate to make further recommendations. Not all formal reports make a recommendation.

In the rationale, explain your recommendation by showing how the "mix" of the criteria supports your conclusions. Follow these guidelines:

- Number each recommendation.
- Make the solution to the problem the first recommendation.
- If the rationale section is brief, add it to the appropriate recommendation.
- If the rationale section is long, make it a separate section.

RECOMMENDATIONS

1. XYZ should implement a spousal employment assistance program. This program is feasible and should eliminate much of the stress that has caused some of the personal anxiety and productivity decreases we have felt with the recent expansion.	Solution to the basic problem
2. The Executive Committee should authorize Human Resources to begin the procedure of writing position guidelines and hiring an SEA counselor.	Other recommendations on implementation

THE BODY OF THE FORMAL REPORT

The body of the formal report, like any other report, fills the needs of the reader. Issues of planning and design, covered in other chapters, all apply here. You can use any of the column formats displayed in Chapter 7 for laying out pages. Special concerns in formal reports are paginating and indicating chapter divisions.

Paginating

Be consistent and complete. Follow these guidelines:

- Assign a number to each piece of paper in the report, regardless of whether the number actually appears on the page.
- Assign a page number to each full-page table or figure.
- Place the numbers in the upper right corner of the page with no punctuation, or center them at the bottom of the page either with no punctuation or with a hyphen on each side (-2-).
- Consider the title page as page 1. Do not number the title page. Most word processing systems allow you to delete the number from the title page.

- In very long reports, use lowercase roman numerals (i, ii, iii) for all the pages before the text of the discussion. In this case, count the title page as page i, but do not put the i on the page. On the next page, place a ii.
- Paginate the appendix as discussed in "End Material" (below).
- Use headers or footers (phrases in the top and bottom margins) to identify the topic of a page or section.

Indicating Chapter Divisions

To make the report "more formal," begin each new major section at the top of a page (see Example 14.2, which starts on p. 378).

END MATERIAL

The end material (glossary and list of symbols, references, and appendixes) is placed after the body of the report.

Glossary and List of Symbols

Traditionally, reports have included glossaries and lists of symbols. However, such lists tend to be difficult to use. Highly technical terminology and symbols should not appear in the body of a report that is aimed at a general or multiple audience. Place such material in the appendix. When you must use technical terms in the body of the report, define them immediately; informed readers can simply skip over the definitions. Treat the glossary as an appendix. If you need a glossary, follow these guidelines:

- Place each term at the left margin, and start the definition at a tab (2 or 3 spaces) farther to the right. Start all lines of the definition at this tab.
- Alphabetize the terms.

References

The list of references (included when the report contains information from other sources) is discussed along with citation methods in Appendix B.

Appendix

The appendix contains information of a subordinate, supplementary, or highly technical nature that you do not want to place in the body of the report. Follow these guidelines:

- Refer to each appendix item at the appropriate place in the body of the report.
- Number illustrations in the appendix in the sequence begun in the body of the report.
- For short reports, continue page numbers in sequence from the last page of the body.
- For long reports, use a separate pagination system. Because the appendixes are often identified as Appendix A, Appendix B, and so on, number the pages starting with the appropriate letter: A-1, A-2, B-1, B-2.

■ WORKSHEET FOR PREPARING A FORMAL REPORT

❏ *Determine the audience for this report.*

Who is the primary audience and who the secondary? How much does the audience understand about the origins and progress of this project? How will they use this report? Will it be the basis for a decision?

❏ *Plan the visual aids that will convey the basic information of your report.*

❏ *Construct those visual aids.*

Follow the guidelines in Chapter 8.

❏ *Prepare a style sheet for up to four levels of heads and for margins, page numbers, and captions to visual aids.*

❏ *Decide whether each new section should start at the top of a new page.*

❏ *Create a title page.*

❏ *Prepare the table of contents.*

How many levels of heads will you include? (Two is normal.) Will you use periods for leaders?

❏ *Prepare the list of illustrations.*

❏ *Present figures first, then tables.*

❏ *Determine the order of statements (purpose, scope, procedure, and so forth) in the introduction.*

In particular, where will you place the problem and background statements? in the introduction? in a section in the body?

❏ *Prepare a glossary if you use key terms unfamiliar to the audience.*

❏ *List conclusions.*

❏ *List recommendations, with most important first.*

❏ *Write the rationale to explain how the mix of conclusions supports the recommendations.*

❏ *Write the summary.*

❏ *Prepare appendixes of technical material.*
   Use an appendix if the primary audience is nontechnical or if you have extensive tabular or support material.

EXAMPLES

Example 14.1 is the body of the report whose introduction is explained in this chapter. Example 14.2 is a brief formal report.

EXAMPLE14.1
Formal Report Body

DISCUSSION

In this section, I will describe spousal employment assistance, discuss the advantages and benefits of it, and develop a time schedule for the implementation of it.

NATURE OF THE PROBLEM

Many complex issues arise when relocating a dual-career family. Issues such as a new home, a new mortgage, two new jobs in the family, a new and reliable child care service—to name only a few. These issues, if not dealt with in an efficient manner, can create tremendous stress in the new employee—stress that dramatically affects productivity on the job.

Productivity and protection of our company's human resource investment are the key issues we are dealing with in this program. The intention is that the more quickly the employee can be productive and settled in a new area, the less costly it will be for our company.

DESCRIPTION OF THE PROGRAM

I am proposing a separate office within the company for the SEA program. It would be staffed by a consultant who would research and develop the following areas:

- Home-finding counseling
- Neighborhood finding
- Mortgage counseling
- Spouse and family counseling
- Spouse employment assistance
- Child care referrals
- School counseling
- Cost-of-living differences
- Doctor and dentist referrals

All counseling services would be handled by our SEA office employee except for formal employment assistance, which would be contracted with a third-party employment firm. A third-party firm can provide the advantage of objectivity as well as a proper level of current employment information.

ADVANTAGES OF THE PROGRAM

The program is a service provided by us, and paid for by us, that is for the sole purpose of assisting the new employee. The advantages are increased

EXAMPLE 14.1
(continued)

---

employee morale, increased job satisfaction, and greater company loyalty. The employee feels that the company is concerned with the problems he or she is facing in the relocation process. The assistance the employee receives makes the move easier, so adjusting to the new job is quicker. The result is a more productive employee.

WHAT ARE THE COSTS VERSUS THE BENEFITS?

Costs

The comprehensive program will cost the company approximately $54,500 per year. As illustrated in Table 1, this includes $2,500 for research and development, $27,000 for the SEA consultant, and $25,000 for the third-party employment firm (10 contracts at $2,500 each). This figure doesn't include the cost of office completion, which would run about $1,100 to finish the first-floor office space (room 120), which isn't currently occupied.

    Also in Table 1, I have estimated the dollar amount our company invests yearly on new relocating managers. $54,500 is a drop in the bucket when you realize that we spend at least $290,000 yearly on new hires alone.

TABLE 1
Cost/Employee Investment Comparison

	Estimated Yearly Cost of Program*	Estimated Value of Human Resource Investment	
Research/development	$ 2,500	New relocating managers	
SEA consultant	27,000	Approx. 10 @ $29,000 each	$290,000
Employment firm contracts 10 @ approx. $2,500 each	25,000		
TOTAL	$ 54,500	TOTAL	$290,000

*Doesn't include the one-time cost of office completion (about $1,100).

Benefits

The benefit to our company is the increase in productivity of the management staff. The cost to our company shouldn't be considered a luxury or frill expense, but a way to protect and enhance the company's human resource investment. The yearly cost of the program ($54,500) compared with the estimated yearly cost of new employees who would use it ($290,000) shows that the expense is far outweighed by the investment we've made in new management hires.

EXAMPLE 14.1
(continued)

WHAT ABOUT IMPLEMENTATION?

Implementation time is estimated at six to seven months depending on when the SEA consultant is hired. This is because, after a three-month hiring and selection period, the new consultant would be given three months to begin the research and development of the program. After these three months, research would continue, but client consultation would also begin (refer to Figure 1).

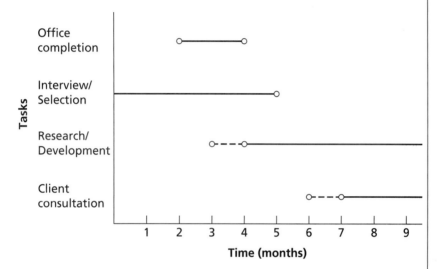

FIGURE 1
Schedule for Program Implementation

EXAMPLE 14.2
Formal Report

FEASIBILITY OF FINDING PROGRAM
LANGUAGE CODE ON THE INTERNET

By
Chad Seichter

May 8, 2000

Prepared for
Kim O'Neil
Program Director

EXAMPLE 14.2
(continued)

TABLE OF CONTENTS

EXAMPLE 14.2
(continued)

ABSTRACT

This report determines whether or not it is feasible for Applied Mathematics majors to find program language code on the Internet. To make this judgment, I looked for two separate programming languages; they were Java and Smalltalk. The pages I looked at were evaluated according to how current they were, if the source was credible, and if there actually was code on them. I found that I was easily able to find code for both of these languages and therefore have concluded that the Internet is a feasible source of information for my major.

INTRODUCTION

Background

Goal. The goal of this project was to decide if the Internet is a feasible source of information for Applied Math majors. I researched to see if I could find source code for Java and Smalltalk. Because of my research, I have come to the conclusion that the Internet is a good source for information for Applied Math majors. The purpose of this report is to explain my research and tell how I came to this decision.

Rationale. For my study I chose two different programming languages to try to find information on. The two languages were Java and Smalltalk. I picked these because writing computer programs is a large part of the Applied Math program. I chose the Java language because it is an up-and-coming language that is very popular right now. I figured it would be easy to find information on this. On the other hand, Smalltalk is a lot less known and used in the present day. I didn't know how much I would find on a language that is not very popular. I figured that choosing languages on the opposite ends of the popularity spectrum would give me a good look at not only these two languages but also all the other ones.

Method

Choosing Topics. My topics of study were whether or not I could find source code for programming languages on the Internet. I focused my search on two separate languages. One was a popular language, Java, and one less popular, Smalltalk. I figured that these two languages would give me a good overview about finding code for all of the different computer languages there are.

Determining Feasibility. I had to research my topics in order to figure out if the Internet was a feasible source of information. I used two separate search engines to do this: WebCrawler and Dogpile. Both of these

EXAMPLE 14.2
(continued)

search engines seemed to give me good information on my topics. Once I did the search, I evaluated the Web sites that came up and based my evaluation on my criteria (see "Explanation of Criteria" section below). In order to conclude that the Internet was useful for me, I needed to find Web sites that met most of the criteria for each topic.

Explanation of Criteria. I used the following criteria to come up with a conclusion:

1. Current For the Java language, I chose that the pages had to have been updated sometime within the last six months because many changes are still being done to this language. For the Smalltalk language, I decided that anything within the last two years was good because it is an older language with fewer revisions still taking place.

2. Credible In order for the source to be credible, it couldn't be someone's personal Web page. I also tried out the code myself to see if the page was credible. If it didn't work for me, then I considered it noncredible.

3. Was there code? To meet this criterion, the Web page had to have actual examples of source code on it that could be used by others.

Conclusion

After doing my searches using WebCrawler and Dogpile, I am able to conclude that the Internet is a feasible source of information for Applied Math majors. I was able to find numerous Web pages that met my three criteria for both the Java language and the Smalltalk language.

EXAMPLE 14.2
(continued)

DISCUSSION

Finding Java Code on the Web

Introduction.   I am an Applied Math major and am trying to figure out if the Internet and my major are interrelated. The purpose of this search is to find code that I could use to assist me in making computer programs. The language of code I would like to find is Java code. Specifically, I want to find Java applets that can be inserted into my programs. To help answer my question, I used the WebCrawler search engine. I checked the first five sites and evaluated them according to my criteria. If I could find at least five sites that had code, I could come to the conclusion that the Web is useful for finding Java code.

Findings.   Using the WebCrawler search engine, I typed in the keywords "java applets" and then looked at the sites that came up. Over 45,000 sites came up using this search, so I started looking at them starting at the beginning. I found that all of the first five sites met my criteria. Table 1 below shows my results using my criteria.

TABLE 1
Java Code Sites on the Internet

	Current	*Credible*	*Were There Applets?*
http://java.sun.com/starter.html	Yes	Yes	No, but had links to some
http://www.javasoft.com/applets/index.html	Yes	Yes	Yes
http://javapplets.com/	Yes	Yes	Yes
http://www.conveyor.com/conveyor-java.html	Yes	Yes	Yes
http://javaboutique.internet.com/	Yes	Yes	Yes

Conclusion.   After doing this search and going through these top five sites, I have concluded that the Internet is very helpful for me to find applets for Java. All these pages appeared to be very recent. Most of them had a copyright in the year 2000, so I know they would still be useful now. I wanted to check to see if the code was correct, so I moved some of the applets off these Web pages onto one that I had created, and they all worked in my code as well. Therefore I knew that these sites were credible.

EXAMPLE 14.2
(continued)

Java has become such a big language to program that there appears to be an almost unlimited amount of code on the Web for it. I think that the sites that I checked out were probably above-average sites, because all the code I used worked correctly. I'm sure that there are some sites that aren't as good as these and could have bad code. If I was ever to use any of these pages, I would make sure I understood the code and made sure it was an efficient way to do the task. At worst, there are many examples to give you an idea of how to create an applet, so this search was very helpful to me.

EXAMPLE 14.2
(continued)

Finding Smalltalk Code on the Web

Introduction.   I am an Applied Math major and am trying to figure out if
the Internet and my major are interrelated. The purpose of this search is
to find code that I could use to assist me in making computer programs.
The language of code I would like to find is Smalltalk. I chose this language because it isn't very popular, so I figure if I can find this, then I
should be able to find almost any other language. To help answer my
question, I used the Dogpile search engine. I checked the first five sites
and evaluated them according to my criteria. If I could find at least five
sites that had code, I could come to the conclusion that the Web is useful
for finding Java code.

Findings.   Using the Dogpile search engine, I typed in the keywords
"Smalltalk example code" and then looked at the sites that came up.
There weren't a whole lot of sites, but the ones that came up usually had
good information and links to other good pages. Table 2 below shows
my results from the five Web sites I looked at.

TABLE 2
Smalltalk Code Sites on the Internet

	Current	Credible	Code on the Page?
www.site.gmu.edu	1995, but information was still useful	Yes	Yes
www.mk.dmu.ac.uk	No date given	Yes	Yes
www.ics.hawaii.edu	Yes	Yes	Yes
www.phaidros.com	Yes	Yes	Yes
www.objectconnect.com	No date given	Yes	Yes

Conclusion.   After doing this search and going through these top five
sites, I have concluded that the Internet is helpful for me to find Smalltalk code. Some of the pages weren't very current or didn't have a date,
but because there haven't been too many changes to this language recently, that isn't a big issue. Most of them were within the last couple of
years, so that was sufficient. I wanted to check to see if the code was correct, so I used some of the code in other programs I have written in the
past, and it all seemed to work. Therefore, I knew that these sites were

EXAMPLE 14.2
(continued)

credible. Also, because Smalltalk isn't a popular language to program in, I feel that because I can use the Internet as a tool for this language, I can probably also use it for almost any other. Besides having code, I found several other helpful tools while using the Web that related to the programming language that could help me in writing my own programs.

▪ EXERCISES

1. In groups of two to four, discuss whether the conclusions and recommendations in Example 14.1 should appear at the beginning. Be prepared to give an oral report to the class. If your instructor requires, rewrite the introductory material so it follows the pattern of the human resources proposal (p. 368) Alternate: Rewrite the human resources introduction by using the executive summary method.

2. Redo this table of contents to make it more readable.

Introduction	2–3	chefmate	6
LIST OF FIGURES	2	conclusion	page 5
recommendation	4	table 1 cost	page 6
discussion	5–12	cost	7–8
width of front panel	5	hitachi	7
hitachi	5		

3. For Exercise 8, Chapter 7 (pp. 165–166), create one or all of the following: a title page, table of contents, summary, conclusion, and recommendation.

4. For Exercise 8, Chapter 7 (pp. 165–166), create a page layout.

5. Your instructor will hand out a sample report from the *Instructor's Manual*. In groups of two to three, edit it into a formal report. Change introductory material as necessary.

6. Edit the following selection, which is taken from the discussion section of a formal report. Add at least two levels of heads, and construct one appropriate visual aid. Write a one- or two-sentence summary of the section.

   The cost of renting a space will not exceed $150. Our budget allows $140 per month investment at this time for money available from renting space. The cost of renting a space is $175 per month for 100 square feet of space at Midtown Antique Mall. This exceeds the criteria by a total of $25 per month. The cost for renting 100 square feet of space at Antique Emporium is $100 per month, which is well within our criteria based on our budget. Antique Emporium is the only alternative that meets this criterion. The length of the contract cannot exceed 6 months because this is what we have established as a reasonable trial period for the business. Within this time, we will be able to calculate average net profit (with a turnover time no longer than 3 months) and determine if it is worth the time invested in the business. We will also be able to determine if we may want to continue the business as it is or on a larger scale by renting more floor space. The Midtown Antique Mall requires a 6-month contract. The Antique Emporium requires an initial 6-month contract which continues on a month-to-month basis after the contract is fulfilled. Both locations fulfill the contract length desired in the criteria. The possibility of continuing monthly at the Antique Emporium is an attractive option compared with renewing contracts bi-yearly.

7. If you are working on formal format elements, bring a draft of them to class. In groups of two or three, evaluate each other's material. Use the guidelines (for Title Page, Table of Contents, Summary, Introduction, Conclusion, Recommendation) in this chapter as your criteria. Rewrite your material as necessary.

▪ WRITING ASSIGNMENTS

1. Create a formal report that fulfills a recommendation, feasibility, proposal, or research assignment, as given in other chapters of this book.
    a. Create a template for your formal report. Review Chapter 7, pages 152–155, and Chapter 17, pages 454–457.
    b. Choose an introductory combination and write it.
    c. Write the conclusions and recommendations/rationale sections.
    d. Divide into groups of two. Read each other's draft from the point of view of a manager. Assess whether you get all the essential information quickly. If not, suggest ways to clarify the material.

2. Write a learning report for the writing assignment you just completed. See Chapter 5, Writing Assignment 7, page 123, for details of the assignment.

▪ WEB EXERCISE

Review two or three Web sites of major corporations in order to determine how they use the elements of format. Review the home page, but also review pages that are several layers "in" (e.g., Our Products/Cameras/Ultra-Compacts) in the Web; typically, pages further "in" look more like printed pages. Write a brief analytical or IMRD report discussing your results.

▪ WORKS CITED

American National Standards Institute (ANSI). *Guidelines for Format and Production of Scientific and Technical Reports*. ANSI 239. 18-1974. NY: Author, 1974.

General Motors. *Writing Style Guide*. Rev. ed. GM1620. By Lawrence H. Freeman and Terry R. Bacon. Warren, MI: Author, 1991.

15 Recommendation and Feasibility Reports

CHAPTER CONTENTS

Chapter 15
IN A NUTSHELL

Feasibility studies and recommendations present a position based on credible critera and facts. *Feasibility studies* use criteria to investigate an item in order to tell the reader whether or not to accept the item. *Recommendations* use criteria to compare item A to item B in order to tell the reader which one to choose. To decide whether or not to air condition your house is a feasibility issue; to decide which air conditioning system to purchase is a recommendation issue.

Report strategy.   In the introduction, *set the context:* tell the background of the situation, explain the methods you used to collect data, and state why you chose these criteria. In the body, *deal with one criterion per section*. A helpful outline for a section is

- Brief introduction to set the scene
- Discussion of data, often subdivided by alternative
- A helpful visual aid
- A brief, clear conclusion

Basis on criteria.   Criteria are the framework through which you and the reader look at the subject.

- Select topics that an expert would use to judge the situation. (For the air conditioner, a criterion is cost.)
- Select a standard, how you limit the criterion. (The limitation is "the system may not cost more than $6000.")
- Apply the criteria. (Look at the sales materials of two reputable systems.)
- Present the data and conclusion clearly. Report the appropriate facts from your investigation, create a useful visual aid, and use heads and chunks to guide the reader through the subsections.

Professionals in all areas make recommendations. Someone must investigate alternatives and say "choose A" or "choose B." The "A" or "B" can be anything: which type of investment to make, which machine to purchase, whether to make a part or buy it, whether to have a sale, or whether to relocate a department. The decision maker makes a recommendation based on *criteria:* standards against which the alternatives are judged.

For professionals, these choices often take the form of *recommendation reports* or *feasibility reports.* Although both present a solution after alternatives have been investigated, the two reports are slightly different. Recommendation reports indicate a choice between two or more clear alternatives: this distributor or that distributor, this brand of computer or that brand of computer (Markel). Feasibility reports investigate one option and decide whether it should be pursued. Should the client start a health club? Should the company form a captive insurance company? Should the company develop this prototype? (Alexander and Potter; Bradford; Angelo). This chapter explains how to plan and write both types of reports.

PLANNING THE RECOMMENDATION REPORT

In planning a recommendation, you must consider the audience, choose criteria for making your recommendations, use visual aids, and select a format and an organizational principle.

Consider the Audience

In general, many different people with varying degrees of knowledge (a multiple audience) read these reports. A recommendation almost always travels up the organizational hierarchy to a group—a committee or board—that makes the decision. These people may or may not know much about the topic or the criteria used as the basis for the recommendation. Usually, however, most readers will know a lot about at least one aspect of the report—the part that affects them or their department. They will read the report from their own point of view. The personnel manager will look closely at how the recommendation affects workers, the safety manager will judge the effect on safety, and so on. All readers will be concerned about cost. To satisfy such readers, the writer must present a report that enables them all to find and glean the information they need.

Choose Criteria

To make data meaningful, analyze or evaluate them according to criteria. Selecting logical criteria is crucial to the entire recommendation report because you will make your recommendation on the basis of those criteria and because your choice of the "right" criteria establishes your credibility.

The Three Elements of a Criterion.   A *criterion* has three elements: a name, a standard, and a rank (Holcombe and Stein). The *name* of the criterion, such as "cost," identifies some area relevant to the situation. The *standard* is a statement that establishes the limit of the criterion—for instance, "not to exceed $500.00." The standard heavily influences the final decision. Consider two very different standards that are possible for cost:

1. The cost of the water heater will not exceed $500.
2. The cheapest water heater will be purchased.

If the second standard is in effect, the writer cannot recommend the more expensive machine even if it has more desirable features.

The *rank* of the criterion is its weight in the decision relative to the other criteria. "Cost" is often first, but it might be last, depending on the situation.

Discovering Criteria.   Criteria vary according to the type of problem. In some situations, a group or individual will have set up all the criteria in rank order. In that case, you show how the relevant data for the various alternatives measure up to these criteria.

When criteria have not been set up, you need to discover them by using your professional expertise and the information you have about needs and alternatives in the situation. One helpful way of collecting relevant data is to investigate appropriate categories: technical, management/maintenance, and financial criteria (Markel).

Technical criteria apply to operating characteristics such as the necessary heat and humidity levels in an air-moving system. *Management/ maintenance criteria* deal with concerns of day-to-day operation, such as how long it will take to install a new air-moving system. *Financial criteria* deal with cost and budget. How much money is available, and how much system will it purchase?

Applying Criteria.   Suppose you were to investigate which of two jointers to place in a high school woods lab. To make the decision, you need to find the relevant data and create the relevant standards. To find relevant data, answer questions derived from the three categories.

- Technical—Does the jointer have appropriate fence size? table length? cutting capacity?
- Financial—How much does each jointer cost? How much do optional features cost? How much money is available? What is the standard?

▨ Management/Maintenance—Which one is safer? Will we need to reconfigure the lab or its electrical service? Will the jointers be available by the start of school in August?

To create standards, you must formulate statements that turn these questions into bases for judgment. You derive these standards from your experience, from an expert authority (such as another teacher), or from policy. For instance, because you know from your own experience the length of your typical stock, your standard will read "Must be able to handle up to 52 inches." Another teacher who has worked with these machines can tell you which features must be present for safety. School policy dictates how you should phrase the cost standard.

Use Visual Aids

Although you might use many kinds of visuals—maps of demographic statistics, drawings of key features, flow charts for procedures—you will usually use tables and graphs. With these visuals you can present complicated information easily (such as costs or a comparison of features). For many sections in your report, you will construct the table or figure first and then write the section to explain the data in it. Visual aids help overcome the problem of multiple audiences. Consider using a visual with each section in your report.

In the following example, the author first collected the data, then made the visual aids, and *then* wrote the section. Note that the table combines data from several criteria; this technique avoids many small, one-line tables. (The entire report appears as Example 15.1 at the end of the chapter.)

Fence Size

The fence serves as a guide for planing face and edge surfaces. The size of the fence, width and length, is directly related to cutting efficiency. The fence size of the jointer currently in operation is 3" × 28". In purchasing a new jointer the fence size should be increased for improved accuracy and squaring efficiency.

■ Delta DJ-20. As Table 1 shows, the Delta fence size is 5" × 36". These dimensions represent a 2" × 8" increase, which will result in more efficient operations.

■ Powermatic-60. The Powermatic fence is 4" × 34½", a 1" × 6½" increase over that of the existing fence (see Table 1).

Conclusion. Both machines exceed the fence size criterion of 3" × 28". Delta DJ-20 has the greatest increase, 2" × 8", and will result in greater squaring accuracy and longitudinal control when jointing edge surfaces.

TABLE 1
8" Jointer Capabilities Comparison

Criteria	Standard	Delta DJ-20	Powermatic-60
Fence size	Minimum of 3" wide × 28" long	5" × 36"	4" × 34½"
Table length	Minimum of 52"	76½"	64"
Cutting capacity	Minimum depth of ⅜"	⅝"	½"
Cost	Not to exceed $2300	$2128.00	$2092.00

Select a Format and an Organizational Principle

As you plan your report, you must select a format, an organizational principle for the entire report, and an organizational principle for each section.

Select a Format.   Your choice of format depends on the situation. If the audience is a small group that is familiar with the situation, an informal report will probably do. If your audience is more distant from you and the situation, a formal format is preferable. The informal format is explained in Chapter 12, the formal format in Chapter 14.

In addition to selecting format type, create a style sheet of heads and margins. Review Chapter 7 and the examples in Chapters 12 and 14. Your style sheet should help your audience find what they need to do their job.

Organize the Discussion by Criteria.   Organize the discussion section according to criteria, with each criterion receiving a major heading. Review Examples 15.1 and 15.2; each major section is the discussion of one criterion. Your goal is to present comparable data that readers can evaluate easily.

Organize Each Section Logically.   Each section deals with one criterion and evaluates the alternatives in terms of that criterion. Each of these sections should contain three parts: an introduction, a body, and a conclusion. In the introduction, define the criterion and discuss its standard, rank, and source, if necessary. (If you discuss the standard, rank, and source somewhere else in the report, perhaps in the introduction, do not repeat that information.) In the body, explain the relevant facts about each alternative in terms of the criterion; in the conclusion, state the judgment you have made as a result of applying this criterion to the facts. You will find a sample section on page 396.

WRITING THE RECOMMENDATION REPORT

As you write the recommendation report, carefully develop the introduction, conclusions, recommendations/rationale, and discussion sections.

Introduction

After you have gathered and interpreted the data, develop an introduction that orients the readers to the problem and to the organization of the report. Your goal is to make readers confident enough to accept your recommendation. In recommendation reports, as in all reports, you can mix the elements of the introduction in many ways. Always include a purpose statement and add the other statements as needed by the audience. Four common elements in the introduction are

- Statement of purpose.
- Explanation of method of investigation.
- Statement of scope.
- Explanation of the problem.

Purpose. Begin a recommendation report with a straightforward statement, such as "The purpose of this report is . . . " or, more simply, "This report recommends. . . . " You can generally cover the purpose, which is to choose an alternative, in one sentence.

Method of Gathering Information. State your method of gathering information. As explained in Chapter 5, the four major methods of gathering data are observing, testing, interviewing, and reading. Stating your methodology not only gives credit where it is due but also lends authority to your data and thus to your report.

In the introduction, a general statement of your model of investigation is generally sufficient: "Using lab and catalog resources here at the university and after discussion with other Industrial Arts teachers in this area, I have narrowed my choices to two: Delta Model DJ-20 and Powermatic Model 60."

Scope. In the scope statement, cite the criteria you used to judge the data. You can explain their source or their rankings here, especially if the same reasons apply to all of them. Name the criteria in the order in which they appear in your report. If you have not included a particular criterion because data are unavailable or unreliable, acknowledge this omission in the section on scope so that your readers will know you have not overlooked that criterion. Here is an example:

Each machine has been evaluated using the following criteria, in descending order of importance:

1. Fence size
2. Table length
3. Cutting capacity
4. Cost

Background.   In the background, discuss the problem, the situation, or both. To explain the problem, you must define its nature and significance: "Considering that the machine has been under continuous student use for 27 years and has reduced accuracy because of the small table and fence size, I indicated I would contact you regarding a new jointer." Depending on the audience's familiarity with the situation, you may have to elaborate, explaining the causes of various effects (Why does it have reduced accuracy? Just what is the relationship of the table and the fence? What are tables and fences?).

To explain the situation, you may need to outline the history of the project, indicate who assigned you to write the report, or identify your position in the corporation or organization.

The following informal introduction effectively orients the reader to the problem and to the method of investigating it.

SAMPLE INFORMAL INTRODUCTION

Date:	December 2, 2004	Memo head
To:	Joseph P. White, Superintendent of Schools	
From:	David Ayers	
Subject:	Purchase recommendation for 8" jointer	

Recently, Jim DeLallo and I discussed at length the serious problems he was having in operating the jointer at the high school. Considering that the machine has been under continuous student use for 27 years and has reduced accuracy because of the small table and fence size, I indicated I would contact you regarding a new jointer. You asked that I forward 2005–2006 budget requests by December 15.

Situation and background

Cause of writing

Therefore, I have prepared this recommendation report for choosing a new 8" jointer. Using lab and catalog resources here at the university and after discussion with other Industrial Arts teachers in this area, I have narrowed my choices to two: Delta Model DJ-20 and Powermatic Model 60. Each machine has been evaluated

Method

using the following criteria, in descending order of importance:

1. Fence size   Scope
2. Table length
3. Cutting capacity
4. Cost

The remainder of the report will compare both machines   Preview
to the criteria.

Conclusions

Your conclusions section should summarize the most significant information about each criterion covered in the report. One or two sentences about each criterion are usually enough to prepare the reader for your recommendation. Writers of recommendation and feasibility reports almost always place these sections in the front of the report. Remember, readers want the essential information quickly.

All elements in the criteria have been met. The slightly higher cost of the Delta, $36.00, is more than offset by increased efficiency and capacity as noted below:

1. A larger fence size—for better control of stock when squaring
2. A larger table size—resulting in more efficient planing
3. A greater depth of cutting capacity—for improved softwood removal and increased rabbeting capacity

Recommendations/Rationale Section

The recommendation resolves the problem that occasioned the report. For short reports like the samples presented here, one to four sentences should suffice. For complex reports involving many aspects of a problem, a longer paragraph (or even several paragraphs) may be necessary.

It is recommended that the district budget for capital   Recommendation
purchase of the Delta Model DJ-20 8" Jointer in
2005–2006. Selection of the Delta jointer is a departure
from the practice of purchasing Powermatic equipment
for the woodworking shop. It is my feeling that the Delta
Jointer is best suited for the current and future needs of
the woodworking program. Service and repair will not   Possible negative
be a problem in changing equipment manufacturers,   factor explained
since N. H. Bragg services both lines of equipment.

Discussion Section

As previously noted, you should organize the discussion section by criteria, from most to least important. Each criterion should have an introduction, a body discussing each alternative, and a conclusion. Here is part of the discussion section from the recommendation report on ink-jet printers. (The full report appears as Example 15.2 at the end of the chapter.)

Memory

Memory affects the way a plotter functions. The more standard memory a plotter has, the easier it is for it to perform the plotting process. After speaking with product representatives and other individuals, I would recommend a minimum of 4 MB RAM standard for any plotter.

CalComp. The TechJet plotter comes standard with 4 MB RAM and is upgradable to 20 MB.

HP. The DesignJet plotter only comes with 2 MB RAM standard, and to meet the requirement for this criterion it would be necessary to add an additional 2 MB of memory. This addition in memory will add to the overall cost of the DesignJet. The price for this expansion will be shown in the cost criteria section.

Conclusion. Both plotters would work with their standard memory, but the best bet would be to start out with 4 MB RAM minimum. It may be necessary to expand even more, depending on the types of plots that will be done with the plotter.

PLANNING THE FEASIBILITY REPORT

Feasibility reports investigate whether to undertake a project. They "size up a project before it is undertaken and identify those projects that are not worth pursuing" (Ramige 48). The project can be anything: place a golf course at a particular site, start a capital campaign drive, or accept a proposal to install milling machines. The scope of these reports varies widely, from analyses of projects costing hundreds of thousands of dollars to informal reviews of in-house proposals. Your goal is to investigate all relevant factors to determine whether any one will prevent the project from continuing. Basically you ask, "Can we perform the project?" and you answer yes or no. Follow the same steps as for planning recommendation reports. In addition, consider the following guidelines:

■ Consider the audience.
■ Determine the criteria.
■ Determine the standards.
■ Structure by criteria.

Consider the Audience

Generally, the audience is familiar with the situation in broad outline. Your job is to give specific information. They know, for example, that in any project a certain time is allowed for cost recovery, but they do not know how much time this project needs. Your goal is to make them confident enough of you and the situation to accept your decision.

Determine the Criteria

Criteria are established either by a management committee or by "prevailing practice." Either a group directs investigators to consider criteria such as cost and competition level, or "prevailing practice"—the way knowledgeable experts investigate this type of proposed activity—sets the topics. For instance, cost recovery is always considered in the evaluation of a capital investment project.

If you have to discover the topics yourself, as you often do with small projects, use the three categories described on page 390—technical, management/maintenance, and financial criteria. The criteria you choose will affect the audience's sense of your credibility.

Determine the Standards

To determine standards is to state the limits of the criteria. If the topic is reimbursement for acceptable expenses, you must determine the standards to use to judge whether the stated expenses fall within the acceptable limit. These standards require expert advice unless they exist as policy. If the policy is that a new machine purchase must show a return in investment of 20 percent, and if the machine under consideration will return 22 percent, buying the machine is feasible.

Structure by Criteria

The discussion section of a feasibility report is structured by criteria. The reimbursement report could include sections on allowable growth, time of recovery of investment, and disposal costs.

WRITING THE FEASIBILITY REPORT

To write the feasibility report, choose a format and write the introduction and the body.

Choose a Format

The situation helps you determine whether to use a formal or an informal format for your feasibility studies. As a rule of thumb, use the formal format for a lengthy report intended for a group of clients. The informal format is suitable for a brief report intended to determine the feasibility of an internal suggestion.

Write the Introduction and Body

In the introduction, present appropriate background, conclusions, and recommendations. Treat this introduction the same as a recommendation introduction. In the discussion, present the details for each topic. As in the recommendation report, you should present the topic, the standard, relevant details, and your conclusion. Organize the material in the discussion section from most to least important. As with all reports, use appropriate visual aids, including tables, graphs, and even maps, to enhance your readers' comprehension.

The following section from an informal internal feasibility report presents all four discussion elements succinctly:

SAMPLE FEASIBILITY SECTION

TOTAL COST

The total cost of a new lathe will include machine and installation costs. Our standard is that the total cost of the lathe must be less than $7500. The budget for the JIT Project is $25,000; up to $10,000 for JIT training, and $14,000 for capital equipment purchases. A quick sample of companies listed in the *Thomas Register* showed that we can find a lathe that meets our budgetary need. **Proposal meets criterion.**	Topic Standard Details Conclusion

Several brief informal feasibility reports appear in the examples and exercises of this chapter.

■ **WORKSHEET FOR PREPARING A RECOMMENDATION/FEASIBILITY REPORT**

❑ *Analyze the audience.*
Who will receive this report?
Who will authorize the recommendation in this report?
How much do they know about the topic?
What is your purpose in writing to them? How will they use the report?

What will make you credible in their estimation?

❏ *Name the two alternatives or name the course of action that you must decide whether to take.*

❏ *Determine criteria.*
Ask technical, management/maintenance, and financial questions.

❏ *For each criterion provide a name, a standard, and a rank.*

❏ *Rank the criteria.*

❏ *Prepare background for the report.*
Who requested the recommendation report? Name the purpose of the report. Name the method of investigation. Name the scope. Explain the problem. What is the basic opposition (such as need for profit versus declining sales)?
What are the causes or effects of the facts in the problem?

❏ *Select a format—formal or informal.*

❏ *Prepare a style sheet including treatment of margins, headings, page numbers, and visual aid captions.*

❏ *Select or prepare visual aids that illustrate the basic data for each criterion.*

❏ *Select an organizational pattern for each section, such as introduction, alternative A, alternative B, visual aid, conclusion.*

■ WORKSHEET FOR A SELF-EVALUATION REPORT

❏ *Evaluate your report. Answer these questions:*

❏ *Evaluate the introduction.*

  ■ Does the introduction give you the gist of the report?

  ■ Does the introduction give you the context (situation, criteria, reason for writing) of the report?

  ■ Do you know the recommendation after 5 to 10 lines?

❏ *Evaluate the criteria.*

  ■ Do they seem appropriate?

  ■ Are all the appropriate ones included? If not, which should be added?

■ Can you find a statement of the standard for each one? If no, which ones?

■ Can you really evaluate the data on the statement of standard?

■ Do you understand why each criterion is part of the discussion?

■ Do you understand the rank of each criterion?

❏ *Evaluate the discussion.*

■ Is the standard given so you can evaluate?

■ Are there enough data so you can evaluate?

■ Do you agree with the evaluation?

■ Do you understand where the data came from?

❏ *Evaluate the visual aid and the paper's format.*

■ Are the two levels of heads different enough? See pages 148–153.

■ Is the discussion called "discussion"?

■ Does a visual appear in each spot where one would help communicate the point?

■ Are any of the visuals more or less useless; that is, they really don't explain anything?

■ Is the visual clearly titled and numbered?

■ Is the visual on the same page as the text that describes it?

■ Does the text tell you what to see in the visual?

■ WORKSHEET FOR EVALUATING A PEER'S REPORT

❏ *Answer the following questions about a peer's paper:*

❏ *Recommendation Rough Draft.*
Read your partner's paper. Ask the following questions:

1. Why did you include each sentence in the introduction? (Explain the reason for each one.)

2. Why did you use the head format you used? Do you think our instructor will like it?

3. Why did you choose each criterion?

4. Why did you write the first sentence you wrote in each criterion section? Do you think our instructor will like them?

5. Why did you organize each section the way you did? Do you think a reader would like to read it this way?

6. What one point have you made with the visual aid? Why did you construct it the way you did and place it where you did? Will our instructor be happy about that?

7. If you had to send this paper to someone who paid you money regularly for doing a good job, would you? If not, what would you do different? Why don't you do that for the final paper?

8. Are you happy with the level of writing in this paper? I mean, do you think these sentences are appropriately professional, the kind of thing you could bring forward as support for your promotion? If not, how will you fix them? If you try to fix them, do you know what you're doing?

EXAMPLES

Examples 15.1–15.3 illustrate informal recommendation and feasibility reports. For other recommendation examples, see "Brief Analytical Reports," Chapter 12, pages 298–300. For another feasibility example, see "Feasibility of Finding Language Program Code on the Internet," Chapter 14, Example 14.2, pages 378–385.

EXAMPLE 15.1
Informal Recommendation Report

Date: December 2, 2003
To: Joseph P. White, Superintendent of Schools
From: David Ayers
Subject: Purchase recommendation for 8" jointer

Recently, Jim DeLallo and I discussed at length the serious problems he was having in operating the jointer at the high school. Considering that the machine has been under continuous student use for 27 years and has reduced accuracy because of the small table and fence size, I indicated I would contact you regarding a new jointer. You asked that I forward 2004–2005 budget requests by December 15.

Therefore, I have prepared this recommendation report for choosing a new 8" jointer. Using lab and catalog resources here at the university and after discussion with other Industrial Arts teachers in this area, I have narrowed my choices to two: Delta Model DJ-20 and Powermatic Model 60. Each machine has been evaluated using the following criteria, in descending order of importance:

1. Fence size
2. Table length
3. Cutting capacity
4. Cost

RECOMMENDATION

It is recommended that the district budget for capital purchase of the Delta Model DJ-20 8" jointer in 2004–2005. Selection of the Delta jointer is a departure from the practice of purchasing Powermatic equipment for the woodworking shop. It is my feeling that the Delta jointer is best suited for the current and future needs of the woodworking program. Service and repair will not be a problem in changing equipment manufacturers, since N. H. Bragg services both lines of equipment.

All elements in the criteria have been met. The slightly higher cost of the Delta, $36.00, is more than offset by increased efficiency and capacity, as noted below.

1. A larger fence size—for better control of stock when squaring
2. A larger table size—resulting in more efficient planing
3. A greater depth of cutting capacity—for improved softwood removal and increased rabbeting capacity

The remainder of the report will compare both machines to the criteria.

EXAMPLE 15.1
(*continued*)

CRITERIA

Fence Size

The fence serves as a guide for planing face and edge surfaces. The size of the fence, width and length, is directly related to cutting efficiency. The fence size of the jointer currently in operation is 3" × 28". In purchasing a new jointer the fence size should be increased for improved accuracy and squaring efficiency.

- Delta DJ-20. As Table 1 shows, the Delta fence size is 5" × 36". This represents a 2" × 8" increase, which will result in more efficient operations.
- Powermatic-60. The Powermatic fence is 4" × 34½", a 1" × 6½" increase over that of the existing fence (see Table 1).

Conclusion. Both machines exceed the fence size criterion of 3" × 28". Delta DJ-20 has the greatest increase, 2" × 8", and will result in greater squaring accuracy and longitudinal control when jointing edge surfaces.

TABLE 1
8" Jointer Capabilities Comparison

Criteria	Standard	Delta DJ-20	Powermatic-60
Fence size	Minimum of 3" wide × 28" long	5" × 36"	4" × 34½"
Table length	Minimum of 52"	76½"	64"
Cutting capacity	Minimum depth of ⅜"	⅝"	½"
Cost	Not to exceed $2,300	$2,128.00	$2,092.00

Table Length

In-feed and out-feed tables are combined and referred to as table length. Increased table length improves accuracy when jointing and provides greater stability when planing face surfaces. On the existing machine, the table length is 52". When planing and jointing stock over 40", it is difficult to maintain accuracy. To realize improved handling and accuracy on a new jointer, the table length should be above 52".

- Delta DJ-20. As Table 1 shows, the table length of the Delta is 76½", a 24½" increase. This increased size will allow for greater efficiency when planing stock to approximately 60".

EXAMPLE 15.1
(continued)

- Powermatic-60. As Table 1 shows, the table length of this jointer exceeds the minimum length by 12″. Improved planing can be increased to approximately 50″.

Conclusion. Both jointers exceed the 52″ minimum table length size. The significant increase in the Delta jointer table length will offer improved planing and jointer accuracy and increased handling capacity.

Cutting Capacity (Depth of Cut)

Jointer cutting capacity is determined by the maximum depth of cut. This depth of cut is created when the in-feed table is lowered. For production work with softwoods and edge rabbeting, a large depth of cut is desired. The existing jointer has a ⅜″ maximum depth of cut. This is a limiting factor when doing softwood production work and constructing edge rabbets over ⅜″. When purchasing a new machine, the depth of cut should be at least ⅜″.

- Delta DJ-20. As Table 1 shows, the depth of cut on this machine is ⅝″, ¼″ above the minimum standard. This will be an important feature when edge rabbeting and doing softwood production work.
- Powermatic-60. As Table 1 shows, the depth of cut for this machine is ½″, a ⅛″ increase above the minimum standard.

Conclusion. Both machines exceed the ⅜″ minimum criterion set. The Delta jointer has the greatest depth of cut, ⅝″, which will allow for greater softwood removal and maximum rabbeting.

Cost

The jointer is a capital equipment item and the cost cannot be department budgeted if in excess of $2,300, unless prior approval is granted by the secondary committee. Costs (including shipping, stand, and three-phase conversion) are

- Delta DJ-20: $2,128.00
- Powermatic-60: $2,092.00

Conclusion. Both machines meet the fourth criterion. The Powermatic is slightly lower in cost, but does not have all the capacity and features of the Delta model. The additional cost of the Delta jointer ($6.80 on a 20-year depreciation schedule) is more than offset by the increase in table and fence size and improved cutting depth.

EXAMPLE 15.2
Informal Recommendation Report

Date: 4/23/03
To: Pete Boyer
From: Kevin Albinson
Subject: Table saws

This is regarding your question on which table saw to buy for your company. I narrowed my options down to two saws after knowing your criteria: the Rugged 22172 and the Powermate 3400. In order to decide between these two, I found an article in *The Woodworkers Journal*, October 1993, comparing them. After studying the article, I decided that the Powermate 3400 would be the best table saw for you.

CRITERIA

Here are the criteria you gave me in descending order of importance. (See the "Standard" column in Tables 1 and 2 for specifics on the criteria.)

1. Machine capabilities
2. Machine features
3. Cost

MACHINE CAPABILITIES

Table 1 compares the capabilities of the saws.

TABLE 1
Machine Capabilities

Capabilities	Standard	Rugged	Powermate
1. Portable	Yes	Yes	Yes
2. Left rip cap.	10"	13"	11"
3. Right rip cap.	20"	15"	28"
4. Depth of cut	3"	2½"	3"
5. Speed (rpm)	4000	5000	4800

Powermate 3400

As you can see in the table, the Powermate fulfills every requirement needed. The most impressive is the right rip cut, because it will help when cutting plywood or large objects.

Rugged 22172

This saw does fulfill many of the requirements. In fact, it even has a faster speed than the Powermate. It does, however, fall short in the right

EXAMPLE 15.2
(continued)

rip capacity and the depth of the cut, which are important and can't be overlooked.

MACHINE FEATURES

Table 2 compares the features of the saws.

TABLE 2
Features

Features	Standard	Rugged	Powermate
1. Blade size	10″	10″	10″
2. Rip fence	Yes	Yes	Yes
3. Miter gauge	Easy to read	No	Yes
4. Dust control	Yes	No	Yes

Powermate 3400

Once again, this saw fulfills all the standards needed. The article talked about how easy it was to read and use the miter gauge, which is very important for some of the jobs that you do.

Rugged 22172

This saw did not fulfill all the requirements once again. The article stated that this miter gauge was hard to use and didn't have a dust output.

COST

The cost must not go over $300, and neither of the saws does. The most expensive saw is the Rugged 22172 at a price of $199.99. For a little cheaper you get the Powermate 3400 for $179.00, and it is a better saw.

EXAMPLE 15.3
Informal Feasibility Report

WEB FEASIBILITY STUDY FOR PRODUCT DEVELOPMENT

By

Brandon McCartney

Student, Technical Writing, UW-Stout

December 9, 2003

Prepared for

Kong Mua

Coordinator

Product Development Curriculum

EXAMPLE 15.3
(continued)

ABSTRACT
The purpose of this project is to find out if the Web is a feasible source of information for product development. Two areas of product development that I am researching are rapid prototyping (RP) and concurrent engineering (CE). I want to know what the different types of rapid prototyping are and how concurrent engineering can help reduce the time to market of new products. From my research I believe that the Web is a very useful source of information for product development.

EXAMPLE 15.3
(*continued*)

INTRODUCTION

I performed the research to decide whether or not the Web is a valuable research tool for product development. This report describes what information I found and the conclusions I made. The reason that I am searching for rapid prototyping and concurrent engineering is because these two topics are going to change the way products are developed and manufactured.

Criteria

To determine if the Web sites I found are feasible, I set three criteria: recency, credibility, and the site should not be trying to sell services. Also, I want at least five sites that meet all of my criteria.

- Recency—The informaton on the site needs to have been updated within the last 2 years. Because these two topics are fairly new I should have no problem finding information that was published in the last two years.

- Credibility—For the site to meet this criterion, it needs to have contact information, list of references, pictures of parts if it is an RP site, and links to other related sites.

- Site needs to be a professional organization, institute, or university—I do not want company pages telling me how great their business is. If there is a business site, then I want reference to where they got the information. I am assuming that any address that has ".com" is a company.

Because I was able to find five Web sites that met all three criteria, I concluded that the Web is a valuable source of information for rapid prototyping and concurrent engineering.

Method

I used various search engines to search the Web; however, the two main search engines used were Hot Bot and Yahoo. I picked these two because I have used them in the past and they have returned good results. Also, Hot Bot was the *PC Magazine* editor's choice in the December 2 issue. The keywords I used for my rapid prototyping search were "rapid prototyping and product development." I received usable results from this search, so I did not think it was necessary to do advanced searches. Once resuls were returned, I scanned the titles and description of the sites. I went to sites that I thought would meet my criteria. I skimmed the site deciding if it met the recency and credibility criteria. Usually the title told me if it was a company's page. If the site looked good, I bookmarked it for further review.

EXAMPLE 15.3
(continued)

When I performed the searches for concurrent engineering, I used the same technique but used different keywords. I used "concurrent engineering and product development" as keywords.

Another way I searched for sites was to use related links of pages. When I scanned the site, I looked for links of related sites. Most of the time, pages refer to other valuable pages they have found. I have found lots of good sites using this method.

CONCLUSION

I was able to find five Web sites that met all three criteria for rapid prototyping and concurrent engineering. I conclude that the Web is a valuable source of information for my area of product development.

DISCUSSION

Rapid Prototyping

Introduction.   Rapid prototyping is helping companies reduce the time to market of new products. This is increasing their profit margins. Engineers can export their three-dimensional CAD models into an RP machine, and within minutes to hours, they can have a working prototype. This is changing the way products are being designed. There is some talk about RP here at Stout, but not enough. I wanted to explore the Net to see what different types of rapid prototyping are being used in industry.

From my search of the Web, I believe that it is a valuable tool for rapid prototyping. I was able to find many sites that met my criteria.

What I Found.   I found numerous Web pages dealing with rapid prototyping that met all of my criteria. A rapid prototyping consultant published one of the best RP sites. The title of the page is "Wohlers Web World." At first I did not think this site offered any useful information. I was wrong. This site was loaded with links to other prototyping pages, technical papers, and reports. There are over 40 articles on-line for free and 124 related links. The purpose of this page was to give people prototyping information. I found this site by following a link from another page. I had seen it referred to on other pages as well, so I decided to see what was on it. It was last updated on November 8, 2003. There were contact information and E-mail addresses posted at the top of the page. I feel that this site was very credible, because all of the information was there for me to research for free, and many other pages used it as a reference.

EXAMPLE 15.3
(continued)

TABLE 1
Rapid Prototyping Web Pages

Title	Address	Last Update	Credible	Related Links
Wohlers Web World	*lamar.colostate. edu/~wohlers/*	Nov. 8, 2003	Very	Yes
Rapid Prototyping Home Page	*stress.mech.utah.edu/ home/novac/rapid.html*	Dec. 7, 2003	Yes	Yes
The Rapid Prototyping Development Laboratory	*www.udri.udayton.edu/ mat_eng/rpdl.htm*	March 20, 2003	Yes	Yes
Rapid Prototyping Laboratory	*cadserv.cadlab.vt.edu/ bohn/RP.html*	Dec. 1, 2003	Yes	Yes
Center of Advanced Manufacturing: Rapid Prototyping	*www.eng.clemson.edu/ ~apapada/SLS/main.html*	April 22, 2003	Yes	Yes

Conclusion.   From my research of the Web pages, I believe that the Web is a valuable source of information for rapid prototyping. There were still plenty of companies' Web pages that I had to scan at first, but when I found a good site, there were other links to other RP-related sites. I think some of the search time was due to the keywords I searched for. I feel that, if I narrowed down the search, I would get results faster.

Concurrent Engineering

Introduction.   Concurrent engineering is a systematic approach of involving all departments in the development of a new product at the same time. I believe that the Web is a useful source of information for concurrent engineering. I found sites that met the criteria of recency, credibility, and not a company site.

What I Found.   From my search of the Net, I was able to find many good sites on concurrent engineering. The best site was the Society of Concurrent Engineers Home Page. It was last updated on 11/22/03. Contact information was on the Board of Directors page, which is a link off the main page telling readers who the directors are and how they can be contacted. Finally, it is not a company's Web advertisement.

    This site has many different areas to gather information. For example, there is a link called "Discussion Web." Discussion Web is an on-line discussion forum where engineers can post letters about concurrent

EXAMPLE 15.3
(continued)

engineering. There was a link to the "SOCE Bookstore," where you can purchase books on CE. Any good Web site has links to other related sites. The SOCE Home Page has 13 different related links. Also, there are links to magazines, associations, universities, and businesses. Another link I liked was "Paper & News Articles." Here there are various papers and news articles that members of SOCE have submitted for reading. This site was a one-stop concurrent engineering page.

TABLE 2
Concurrent Engineering Web Pages

Title	Address	Recency	Credible
SOCE Home Page	*www.soce.org/*	11/22/03	Yes
CERC	*www.cerc.wvu.edu/*	2003	Yes
CERG/SMIC Concurrent Engineering Information Center	*www.mor.itesm.mx/~ smic/ceic/*	2003	Yes
CERG	*www.mor.itesm.mx/ EVENTOS/CERG/CERG.html*	2/14/02	Yes
Oak Ridge Centers for Manufacturing Technology	*cewww.eng.ornl.gov/*	6/19/02	Yes

Conclusion.   I feel that the Web is a valuable source of information for concurrent engineering. The sites all had useful information. I did come across some company Web sites advertising their services. From the information posted on the Web, I was able to find out how concurrent engineering is changing the rate at which new products are being developed.

■ EXERCISES

1. In groups of two to four, analyze the community attitudes that are addressed by the authors of Examples 15.1–15.3 or of the examples in Exercises 2 and 3 below. What factors have the writers obviously tried to accommodate? What kind of memo is expected? What length? Do they desire to prove conclusively that the material is accurate? Or is there an informal understanding that only a few words are necessary?

    Alternate: In the groups, role-play the sender and receiver of the reports. Receivers interview the senders to decide whether to implement the recommendation.

2. Analyze this sample for organization, format, depth of detail, and persuasiveness. If necessary, rewrite the memo to eliminate your criticisms. Create the visual aid that the author mentions at the end of the report. Alternate: Rewrite the memo as a much "crisper," less chatty document. Alternate: Construct a table that summarizes the data in the report.

    The purpose of this report is to determine from which insurance company I should purchase liability insurance for my 1994 Pontiac 6000. Data for this report were gathered from personal interviews with agents representing their companies. After comparing different companies, I narrowed my choice to decide which one I should buy. I evaluated Ever Safe and Urban Insurance using the following criteria, which are ranked in importance:

    1. Cost—Could annual insurance of liability be less than $250?
    2. Payments—Could it be paid semiannually?
    3. Service—Is the agent easily accessible?

    After this evaluation, I concluded that Ever Safe was the best company to purchase my liability insurance. First, this insurance company costs $245, which is less than the $250 limit that I proposed to spend. Second, it can be paid semiannually. And, third, Ever Safe offers toll-free claim service 24 hours a day.

    Ever Safe costs $245 a year, with Urban Insurance costing $240 a year, which both met my required criteria of purchasing liability insurance for under $250. Urban Insurance is $5 less; however, Ever Safe does have other options that are worth the extra money in means of purchasing.

    Ever Safe and Urban Insurance both offer semiannual payments. In terms of this aspect, they are both weighted the same.

    Ever Safe offers toll-free claim service 24 hours a day. Urban Insurance is long distance with limited working hours. They are available after working hours but only through an answering machine that will record your message for the agent to get in touch with you on the following day.

In the decision of an insurance company, it is plain to see that Ever Safe meets the requirements of my criteria and that Urban Insurance does not. Urban Insurance is cheaper, allows semiannual payments, but does not fulfill the service that I was looking for. For the extra dollars of payment, the service in Ever Safe is worth it.

---

3. Analyze this sample for organization, format, depth of detail, and persuasiveness. Rewrite the memo, if necessary, to eliminate your criticisms. Create a visual aid that the author mentions at the end of the report. Summarize the data that support the recommendation. Alternate: Rewrite the memo as a much "crisper," less chatty document. Alternate: Construct a table or figure that effectively summarizes the data in the report.

DATE: December 1, 2005
TO: Dan Riordan
FROM: Tim Maple
SUBJECT: Buying New Negative Air Machines vs. Reconditioning Current Machines

INTRODUCTION

Two of our negative air machines are in poor condition and will need major repairs or replacing within the next month. I have suggested buying new machines or having the bad machines reconditioned. In response to your request that I research the two alternatives, the following report will support my recommendation to buy two new machines.

Two of our negative air machines are in poor working condition. One machine is six years old, and the other is seven. This means they have no value after being depreciated for five years. The warranties are void, and both stand a high chance of breakdown in the near future. If these machines break down on a job site, the cost could be very high due to the job becoming behind schedule and due to the cost of cleaning up contamination. If contamination results, the fines from OSHA and the EPA could put our business into bankruptcy. It is imperative that the machines be reliable and in good working order.

I have evaluated the two proposals using information obtained from vendors and repairmen. All information was compared based on the following criteria:

1. Machines must have warranties.
2. Stay within the $10,000 budget.
3. Machines must be able to move 600 cfm of air per machine.
4. Machines must have at least a two-stage filter.

COMPARISON OF THE PROPOSALS RELATIVE TO THE CRITERIA

My recommendation is to buy two new machines. All of the information on the new machines is for a model made by SurVac—the SV-800. This is the particular machine that I recommend.

All criteria are met by both proposals. I have based my recommendation on how strongly each criterion is met.

The SV-800 have a five-year warranty on parts and labor. A new machine is more reliable than a used machine, and the five-year warranty spans the useful life of the machine. It will be depreciated over a five-year period. The reconditioned machines would have to be depreciated over a three-year period, and the warranty on the reconditioned machine is only one year.

Two new machines will cost $6,400, and the reconditioning of two machines will cost $3,000.

The new machines will be able to move 800 cfm of air, which provides quicker total air exchange. This provides a safer working environment and allows us to do larger jobs. We would be able to meet the minimum of three total air exchanges per hour for most large jobs.

The three-stage filter is an added advantage over the two-stage filter because it will not plug as often. This enables the machine to create a safer discharge air and to prolong the life of the expensive HEPA filters.

Serviceability, meaning how easy repairs are on the machine, is greater for the new machines due to the design of the machines. It is easier to repair in the field and major repairs take less time. Changing of the filters and maintenance are also easier due to the design of the new machines. The reconditioned machines are lighter, but this does not support reconditioning because the new machines are just as mobile and easy to handle. The shut-down warning of the new machines has a light and a buzzer. This provides warning in noisy environments and where the machine is not visible.

---

4. Combine the following text and table into a table, and then write a brief section in which you compare the two machines and recommend one of them.

Machine Capabilities

Capabilities of the new machine must meet our tooling engineer's specified criteria. His criteria are:

1. Accuracy: Material movement on the x/y table shall be a minimum of + or − 2.005 in. on hole centers.
2. Linear table speed: Minimum table speed must be more than 1000 in. per minute (IPM).
3. Tonnage: The punching tonnage shall equal or exceed 20 tons.

4. Tool loading: Tools shall have the ability to be preloaded into a turret that will automatically feed tools into the machine punching head.

5. Indexing punch head: The punching head of the machine shall have the ability to index 360 in both directions.

6. Laser/plasma capabilities: The machine shall have the designed-in capability to add laser or plasma cutting.

The following table shows how both machines measure up to these criteria. It is important to note the outstanding accuracy and speed of the Magnum XQF.

TABLE 1
Machine Capabilities Comparison

Criteria	Wardell Magnum XQF	Williamson Model 150B
Accuracy	± .002 in.	± .005 in.
Table speed	2400 IPM	1200 IPM
Tonnage	45 tons	30 tons
Tool loading	Yes	No
Indexing punch head	Yes	No
Laser capabilities	Yes	Yes
Plasma capabilities	Yes	Yes

5. As your instructor requires, perform the following exercises in conjunction with one of this chapter's Writing Assignments.

   a. Perform the actions required by the worksheet.

   b. Write a discussion section. Construct a visual aid that depicts data for each criterion. Write an introduction for the section: define the criterion and tell its significance, rank, and source. Point out the relevant data for each section. Write a one-sentence conclusion. Word it positively. (Say X is cheaper than Y, not Y is more expensive than X.)

   c. Write an introduction that orients the reader to the situation and to your recommendation. Choose one of the several methods shown in this chapter and Chapter 12.

   d. In groups of two or three, review each other's problem statements and the criteria derived from them. Make suggestions for improvement.

   e. In groups of two or three, read a body section from each other's reports. Assess whether it presents the data that support the conclusion.

f. In groups of two or three, compare conclusions to the recommendations. Do the conclusions support the recommendations?

g. In groups of two or three, assess each other's introductions. Do they contain enough information to orient the reader to the situation and the recommendation?

h. In groups of two or three, read the near-final reports for consistency of format. Are all the heads at the appropriate level? Are all the heads really informative? Is the style sheet applied consistently? Does it help make the contents easy to group? Do the visual aids effectively communicate key points?

■ WRITING ASSIGNMENTS

1. Assume that you are working for a local firm and have been asked to evaluate two kinds, brands, or models of equipment. Select a limited topic (for instance, two specific models of 10-inch table saws, the Black and Decker model 123 and the Craftsman model ABC), and evaluate the alternatives in detail. Write a report recommending that one of the alternatives be purchased to solve a problem. Be sure to explain the problem. Both alternatives should be workable; your report must recommend the one that will work better.

    Gather data about the alternatives just as you would when working in industry—from sales literature, dealers, your own experience, and the experience of others who have worked with the equipment. Select a maximum of four criteria by which to judge the alternatives and use a minimum of one visual aid in the report. Aim your report at someone not familiar with the equipment. Fill out the worksheet in this chapter, and perform the parts of Exercise 5 that your instructor requires.

2. Assume that you are working for a local firm that wants to expand to a site within 50 miles. Pick an actual site in your area. Then write a feasibility report on the site. Devise criteria based on the situation. Do all the research necessary to discover land values, transportation systems, governing agencies, costs, and any other relevant factors. Your instructor will provide you with guidance about how to deal with the local authorities and how to discover the facts about these topics. Use this chapter's worksheet, and perform those parts of Exercise 5 that your instructor requires.

3. Assume that you have been asked to decide on the feasibility of a proposed course of action. Name and describe the proposal. Then establish the relevant criteria to determine feasibility. Apply the criteria and write an informal report. Use this chapter's worksheet, and perform those parts of Exercise 5 that your instructor requires.

4. Find a firm or agency in your locale that has a problem that it will allow you to solve. Research the problem, and present the solution in a report. The report may be either formal or informal, recommendation or feasibility. Your instructor will help you schedule the project. This project should not be an exercise in format and organization, but a solution that people need in order to perform well on their jobs. Use this chapter's worksheet, and perform those parts of Exercise 5 that your instructor requires.

5. Assume that your manager wants to create a Web page. Investigate the situation, and write a report explaining the feasibility of creating and maintaining a Web site.

6. Write a learning report for the writing assignment you just completed. See Chapter 5, Writing Assignment 7, page 123, for details of the assignment.

■ WEB EXERCISES

1. Assume that your manager wants to create a Web page. Investigate the situation and write a report explaining the feasibility of creating and maintaining a Web site.

2. Write a report on whether or not the Web is a feasible source of information that you can use to perform your duties as a professional in your field. For instance, is the Web a more feasible source than hard copy of OSHA regulations or ASTM standards?

■ WORKS CITED

Alexander, Heather, and Ben Potter. "Case Study: The Use of Formal Specification and Rapid Prototyping to Establish Product Feasibility." *Information and Software Technology* 29.7 (1987): 388–394.

Angelo, Rocco M. *Understanding Feasibility Studies.* East Lansing, MI: Educational Institute of the American Hotel and Motel Association, 1985.

Bradford, Michael. "Four Types of Feasibility Studies Can Be Used." *Business Insurance* 19 June 1989: 16.

Holcombe, Marya W., and Judith K. Stein. *Writing for Decision Makers: Memos and Reports with a Competitive Edge.* Belmont, CA: Lifelong, 1981.

Markel, Mike. "Criteria Development and the Myth of Objectivity." *The Technical Writing Teacher* 18.1 (1991): 37–47.

Ramige, Robert K. "Packaging Equipment: Twelve Steps for Project Management." *IOPP Technical Journal* X.3 (1992): 47–50.

16 Proposals

Chapter 16
IN A NUTSHELL

The goal of a proposal is to persuade readers to accept a course of action as an acceptable way to solve a problem or fill a need. Internal proposals show that the situation is bad and your way will clearly make it better. External proposals show that your way is the best.

Basic proposal issues.   Four issues for you to discuss convincingly in a proposal are

- The *problem*—how some fact negatively affects positive expectations (high absenteeism on manufacturing line 1 is causing a failure to meet production goals) and that you know the cause (workers are calling in sick because of sore backs).
- The *solution*—actions that will neutralize the cause (eliminate bending by reconfiguring the work tables and automating one material transfer point).

- The *benefits* of the solution—what desirable outcome each person or group in the situation will obtain.
- The *implementation*—who will do it and how, how long it will take.

Develop credibility.   To accept your solution, your readers must feel you are credible. Your methods must be clear and normal—what a person would expect of an expert in this situation. Your analyses of the problem, the cause, the benefits, how long it will take, the cost, etc., must show a reasonable way to regard each concern, one that will not cause surprises later on.

Basic guidelines.   Follow these guidelines:

- Use a top-down strategy.
- Use clear heads and visual aids.
- Provide context in the introduction.
- Provide a summary that clearly states the proposed solution.

419

A proposal persuades its readers to accept the writer's idea. There are two kinds of proposals: external and internal. In an *external proposal,* one firm responds to a request—from another firm or the government—for a solution to a problem. Ranging from lengthy (100 pages or more) to short (4 or 5 pages), these documents secure contracts for firms. In an *internal proposal,* the writer urges someone else in the company to accept an idea or to fund equipment purchases or research.

THE EXTERNAL PROPOSAL

A firm writes external proposals to win contracts for work. Government agencies and large and small corporations issue a *request for proposal (RFP),* which explains the project and lists its specifications precisely. For example, a major aircraft company, such as British Airlines, often sends RFPs to several large firms to solicit proposals for a specific type of equipment—say, a guidance system. The RFP contains extremely detailed and comprehensive specifications, stating standards for minute technical items and specifying the content, format, and deadline for the proposals.

The companies that receive the RFP write proposals to show how they will develop the project. A team assembles a document demonstrating that the company has the technical know-how, managerial expertise, and budget to develop the project.

After receiving all the proposals, the firm that requested them turns them over to a team of evaluators, some of whom helped write the original specifications. The evaluators rate the proposals, judging the technical, management, and cost sections in order to select the best overall proposal (Bacon).

Not all proposals are written to obtain commercial contracts. Proposals are also commonly written by state and local governments, public agencies, education, and industry. University professors often write proposals, bringing millions of dollars to campuses to support research in fields as varied as food spoilage and genetic research.

Discussion of a lengthy, 50- to 200-page proposal is beyond the scope of this book; it is a subject for an entire course. But brief external proposals are very common. They require the same planning and contain the same elements as a lengthy proposal. The following sections illustrate the planning and elements of a brief external proposal. A sample external proposal appears in the Instructors Resource Manual.

PLANNING THE EXTERNAL PROPOSAL

To write an external proposal, you must consider your audience, research the situation, use visual aids, and follow the usual form for this type of document.

Consider the Audience

The audience for an external proposal consists of potential customers. These customers know that they have a need, and they have a general idea of how to fill that need. Usually they will have expressed their problem to you in a written statement (an RFP) or in an interview. Generally, a committee decides whether to accept your proposal. Assess their technical awareness and write in such a way that not only do they understand your proposal, but they also have confidence in it and in you. To write to them effectively, you should follow these guidelines:

- Address each need they have expressed.
- Explain in clear terms how your proposal fills their needs.
- Explain the relevance of technical data.

For instance, if you want to sell a computer system to a nonprofit arts organization, you cannot just drop code names for microprocessors—say, an 80486 chip—and expect them to know what that means. You need to explain the data so that the people who make the decision to commit their money will feel comfortable.

Research the Situation

To write the proposal effectively, understand your customer's needs as well as the features of your own product or service. Your goal is to show how the features will fill the needs. Discover this by interviewing the customer or by reading their printed material. Showing that you understand the situation and have taken proper research steps enhances your credibility.

Writers devise different ways to develop their research. To relate needs and features, many writers compile a two-column table like this:

Need	Feature That Meets Need
Director must be able to access latest financial data and public relations data.	Available on Appletalk network, hard disk.
Director must be able to access data at any time.	Director needs workstation in her office.
Secretary enters data, but not continuously.	Secretary needs access to workstation.
Secretary does accounting.	Secretary can use Accountant Inc. 2.1c.
Artist enters data.	Artist needs access to workstation.
Artist does desktop publishing.	Artist needs Aldus Pagemaker and laser printer.

Need	*Feature That Meets Need*
$15,000 maximum.	2 lower end computers, 1 laser printer; software for artwork, word processing, accounting, and desktop publishing.

Once you establish the client's needs, you can easily point out a reasonable way to meet them.

Use Visual Aids

Many types of visual aids may be appropriate to your proposal. Tables might summarize costs and technical features. Maps (or layouts), for instance, might show where you will install the workstation and the electrical lines in the office complex. Illustrations of the product with callouts can point out special features. Remember that your goal is to convince the decision makers that your way is the best; good visuals are direct and dramatic, drawing your client into the document.

WRITING THE EXTERNAL PROPOSAL

To write an external proposal, follow the usual form for writing proposals. The four main parts of a proposal are an executive summary and the technical, managerial, and financial sections. An external proposal appears in the student sample section of the Instructor's Manual.

The Executive Summary

The executive summary contains information designed to convince executives that the proposers should receive the contract. In short external proposals, this section should be reduced in proportion to the body (see Chapter 6). It should succinctly present the contents of the technical, managerial, and financial sections. Generally write this section last.

The Technical Section

A proposal's technical section begins by stating the problem to be solved. The proposers must clearly demonstrate that they understand what the customer expects. The proposal should describe its approach to solving the problem and present a preliminary design for the product, if one is needed. Sometimes the firm offers alternative methods for solving the problem and invites the proposal writer to select one. In the computer network example, the proposal might explain three different configurations that fulfill needs slightly differently but still stay within the $15,000 maximum cost.

The Management Section

The management section describes the personnel who will work directly on the project. The proposal explains the expertise of the people responsible for the project. In a short proposal, this section usually explains qualifications of personnel, the firm's success with similar projects, and its willingness to service the product, provide technical assistance, and train employees. This section also includes a schedule for the project, sometimes including deadlines for each phase.

The Financial Section

The financial section provides a breakdown of the costs for every item in the proposal. This section varies in depth. Often a brief introduction and table may be sufficient, but if you need to explain the source or significance of certain figures, do so.

THE INTERNAL PROPOSAL

The internal proposal persuades someone to accept an idea—usually to change something, or to fund something, or both. Covering a wide range of subjects, internal proposals may request new pieces of lab equipment, defend major capital expenditures, or recommend revised production control standards. The rest of this chapter explains the internal proposal's audiences, visual aids, and design.

PLANNING THE INTERNAL PROPOSAL

The goal of a proposal is to convince the person or group in authority to allow the writer to implement his or her idea. To achieve this goal, the writer must consider the audience, use visual aids, organize the proposal well, and design an appropriate format.

Consider the Audience

Writers consider the audience of a proposal in at least three ways: in terms of their involvement, their knowledge, and their authority.

How Involved Is the Audience?   In most cases, readers of a proposal either have assigned the proposal and are aware of the problem or have not assigned the proposal and are unaware of the problem. For example, suppose a problem develops with a particular assembly line. The production engineer in charge might assign a subordinate to investigate the situation and recommend a solution. In this assigned proposal, the writer does not have to establish that a problem exists, but he or she does have to show how the proposal will solve the problem.

More often, however, the audience does not assign the proposal. For instance, a manager could become aware that a new arrangement of her floor space could create better sales potential. If she decides to propose a rearrangement, she must first convince her audience—her supervisor—that a problem exists. Only then can she go on to offer a convincing solution.

How Knowledgeable Is the Audience?   The audience may or may not know the concepts and facts involved in either the problem or the solution. Learn to estimate your audience's level of knowledge. If the audience is less knowledgeable, take care to define terms, give background, and use common examples or analogies.

How Much Authority Does the Audience Have?   The audience may or may not be able to order the implementation of your proposed solution. A manager might assign the writer to investigate problems with the material flow of a particular product line, but the manager will probably have to take the proposal to a higher authority before it is approved. So the writer must bear in mind that several readers may see and approve (or reject) the proposal.

Use Visual Aids

Because the proposal is likely to have multiple audiences, visual aids are important. Visuals can support any part of the proposal—the description of the problem, the solution, the implementation, and the benefits. In addition to the tables and graphs described in Chapter 8, Gantt charts and diagrams can be very helpful.

Gantt Charts.   As described in Chapter 8, Gantt charts visually depict a schedule of implementation. A Gantt chart has an X axis and a Y axis. The horizontal axis displays time periods; the vertical axis, individual processes. Lines inside the chart show when a process starts and stops. By glancing at the chart, the reader can see the project's entire schedule. Figure 16.1 is an example of a Gantt chart.

Diagrams.   Many kinds of diagrams, such as flow charts, block diagrams, organization charts, and decision trees, can enhance a proposal. Layouts, for instance, are effective for proposals that suggest rearranging space.

Organize the Proposal

The writer should organize the proposal around four questions:

FIGURE 16.1
Gantt Chart

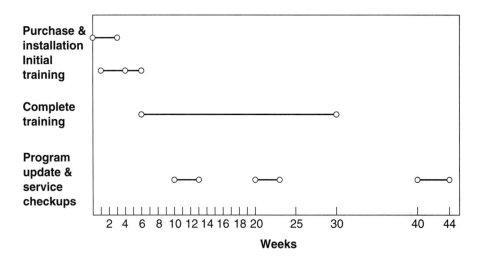

1. What is the problem?
2. What is the solution?
3. Can the solution be implemented?
4. Should the solution be implemented?

What Is the Problem? Describing the problem is a key part of many proposals. You must establish three things about the problem:

- The data
- The significance
- The cause

The *data* are the actual facts that a person can perceive. The *significance* is the way the facts fail to meet the standard you hope to maintain. To explain the significance of the problem, you show that the current situation negatively affects productivity or puts you in an undesirable position. The *cause* is the problem itself. If you can eliminate the cause, you will eliminate the negative effects. Of course, almost every researcher soon discovers that there are chains of causes. You must carry your analysis back to the most reasonable cause. If the problem is ultimately the personality of the CEO, you might want to stop the chain before you say that. To be credible, you must show that you have investigated the problem thoroughly by talking to the right people, looking at the right records, making the right inspection, showing the appropriate data, or whatever. In the following section from a proposal, the writers describe a problem:

CONFUSING PARKING SIGNS

Table 1 shows a big jump in the number of parking tickets given out in 2002–2003, an increase of over 3000 tickets. We feel that the increase occurred because of the inadequate parking lot signs. The current signs are old, plain, vague, and not very sensible. They only state that a permit is required, and one often does not know what kind of permit is needed. The signs don't specify whether they are for faculty, students, or commuters. In addition, the current signs are only 12 inches by 18–24 inches and can be overlooked if people are unaware of them.

 In our survey of some West Central University students, we found that many students who received tickets either did not know that they could not park in the specific lot, were unsure of which lot they were able to park in, or did not see any specific signs suggesting that they could not park there.

Significance

Cause
Data

Significance

TABLE 1
Tickets Given Out per 2500 Parking Stalls at
West Central University

Year	No. of Tickets
2000–2001	13,202
2001–2002	13,764
2002–2003	16,867

What Is the Solution? To present an effective solution, explain how it will eliminate the cause, thus eliminating whatever is out of step with the standard you hope to maintain. If the problem is causing an undesirable condition, the solution must show how that condition can be eliminated. If the old signage for parking lots gives insufficient information, explain how the solution gives better information. A helpful approach is to analyze the solution in terms of its impact on the technical, management/maintenance, and financial aspects of the situation.

NEW SIGNS FOR ENTRANCE

Our solution is to create new permanent signs which will be installed at the entrance of each parking lot. The new signs (in their entirety) will measure 3 feet by 4 feet so

Solution named

they will be visible to anyone entering the lot. Each sign will include the name of the lot; a letter to designate if the lot is for students (S), faculty (F), or administration (A); a color code for the particular permit needed; and the time and the days that the lot is monitored. The signs will not only present the proper information but will also look nice, making the campus more appealing. See Figure 1 for the proposed design.

Details show how the solution solves the problem.

Benefits

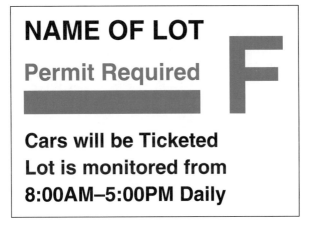

FIGURE 1
Entrance Sign

Can the Solution Be Implemented?   The writer must show that all the systems involved in the proposal can be put into effect. To make this clear to the audience, you would explain

- The cost.
- The effect on personnel.
- The schedule for implementing the changes.

This section may be difficult to write because it is hard to tell exactly what the audience needs to know.

IMPLEMENTATION

The businesses we suggest that you deal with are Fulweil Structures, CE Signs, and University Grounds Services. The reason for choosing these businesses is that you will please the community of Menomonie by doing business in town and these businesses have good prices for a project like this. Also, these companies can provide services over the summer.

Agents involved in implementation

Schedule

Implementation of the new signs will take approximately one summer.

A suggested schedule is

1. Order signs from Fulweil.   1 week ˙
2. Fulweil constructs signs.   1 week
3. CE paints signs.   1 week
4. Grounds crew erects signs.   2 weeks

If you compare this schedule to the estimates below, you will see that we have built in some time for delays. The project can be easily finished in a month. We suggest June because it has the fewest students for the most weeks; our second suggestion is August, but then you will have to finish by about the 20th or risk much confusion when school starts on the 25th.

Schedule explained

Cost

Below is a list of supplies and approximate costs from Fulweil Structures and CE Signs. The total project cost is $13,892.16. Fulweil Structures asked us to inform you that these prices are not binding quotes.

Cost background

TABLE 2
List of Supplies and Approximate Costs for New Entrance Signs

Fulweil Structures (each sign)

6′ × 2″ × 2″ solid bar aluminum (2 in quantity)		
3′4″ × 3′4″ aluminum sheet (1 in quantity)	$183.84	
3 hours of labor at $25/hour	75.00	
Total cost		$ 258.84

Table presents all cost figures

CE Signs (each sign)

3′ × 3′ Reflective Scotchguard	$ 50.00	
10–15 letters painted	125.00	
2½ hours labor at $34/hour	85.00	
Total cost		$ 260.00
Total cost of each sign		518.84
Total cost of 24 signs		12,452.16
Projected cost of erecting signs		
2 hours/sign @ 25.00/hr (24 signs)	1200.00	
Materials/sign @ 10.00 (24 signs)	240.00	
Total cost of erecting signs		1440.00
Total cost of project (24 signs)		$13,892.16

Should the Solution Be Implemented?   Just because you can implement the solution does not mean that you should. To convince someone that you should be allowed to implement your solution, you must demonstrate that the solution has benefits that make it desirable, that it meets the established criteria in the situation, or both.

THE BENEFITS OF THIS PROJECT

The benefits of the signs will be felt by you, the students, the faculty, and the administration. You will see the number of appeals decline because the restrictions will be clearly visible, saving much bookwork and time for appeals. You will also answer fewer phone calls from persons needing to know where to park and you will write fewer tickets, thus saving much processing time.

   The students, faculty, and administration will be happier because they will know exactly where and when they can and cannot park. Students will not receive as many parking tickets and will save money. Faculty and administration will also benefit by not having students park in their reserved parking spots (or at least not as often).

List of people who benefit

Discussion of each area of benefit

Design the Proposal

To design a proposal, select an appropriate format, either *formal* or *informal*. A formal proposal has a title page, table of contents, and summary (see Chapter 14). An informal proposal can be a memo report or some kind of preprinted form (see Chapter 12). The format depends on company policy and on the distance the proposal must travel in the hierarchy. Usually the shorter the distance, the more informal the format. Also, the less significant the proposal, the more informal the format. For instance, you would not send an elaborately formatted proposal to your immediate superior to suggest a $50 solution to a layout problem in a work space.

WRITING THE INTERNAL PROPOSAL

Use the Introduction to Orient the Reader

The introduction to a proposal demands careful thought because it must orient the reader to the writer, the problem, and the solution. The introduction can contain one paragraph or several. You should clarify the following important points:

- Why is the writer writing? Is the proposal assigned or unsolicited?
- Why is the writer credible?
- What is the problem?
- What is the background of the problem?

- What is the significance of the problem?
- What is the solution?
- What are the parts of the report?

An effective way to provide all these points is in a two-part introduction that includes a context-setting paragraph and a summary. The context-setting paragraph usually explains the purpose of the proposal and, if necessary, gives evidence of the writer's credibility. The summary is a one-to-one miniaturization of the body. (Be careful not to make the summary a background; background belongs in a separate section.) If the body contains sections on the solution, benefits, cost, implementation, and rejected alternatives, the summary should cover the same points.

A sample introduction follows.

DATE:	April 8, 2003
TO:	Jennifer Williamson
FROM:	Steve Vinz
	Mike Vivoda
	Michele Welsh
	Marya Wilson
SUBJECT:	Installing new parking lot signs

Parking on campus has been a topic of many discussions here at West Central University and one of much concern. The topics on parking include what lots students are able to park in, when students can park in the lots, and the availability of parking on campus. We believe that students do not know exactly when and where they can park in the campus lots because of the vague and confusing signs.

Reason for writing: sets context

We feel that the school should post at each entrance new, more informative, and more readable signs containing all the rules and regulations. These signs would say exactly who can and cannot park in the lot, the times when the lots are patrolled, and what type of permit is needed. The project could be completed in 5 weeks and would cost $13,892.16. Major benefits include fewer administrative hassles and happier university community members. This memo will first discuss the problem, then the solution, implementation, and the benefits.

Summary

Preview of sections

Use the Discussion to Convince Your Audience

The discussion section contains all the detailed information that you must present to convince the audience. A common approach functions this way:

The problem

- Explanation of the problem
- Causes of the problem

The solution

- Details of the solution
- Benefits of the solution
- Ways in which the solution satisfies criteria

The context

- Schedule for implementing the solution
- Personnel involved
- Solutions rejected

In each section, present the material clearly, introduce visual aids whenever possible, and use headings and subheadings to enhance page layout.

Which sections to use depends on the situation. Sometimes you need an elaborate implementation section; sometimes you don't. Sometimes you should discuss causes, sometimes not. If the audience needs the information in the section, include it; otherwise, don't.

The section above (pp. 425–429) illustrates one approach to the body. Other examples appear in the examples.

■ WORKSHEET FOR PREPARING A PROPOSAL

❏ *Determine the audience for the proposal.*
Will one person or group receive this proposal?
Will the primary audience decide on the recommendations in this proposal?
How much do they know about the topic?
What information do you need to present in order to be credible?

❏ *Prepare background.*
Why did the proposal project come into existence?

❏ *Select a format—formal or informal.*

❏ *Prepare a style sheet of margins, headings, page numbers, and visual aid captions.*

EXTERNAL PROPOSAL

❏ *Write a statement of the customer's needs.*

❏ *Prepare a two-column list (pp. 421–422) of the customer's needs and the ways your proposal meets those needs.*

❏ *Present your features in terms of the customer's needs, using the customer's terminology.*

❏ *Clearly explain the financial details.*

❏ *Explain in detail why your company has the expertise to do the job.*

❏ *Prepare a schedule for implementing. Assess any inconveniences caused by implementation.*

INTERNAL PROPOSAL

❏ *Define the problem.*
Tell the basic standard that you must uphold (we must make a profit). Cite the data that indicate that the standard is not being upheld (we lost 5 million dollars last quarter). Explain the data's causes (we lost three large sales to competitors) and significance (we can sustain this level of loss for less than another year).

❏ *Construct a visual aid that illustrates the problem or the solution.*
Write a paragraph that explains this visual aid.

❏ *List all the parameters within which your proposal must stay.*
Examples include cost restrictions, personnel restrictions (can you hire more people?), and space restrictions.

❏ *Outline your methodology for investigating the situation.*

❏ *Prepare a list of the dimensions of the problem, and show how your proposed solution eliminates each item.*
(This list is the basis for your benefits section.)

❏ *Write the solution section.*
Explain the solution in enough detail so that a reader can fully understand what it entails in terms of technical aspects, management/

maintenance, and finances. Also clearly show how it eliminates the causes of the undesirable condition.

❏ *Construct the benefits section.*
Clearly relate each benefit to some aspect of the problem. A benefit eliminates causes of the problem (the bottleneck is eliminated) or causes the solution to affect something else positively (worker morale rises).

❏ *Prepare a schedule for implementation.*
Assess any inconveniences.

❏ *List rejected alternatives, and in one sentence tell why you rejected them.*

■ WORKSHEET FOR EVALUATING A PROPOSAL

❏ *Answer these questions about your paper or a peer's. You should be able to answer "yes" to all of the following questions. If you receive a "no" answer, you have a section to revise.*
   a. Is the problem clear?
   b. Is the solution clear?
   c. Do you understand (and believe) the benefits?
   d. Does the implementation schedule deal with all aspects of the situation?
   e. Does the introduction give you the basics of the problem, the solution, and the situation?
   f. Is the style sheet applied consistently? Does it help make the contents clear?
   g. Do the visual aids communicate key ideas effectively?

EXAMPLES

These examples illustrate three different methods of handling internal proposals.

EXAMPLE 16.1
Internal Proposal

Date: November 7, 2004
To: George Schmidt, Chief Engineer
From: Greg Fritsch, Assistant Engineer
Subject: Unnecessary shearing from joint welds

After talking to you on the phone last week, I mentioned that the Block Corporation is having difficulties with shearing on their engine mount supports. I contacted Mr. Jackson, a research expert, who said the stress from the weight of the engine causes the weld to shear. The shearing then causes the motor to collapse onto the engine mount supports. He advised me to purchase a higher-tensile-strength weld. The new weld I propose will reduce the defect rate from 10% to 0%. This memo includes the following information: weld shearing, weld constraints, and shearing solution.

WELD SHEARING

Unnecessary weld shearing of the engine mount supports has been a problem for the Block Corporation since 1989. The company is suffering a 10% defective rate on every 100 engine mounts welded.

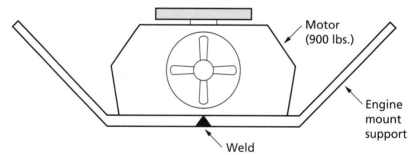

FIGURE 1
Engine Mount Weld

As seen in Figure 1, the weld must hold together when 900 lbs. of force are applied to the motor mount supports. A quality weld with a high tensile strength should withstand temperature fluctuation without shearing.

WELD CONSTRAINT

The Block Corporation listed the following constraints for implementing a new weld:

1. Material costs must increase by less than .01¢ per engine mount support welded.

EXAMPLE 16.1
(continued)

2. Welding machines must not exceed 240 volts.

3. Current welding machines have to be used.

4. Each electrical outlet has to have a separate transformer.

SHEARING SOLUTION

The solution to the company's problem is to implement a higher-tensile-strength weld. The weld is projected to increase material and electrical costs, but is not expected to exceed the company's 1% budget increase for the 2005 fiscal year.

Cost

New welding wire with a higher tensile strength will increase 2¢ for every 100 yards of wire. All engine mount welds require 3 yards of wire to secure a solid weld. The overall cost increase per engine mount welded will be only .006¢.

Voltage

There will be an increase in the amount of electricity used in the new welding process. The welding machines will be required to switch from 120 to 240 volts.

Use of Current Machines

The welders will use the same welding machines as in the past. The welding machines are compatible with the new welds and do not need to be replaced.

Separate Transformers

An electrical hookup from 120 to 240 volts will be needed at each electrical outlet. A transformer will be required at each individual box to ensure an increase in voltage flow.

EXAMPLE 16.2
Internal Proposal

Date: February 14, 2000
To: Irene Gorman
From: Chris Lindblad
Subject: Replacing Voltage Buss Bars

INTRODUCTION

Presently the voltage buss bars on the C90 modules are not ohmed until after all of the option chips have been bonded to the circuit board. If a voltage buss-to-ground short is found after the bonding process, the short must be located, which takes an average of over 10 hours.

RECOMMENDATION

Based on time savings, cost, space available on the bonders, training involved, and savings to the company, I recommend installing a Fluke model 73 multimeter at each bonding station and to have operators ohm the buss bars after each option is bonded to the circuit board.

TIME SAVINGS WILL RESULT

Installing a Fluke model 73 multimeter at each bonding station would have a positive effect on the time spent on locating voltage buss-to-ground shorts, as shown in Table 1. It also shows that ohming the voltage buss bars after each bond would increase the bonding process time but would result in a time savings of 7.1 hours per module.

TABLE 1
Time Savings with Ohming Capabilities Installed at Bonding Stations

Time	Without Using a Fluke 73 (in hours)	Using a Fluke 73 (in hours)
Average time required to bond all options on circuit board	49.5	51.9
Average time required to locate buss-to-ground shorts	10.0	0.5
Total time required	59.5	52.4
Time savings	—	7.1

WITHIN ALLOWED BUDGET

Currently the budget allows for $5000.00 in bonder improvements. The cost of equipping each bonding machine with a Fluke model 73 multime-

EXAMPLE 16.2
(continued)

ter and associated test leads would amount to $350.00. The total cost of equipping the four option bonders would be $1400.00. This cost is well within the allowed budget and would also allow any future bonders to be installed with this equipment.

THE SPACE IS AVAILABLE

The space required for the installation of the ohming equipment is minimal, and it can easily be installed at the base of the bonder at the buss bar end of the module without any loss of mobility of the bonding head. It would also be within easy reach of the operator and cause no safety hazards. Also, no special power requirements are necessary because the Fluke 73 operates on an internal battery source.

TRAINING IS MINIMAL

The training required by the operator to learn how to use the Fluke 73 could be handled by the company's training department, which already has training in place for its use. Only one hour of class time is required with three hours on-the-job training to become proficient in its use.

SAVINGS ARE SIGNIFICANT

By installing a Fluke model 73 multimeter at each of the option bonding stations, the company could save a considerable amount of money. The current cost of troubleshooting a voltage buss-to-ground short is $130.00. This cost, with ohming equipment installed, would drop to around $13.00 per voltage buss-to-ground short, with a savings of $117.00.

CONCLUSION

If you require any further information or documentation on my recommendation, please contact me at the module test department.

EXAMPLE 16.3
Internal Proposal

Date: November 11, 2000
To: Dr. Vanhtha Rasavong
From: Concerned dietetic students
           Michelle Royer
           Kim Bloss
           Kimberly Kainz-Poplawski
Subject: Implementation of a new nutrition education program at RDS

INTRODUCTION

This memo proposes implementing a new nutrition education program at the Residence Dining Services (RDS). Our educational background and experience are in the area of dietetics, so we have a special interest in nutrition education for the student community.

Recently we conducted a survey concerning the current program, Dietary Guidelights, that is in place at the Commons and Tainter. The survey revealed that the current program is confusing and does not meet the needs of the students. We have devised an alternative nutrition education program that is easy to follow and will meet the students' needs.

The remainder of this memo discusses background information regarding the survey, the problems with the existing program, our proposal, and the steps involved for implementation of our program. The memo also points out why the proposed program should be implemented through a discussion of the benefits.

BACKGROUND

People We Surveyed

Fifteen students, all of whom eat at the Commons or Tainter, completed the survey. Among the students surveyed, the number of meals eaten per day and per week at the residence dining facilities averaged 1.73 and 9.4, respectively. When asked if they were aware of the Guidelights program, 73% (11 of 15) stated yes. However, only 27% (4 of 15) of the students indicated knowledge of how the Guidelights program works, and only 33% (5 of 11) indicated using the Guidelights when making food choices.

What We Found

On a scale of 1 to 5, 1 being highly concerned, the students rated themselves as somewhat concerned with overall nutrition (2.07). They indicated an average satisfaction (2.47 on a scale of 1–5, 1 being highly satisfied) when asked if RDS met their nutrition education needs. Five individuals specifically suggested posting the actual fat/calorie content next to the food item in the serving area.

EXAMPLE 16.3
(continued)

We feel that student unwillingness to use the Guidelights program, despite awareness and nutritional concern, can be attributed to the confusing nature of the Guidelights program. The fact that five individuals requested posting the actual fat/calorie contents leads us to believe that the needs of the students would be better met by implementing a more simplified program.

CURRENT SITUATION

The purpose of the Dietary Guidelights program is to inform the students of the fat content of the menu items. The current program provides the information to the students. However, as discovered from our survey, the information is not being utilized.

The current program provides the user with the food's fat content percentage range by posting colored dots next to the menu item on a sign in the serving area. To determine the percentage of fat in foods, one must match the colored dot with dots on a poster hanging in the serving area. For instance, the yellow dot represents a range of 30–60%. The problem is that 30–60% is a very wide range; most of the items served at the dining facility are included in this range. According to the American Heart Association, the items in the low end of this range may be eaten on a regular basis, whereas foods at the high end of the range may be eaten less frequently. However, the current program does not tell the student if the food is at the high or low end of the range.

PROPOSAL

The solution to the problems mentioned is to post the actual fat grams and total calories on the sign. This sign will provide the students with precise and useful information they can easily understand. The confusion associated with the current program will be eliminated by this simple change, which will allow the students to track their daily intake. Figure 1 displays an example of what the signs will look like.

EXAMPLE 16.3
(continued)

Menu Item	Fat Grams/Calories
Pasta	
Spaghetti	2/132
Mostaccioli	5/226
Rotini	8/186
Sauces	
Vegetarian sauce	4/83
Italian hamburger sauce	8/142
White clam sauce	8/122

FIGURE 1
Proposed Nutrition Education Sign

IMPLEMENTATION AND COSTS

Implementation of the proposed program will be quite simple and require minimal time and resources. The time involved with the startup of this program is six working days. During this time, the current program can remain in place. Cost is minimal.

The Schedule

The schedule for implementing is as follows:

1. Obtain nutritional analysis from the *Guide to Eating for a Healthy You* booklet (Day 1).
2. Enter nutritional data into the RDS computer, design signs (Day 1 through 4).
3. Print new signs on computer printer (Day 4).
4. Have signs laminated at ITS-Graphics (Day 5–6).
5. Remove old signs from plastic sleeves and replace with new signs (Day 6).

Explanation of Schedule and Costs

To implement the new program we must obtain the nutritional data needed for the signs. This information is available from the booklet *Guide to Eating Right for a Healthy You,* which RDS distributed to the

EXAMPLE 16.3
(*continued*)

students approximately four weeks ago. Thus there are no costs associated with obtaining the information.

To enter the nutritional data we can use the computer software used to produce the signs for the Guidelights program. The addition of a second column to the sign format is necessary. This column is where the fat and calorie data for each item will appear. Four 4-hour days, for a total of 16 hours, should be sufficient time to complete this process. To keep labor costs down, a currently employed dietetic student can perform this task.

To print the new signs we will use RDS's computer, so the cost of the paper is the only expense associated with this step.

Laminating the signs may be done for the lowest cost at Instructional Technology Services (ITS-Graphics). Once the signs are printed, someone needs to drop them off at ITS-Graphics for lamination. It will take approximately two days for the signs to be completed.

Removing the old signs from the plastic sleeves and replacing them with the new signs can be done, as currently, by a student employee on a meal-to-meal basis. No additional expenses accrue.

Cost

Expenses for implementing this proposed program are minimal: paper, lamination, and labor costs. The total cost involved with initiating the proposed program is $106.10. A breakdown of the expenses is shown in Table 1. To compile this table, price inquiries were made by telephone.

TABLE 1
Expenses Associated with Implementing New Program

	Number	*Price/Unit*	*Cost*
Paper	217 sheets	$7.14/1000 sheets	$ 1.55
Lamination	217 sheets	$.30/ft (2 sheets/ft)	32.55
Labor	16 hours	$4.50/hr	72.00
Total			$106.10

Sources: Maryanne Sherman, RDS director
ITS-Graphics
Wal-Mart

EXAMPLE 16.3
(continued)

BENEFITS

Gives Precise Information

Replacing the Guidelights program with the proposed program will provide the students with precise nutritional information. If the exact amount of fat and calories is posted, students have the necessary information directly in front of them to make good nutritional food choices and track their daily intake. Because a number of individuals specifically requested this type of program, the satisfaction rating with RDS meeting the students' needs should improve.

Is Simple to Use

The proposed program is very simple and easy to follow. Implementation of the program will eliminate the confusion associated with the Guidelights, which should increase utilization of the nutrition education materials. Because the students will be utilizing this program, they will be informed. Thus the program will serve its purpose.

Improves Economics

Implementing the proposed program will benefit the economic efficiency of RDS. Because students will be more knowledgeable of the nutritional content of foods with the new program, they will be more likely to try the low-fat foods. Increased demand for these items will require purchasing larger quantities of food ingredients. Being able to purchase in bulk quantities will decrease the cost of the ingredients, thus decreasing the total food bill for RDS.

■ EXERCISES

1. Create a visual aid that demonstrates that a problem exists.

2. With the visual aid from Exercise 1, write a paragraph that includes the data, the significance, and the cause of the problem, and write a second paragraph that suggests a way to eliminate the problem.

3. Make a Gantt chart of a series of implementation actions. Write a paragraph that explains the actions.

4. In groups of two to four, discuss one of the proposals given in this chapter. What do you like? dislike? Would you agree to implement the solution? Report your results to the class.

5. In groups of three or four, analyze Example 16.3. Prepare a memo to your class that pinpoints its weaknesses and strengths. Focus on depth of detail, appropriateness for audience, and unnecessarily included items.

6. Analyze Examples 16.1 and 16.2. Follow the instructions for Exercise 5. Alternate: If your instructor requires, rewrite and redesign it.

7. In groups of three or four, write a proposal using the details given for a nonprofit organization's need for a computer system (pp. 421–422).

8. Create two different page designs for the proposal about parking signs on campus (pp. 426–429).

9. Rewrite the following paragraphs. The writer is a recreation area supervisor who has discovered the problem; the reader is the finance director of a school district. Shorten the document. Make the tone less personal. Make a new section if necessary. Adopt the table or create new visual aids. If your instructor requires, also add an introduction and summary.

    ### DISCUSSION OF TRENDS

    I have data that establishes trends in the building's use (see Table 1). These data show peak adult and student use during the winter months. When school is out (June–August), we have more students and children using the building. Our slow months are in the Spring (April and May) and in the Fall (September and October). These trends coincide with what we know to be true about revenue loss. I have a more difficult time controlling the adult and student population using the building during the winter months. This results in a higher (25%) revenue loss for these months. On the other end, the children and students using the building during the summer are easier to control. This results in a lower (10%) revenue loss.

TABLE 1
Building Use for Open Recreation

	Adults	Students (Grades 7–12)	Children (Grade 6 & Under)	Total
January	621	583	412	1616
February	645	571	407	1623
March	597	545	393	1535
April	428	372	279	1070
May	210	330	239	779
June	365	701	587	1653
July	276	823	650	1749
August	327	859	718	1904
September	189	268	225	682
October	226	314	275	815
November	398	292	412	1102
December	589	494	384	1467

PROBLEM

The problem of revenue loss really involves two issues. The loss of revenue leads directly to a secondary issue, which is loss of control. When I cannot control the people entering the building, we lose revenue. When these people assume they can get in free, they also assume I cannot control their actions thereafter.

As a supervisor I have many duties. During open rec. I am expected to be at the office window collecting fees. This is all well and fine *if* I could stay there the entire time! Unfortunately, I must occasionally check activities in the weight room, the fieldhouse, the pool, and the locker rooms. At these times I am out of the office and cannot control people from just walking in. Even answering the phone causes problems. I must cross the office to the desk, and then I lose direct eye contact to the front entrance.

I really have no good explanation for why I have more problems with the adult-student users during the winter months as compared to the student-children users in the summer. All I know is that when these winter "bucket shooters" start pouring in for open rec., control goes right out the window. The only answer is a barrier to contain them in the lobby area until they have paid.

SOLUTION

The solution is a barrier that extends from the entrance door into the lobby, to the office wall. This is a length (open space) of about 14 feet. I suggest a chain as a temporary solution. Attached at the entrance door frame, it should extend 5½ feet to a stationary post (nonpermanent support), feed through an opening at the top of this post, and continue on another 5½ feet to another post. The remaining 3 feet to the office wall will be the entrance area. This will be chained off as well, and passage will be allowed only after paying the open rec. fee. A sign that reads "DO NOT ENTER" should be attached to the chain at the entrance area by the office. When I am out of the office, people may think twice and remain in the lobby until I return.

The cost in hardware for this barrier will be minimal, and I suggest it only as a temporary measure. I would like to establish the effectiveness of a simple barrier before considering a more permanent structure. There will always be some who ignore the barrier. There is never a perfect solution.

■ WRITING ASSIGNMENTS

For each of the following assignments, first perform the activities required by the worksheet (pp. 431–433).

1. Write a proposal in which you suggest a solution to a problem. Topics for the assignment could include a problem that you have worked on (and perhaps solved) at a job or a problem that has arisen on campus, perhaps involving a student organization, or at your workplace. Explain the problem and the solution. Show how the solution meets established criteria or how it eliminates the causes of the problem. Explain cost and implementation. If necessary, describe the personnel who will carry out the proposal. Explain why you rejected other solutions. Use at least two visual aids in your text. Your instructor will assign either an informal or a formal format. Fill out the worksheet from this chapter, and perform the exercises that your instructor requires.

   Your instructor may make this a group assignment. If so, follow the instructions for developing a writing team (Chapter 2), and then analyze your situation and assign duties and deadlines.

---

2. In groups of three or four, write a simple request for a proposal (RFP). Ask for a common item that other people in your class could write about. (If you've all taken a class in computerized statistics, for example, ask for a statistics software program.) Try to find a real need in

your current situation. Interview affected people (such as the statistics instructor) to find out what they need. Then trade your RFP with that of another group. Your group will write a proposal for the RFP you receive. Your instructor will help you with the day-to-day scheduling of this assignment.

3. Write a learning report for the writing assignment you just completed. See Chapter 5, Writing Assignment 7, page 123, for details of the assignment.

WEB EXERCISE

Write a proposal suggesting that you create a Web site for a campus club or a company division (including a "special interest" site, such as for the company yoga club). Explain how you will do it, why you are credible, the cost, the benefits to the company, and the schedule for production.

WORKS CITED

Bacon, Terry. "Selling the Sizzle, Not the Steak: Writing Customer-Oriented Proposals." *Proceedings of the First National Conference on Effective Communication Skills for Technical Professionals.* Greenville, SC: Continuing Engineering Education, Clemson University, November 15–16, 1988.

17 User Manuals

CHAPTER CONTENTS

Chapter 17
IN A NUTSHELL

A manual should make the readers comfortable enough with the machine or object so that the know-how for interacting with the machine is in them, not just in the manual. Effective manuals show readers that the machines are just objects that humans use and control. Your readers can achieve this position if you help them relate to the machine.

Supply context. Help them see the machine from the designer's point of view. What does this machine or this part do, and why, and what kinds of concerns does that function imply? Once readers get the big picture, they will usually try to use the item for its intended purpose.

Explain what the parts do. List all the visible parts, and explain what they cause, how to stop or undo what they cause, what other parts work in sequence with them.

Explain how to perform the sequences. Think of readers as users or doers. What actions will they perform? Think of common ones like turning the machine on and off. Spend time working on the machine so you can tell someone else how to work it.

Use visual logic. One major section should discuss each of the three areas mentioned above. Divide each section into as many subsections as needed. Use heads and white space so readers can find sections and subsections easily. Use clear text and visual aids so readers figure out how to do the actions confidently.

Develop credibility. Give brief introductions that tell the end goal of a series of steps; give warnings before you explain the step; state the results of actions or give clear visual aids so that readers can decide if they did the right thing.

Companies sell not only their products but also knowledge of how to use those products properly. This knowledge is contained in manuals. Both the manufacturer and the buyer want a manual that will allow users safely and successfully to assemble, operate, maintain, and repair the product.

Very complex mechanisms have separate multivolume manuals for different procedures such as installation and operation. The most common kind of manual, however, is the user's manual, which accompanies almost every product.

User's manuals have two basic sections: descriptions of the functions of the parts and sets of instructions for performing the machine's various processes. In addition, the manual gives information on theory of operation, warranty, specifications, parts lists, and locations of dealers to contact for advice on parts. This chapter explains how to plan and write an operator's manual.

PLANNING THE MANUAL

Your goal for the manual is that it help readers achieve their goals with your product. To plan effectively, determine your purpose, consider the audience, schedule the review process, discover sequences, analyze the steps, analyze the parts, select visual aids, and format the pages.

Determine Your Purpose

The purpose of a manual is to enable its readers to perform certain actions. But manuals cannot include everything about any system or machine. Decide which topics your readers will need, or can deal with. For example, you would choose to explain simple send and receive commands for E-mail beginners, not complicated directory searching.

Decide the level of detail. Will you provide a sketchy outline, or will you "hand-hold," giving lots of background and explanation? To see the results of a decision to "hand-hold," follow the "Background Sound" instructions in Chapter 11, pages 278–279. Making these key decisions will focus your sense of purpose, allowing you to make the other planning decisions detailed in this chapter.

Consider the Audience

Who is your audience? Your goal is to characterize your readers and their situation so that you can include text, visuals, and page design that give them the easiest access to the product. First, determine how much they know about general terms and concepts. Readers who are learning their first word processing program know nothing about "save," "cut," "paste," "open," "close," and "print." Readers learning their fifth program, however, already understand basic word processing concepts. Early in the planning process, make a list of all the words the readers must understand.

Second, consider your goal for your readers. What should they be able to do as a result of reading the manual? A common answer, of course, is to be able to operate the product, but what are the key abilities, the ones they must have? Those abilities will help you decide what sections to include and how to write them.

Third, consider how your readers will read the manual. Both beginning and expert audiences usually are "active learners." They do not want to read; instead, they want to accomplish something relevant quickly (Redish). When they do read, they do not read the manual like a story, first page to last. Instead, they go to the section they need. To accommodate these active learners who differ widely in knowledge and experience, use format devices—such as heads and tables of contents—that make information accessible and easy to find. This type of thinking will help you with the layout decisions you must make later and will help you decide what information to include in the text.

Fourth, consider where the audience will use the manual. This knowledge will help you with page design. For instance, manuals used in poor lighting might need big pages and typefaces, whereas manuals used in constricted spaces or enclosed in small packages need small pages and typefaces.

Fifth, consider your audience's emotional state. For various reasons, many, if not most, users do not like, or even trust, manuals (Cooper). Further, users are often fearful, hassled, or both. Your goal is to both allay their fears and develop their confidence. The presentation of your manual—its sequence and format—and of your identity as a trustworthy guide will develop a positive relationship.

Determine a Schedule

Early in your planning process, set up a schedule of the entire project. Typically, a manual project includes not just you, the writer, but also other people who will review it for various types of accuracy—technical, legal, and design. In industrial situations, this person might be the engineer who designed the machine. If you write for a client, it will be the client or some group designated by the client.

Think of each draft as a cycle. You write, and then someone reviews, and as a result of their review you rewrite or redesign. At the outset of the project, set dates for each of these reviews and decide who will be part of the review team. In addition, agree with your reviewers on when you expect them to return the draft and on what types of comments they are to make. You can handle the actual schedule in several ways, perhaps write in the actions you will perform during various weeks on a calendar. Or you could make a Gantt chart (see below).

Suppose your tasks are to interview an engineer, create a design, write a draft, have a reader's review, write a second draft, have a second review, and print the manual. Suppose also that your schedule allows you 8 weeks. Your Gantt chart might look like Figure 17.1.

Discover Sequences

Discovering all the sequences means that you learn what the product does and what people do as they use it (Cohen and Cunningham). To learn what the product does, learn the product so thoroughly that you are expert enough to talk to an engineer about it. Because this process takes a good deal of time, you need to plan the steps you will take to gain all this knowledge. Schedule times to use the product. Talk to knowledgeable people—either users or designers, or both. Your goal is to learn all the procedures the product can perform, all the ways it performs them, and all the steps users take as they interact with the product.

For example, the writer of a manual for a piston filler, a machine that inserts liquids into bottles, must grasp how the machine causes the bottle to reach the filling point and how the machine injects the liquid into the bottle. Gaining this knowledge requires observing the machine in action, interviewing engineers, and assembling and disassembling sections.

FIGURE 17.1
Gantt Chart

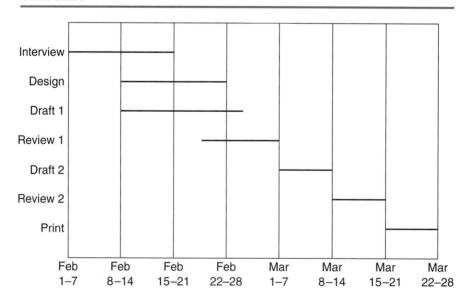

But the writer must also know what people do to make the machine work. The most practical way to gain this knowledge is to practice with the product. These acts become the basis for the sections in the procedures section. As you practice, make flow charts and decision trees. In your flow charts, list each action and show how it fits into a sequence with other actions (see Figure 17.2).

The sequences your manual must teach the user typically include

- How to assemble it.
- How to start it.
- How to stop it.
- How to load it.
- How it produces its end product.
- How each part contributes to producing the end product.
- How to adjust parts for effective performance.
- How to change it to perform slightly different tasks.

Analyze the Steps

To analyze the steps in each sequence means to name each individual action that a user performs. This analysis is exactly the same as that for writing a set of instructions (review Chapter 11). In brief, determine both the end goal and the starting point of the sequence, and then provide all the intermediary steps to guide the users from start to finish. Try constructing a decision tree. Make a flow chart for the entire sequence, and then convert the chart into a decision tree.

For an example of such a conversion, compare Figures 17.2 and 17.3. In these steps, taken from a piston filler manual, the writer wants to explain how to insert a specified amount of liquid into a bottle. Figure 17.2 shows the flow chart; Figure 17.3 shows a decision tree based on the flow chart.

FIGURE 17.2
Flow Chart

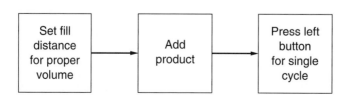

FIGURE 17.3
Decision Tree Based on Flow Chart

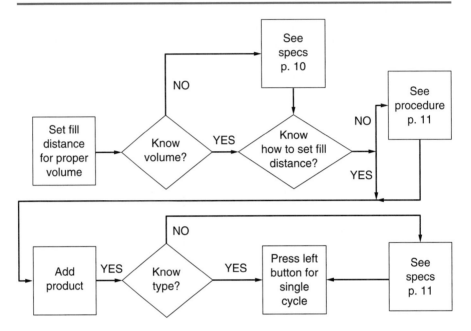

Here is the text developed from the two figures:

1. Set the fill distance for the proper volume.
   a. Check specifications for bottle volumes (p. 10).
   b. To determine this distance, find out the diameter of your piston.
   c. Go to the volume chart on p. 11.
   d. Find the piston diameter in the left column.
   e. Read across to the volume you need.
   f. Read up to determine the length you need.
   g. Adjust the distance from *A* to *B* (Figure 6 [not shown]) to the length you need.
2. Add the product to the hopper. If you are unsure of the product type, see specifications (p. 11).
3. Press the left button (*A* on Figure 6 [not shown]) for single cycle.

Analyze the Parts

To analyze the parts, list each important part and explain what it does. Then convert these notes into a sentence. If you look at a few common user manuals, say for a VCR, you will always find this section in the front of the manual. A helpful method is to make a three-part row for each part. Name the part, write the appropriate verb, and write the effect of the verb. Then turn that list into a comprehensible sentence. Here is the list for a stop button:

Name of Part	Verb	Effect
stop button	stops/ends	all functions stop

Here is the sentence for the button:

The red emergency stop button immediately stops all functions of the machine.

Select Visual Aids

Visual aids—photographs, drawings, flow charts, and troubleshooting charts—all help the reader learn the product. In recent years, with the advent of desktop publishing and many graphics software and hardware programs, the use of visual aids has proliferated. Many visuals are now the norm. Many manuals have at least one visual aid per page; many have one per step.

Your goal is to create a text-visual interaction that conveys knowledge both visually and textually. Consider this aspect of your planning carefully. If you can use a visual aid to eliminate text, do so. Notice one key use of visual aids in manuals. Visuals give permission. Although many visual aids are logically unnecessary because the text and the product supply all the knowledge, they are still useful. Consider, for instance, Figure 9 on page 461 of the Dewpointer manual or the phone visuals on page 469 of the telephone manual. Neither of these is strictly needed because the user could read the text and look at the machine and see what is described in the text. But the visual reassures the readers that they are "in the right place." Use visuals liberally in this manner. Your readers will appreciate it.

You must decide whether each step needs a visual aid. Most manual writers now repeat visual aids. (Notice that the meter selector switch appears twice in the Dewpointer manual.) As a result, the reader does not have to flip back and forth through pages. To plan the visual image needed to illustrate a step, decide which image to include and from which angle users will view it. If they will see the part from the front, present a picture of it from the front. Use a storyboard (Riney), such as the one shown in Figure 17.4, to plan the visual aid. Storyboards are discussed in Chapter 18.

FIGURE 17.4
Storyboard

1. Pull out the stop switch (C).	Photo of top switch Pulled out 3/4 view from front top

Format the Pages

The pages of a manual must be designed to be easy to read. Create a style sheet with a "visual logic" (see Chapters 7 and 8) that associates a particular look or space with a particular kind of information (all figure captions italic, all page numbers in the upper outside corner, and all notes in a different typeface). You must also design a page that moves readers from left to right and top to bottom. (Review Chapter 7 for format decisions.) This process is more complex than you might think, so carefully consider your options. You might review several consumer manuals that accompany software products or common home appliances.

To produce effectively laid out pages, use a grid and a template. A *grid* is a group of imaginary lines that divide a page into rectangles (see Figure 17.5). Designers use a grid to ensure that similar elements appear on pages in the same relative position and proportion. One common grid divides the page into two unequal columns. Writers place text in the right column and place subordinate notes or emphasized warnings in the left column, as shown on pages 460–461.

A *template* is an arrangement of all the elements that will appear on each page, including page numbers, headers, footers, rules, blocks of text, headings, and visual aids. Figure 17.6 is a template of a page. The arrows indicate all the spots at which the author made a deliberate format decision. Create a tentative template before you have gone very far with your writing because your visual logic is part of your overall strategy (see p. 456) and will influence your word choice dramatically.

The following notes list all the format decisions that the author made for Figure 17.6:

1.   Special treatment of header rule to set off header text
2.   Type, font, size, and position of header information
3.   Length and width of rule and its distance from the top of the page

FIGURE 17.5
Page Grids

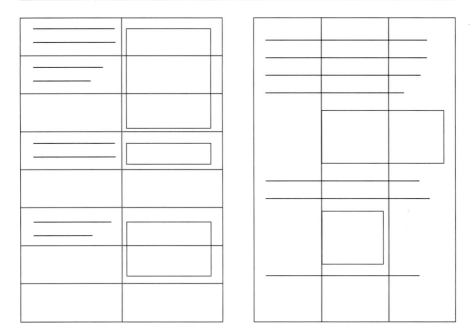

4. Size, type font, position, and grammatical form (*-ing* word) of level 1 heads

5. Size, type font, and position of level 1 introductory material; distance of this material below the level 1 head

6. Size, type font, and position of level 2 heads; also the grammatical form (*-ing* word) of the head; distance of the head below previous text

7. Size, type font, and position of instructional text; space between head and next line of text (leading)

8. Size, type font, and position of numeral for instructional step

9. Punctuation following the numeral

10. Position of second line of text

11. Space between individual instructions

12. Size, type font, and position of notes or warnings

13. Space between text and visual aid

14. Width (in points) and position of frame for visual aid

FIGURE 17.6
Page Template with Decision Points

Chapter 3
Macintosh

Learning the Basics of Macintosh

This section is for the Macintosh beginner; it covers the basic functions: *Moving the pointer, clicking, double-clicking,* and *selecting icons.*

Moving the pointer

The pointer is the black arrow you see on the screen.

1. Watch the screen while you roll the mouse. Every move you make with the mouse moves the pointer in exactly the same way.

2. Lift the mouse up and put it down in a different place. Notice that lifting the mouse doesn't move the pointer; therefore, when you run out of room for the mouse, you can lift it up and put it down where you have more room.

Clicking

Press and quickly release the mouse button.

Double-clicking

Press and release the mouse button twice in quick succession.

Note: Double-clicking is a handy way to open a folder, application, or document.

Selecting icons

1. Position the pointer on an icon.

2. Click the icon by pressing and immediately releasing the mouse button. The icon becomes highlighted. What was black is now white and vice versa (Fig. 3-5).

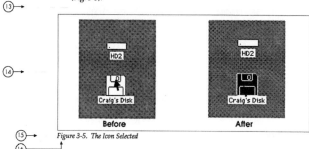

Before | After

Figure 3-5. The Icon Selected

15. Size, type font, and treatment of visual aid caption
16. Position of caption relative to frame
17. Size, type font, and position of page number

WRITING THE MANUAL

The student sample shown in Figure 17.7 is taken from a user's manual for a lab machine, a Dewpointer. The sections included here—the parts and functions section and one section of the operating instructions—are found in all manuals. The full manual included a title page, a table of contents, a six-part section on using the Dewpointer, and an appendix of mathematical values that a researcher needs. This manual uses a two-column page, with notes and warnings in the left column. All the visual aids were produced on a computer.

Introduction

In the introduction explain the manual's purpose and whatever else the reader needs to become familiar with the product: how to use the manual, the appropriate background, and the level of training needed to use the mechanism.

The introduction, which appears on the first page of the sample, tells the purpose of the machine, states the purpose and divisions of the manual, and explains why a user needs the machine.

Arrange the Sections

A manual has two major sections:

- Description of the parts (for example, the function of all the buttons on the control panel)
- Instructions for all the sequences (for example, how to start the machine from the control panel)

The Parts Section.   The parts and functions section provides a drawing of the machine with each part clearly labeled. The description explains the function of each item. This section answers the question: What does this part do? or What happens when I do this? An easy, effective way to organize the parts description is to key the text to a visual aid of the product. Most appliance manuals (as for VCRs) have such a section.

The Sequences Section.   The sequences section enables users to master the product. Arrange this section by operations, not parts. Present a section for each task. Usually the best order is chronological, the order in which readers will encounter the procedures. Tell first how to assemble,

FIGURE 17.7
Excerpts from an Operator's Manual

Introduction

The Alnor Dewpointer measures the relative dewpoint of almost any gas. In this manual you will learn how to properly adjust the Dewpointer before you take any measurements. Then you will be given a step-by-step process for finding the exact dewpoint of the gas you are testing.

Knowing the exact dewpoint of a gas will allow you to weld different metals with more accuracy.

Adjusting the Dewpointer

WARNING:
Never depress the gauge valve when the purging valve is closed. Oil will shoot out of the gauge valve.

Adjusting for Unity

1. Pull out the *operating valve* (See Figure 1).

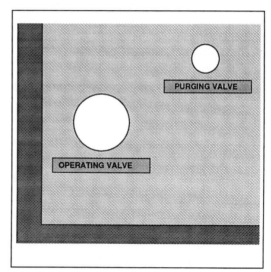

Figure 1. Location of the purging valve.

Note:
This step releases all internal pressure.

2. Open the *purging valve* (See Figure 1).

FIGURE 17.7
(continued)

Parts and Functions

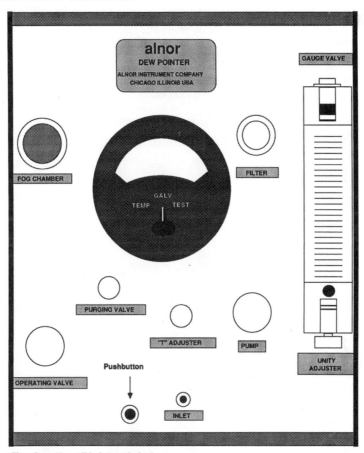

1. **Fog Chamber** - You will look in to find a fog.
2. **Operating Valve** - Pushing in initiates a test.
3. **Purging Valve** - Allows the system to be pressurized and depressurized. Turn to the left to open. Turn to the right to close.
4. **T-Adjuster** - Fine tuner for the pointer, located on the meter.
5. **Pump** - Pumps pressure into the system, much like a hand pump fills a football.
6. **Gauge Valve** - Releases the pressure in the pressure ratio gauge. *Never* press the gauge valve unless the purging valve is open, because oil will shoot out.
7. **Unity Adjuster** - Adjusts the oil level of the pressure ratio gauge.
8. **Pressure Ratio Gauge** - Measures the dewpoint pressure.
9. **Meter Selector Switch** - Allows you to test for accuracy and read the fog chamber temperature.

FIGURE 17.7
(continued)

Using the Dewpointer

The *Alnor Dewpointer* can measure the relative dewpoint of almost any gas. The gas to be tested is stabilized to room temperature in a fog chamber, then suddenly cooled. If the gas is cooled to or below the dewpoint a fog will appear in the fog chamber. You will have to record several readings in order to determine the exact dewpoint. You will need a pencil and paper to record values.

Purging the system

WARNING:
Do not hook the gas up. Your instructor must hook the gas line up to the Dewpointer.

1. Open the *purging valve* (See Figure 7).

2. Pull open the *operating valve* (See Figure 7).

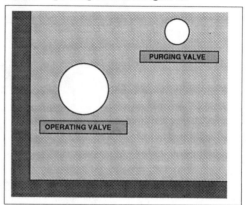

Figure 7. Location of the operating and purging valves.

Note:
Purging removes the existing gas and fills the dewpointer with the gas you want to test.

3. Using the *pump knob*, purge the system with 15 to 20 strokes of the pump (See Figure 8).

4. Close the *purging valve*.

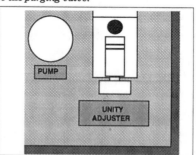

Figure 8. Location of the pump knob.

FIGURE 17.7
(continued)

Setting up the Dewpointer

1. Using the pump knob raise the pressure in the *pressure ratio gauge* to the **0.7** mark.

2. Turn the *meter selector switch* to **GALV**. The pointer will return to **Z** (See Figure 9).

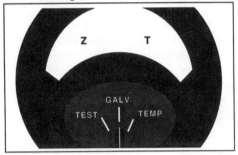

Figure 9. The meter selector switch.

Note:
If necessary, use the T-Adjuster Knob to center the pointer on **T**.

3. Turn the *meter selector switch* to **TEST**. The pointer should reach **T** (See Figure 9).

4. Press and hold the *pushbutton*.

Note:
This temp. will be used in the final calculation.

5. Turn the *meter selector switch* to **TEMP** (See Figure 9).

6. Read and record as the *Initial Temperature*.

7. Release the *pushbutton*.

Running the test

Running the test will require you to push down the operating valve while looking in the fog chamber. When the operating valve is pushed in, a light will appear in the fog chamber. The fog will be a fine mist. You will have to take several readings to close in on the exact dewpoint. When measuring very low dewpoints, allow the gas to stabilize for two minutes before continuing with step 1.

Note:
If a fog appears, it will be a fine mist.

1. Look in the fog chamber and push down the operating valve.

2. If you see a fog, go directly to step **4**, page **9**.

3. If you don't see a fog, you must purge the system.

then how to check out, then how to start, to perform various operations, and to maintain. However, be aware that readers seldom read manuals from beginning to end, so you must enable them to find the information they need. Make the information easy to locate and use by cross-referencing to earlier sections. Never assume that readers will have read an earlier section.

In addition, as mentioned earlier, repeat key instructions or visuals. Do not make readers flip back and forth between pages. Rather, place the appropriate information where readers will use it (Rubens).

Assume Responsibility.   All manual writers have an ethical responsibility to be aware of the dangers associated with running a machine. Keep in mind that if you leave out a step, the operator will probably not catch the error, and the result may be serious. Also, you must alert readers to potentially dangerous operations by inserting the word WARNING in capital letters and by providing a short explanation of the danger. These warnings should always appear before the actual instruction.

Other Sections.   Manuals traditionally have a number of other sections, though not all of them appear in all manuals or in the exact arrangement shown here. These sections are the front matter, the body, and the concluding section. The front matter includes such elements as

- Title page.
- Table of contents.
- Safety warnings.
- A general description of the mechanism.
- General information, based on estimated knowledge level of the audience.
- Installation instructions.

The body includes this element:

- A theory of operation section

The concluding section includes such elements as

- Maintenance procedures.
- Troubleshooting suggestions.
- A parts list.
- The machine's specifications.

Usability

Usability testing helps writers find the aspects of the manual that make it easier or harder to use, especially in terms of the speed and accuracy with which users perform tasks (Craig). You need to plan, conduct, and evaluate a usability test (Brooks).

Planning a Usability Test.   *Planning* the test is selecting what aspects of the manual you want to evaluate, what method you will use, and who will be the test subjects.

Select the aspects of the manual that you want to study. The most important question is: Does this manual allow the readers to use the object easily and confidently? Consider using some or all of these questions (Queipo; Bethke et al.):

- *Time*
  How long did it take to find information? to perform individual tasks? to perform groups of tasks?
- *Errors*
  How many and what types of errors did the subject make?
- *Assistance*
  How often did the subject need help?
  At what points did the subject need help?
  What type of help did the subject need?
- *Information*
  Was the information easy to find? easy to understand? sufficient to perform the task?
- *Format*
  Is the format consistent?
  Are the top-down areas (headings, introductions, highlighters) helpful?
  Is the arrangement on the page helpful?
- *Audience Engagement*
  Is the vocabulary understandable?
  Is the text concrete enough?
  Is the sequence "natural"? Does it seem to the learner that this is the "route to follow" to do this activity?

Select the method you will use to find the answers to your questions. Some questions need different methods. One method often is not sufficient to derive all the information you want to obtain. Test methods (Sullivan) include

- *Informal observation*—watching a person use the manual and recording all the places where a problem (with any of the topic areas you selected to watch for) arose.

▪ *User protocols*—the thoughts that the user speaks as he or she works with the manual and that an observer writes down, tapes, or video records.

▪ *Computer text analysis*—subjecting the text to evaluation features that a software program can perform, including word count, spelling, grammar, and readability scores (i.e., at what "grade level" is this material?)

▪ *Editorial review*—knowledgeable commentary from a person who is not one of the writers of the text.

▪ *Surveys and interviews*—a series of questions that you ask the user after he or she has worked with the manual.

Your goal is to match the test method with the kind of information you want. For instance, an editorial review would produce valuable information on consistency. User protocols or survey/interviews would help you determine if the vocabulary was at the appropriate level or if the page arrangement was helpful. Observation would tell you if the information given was sufficient to perform the task.

Select the test subjects. The test subjects are most often individuals who are probable members of the manual's target audience but who have not worked on developing the manual.

Conducting a Usability Test.   *Conducting* the test is administering it. The key is to have a way to record all the data—as much feedback as possible as quickly as possible. You can use several methods:

▪ If you do an informal observation, you can use a tally sheet (Rubin) that has three columns—Observation, Expected Behavior or User Comment, and Design Implications. Fill out the observation column as you watch and the other two columns later.

▪ For user protocols, you can design a form like the one you use for informal observations, or you can audio or video record, though the difficulties with taping methods—setup procedure, use of the material after the session—require a clear decision on your part of whether or not you will really use the data you record.

▪ Computer and editorial analysis will tell you about the features of the text but will not tell the audience's reaction; these tests are relatively simple to set up, although telling an editor what to look for and setting a grammar checker to search for only certain kinds of problems are essential.

▪ For surveys and interviews, you can design a form (as outlined in Chapter 5) and administer it after the subject has finished the session. Sample questions include:

Were you able to find information on X quickly?

Did the comments in the left margin help you find information?

Did you read the introductions to the sequences?

Did the introduction to each sequence make it easier for you to grasp the point of sequence?

A typical way to record the answers is either yes/no/comments or some kind of recording scale (1 = highly agree, 5 = highly disagree).

Evaluating a Usability Test. *Evaluating* the test is determining how to use the results of the test (Sullivan). Your results could indicate a problem with

- The text (spelling, grammar, sufficiency of information).
- The text's design (consistency, usefulness of column arrangement or highlighting techniques).
- The "learning style" of the audience (sequence of the text, basic way in which you approach the material).

If you have determined beforehand what is an acceptable answer (e.g., this procedure should take X minutes; this word is the only one that can be used to refer that object), you will be able to make the necessary changes. For more help on this topic, consult Craig.

■ WORKSHEET FOR PREPARING A MANUAL

❑ *Consider the audience.*
How much do readers know about the general terms and concepts?
Where and when will they use the manual?
What should they be able to do after reading the manual?
List all the terms a user must comprehend. Define each term.

❑ *Determine a schedule.*
On what date is the last version of the manual due?
Who will review each stage?
How long will each review cycle take?

❑ *List where you can obtain the knowledge you need to write the manual.*
A person? Reading? Working with the mechanism?

❑ *Analyze the procedures a user must follow to operate the product.*
What must be done to install it, to turn it on, to turn it off, and to do its various tasks?
List the sequence for presenting the processes.

Choose an organizational pattern for the sequence—chronological or most important to least important.

Create a flow chart for each procedure the machine follows.

Create a decision tree for each procedure the user follows.

Name each part and its function.

For a complicated product, you will discover far too many parts to discuss. Group them in manageable sections. Decide which ones your audience needs to know about.

❏ *Choose a visual aids strategy.*

Will you use drawings or photographs?

Will you use a visual aid for each instruction?

Will you use a visual aid on each page?

Will you use callouts?

❏ *Create a storyboard for your manual.*

❏ *Write step-by-step instructions.*

Clearly label any step that could endanger the person (WARNING!) or the machine (CAUTION!).

❏ *Design pages by preparing a style sheet of up to four levels of heads, captions for visual aids, margins, page numbers, and fonts (typefaces).*

Select rules, headers, and footers as needed to help make information easy to find on pages.

❏ *Field-test the manual.*

Select the features of the manual you want to field-test.

Select a method of testing those features. Be sure to create a clear method for recording answers. Determine what you think are acceptable results for each feature (e.g., How long should it take to perform the process?).

Select subjects to use the manual.

EXAMPLE

The excerpts shown in Example 17.1 are several sections of an operator's manual for a telephone. The entire manual is a one-page foldout, with seven sections including one in Spanish. Presented here are the table of contents, the parts and functions section (1-B, "Location of Controls"; 3, "Speed Dialer"; and 4, "One-Touch Dialer,"), two sections of operating instructions, and one page of troubleshooting. These pages represent sections you will find in almost all manuals written for consumers.

EXAMPLE 17.1
Excerpts From an Operator's Manual
Source: Reprinted by permission of Matsushita Electric Corporation of America.

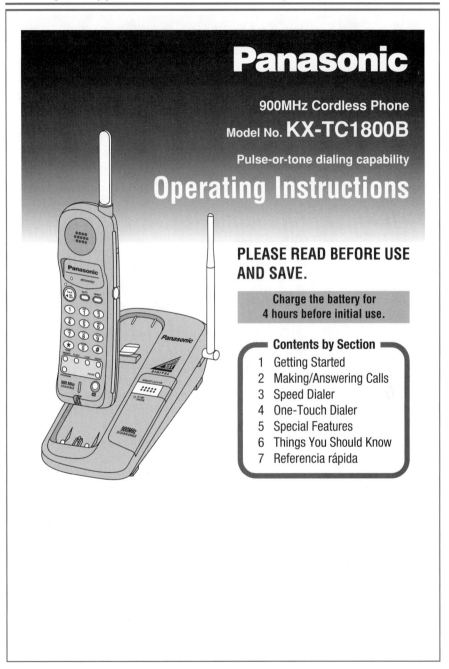

Panasonic

900MHz Cordless Phone

Model No. **KX-TC1800B**

Pulse-or-tone dialing capability

Operating Instructions

PLEASE READ BEFORE USE AND SAVE.

Charge the battery for
4 hours before initial use.

Contents by Section

1 Getting Started
2 Making/Answering Calls
3 Speed Dialer
4 One-Touch Dialer
5 Special Features
6 Things You Should Know
7 Referencia rápida

EXAMPLE 17.1
(continued)

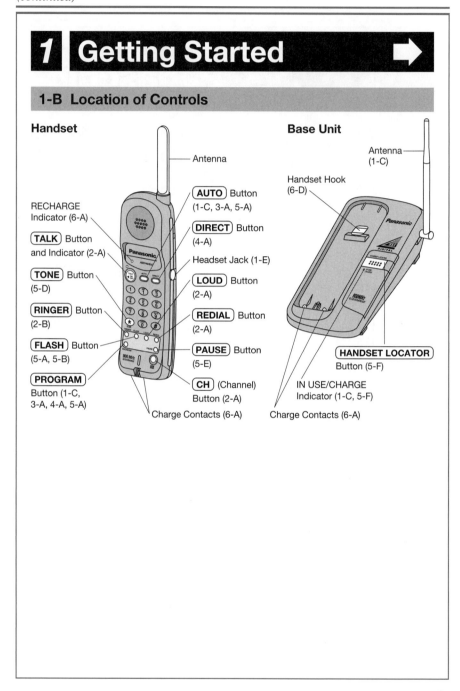

1 | Getting Started ➡

1-B Location of Controls

Handset

Antenna

RECHARGE
Indicator (6-A)

TALK Button
and Indicator (2-A)

TONE Button
(5-D)

RINGER Button
(2-B)

FLASH Button
(5-A, 5-B)

PROGRAM
Button (1-C,
3-A, 4-A, 5-A)

AUTO Button
(1-C, 3-A, 5-A)

DIRECT Button
(4-A)

Headset Jack (1-E)

LOUD Button
(2-A)

REDIAL Button
(2-A)

PAUSE Button
(5-E)

CH (Channel)
Button (2-A)

Charge Contacts (6-A)

Base Unit

Antenna
(1-C)

Handset Hook
(6-D)

HANDSET LOCATOR
Button (5-F)

IN USE/CHARGE
Indicator (1-C, 5-F)

Charge Contacts (6-A)

EXAMPLE 17.1
(continued)

---

3 | Speed Dialer   Section 3

3-A Storing Phone Numbers in Memory

You can store up to 10 phone numbers in the handset. The dialing buttons ((0) to (9)) function as memory stations. **The TALK indicator light must be off before programming.**

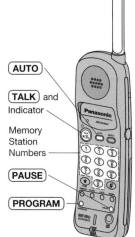

AUTO

TALK and Indicator

Memory Station Numbers

PAUSE

PROGRAM

1 Press (PROGRAM).
  • The TALK indicator flashes.

2 Enter a phone number up to 22 digits.

3 Press (AUTO).

4 Press a memory station number ((0) to (9)).
  • A beep sounds.
  • To store other numbers, repeat steps 1 through 4.

If you misdial
Press (PROGRAM) to end storing. ➡ Start again from step 1.

To erase a stored number
Press (PROGRAM) ➡ (AUTO) ➡ the memory station number ((0) to (9)) for the phone number to be erased.
  • A beep sounds.

• If a pause is required for dialing, press (PAUSE) where needed. Pressing (PAUSE) counts as one digit (5-E).

3-B Dialing a Stored Number

Press (TALK) ➡ (AUTO) ➡ The memory station number ((0) to (9)).
• If your line has rotary or pulse service, any access numbers stored after pressing (TONE) will not be dialed.

EXAMPLE 17.1
(continued)

4 | One-Touch Dialer

4-A Storing a Phone Number in the DIRECT Button

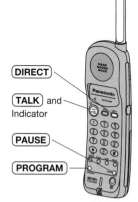

DIRECT

TALK and
Indicator

PAUSE

PROGRAM

A phone number stored in the (DIRECT) button can be dialed with a one-touch operation. **The TALK indicator light must be off before programming.**

1 Press (PROGRAM).
   • The TALK indicator flashes.

2 Enter a phone number up to 22 digits.
   • If you misdial, press (PROGRAM), and start again from step 1.

3 Press (DIRECT).
   • A beep sounds.

• If a pause is required for dialing, press (PAUSE) where needed. Pressing (PAUSE) counts as one digit (5-E).

4-B Dialing the Stored Number in the DIRECT Button

Press (TALK) ➡ (DIRECT).

• If your line has rotary or pulse service, any access numbers stored after pressing (TONE) will not be dialed.

To erase a stored number: press (PROGRAM) ➡ (DIRECT).

EXAMPLE 17.1
(continued)

Things You Should Know   Section 6

6-E Before Requesting Help

Problem	Remedy
The unit does not work.	• Check the settings (1-C). • Charge the battery fully (6-A). • Clean the charge contacts and charge again (6-A). • Install the battery properly (1-C, 6-B). • Place the handset on the base unit and unplug the AC adaptor to reset. Plug in and try again. • Re-insert the battery and place the handset on the base unit. Try again.
An alarm tone sounds.	• You are too far from the base unit. Move closer and try again. • Place the handset on the base unit and try again. • Plug in the AC adaptor. • Raise the base unit antenna.
Static, sound cuts in/out, fades. Interference from other electrical units.	• Locate the handset and the base unit away from other electrical applicances (6-C). • Move closer to the base unit. • Raise the base unit antenna. • Press (CH) to select a clearer channel.
The unit does not ring.	• To ringer volume is set to OFF. Press (RINGER) while the TALK indicator light is off (2-B).
While storing a number, the unit starts to ring.	• To answer the call, press (TALK). The program will be cancelled. Store the number again.
You cannot store a phone number in memory.	• You cannot store a number while the unit is in the talk mode. • Do not pause for over 60 seconds while storing. • Move closer to the base unit.
Previously programmed information is erased.	• If a power failure occurs, programmed information may be erased. Reprogram if necessary.
You cannot redial by pressing (REDIAL).	• If the last number dialed was more than 32 digits long, the number will not be redialed.
(HANDSET LOCATOR) does not function.	• The handset is too far from the base unit or is engaged in an outside call.
The RECHARGE indicator flashes or the unit beeps intermittently.	• Charge the battery fully (6-A).
You charged the battery fully, but the RECHARGE indicator flashes.	• Clean the charge contacts and charge again (6-A). • Install a new battery (6-B).
The IN USE/CHARGE indicator light does not go out while charging	• This is normal.
If you cannot solve your problem	• Call our customer call center at 1-800-211-PANA (7262).

■ EXERCISES

1. Collect one or two professional manuals. Bring a manual to class. Good examples include VCR, stereo, CD, automobile, appliance, or computer manuals. Analyze them for page design, visual logic, text-visual interaction, sequence of parts, and assumptions made about the audience. Discuss these topics in groups of two to four, and then report to the class the strategies that you find most helpful and are most likely to use in Writing Assignment 1.

2. In groups of two to four, analyze the page layout of one of the manuals that appear in this chapter. Write a brief description of and reaction to this layout and share your reactions with the group. Your instructor will ask some groups to report their results.

3. Using any machine or software program you know well, write a parts description.

4. Using any machine or software program you know well, create a flow chart for the sequences you want a reader to learn. Convert that flow chart into step-by-step instructions.

5. Review the types of decisions included in creating a template (pp. 454–457). Then create your own design for what you wrote in Exercise 3 or 4.

6. For the manual you are creating for Writing Assignment 1 or for the section you wrote for Exercise 4, create a storyboard.

7. Write the introduction to the parts description and sequences you created in Exercises 3 and 4.

8. For the manual you are creating for Writing Assignment 1, complete the following exercises. Your instructor will schedule these steps at the appropriate time in your project.
   a. Consider how consistently it handles all details of format.
   b. Consider how precisely it explains how to perform an action. Read closely to see whether everything you need to know is really present.
   c. Conduct a field test by asking a person who knows almost nothing about the product to follow your manual. Accompany the tester, but do not answer questions unless the action is dangerous or the tester is hopelessly lost (say, in a software program). Note all the

problem areas, and then make those changes. Discuss changes that would help the user.

■ WRITING ASSIGNMENTS

1. Write an operator's manual. Choose any product that you know well or one you would like to learn about. The possibilities are numerous—a bicycle, a sewing machine, part of a software program such as Front-Page® or Dreamweaver®, a computer system, any laboratory device, a welding machine. If you need to use high-quality photographs or drawings, you may need help from another student who has the necessary skills. Your manual must include at least an introduction, a table of contents, a description of the parts, and the instructions for procedures. You might also include a troubleshooting section. Give warnings when appropriate. Complete this chapter's worksheet or the appropriate exercises.

2. Write a learning report for the writing assignment you just completed. See Chapter 5, Writing Assignment 7, page 123, for details of the assignment.

■ WEB EXERCISE

Create a minimanual to publish on a Web site. Use a simple machine, say, a flashlight. Include one section describing the parts and one section presenting the appropriate sequences for operating. Include several visual aids.

■ WORKS CITED

Bethke, F. J., W. M. Dean, P. H. Kaiser, E. Ort, and F. H. Pessin. "Improving the Usability of Programming Publications." *IBM Systems Journal* 20.3 (1981): 306–320.

Brooks, Ted. "Career Development: Filling the Usability Gap." *Technical Communication* 38.2 (April 1991): 180–184.

Cohen, Gerald, and Donald H. Cunningham. *Creating Technical Manuals: A Step-by-Step Approach to Writing User-Friendly Manuals.* NY: McGraw-Hill, 1984.

Cooper, Marilyn. "The Postmodern Space of Operator's Manuals." *Technical Communication Quarterly* 5.4 (1996): 385–410.

Craig, John S. "Approaches to Usability Testing and Design Strategies: An Annotated Bibliography." *Technical Communication* 38.2 (April 1991): 190–194.

Queipo, Larry. "Taking the Mysticism Out of Usability Test Objectives." *Technical Communication* 38.2 (April 1991): 190–194, 185–189.

Redish, Virginia. "Writing for People Who Are 'Reading to Learn to Do.'" *Creating Usable Manuals and Forms: A Document Design Symposium.* Technical Report 42. Pittsburgh, PA: Carnegie-Mellon Communications Design Center, 1988.

Riney, Larry A. *Technical Writing for Industry: An Operations Manual for the Technical Writer.* Englewood Cliffs, NJ: Prentice-Hall, 1989.

Rubens, Phillip M. "A Reader's View of Text and Graphics: Implications for Transactional Text." *Journal of Technical Writing and Communication* 16.1/2 (1986): 73–86.

Rubin, Jeff. "Conceptual Design: Cornerstone of Usability." *Technical Communication* 43.2 (May 1996): 130–138.

Sullivan, Patricia. "Beyond a Narrow Conception of Usability Testing." *IEEE Transactions of Professional Communication* 32.4 (December 1989): 256–264.

18 Oral Reports

Chapter 18
IN A NUTSHELL

Oral reports range from brief answers to questions at meetings to hour-long speeches to large audiences.

Follow these guidelines:

- Speak in a normal voice. Help yourself speak normally by not memorizing—practice enough so you can speak from notes. Present a visual aid and then explain it to the audience.
- Arrange your speech top-down. Use topic sentences to begin sections so that you are constantly telling the audience where they are in the sequence.
- Make visual aids large enough to see and focus each one on just one point.
- Practice with any technology (laptops, computer slide presentations) before you give the speech.
- Be presentable. You should dress appropriately. If you don't know what a professional should wear in this situation, ask someone who does. Avoid irritating mannerisms (smacking lips, shaking keys in pockets, saying "um" repeatedly).

Throughout your career, you will give oral reports to explain the results of investigations, propose solutions to problems, report on the progress of projects, make changes to policy, or justify requests for such items as more employees and equipment. Sometimes these presentations are impromptu; sometimes they are elaborately planned. An oral report may supplement a written one or may replace it entirely. This chapter explains how to plan, organize, and present an oral report.

PLANNING THE ORAL REPORT

Planning includes decisions about your audience and your visual aids.

Consider the Audience

Your oral report must engage your audience, who will have various levels of knowledge and emotional involvement with your topic. Your speeches will reach listeners more effectively if you understand a few essential differences between a reading and a listening audience.

Speakers Use Personal Contact.   A speech allows you to have personal contact with listeners. You can make use of personality, voice, and gestures, as well as first-person pronouns, visuals, and feedback from listeners. If you are a person speaking to people, your audience will react positively.

Listeners Are Present for the Entire Oral Report.   That listeners are present for the entire report may seem advantageous, but it also may make communication more difficult. Many listeners want to hear only selected parts of a report—the parts that apply directly to them. If, for instance, your listeners are the plant manager and her staff, the plant manager would probably prefer a capsule version of the report, which a short abstract would provide, and would rather leave the details for staff members to examine. The oral report gives her no choice but to listen to all your detailed information, a situation that might put her in a negative frame of mind.

Listeners Do Not Have the Benefit of Formatted Pages.   The oral report does not provide headings to identify sections of particular interest to the listeners and to indicate parallel and subordinate ideas. Instead, you have to provide oral cues or use visual aids to help an audience understand when one section ends and another begins.

Select Visual Aids

Visual aids can reinforce major points and clarify complex ideas in an oral report. As you construct an outline, ask yourself whether a visual aid will help listeners grasp the point or the section, and then organize the report with all your visual aids in mind. Good visual aids are often the difference between an effective and an ineffective presentation. Research also shows that visuals make speakers appear better prepared and more professional. Color graphics are especially impressive (Meng). Learn the types of visual aids, and know how to use, create, and display them.

Types of Visual Aids. Appropriate visual aids for a speech include outlines; slides or drawings; tables, graphs, and charts; and handouts.

The basic *outline* shows listeners the sections and subsections of the report. This device orients the audience to the relationship among sections in the speech—what is a major section, what is a subsection—as well as to the sequence of sections. Remember, though, that outlines are boring to look at for any length of time.

Slides and *drawings* can introduce listeners to important images. High-quality slides can present exact representations. Drawings are good for procedures, such as the path products follow through a sterilizing machine.

Tables, graphs, and *charts* can present data in a way that enables listeners to grasp relationships right away. An oral explanation of the relationship among the percentages that affect a pay increase is hard to follow, but a table or graph makes it crystal clear. (See Chapter 8 for more on tables and graphs.)

A *handout* can replace or supplement projected visual aids. Often a handout of the outline is effective (use an outline report as explained in Chapter 12). You could also pass out copies of a key image, perhaps a table. Listeners can make notes on it as you speak.

Uses of Visual Aids. Decide how you will use visual aids. They can be used

■ To illustrate a point.
■ To begin a lengthy explanation.

For instance, if the writer of the spousal employment assistance proposal discussed in Chapter 14 were giving an oral presentation and wanted to dramatize the need for the program, she might use a bar graph that contrasted total new hires to total new hires who quit within six months. On the other hand, if she wanted to emphasize the causes of this exodus, she might project a list of common reasons given for departure.

If a section of your speech contains a complicated explanation of a process, a mechanism, or an abstract relationship, a visual aid always helps listeners. Project the image first: then explain it in detail.

Use a Storyboard to Choose Visual Aids. Experienced speakers use storyboards to determine which visual aids they will use. A storyboard is simply a list of topics arranged opposite a list of visual aids. To make a storyboard, follow these guidelines:

▧ Determine the major points of your presentation and list them down the left side of a sheet of paper.

▧ List down the right side the visual aids you plan to use to illustrate each point.

Here is an example of a storyboard:

Point	*Visual Aid*
Introduction	
Source of assignment	
Recommendation	List of recommendations
Preview	Outline of main topics
Section 1	
Method of researching	List of main methods
Section 2	
Three types of laminates	For each type:
Advantages of each	Cross-sectional view
	List of advantages
	(both on same page)
Section 3	
Cost	Table of costs

Creating Visual Aids.   You can create visual aids manually or with a computer. After you design your visuals, make overhead transparencies from them, duplicate them to hand out as notes, or make slides from them. Many computer programs allow you to design visuals. Most of them enable you to start from an outline and use a storyboard.

The following guidelines will help you design effective computer visuals (Scoville; Tessler; Welsh).

1. Know the parts of the visual—title, text or graphics, and border (see Figure 18.1).

   The *title* appears at the top, usually in the largest type size. Use it to identify the contents of the visual explicitly. A rule (½ or 1 point) separates the title from the text or graphic.

   The *text* makes the points you want to highlight. Use phrases that convey specific content rather than generic topics.

   The *graphic* consists of a table, chart, or drawing.

   The *border* is a line that provides a frame around the visual.

FIGURE 18.1
Parts of a Visual

2. Create a template, or "master." Make all the visuals consistent, with the same elements in the same place and in the same color. For instance, make all titles 24 point, black, and centered at the top.
3. Use only one main idea per visual.
4. For text visuals (visuals that use only words):

    Use no more than seven lines of text.

    Restrict each line to seven words or less.

    Use initial capitals followed by lower-case letters.

    Use 18-point type for body text, 24-point type for titles.
5. For graphic visuals (tables, charts, pictures):

    Simplify the chart so that it makes only one point.

    Use charts for dramatic effect. A line graph that plunges sharply at one point calls attention to the drop. Your job is to interpret it.

    Use tables for presenting numbers. Be prepared to point out the numbers you want the audience to notice.

    Use pictures to illustrate an object that you want to discuss, for instance, the control panel of a new machine.
6. Use color intelligently.

    Give each item (title, test, border) in the template its own color.

    Use a background color; blue is commonly used.

Use contrasting colors—white or yellow text on green or blue background.

Use red sparingly; it focuses attention on itself. Long passages in red are hard to read.

Avoid hard-to-read color combinations, such as yellow on white and black on blue. Violet can be very hard to read.

ORGANIZING THE ORAL REPORT

Effective oral reports contain an introduction, body, and conclusion. The audience should easily recognize each of these sections.

Develop the Introduction

The introduction establishes both the tone and the topic of the speech. Your *tone* is your attitude toward the listeners and the subject matter. Be serious but not dull. Avoid being so intense that no one can laugh or so flip that the topic seems insignificant. Introduce your topics succinctly. Be explicit about your purpose. The best speakers focus on one or two points and list them in the introduction.

Follow these guidelines:

- You do not need to begin your report with a joke, a quotation by an authority, or an anecdote, but a well-chosen light story often helps relax you and the audience.
- Explain why your report is important to your audience.
- Present your conclusions or recommendations right away. Then the audience will have a viewpoint from which to interpret the data you present.
- Explain how you assembled your report.
- Indicate your special knowledge of or concern with the subject.
- Identify the situation that required you to prepare the report (or the person who requested it).
- Preview the main points so your listeners can understand the order in which you will present your ideas.

Develop the Body

Many studies have shown that listeners simply do not hear everything the speaker says. Therefore, you should give several minutes to each main idea—long enough to get each main point across, but not long enough to labor it.

Choose an Effective Principle of Organization.   The order in which you present your ideas should be appropriate to the subject. Most subjects can be structured into chronological order, problem-to-solution order, least-to-most-important order, or spatial order, such as from outside to inside or from north to south. If your preview is clear, the listeners will be able to follow and understand the major points in the report.

Use Transitions Liberally.   Clear transitions are very helpful to an audience of listeners. Your transitions remind the audience of the report's structure, which you established in the preview. Indicate how the next main idea fits into the overall report and why it is important to know about it. For instance, a proposal may seem very costly until the shortness of the payback period is emphasized.

Select Important Details.   Although providing extensive details to support main ideas is not possible in the time permitted for an oral report, you should select enough significant details to show that your point is valid. Choose details that are especially meaningful to the audience. Explain any anticipated changes in equipment, staff, or policy, and show how these changes will be beneficial.

Impose a Time Limit.   Find out how long the audience expects the speech to last and fit your speech to that time frame. If they expect 15 minutes and you talk 15, they will feel very good. Generally, speak for less time. It is much better to present one or two main ideas carefully than to attempt to communicate more information than your listeners can grasp.

Develop a Conclusion

The conclusion section restates the main ideas presented in the body of the report. Follow these guidelines:

- As you conclude your report, you should actually say, "In conclusion . . ." to capture your listeners' interest.
- For a proposal, stress the main advantages of your ideas, and urge your listeners to take specific action.
- For a recommendation report, emphasize the most significant data presented for each criterion, and clearly present your recommendations.
- Use a visual to summarize the important data.
- End the report by asking whether your listeners have any questions.

PRESENTING THE ORAL REPORT EFFECTIVELY

The best long oral report is extemporaneous rather than read or memorized. An extemporaneous report, however, is not a spontaneous, off-the-top-of-your-head presentation. Rather, the speaker follows a prepared outline and supplies appropriate detail and explanation as needed. In fact, an extemporaneous report is carefully rehearsed and delivered.

Rehearse Your Presentation

During rehearsals, go straight through the speech, using note cards. At least once, wear the same clothes you will wear in the actual presentation.

Practice Developing a Conversational Quality. Make your speech sound like a person speaking to people, and use both voice and gestures to emphasize important points. Even the best information will fall on deaf ears if it is delivered like a robotic time-and-weather announcement. Rehearse until you feel secure with your report, but always stop short of memorizing it. If you memorize, you will tend to grope for memorized words rather than concentrating on the listeners and letting the words flow.

Practice Handling Your Visual Aids. Arrange your visual aids in the correct order, and decide where you will place them as you finish with them. If a listener asks you to return to a visual, you want to be able to find it easily. If you are using handouts, decide whether to distribute them before or during the presentation. Distributing them before the presentation eliminates the need to interrupt your flow of thought later, but because the listeners will flip through the handouts, they may be distracted as you start. Distributing them during the presentation causes an interruption, but listeners will focus immediately on the visual.

Rehearse. Present your speech at least once in a situation that simulates the conditions under which you will make the speech, particularly for reports to large groups. Use a room of approximately the same size, with the same type of equipment for projecting your voice and your visuals. Practice with a microphone if you have never used one.

Deliver Your Presentation

You will increase your effectiveness if you use notes and adopt a comfortable extemporaneous style.

Use Notes. Experienced speakers have found that outlines prepared on a few large note cards (5 by 8 inches, one side only) are easier to handle than outlines on many small note cards. Some speakers even prefer outlines on one or two sheets of standard paper, mounted on light cardboard for easier handling.

The outline should contain clear main headings and subheadings. Make sure your outline has plenty of white space so you can keep your place.

Adopt a Comfortable Style. The extemporaneous method results in natural, conversational delivery and helps you concentrate on the audience. Using this method, you can direct your attention to the listeners, referring to the outline only to jog your memory and to ensure that ideas are presented in the proper order. Smile. Take time to look at individual people and to collect your thoughts. Instead of rushing to your next main point, check whether members of the audience understood your last point. Your word choice may occasionally suffer when you speak extemporaneously, but reports delivered in this way still communicate better than those memorized or read.

The following suggestions will help as you face your listeners and deliver the speech:

1. Look directly at each listener at least once during the report. With experience, you will be able to tell from your listeners' faces whether you are communicating well. If they seem puzzled or inattentive, repeat the main idea, give additional examples for clarity, or solicit questions. Don't proceed in lock step through your notes. Adapt.

2. Make sure you can be heard, but try to speak conversationally. You should feel a sense of a round, full voice in your rib cage. You should also feel that your voice fills the space of the room, with the sound of your voice bouncing back slightly to your own ears. The listeners should get the impression that you are talking to them rather than just presenting a report. Inexperienced speakers often talk too rapidly.

3. Try to become aware of—and to eliminate—your distracting mannerisms. No one wants to see speakers brush their hair, scratch their arms, rock back and forth on the balls of their feet, smack their lips. If the mannerism is pronounced enough, it may be all the audience remembers. Stand firmly on both feet without slumping or swaying.

4. To point out some aspect of a visual projected by an overhead projector, lay a pencil or an arrow made of paper on the appropriate spot of the transparency.

5. When answering questions, make sure everyone hears and understands each question before you begin to answer it. If you cannot answer a question during the question-and-answer session, say so, and assure the questioner that you will find the answer.

▦ WORKSHEET FOR PREPARING AN ORAL REPORT

❏ *Identify your audience.*
What is your listeners' level of knowledge about the topic?
What is their level of interest in the entire speech?

❏ *Create an outline showing the main point and subpoints.*

❏ *Assign a time limit to each point.*

❏ *Create a visual aid storyboard.*
What visual aid will illustrate each subpoint most effectively?

❏ *Decide whether you need any kind of projection or display equipment.*
Slide projector? flip chart?

❏ *Review the speaking location. Be sure you have enough room at the speaking location for at least two piles of visual aids: "to use" and "already used."*

❏ *Select a method for pointing to the screen.*

❏ *Prepare clearly written note cards—with just a few points on each.*

❏ *Rehearse the speech several times, including how you will actually handle the visual aids.*

❏ *For computer-projected visuals, check the compatibility of hardware and software at the site where you will speak.*

▦ WORKSHEET FOR EVALUATING AN ORAL REPORT

❏ *Answer these questions:*

1. Clarity
   Did the speaker tell you the point early in the speech? Could you tell when the speaker moved to a new subpoint?
2. Tone
   Did the speaker sound conversational? Did the speaker go too fast? go too slow? speak in a monotone?
3. Use of Visual Aid
   Was the visual aid clear enough to understand? Did the speaker use the visual aid effectively?

■ EXERCISES

1. Create a visual aid that illustrates a problem in one of your current projects. Give a brief speech (2 to 3 minutes) explaining the problem. Alternate 1: Prepare a second visual aid that illustrates the solution or its effects, and present both visuals to the class in a 2- to 3-minute speech. Alternate 2: Prepare the visuals in groups of two to four. Select a speaker for the group. Give the speech.

2. Report on a situation with which you are involved. Your work on an assignment for this class is probably most pertinent, but your instructor will provide his or her own requirements. Depending on the available time, draw a visual on the board, make a transparency, or create a handout. In 2 minutes, explain the point of the visual aid. Class members will complete and/or discuss the evaluation questions above.

3. For Exercises 1 and 2, each member of the audience should prepare a question to ask the speaker. Conduct a question-and-answer session. When the session is finished, discuss the value and relevance of the questions that were asked. What constitutes a good question? Also evaluate the answers. What constitutes a good answer?

4. Make a storyboard for the speech you will give for the following Speaking Assignment. Divide a page into these three columns and fill them in, following this example:

Point	Visual Aid	Time
Method of extrusion	Cross section of laminate	2 minutes

5. Use the generic graph on page 486 to make a 2-minute speech. Title the graph and explain its source, its topic, and the significance of the pattern. Choose any topic that would change over time.

6. Give a brief speech in which you freely use technical terms. The class will ask questions that will elicit the definitions. If there is time, redeliver the speech at a less technical level.

■ SPEAKING ASSIGNMENT

Your instructor may require an oral presentation of a project you have written during the term. The speech should be extemporaneous and should conform to an agreed-upon length. Outline the speech, construct a storyboard,

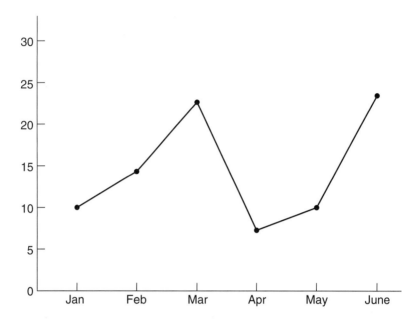

make your visuals, and rehearse. Follow your presentation with a question-and-answer session.

▪ WRITING ASSIGNMENT

Write a learning report for the speaking assignment you just completed. See Chapter 5, Writing Assignment 7, page 123, for details of the assignment.

▪ WEB EXERCISE

Using screens that you download from the Web, give a speech or a Power-Point presentation to your classmates in which you do either of the following:
   a. Explain the effective elements of a well-designed screen.
   b. Explain how to use the screen to perform an activity (order plane tickets, contact a sales representative, perform an advanced search).

▪ WORKS CITED

Meng, Brita. "Get to the Point." *Macworld* 5.4 (1988): 136–143.

Scoville, Richard. "Slide Rules." *Publish!* 4.3 (1989): 51–53.

Tessler, Franklin. "Step-by-Step Slides." *Macworld* 5.12 (1988): 148–153.

Welsh, Theresa. "Presentation Visuals: The Ten Most Common Mistakes." *Intercom* 43.6 (1996): 22–43.

Focus on ELECTRONIC PRESENTATIONS

Since 1990, enormous strides have been made in the direction of multimedia productions for business meetings. Before the advent of computer programs like PowerPoint, most business presentations were made using overhead transparencies, flip charts, or colored 35mm slides. All this changed when portable computers, LCD projectors, and user-friendly multimedia programs became popular.

Most presenters today create their own multimedia presentations and if the creator/presenter pays attention to how the special effects are used, the presentation can be enhanced tremendously. What follows are suggestions that work; but remember, the best way to make a presentation work effectively is to know the audience. Listed below are six specific areas of the multimedia presentation that require special attention, particularly in the creation stage.

Fonts. Carefully consider the font with which you will create your text. Keep the font simple yet elegant, subtle yet striking. Typefaces can portray a wide range of emotions from casual to authoritative, from serious to comic. Selecting and using a typeface that will bring about the desired response from your audience is important. Follow these three guidelines when selecting fonts:

- Use only one font, preferably a sans serif font like Helvetica or Arial.
- For impact, use different sizes, boldface, or italics sparingly. Even the simplest font, when italicized, can become difficult to read. Too much boldface or too many different sizes give the cluttered "ransom note" effect that is very distracting.
- Use larger fonts and/or different colors for your titles. When using larger fonts, be sure to use those sizes that are easily read (18 to 24 point), but not so large that they become distracting.

Use Presentation to Help the Reader. The most important part of any presentation is the content, but do not try to put all of your ideas on slides. Too much text will cause viewers to read slides, not pay attention to you. Follow these guidelines to design the text of your slides:

- Use a landscape layout for your text as opposed to a portrait layout. Landscape makes the longer lines of text easier to read, and columns easier to use.

- Title each slide so your audience will have a quick reference to the topic at hand.

- Use only enough text to clearly label the graphic. Minimum text will allow the graphics to speak for themselves.

- Keep running text to a minimum. Try to keep text to no more than six to eight lines per slide, fewer if possible.

Colors. Use color to enhance your presentation. Color combinations should help viewers focus on key points, not on the combination itself. To use color effectively, consider these guidelines:

- Use color consistently to establish "visual logic." Use only one color for titles, and only for emphasizing key words. (See Focus on Color, pp. 169–178).

- Use green and red sparingly. Ten percent of all people suffer from color blindness, difficulty distinguishing between red or green. It is best to assume that at least one person in every ten of your audience will be limited in his or her ability to translate color.

- Select combinations with an awareness of technology. Colors that look well together in a sign or in print, as in a magazine or newspaper, will probably not work the same way on a screen. For example, ambient light, which is what is produced by an LCD projector, will affect contrast greatly; it will turn a color such as deep burgundy or deep green into a pastel color.

- Use what is known to work well. Yellow backgrounds with black lettering work well in most situations (think about school buses). Other good combinations are deep blue backgrounds with yellow letters, or gray backgrounds with black letters.

- Evaluate templates before using them. Current programs, such as PowerPoint, have a variety of background templates with color schemes that are handsome and exciting at first glance, but always try to keep your audience in mind when you make your selection. Look at it from the standpoint of your audience—will this combination help them understand your point? If you're not certain about the combination, don't use it.

Animation. Animation is one of the most powerful tools available to the electronically produced presentation. By using animation, we can emphasize important points visually while explaining them verbally. However, the idea is to enhance the production, not provide gimmicky entertainment. Follow these guidelines:

■ Use only one text animation. Remember that the audience should be tracking as closely as possible with the presenter. To keep the audience tracking, use a gradual introduction of text, and pick only one primary reading transition. For example, a simple "wipe-right" text animation will keep the reader's eye going in the normal reading direction.

■ Treat previous lines carefully. Fading or subduing the previous bullets when the new information appears will help to keep the audience focused, but select a subdued tone for the previous bullets. Using an entirely different color will only draw attention away from the new text you are trying to introduce.

■ Use animated graphics to make complex points. The multimedia, electronic presentation can use graphics effectively to show the progression of complicated points. Process steps, time lines, and flow charts all benefit nicely from animated graphics. Keep in mind that being consistent is important when using animated graphics. Your audience will appreciate consistent use of color contrast and special effects.

Sound Effects. New creators of multimedia presentation programs often fall to the temptation to use all of the tricks and gimmicks available, especially for sound effects.

■ Use subdued nondramatic sounds for transition. The first time you use a ricocheting bullet sound, you may get a reaction from your audience, but the second time you use it, the reaction will be greatly diminished, and the third time will be boring.

■ Use the same sound for each transition. If you have a very special point that you want to emphasize, or if you want to use a sound effect for some comic relief in a deadly serious situation, go ahead, but use these strategies sparingly.

Slide Transitions.   The method of making a transition from one slide to the next has become a standard part of the multimedia presentation. The method needs to be considered carefully. Remember, if your audience concentrates on the effect rather than the message, you've lost your audience. Follow this guideline:

■ Use only one or two simple transitions. Select transitions in order to aid the viewer. For example, a transition that "wipes up" will help to guide the watcher's eye back to the top of the slide so that the subject of the slide is immediately identified. A simple fade to black between sections of a presentation signals that a new topic is being considered. If you have analyzed your audience carefully, you should be able to tell the level of consistency and subtlety that will work best.

Professional Communication

19 Letters

Chapter 19
IN A NUTSHELL

Letter format is an agreed-upon set of ways to present the parts of a letter. The quickest way to find out what they are and how they fit on the page is to study Figure 19.1. That figure presents the parts in block format, which arranges all the items at the left margin. Using block format is an easy way to present yourself as a credible professional.

Letters represent you or your com-

pany in professional, often legal and emotional, situations. The key to all types of letters is to treat the reader appropriately. "Appropriately" means to use the "you" attitude—speak to readers in nonjargony, understandable, nonconfrontational words. Write several short paragraphs rather than fewer long ones. Treat readers as you would want yourself or people close to you treated.

Business letters are an important—even a critical—part of any professional's job and are written for many reasons to many audiences. They may request information from an expert, transmit a report to a client, or discuss the specifications of a project with a supplier. Letters represent the firm, and their quality reflects the quality of the firm. This chapter introduces you to effective, professional letter writing by explaining the common formats, the standard elements, the planning required, and several common types of business letters.

THREE BASIC LETTER FORMATS

The three basic formats are the block format, the modified block format, and the simplified format (*Merriam; Webster's*).

Block Format

In the *block format,* place all the letter's elements flush against the left margin. Do not indent the first word of each paragraph. The full block format, shown in Figures 19.1 and 19.3, is widely used because letters in this format can be typed quickly.

Modified Block Format

The *modified block format* (an example appears in Figure 19.3) is the same as the full block format with two exceptions: the date line and closing signature are placed on the right side of the page. The best position for both is five spaces to the right of the center line, but flush right is acceptable. A variation of this format is the *modified semiblock.* It is the same as the modified block, except that the first line of each paragraph is indented five spaces.

Simplified Format

The *simplified format* (see Figure 19.4 for an example) contains no salutation and no complimentary close, but it almost always has a subject line. It is extremely useful for impersonal situations and for situations where the identity of the recipient is not known. In personal situations, writers start the first paragraph with the recipient's name.

ELEMENTS OF A LETTER

Internal Elements

This section describes the elements of a letter from the top to the bottom of a page.

FIGURE 19.1
Block Format

4217 East Eleventh Avenue Post Office Box 2701 Austin, TX 78701	Heading
(skip 3 to 5 lines; varies with letter length)	
February 24, 2003	Date
(skip 3 to 5 lines; varies with letter length)	
Ms. Susan Wardell Director of Planning Acme Bolt and Fastener Co. 23201 Johnson Avenue Arlington, AZ 85322 *(double-space)*	Inside address
Dear Ms. Wardell: *(double-space)*	Salutation, mixed punctuation
SUBJECT: ABC CONTRACT (optional) *(double-space)*	Subject line
_____ _____ _____	Body paragraphs flush left
(double-space between paragraphs)	
_____ _____ _____	
(double-space) Sincerely yours, *(skip 4 lines)*	Closing, mixed punctuation
 *John K. Palmer*	Signature
John K. Palmer	Typed name
Treasurer	Position in company
(double-space) abv *(typist's initials)*	Typist's initials
enc: (2)	Enclosure line
(skip 1 or 2 lines; depends on letter length) c: Ms. Louise Black	Copy line

TIP: PUNCTUATION

Letter items are punctuated by either *open* or *mixed* patterns. You may choose either. Be consistent. In open format, put no punctuation after the salutation and complimentary close. In mixed format, put a colon after the salutation and a comma after the complimentary close.

Heading. The heading is your address.

4217 East Eleventh Avenue
Post Office Box 2701
Austin, TX 78701

■ Spell out words such as *Avenue, Street, East, North,* and *Apartment* (but use *Apt.* if the line would otherwise be too long).
■ Put an apartment number to the right of the street address. If, however, the street address is too long, put the apartment number on the next line.
■ Spell out numbered street names up to *Twelfth.*
■ To avoid confusion, put a hyphen between the house and street number (1021-14th Street).
■ Either spell out the full name of the state or use the U.S. Postal Service zip code abbreviation. If you use the zip code abbreviation, note that the state abbreviation has two capital letters and no periods and that the zip code number follows one space after the state (NY 10036).
■ Note on letterhead: place the date 3 to 5 lines below the last line of the letterhead, in the position required by the format (e.g., flush left for block).

Date. Dates can have one of two forms: February 24, 2003, or 24 February 2003.

■ Spell out the month.
■ Do not use ordinal indicators, such as 1st or 24th.

Inside Address. The inside address is the same as the address that appears on the envelope.

Ms. Susan Wardell
Director of Planning
Acme Bolt and Fastener Co.
23201 Johnson Avenue
Arlington, AZ 85322

■ Use the correct personal title (Mr., Ms., Dr., Professor) and business title (Director, Manager, Treasurer).
■ Write the firm's name exactly, adhering to its practice of abbreviating or spelling out such words as *Company* and *Corporation*.

- Place the reader's business title after his or her name or on a line by itself, whichever best balances the inside address.
- Use the title *Ms.* for a woman unless you know that she prefers to be addressed in another way.

Attention Line.   Attention lines are generally used only when you cannot name the reader ("Attention Personnel Manager"; "Attention Payroll Department").

- Place the line two spaces below the inside address.
- Place the word *Attention* against the left margin. Do *not* follow it by a colon.

Salutation.   The salutation always agrees with the first line of the inside address.

- If the first line names an individual (Ms. Susan Wardell), say, "Dear Ms. Wardell:" If the name is "gender neutral" (Robin Jones), say "Dear Robin Jones:"
- If the first line names a company (Acme Bolt and Fastener Co.), use the simplified format (see Figure 19.4) with a subject line or repeat the name of the company ("Dear Acme Bolt and Fastener Co.:").
- If the first line names an office (Director of Planning), address the office, use an attention line, or use a subject line.

Dear Director of Planning: (*or*)
Attention Director of Planning (*or*)
SUBJECT: ABC CONTRACT

- If you know only the first initial of the recipient, write "Dear S. Wardell," or use an attention line.
- If you know only a Post Office box (say, from a job ad), use a subject line.

Box 4721 ML
The Daily Planet
Gillette, WY 82716
Subject: APPLICATION FOR OIL RIG MANAGER

Subject Line.   Use a subject line to replace awkward salutations, as explained above, or to focus the reader's attention.

SUBJECT: **Request to Extend Deadline**

■ Follow the word *Subject* with a colon.

■ For emphasis, capitalize or boldface the phrase.

■ Use of the word *Subject* is optional, especially in simplified format. If you do not use *Subject,* capitalize the entire line.

Body.   Single-space the body, and try to balance it on the page. It should cover the page's imaginary middle line (located 5½ inches from the top and bottom of the page). Use several short paragraphs rather than one long one. Use 1-inch margins at the right and left.

Complimentary Closing and Signature.   Close business letters with "Sincerely" or "Sincerely yours." Add the company name if policy requires it.

Sincerely yours,
ACME BOLT AND FASTENER CO.

John K. Palmer

John K. Palmer
Treasurer

■ Capitalize only the first word of the closing.

■ Place the company's name immediately below the complimentary closing (if necessary).

■ Allow four lines for the handwritten signature.

■ Place the writer's title or department, or both, below his or her typed name.

Optional Lines.   Place optional lines below the typed signature.

■ Place the typist's initials in lower-case letters, flush left.

■ Add an enclosure line if the envelope contains additional material. Use "Enclosure:" or "enc:". Place the name of the enclosure (résumé, bid contract) after the colon, or put the number of enclosures in parentheses.

enc: (2)
Enclosure: résumé

■ If copies are sent to other people, place "c:" (for copy) at the left margin and place the names to the right.

c: Joanne Koehler

FIGURE 19.2
OCR Area of Envelope

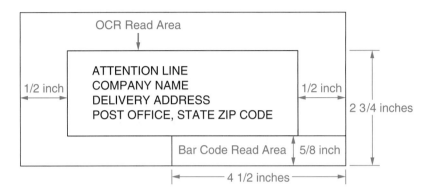

Succeeding Pages. For succeeding pages of a letter, place the name of the addressee, the page number, and the date in a heading.

Susan Wardell   -2-   February 24, 1999

Envelopes

The standard business envelope is 9½ by 4⅟₁₆ inches. Place the stamp in the upper right corner. Place your address (the same one that you used in the heading) in the upper left corner.

Place the address anywhere in the "read area" of the U.S. Postal Service's optical character recognition (OCR) machines (see Figure 19.2). The U.S. Postal Service (USPS) recommends the following descending order:

- Attention line
- Company name
- Street address; on the street address line, also add directions (N, NE, S, etc.), designator (St., Ave., Rd.), and sublocation (Apt., STE [suite], RM [room]). *Note:* The postal service will deliver the mail to the address directly above the city and state.
- City and state
- Zip code to the right of the state; use all 9 digits if you know them

PLANNING BUSINESS LETTERS

In planning your letter, you must consider your audience, your tone, and your format.

Consider Your Audience

Before you begin to write, consider the audience's knowledge level and its specific need for the information. The audience could be a customer who can identify the defective part but who may not know much about how the part fits into the larger system in the machine. The audience could be an expert engineer or manager who understands the general theory of this kind of project (say, constructing a commercial building) but knows little about this particular project.

Also be aware that the audience has various reasons for needing your letter. Assessing that need allows you to write a more effective letter. Your letter may be shown to someone other than just the recipient, usually a person more distant from the situation. And your letter could be used as a basis for decisions, even legal action.

Consider Your Tone

Use Plain English.   You want to sound natural; you are, after all, one human being addressing another. Plain conversational English makes your point better than "businessese." Even if your letter has legal implications, you should use a relaxed, clear tone. Consider this brief passage:

> Pursuant to our discussion of February 3 in reference to the L-19 transistor, please be advised that we are not presently in receipt of the above-mentioned item but expect to have it in stock within one week. Enclosed herewith please find a brochure regarding said transistor as per your request.

Here is the paragraph rewritten in a more direct, conversational style that makes the contents much easier to grasp.

> I've enclosed a brochure on the L-19 transistor we talked about on February 3. Our shipment of L-19s should arrive within a week.

Use the "You" Approach.   The "you" approach is based on the writer's recognition that the recipient is a person who appreciates being approached in a personal way. Applying this approach requires only that you use "I," "we," and "you." Consider the following example, and note how the writer addresses the customer's dissatisfaction both by showing empathy and by proposing solutions to the problem.

> Dear Mr. Hillary:
>
> After my January 27th visit to your complex to investigate the poorly performing laser printers, I talked to our technical support and to Megacorp's customer representative. We have several suggestions for solving

the problem. If they do not work, we will investigate the relatively more difficult task of replacing all ten printers.

Technical support suggests that you discontinue using the printer driver in your desktop publishing program. Hold the shift key down while you select print and you will default to the word processing print driver. In tests we performed here we found that the word processor driver prints about 8–10 times faster. This simple procedure change should solve most of the problems.

The difficulty you have in printing eps images in your desktop publishing program is more complicated. Our simple recommendation is that you convert them to tiff images. We tried this and the documents printed about 3 times faster. Our more involved recommendation is that we upgrade the RAM in the printers to 4 MB Because of the difficulties you have experienced and because of the length of time you have been our customer, we will install them free and charge only our cost.

If none of these suggestions works, we will have to begin to negotiate to return the printers to Megacorp or trade them in. My brief contact with the customer rep at Mega indicates that this option will be more difficult.

I will contact you next week on Tuesday to see if our suggestions have had any effect.

Sincerely,

Marian Goodrich

Marian Goodrich
District Sales Manager

Consider Format

Format can affect the way your audience accepts your message. Use one of the basic formats or one that your company requires. Readers expect you to be a knowledgeable professional; using the correct form helps reinforce that impression. Make careful design decisions. Choose several short paragraphs rather than one long paragraph. Use bullets and indentations to help readers grasp key points easily. Review Chapter 7 to see how format can help presentation.

TYPES OF BUSINESS LETTERS

The rest of this chapter examines several types of business letters and suggests how to structure their contents.

Transmittal Letters

A *transmittal letter* (Figure 19.3) conveys a report from one firm to another. (Transmittal correspondence is explained in Chapter 14.) To write a transmittal letter, follow these guidelines:

- Identify the report enclosed.
- Briefly explain the report's purpose and scope.
- Explain any problems encountered.
- Acknowledge the people who helped.

General Information Letters

General information letters can deal with anything. They serve to keep the writer in touch with the reader (a common public relations device), to send information, or to reply to requests. Figure 19.4 shows an example. To write such a letter, follow these guidelines:

- Use a context-setting introduction.
- If there is an acceptance or rejection, state it clearly.
- Use formatting to highlight the main point.
- Add extra information as needed, but keep it brief.

FIGURE 19.3
Transmittal Letter in Modified Block Format with Closed Punctuation

VINZ CONSULTING
EVERYTHING ABOUT THE SHOP
1021 Portland Drive
East Pines, MD 20840-1461
(307) 432-8866

October 27, 2003

Mr. Charles Lindsay
Mountain Milling
3266 Crestview Drive
Charleston, WV 25301

Dear Mr. Lindsay:

Attached is my final report on the type of milling machine you should purchase for your plant. I recommend that you purchase Ironton's #02119-BTUA.

As we discussed on my site visit last month, I have researched the appropriate literature on this subject, talked to several sales reps, and observed three different demonstrations of the 02119 and its two competitors. You were particularly concerned about size and power— the 02119 will do the job for you.

I have enjoyed our work together and look forward to working with you in the future. I have found your staff particularly helpful in filling my several requests about your plant's capacity and materials flow.

Sincerely,

Steve Vinz

Steve Vinz
Project Manager

FIGURE 19.4
General Information Letter in Simplified Format

Maxwell and Goldman
3227 Girard Avenue South
Minneapolis, Minnesota 55408
608-385-1944 / fax 608-385-1945
www.maxgold.com

July 14, 2004

Mr. Duwan James
James Corporation
4810 River Heights Drive
St. Paul, Minnesota 55106

Duwan, here is the background information on the Adjustable Speed Drive. The cost of this system, as we discussed earlier, is $1000.00 installed.

1. The Adjustable Speed Drive can operate as a clutch to inch and jog your conveyor to the exact assembly position. The operator can control the speed instantly from zero to maximum speed, and any speed in between.

2. The conveyor speed can be varied simply and easily while the motor remains at a constant operating speed. The operator controls the speed by hand with the control lever.

3. This speed drive system offers a speed range of 0 to 160 feet per minute (fpm) for the conveyor. This is approximately 2 miles per hour (mph). You indicated that your average speed is 60 fpm. This speed can be locked in for normal runs or sped up for resupplying the line, and again, slowed down for positioning.

4. The drive system is a compact package weighing 45 pounds and having overall dimensions of 10" x 12" x 32". It won't overload or clutter the conveyor frame. The whole system operates from one power cord and requires no special maintenance. The unit is sealed and prelubricated. The only maintenance necessary would be a periodic check of mounting hardware.

Duwan, if you need more information or have any more questions, call or fax to the numbers above, or email me at goldmans@maxgold.com.

Shana Goldman

■ WORKSHEET FOR WRITING A BUSINESS LETTER

PLANNING

❑ *Analyze the audience.*
Who will receive this letter?
Why do they need it? What will they do as a result of receiving it?

❑ *Name your goal for the reader.*
What do you want to happen after the reader reads the letter?

❑ *Choose a format for the reader.*
Use the simplified format for more impersonal or more routine situations.

GENERATING

❑ *State your main points succinctly.*

❑ *Compose with a "you" attitude.*

FINISHING

❑ *Reread the letter slowly, word for word, to weed out any errors in spelling and grammar.*

❑ *Reread the letter to make sure your facts are accurate.*

❑ *Review each of the following for standard form:*
Your address. Do not use abbreviations, except for the state.
The recipient's name, title, corporation title, and address.
The salutation. Repeat the recipient's name.
If you do not know the recipient's name, use a subject line.
The complimentary closing.
Your typed signature (four spaces below the closing).
Your signature (between the closing and the typed signature).

▪ EXERCISES

1. Rewrite this passage using plain English and a "you" attitude.

   There was a question asked to me in regard to the complete fulfillment of contract 108XB (Manual Effector Arm Robot A). Complete documentation of same has not been fulfilled. The specifications are interpreted by this office to mean that no such documentation was required.

2. Analyze this letter.

   A shredded conveyor belt? What a disaster! And here we were, so happy the last time we talked. Well, while it's always something, there's a silver lining in every cloud, so let's talk about what happened.

   Why did this happen? We haven't had a conveyor belt shred at a customer site in 31 years. You're the first. Have you checked your operating procedures? What do you do for training? These things are practically indestructible—who runs your machines? What do you know about them?

   Anyhow, if that's the cloud, the silver lining is that you get one free. It's in the mail. COD.

   Then I reviewed the problem with our design engineer. She feels that the belt exactly fills the specifications and that the fault probably is with your staff, but there is a slight possibility that there could be a problem with the metal "hooks" that join the two ends of the rubber. As your employees install the new belt, make them check those hooks. They should not "wobble." If they do, call me.

   Our sales representative can get to your place on Friday, June 19. If anything else strange comes up, let her know; she can fix anything—she's a great gal.

   Hope there's no hard feelings. Your business is important to us.

3. a. Write two passages. In the first passage, try to be overtechnical, acting as if you expect that anyone would know the terms and concepts you use. In the second passage, rewrite your text so that it assumes that the technical language is foreign to the reader.

b. In groups of two to four, read your two versions, then discuss your results with the class.

c. Write a memo that tells what you learned from this assignment.

■ WRITING ASSIGNMENTS

1. Write a general information letter to your instructor to give her or him the background details of a report you will write. Explain items that the instructor needs to know to read the report as a knowledgeable member of the corporate community.

2. As part of a research project, write a letter of inquiry to a professional. Ask him or her for information about your topic. Your questions should be as specific as you can make them. Ask questions such as "How does Wheeler Amalgamated extrude the plastic used in the cans for Morning Bright orange juice?" Avoid questions such as "Can you send me all the information you have on the extruding process and any other processes of interest?"

3. As part of an assignment that requires a formal report, write a transmittal letter. Follow Figure 19.3.

4. Write a learning report for the writing assignment you just completed. See Chapter 5, Writing Assignment 7, page 123, for details of the assignment.

■ WEB EXERCISE

Analyze two or three company home pages for the "you" attitude. What happens (or doesn't happen) on the screen to make readers feel that they are being addressed personally?

▦ WORKS CITED

United States Postal Service (USPS). *Addressing for Optical Character Recognition.* Notice 165. June 1981.

United States Postal Service (USPS). *Here's How to Address Your Mail for the Best Mail Service.* Notice 36SUC380. Washington, D.C., n.d.

Webster's New World Office Professionals' Desk Reference. Ed. Anthony S. Vlamis. NY: Macmillan, 1999.

Merriam Webster's Secretarial Handbook. Ed. Sheryl Lindsell-Roberts. 3rd ed. Springfield, MA: Merriam, 1993.

20 Job Application Materials

Chapter 20
IN A NUTSHELL

The goal of the *letter of application* and the résumé is to convince someone to offer you a job *interview*.

Basic letter strategies. Relate to the potential employer's needs. Show how you can fill the need. If, in the job announcement, an employer lists several requirements, you should have a paragraph on each. In those paragraphs, present a convincing and memorable detail: "At Iconglow I was in charge of the group that developed the on-line help screens. Under my direction, we analyzed what topics were needed and which screen design would be most effective."

Write in small chunks, putting the employer's keywords at the beginning of each chunk. Pay close attention to spelling and grammar—mistakes could cost you an interview.

Basic résumé strategies. Design your *résumé* so that key topics jump out. Include sections on

- Your objective (one brief line).
- How to contact you.
- Your education (college only).
- Your work history (most relevant jobs at the top; list job title, employer, relevant duties and responsibilities).

Most résumés place the major heads at the left margin and indent the appropriate text about an inch.

Basic interview strategies. At the *interview,* you talk to people who have the power to offer you the job. Impress them by knowing about their company and by telling the truth—if you don't know the answer, say so.

This chapter explains the process of producing an effective résumé and letter. You must analyze the situation, plan the contents of the résumé and letter, present each in an appropriate form, and perform effectively at an interview.

ANALYZING THE SITUATION

To write an effective résumé and letter of application, you must understand your goals, your audience, the field in which you are applying for work, your own strengths, and the needs of your employers.

Understand Your Goals

Your goals are to get an interview and to provide topics for discussion at that interview. If you present your strengths and experiences convincingly in the letter and résumé, prospective employers will ask to interview you. To be convincing, you must explain what you can do for the reader, showing how your strengths fill the reader's needs.

The letter and résumé also provide topics for discussion at an interview. It is not uncommon for an interviewer to say something like "You say in your résumé that you worked with material requirements planning. Would you explain to us what you did?"

Understand Your Audience

Your audience could be any of a number of people in an organization—from the personnel manager to a division manager, one person or a committee. Whoever they are, they will approach the letter and résumé with a limited amount of time and will expect to see evidence of your skills and professional attitude.

The Reader's Time.   Employers read letters and résumés quickly. A manager might have 100 résumés and letters to review. On the initial reading, the manager spends only 30 seconds to 3 minutes on each application, quickly sorting them into "yes" and "no" piles.

Skill Expectations.   Managers want to know how the applicant will satisfy the company's needs. They look for evidence of special aptitudes, skills, contributions to jobs, and achievements at the workplace (Harcourt and Krizar). Suppose, for instance, that the manager placed an ad specifying that applicants need "experience in materials resource planning." Applications that show evidence of that experience probably will go into the "yes" pile, but those without evidence will go to the "no" pile.

Professional Expectations.   Managers read to see if you write clearly, handle details, and act professionally. Clean, neat documents written in clear, correct English on high-quality paper demonstrate all three of these skills.

Assess Your Field

Find out what workers and professionals actually do in your field, so that you can assess your strengths and decide how you may fill an employer's needs. Answer the following questions:

1. What are the basic activities in this field?
2. What skills do I need to perform them?
3. What are the basic working conditions, salary ranges, and long-range outlooks for the areas in which I am interested?

Talk to professionals, visit your college placement office, and use your library. To meet professionals, set up interviews with them, attend career conferences, join a student chapter, or become a student member of a professional organization. Your college's placement service probably has a great deal of career and employer information available.

In your library two helpful books, among many that describe career areas, are the *Dictionary of Occupational Titles (DOT)* and the *Occupational Outlook Handbook (OOH)*, both issued by the U.S. Department of Labor. *DOT* presents brief but comprehensive discussions of positions in industry, listing the job skills that are necessary for these positions. You can use this information to judge the relevance of your own experience and course work when considering a specific job. Here, for instance, is the entry for manufacturing engineer:

> **012.167-042 MANUFACTURING ENGINEER (profess. & kin.)** Plans, directs, and coordinates manufacturing processes in industrial plant: Develops, evaluates, and improves manufacturing methods, utilizing knowledge of product design, materials and parts, fabrication processes, tooling and production equipment capabilities, assembly methods, and quality control standards. Analyzes and plans work force utilization, space requirements, and workflow, and designs layout of equipment and workspace for maximum efficiency [INDUSTRIAL ENGINEER (profess. & kin.) 012.167-030]. Confers with planning and design staff concerning product design and tooling to ensure efficient production methods. Confers with vendors to determine product specifications and arrange for purchase of equipment, materials, or parts, and evaluates products according to specifications and quality standards. Estimates production times, staffing requirements, and related costs to provide information for management decisions. Confers with management, engineering, and other staff regarding manufacturing capabilities, production schedules, and other considerations to facilitate

production processes. Applies statistical methods to estimate future manufacturing requirements and potential.
GOE: 05.01.06 STRENGTH: L GED: R5 M5 L5 SVP: 8 DLU: 89

OOH presents essays on career areas. Besides summarizing necessary job skills, these essays contain information on salary ranges, working conditions, and employment outlook. This type of essay can help you in an interview. For instance, you may be asked, "What is your salary range?" If you know the appropriate figures, you can confidently name a range that is in line with industry standards.

Assess Your Strengths

To analyze your strengths, review all your work experience (summer, part-time, internship, full-time), your college courses, and your extracurricular activities to determine what activities have provided specific background in your field.

Prepare this analysis carefully. Talk to other people about yourself. List every skill and strength you can think of; don't exclude any experiences because they seem trivial. Seek qualifications that distinguish you from your competitors. Here are some questions (based in part on Harcourt and Krizar) to help you analyze yourself.

1. What work experience have you had that is related to your field? What were your job responsibilities? In what projects were you involved? With what machinery or evaluation procedures did you work? What have your achievements been?

2. What special aptitudes and skills do you have? Do you know advanced testing methods? What are your computer abilities?

3. What special projects have you completed in your major field? List processes, machines, and systems with which you have dealt.

4. What honors and awards have you received? Do you have any special college achievements?

5. What is your grade point average?

6. Have you earned your college expenses?

7. What was your minor? What sequence of useful courses have you completed? A sequence of three or more courses in, for example, management, writing, psychology, or communication might have given you knowledge or skills that your competitors do not possess.

8. Are you willing to relocate?

9. Are you a member of a professional organization? Are you an officer? What projects have you participated in as a member?

10. Can you communicate in a second language? Many of today's firms do business internationally.

11. Do you have military experience? While in the military, did you attend a school that applies to your major field? If so, identify the school.

Assess the Needs of Employers

To promote your strengths, study the needs of your potential employers. At your college's library or placement service, you can find many helpful volumes that describe individual firms. Read annual reports and company brochures, and visit company Web sites. You can easily discover the names of persons to contact for employment information and details describing the company, as well as its locations and the career opportunities, training and development programs, and benefits it offers.

PLANNING THE RÉSUMÉ

Your résumé is a one-page (sometimes two-page) document that summarizes your skills, experiences, and qualifications for a position in your field. Plan it carefully, selecting the most pertinent information and choosing a readable format. Decide what information to include and in which format—chronological or functional—to present that information.

Information to Include in a Résumé

The information to include in a résumé is that which fills the employer's needs. Most employers expect the following information to appear on applicants' résumés (Harcourt and Krizar; Hutchinson and Brefka):

- Personal information: name, address, phone number
- Educational information: degree, name of college, major, date of graduation
- Work history: titles of jobs held, employing companies, dates of employment, duties, a career objective
- Achievements: grade point average, awards and honors, special aptitudes and skills, achievements at work (such as contributions and accomplishments)

The Chronological Résumé

Traditionally, the information required on a résumé has usually been arranged in chronological order, emphasizing job duties. Because employers are accustomed to this order, they know where to find information they need and can focus easily on your positions and accomplishments (Treweek).

The chronological résumé has the following sections:

■ Personal data

■ Career objective

■ Summary (optional)

■ Education

■ Work experience

Personal Data.   The personal data consist of name, address, telephone number (always found at the top of the page), place to contact for credentials, willingness to relocate, and honors and activities (usually found at the bottom of the page).

List your current address and phone number. Tell employers how to acquire credentials and letters of reference. If you have letters in a placement file at your college placement service, give the appropriate address and phone numbers. If you do not have a file, indicate that you can provide names on request.

Federal regulations specify that you do not need to mention your birth date, height, weight, health, or marital status. You can give information on hobbies and interests. They reveal something about you as a person, and they are topics at a surprising number of interviews.

Career Objective.   The career objective states the type of position you are seeking or what you can bring to the company. A well-written objective reads like this: "Management Consulting Position in Information Systems" or "Position in Research and Development in Microchip Electronics" or "To use my programming, testing, and analysis skills in an information systems position."

Summary.   The summary, an optional section, emphasizes essential points for your reader (Parker). In effect it is a minirésumé. List key items of professional experience, credentials, one or two accomplishments, and one or two skills. If you don't have room for the summary in the résumé, consider putting it into your accompanying letter.

SUMMARY

■ Gained extensive co-op experience at IBM sites

■ Worked with Rexx, C. Ada, POSIX

■ Wrote training test case

Education.   The education section includes pertinent information about your degree. List your college or university, the years you attended it, and your major, minor, concentration, and grade point average (if good). If you attended more than one school, present them in reverse chronological order, the most recent at the top. You can also list relevant courses (many employers like to see technical writing in the list), honors and awards, extracurricular activities, and descriptions of practicums, co-ops, and internships. You do not need to include your high school.

Education	B.S. University of Wisconsin-Stout, December 1999
	Major: **Applied Mathematics**
	Concentration: **Business Management**
	G.P.A.: 3.85/4.0

Key courses	Computer Organization	Math Statistics I, II
	Systems Programming	Software Engineering
	C++	Math Models I, II

Work Experience.   The work experience section includes the positions you have held that are relevant to your field of interest. List your jobs in reverse chronological order—the most recent first. In some cases, you might alter the arrangement to reflect the importance of the experience. For example, if you first held a relevant eight-month internship and then took a job as a dishwasher when you returned to school, list the internship first. List all full-time jobs and relevant part-time jobs—as far back as the summer after your senior year in high school. You do not need to include every part-time job, just the important ones (but be prepared to give complete names and dates).

Each work experience entry should have four items: job title, job description, name of company, and dates of employment. These four items can be arranged in a number of ways, as the following examples show. However, *the job description is the most important part* of the entry. Describe your duties, the projects you worked on, and the machines and processes you used. Choose the details according to your sense of what the reader needs.

Write the job description in the past tense, using "action" words such as *managed* and *developed*. Try to create pictures in the reader's mind (Parker). Give specifics that he or she can relate to. Arrange the items in the description in order of importance. Put the important skills first.

The following example illustrates a common arrangement of the four items in the entry:

Unisys, Computer Systems Division, Roseville, MN	Name of company
(5/96–8/96) Function Test Developer	Job title

- Designed test specifications for Unisys POSIX and Ada functions.
- Developed test cases for Unisys Ada functions.
- Wrote a test case development process document to be used for training.

Duties of employment

Order of Entries on the Page.   In the chronological résumé, the top of any section is the most visible position, so you should put the most important information there. Place your name, address, and career objective at the top of the page. In general, the education section comes next, followed by the work section. However, if you have had a relevant internship or full-time experience, put the work section first. Figure 20.1 shows a chronological résumé.

The Functional Résumé

This kind of résumé presents the applicant to the employer in the same way the employer looks at the applicant: in terms of relevant skills. This style allows candidates whose work experience is not relevant to their job area to stress skills learned in classes. If employers cannot easily relate skills to specific jobs, however, functional résumés can produce a negative response (Treweek).

The functional résumé has these sections:

- Personal data
- Objective
- Summary (optional)
- Skills
- Education
- Work

Figure 20.2 shows how to handle each of these sections.

Standard Sections.   Treat the following sections the same as in the chronological résumé (see pp. 513–516):

- Personal data—include your name and address and the address of your placement service.
- Objective—tell your immediate occupational goal.
- Summary—mention your best professional experience, credentials, accomplishments, or skills.
- Education—list your university, major, date of graduation, minors, GPA.

FIGURE 20.1
Chronological Résumé

KEVIN J. CHARPENTIER

Address until December 22, 2001	**Permanent Address**
111½ S. Broadway Apt. #1	1021 Eighth Street
Menomonie, WI 54751	Woodbury, MN 55125
(715) 237-6545	(612) 608-7111

OBJECTIVE — Management Consulting position in Information Systems

SUMMARY
- Extensive co-op experience at 3 IBM sites.
- Worked with Rexx, C, Ada, POSIX.
- Wrote training test case.

EDUCATION — B.S. University of Wisconsin-Stout, December 2001
Major: **Applied Mathematics**
Concentration: **Business Management**
G.P.A.: 3.85/4.0

KEY COURSES

Computer Organization	COBOL	Math Models I, II
Systems Programming	Math Statistics I, II	Management

EXPERIENCE

Project
Development — **Unisys, Computer Systems Division,** Roseville, MN
(5/99- 8/00)
- Designed test specifications for Unisys POSIX and Ada functions.
- Developed test cases for Unisys Ada functions.
- Wrote a test case development process document to be used for training.

Quality
Management — **IBM, Entry Systems Division,** Boca Raton, FL (5/98-8/98)
- Tracked OS/2 development project size and defect data.
- Analyzed data using a quality model. Made recommendations.

Computer
Programming — **IBM, Systems Integration Division,** Oswego, NY (6/97-12/97)
- Designed, coded, and tested software in Rexx and C.
- Analyzed, isolated, and fixed problems in language processor tools.

UW-Stout Student Center, Menomonie, WI (9/00–5/01)
- Developed and supported Dbase III+ software for customers.
- Evaluated customer needs to provide appropriate solution.

Languages and Systems: — Ada, Assembly, C, COBOL, Dbase III+
Unisys 1100/2200, IBM VM

COMMUNICATION
Applied Math Club—President, Vice-President
Volunteer Math Tutor
Chancellor's Award for Academic Excellence (all semesters)

REFERENCES — Available on request

FIGURE 20.2
Functional Résumé

KEVIN J. CHARPENTIER

Address until December 22, 2001	**Permanent Address**
111½ S. Broadway Apt. #1	1021 Eighth Street
Menomonie, WI 54751	Woodbury, MN 55125
(715) 237-6545	(612) 608-7111

CAREER GOAL   Management Consultant

SUMMARY
- Extensive co-op experience at 3 IBM sites.
- Worked with Rexx, C, Ada, POSIX.
- Wrote training test case.

EDUCATION   B.S. University of Wisconsin-Stout, December 2001
Major: **Applied Mathematics**
Minor: **Business Administration and Computer Science**
G.P.A.: 3.85/4.0

SKILLS   **Quality Management.** I have collected actual size and defect information for the OS/2 development project. I used a quality model to track the accuracy of defect rates and made recommendations on process improvement (IBM, ES).

Project Development. I have developed application software for customers in Dbase III+. I have developed requirement documents and design documents. I was the assistant manager for a software engineering project developed in Ada (Unisys).

Computer Programming. I have programmed in the following computer languages: Ada, Vax Assembly, C, C++, Dbase III+, Jovial-J73, Pascal, and Rexx. I have analyzed, isolated, and fixed problems in language processor tools. I have designed programs for automation (IBM, SI).

Communication. I have written a detailed document of a software testing process. I have become an effective speaker through presenting annually at the UW-Stout Applied Mathematics Conference.

CO-OP/INTERN EXPERIENCE

Function Test   **Unisys, Computer Systems Division**, Roseville, MN
  Developer   (5/99-8/00)
Quality Analyst   **IBM, Entry Systems Division**, Boca Raton, FL (5/98-8/98)
Support
  Programmer   **IBM, Systems Integration Division**, Oswego, NY (6/97-12/97)

WORK EXPERIENCE

PASS Advisor   **UW-Stout PASS Office**, Menomonie, WI (9/95-12/95)
Programmer   **UW-Stout Student Center**, Menomonie, WI (9/00-5/01)

HONORS/   Applied Math Club—President, Vice-President,
ACTIVITIES   Chancellor's Award for Academic Excellence (all semesters)

REFERENCES   Available upon request

Work and Skills Sections. You can present the work section as a short list and the skills section as paragraphs.

For the work section, give just the job title, company, and dates for each position you have held.

CO-OP/INTERN
EXPERIENCE

Function Test Developer	Unisys, Computer Systems Division, Roseville, MN (5/96–8/96)	Job title
		Employer
		Dates
Quality Analyst	IBM, Entry Systems Division, Boca Raton, FL (5/95–8/95)	

Present your skills in categories; that is, explain your capabilities and experience after a relevant topic heading. For instance, you might have topic headings for management, research, evaluation, and team membership. Write a paragraph about how you obtained these skills and what level of expertise you have.

SKILLS	Topic heading
Quality Management. I collected actual size and defect information for the OS/2 development project. I used a quality model to track the accuracy of defect rates and made recommendations on process improvement.	Explanatory paragraph

WRITING THE RÉSUMÉ

Drafting your résumé includes generating, revising, and finishing it. Experiment with content and format choices. Ask a knowledgeable person to review your drafts for wording and emphasis. Pay close attention to the finishing stage, in which you check consistency of presentation and spelling.

The résumé must be easy to read. Employers are looking for essential information, and they must be able to find it on the first reading. To make that information accessible, use highlight strategies explained in Chapter 7: heads, boldface, bulleting, margins, and white space. Follow these guidelines (and compare them to the two sample résumés in this chapter):

- Indicate the main divisions at the far left margins. Usually, boldface heads announce the major sections of the résumé.
- Boldface important words such as job titles or names of majors; use underlining sparingly.

- Use bullet lists, which emphasize individual lines effectively.
- Single-space entries, and double-space above and below. The resulting white space makes the page easier to read.
- Control the margins and type size. Use 1 inch for the left margin.
- Use 10- or 12-point type.
- Treat items in each section consistently. All the job titles, for example, should be in the same relative space and in the same typeface and size.
- Print résumés on good-quality paper; use black ink on light paper (white or off-white). Avoid brightly colored paper, which has little positive effect on employers and photocopies poorly.
- Consider using a résumé software program. Actually a database, it provides spaces for you to fill with appropriate data and offers several designs for formatting the page.

PLANNING A LETTER OF APPLICATION

The goal of sending a letter of application is to be invited to an interview. To write an effective letter of application, understand the employer's needs, which are expressed in an ad or a job description. Planning a specific letter requires you to analyze the ad or description and match the stated requirements with your skills.

Analyze the Employer's Needs

To discover an employer's needs, analyze the ad or analyze typical needs for this kind of position. To analyze an ad, read it for key terms. For instance, a typical ad could read, "Candidates need 1+ years of C++. Communication skills are required. Must have systems analysis skills." The key requirements here are 1+ years of C++, communication skills, and systems analysis.

If you do not have an ad, analyze typical needs for this type of job. A candidate for a manufacturing engineer position could select pertinent items from the list of responsibilities printed in the Dictionary of Occupational Titles (see p. 511).

Match Your Capabilities to the Employer's Needs

The whole point of the letter is to show employers that you will satisfy their needs. If they say they need 1+ years of C++, tell them you have it.

As you match needs with capabilities, you will develop a list of items to place in your letter. You need not include them all; discuss the most important or interesting ones.

WRITING A LETTER OF APPLICATION

A letter of application has three parts: the introductory application, the explanatory body, and the request conclusion. You may organize the letter in one of two ways—by skills or by categories. This section first reviews the parts of a letter of application and then presents the same letter organized by skill and by category.

Apply in the Introduction

The application paragraph should be short. Inform the reader that you are applying for a specific position. If it was advertised, mention where you saw the ad. If someone recommended that you write to the company, mention that person's name (if it is someone the reader knows personally or by name). You may present a brief preview that summarizes your qualifications.

I would like to apply for the position of programmer that was advertised in the Sunday, March 1, *Star Tribune.* I feel my education, experience, and career interests are well suited for this position.	Apply Tell source Qualification preview

Convince in the Body

The *explanatory body* is the heart of the letter. Explain, in terms that relate to the reader, why you are qualified for the job. This section should be one to three paragraphs long. Its goal is to show convincingly that your strengths and skills will meet the reader's needs. Write one paragraph or section for each main requirement.

Base the content of the body on your analysis of the employer's needs and on your ability to satisfy those needs. Usually the requirements are listed in the ad. Show how your skills meet those requirements. If the ad mentioned "experience in software development," list details that illustrate your experience. If you are not responding to an ad, choose details that show that you have the qualifications normally expected of an entry-level candidate.

The key to choosing details is "memorable impact." The details should immediately convince readers that your skill matches their need. Use this guideline: In what terms will they talk about me? Your details, for instance, should show that you are the "development person." If you affect your reader that way, you will be in a positive position.

SKILLS SECTION

As a senior graduating this December from the University of Wisconsin-Stout, I have gained skills in software development through my education and work experience. A	Source of skill

few of the courses I have taken are C++, Software Engineering, Systems Programming, Computer Organization, and Simulation.

I have applied these skills in cooperative educational experiences at both Unisys and IBM. I have designed, coded, and tested application software. In addition, I have developed test specifications, test cases, and technical documents in an end-user environment.

Use of skill

Skill activities

Request an Interview

In the final section, ask for an interview and explain how you can be reached. The best method is to ask, "Could I meet with you to discuss this position?" Also explain when you are available. If you need two days' notice, say so. If you can't possibly get free on a Monday, mention that. Most employers will try to work around such restrictions. If no one is at your house or dorm in the morning to answer the phone, tell the reader to call in the afternoon. A busy employer would rather know that than waste time calling. Thank your reader for his or her time and consideration. Readers appreciate the gesture; it is courteous and it indicates that you understand that the reader has to make an effort to fulfill your request.

Could I meet with you to discuss the opening? You may contact me during the evening at (715) 555-5555. Thank you for your time, and I look forward to meeting you in the near future.

Direct question

How to contact writer

Thank you

RESPONSE TO AD FOR REGISTERED DIETITIAN

347 South Hall
Menomonie, WI 54751

February 29, 2003

Tim Jones
Nutrition Services Director
St. Simon's Hospital
4718 Twelfth Avenue
Kenosha, WI 53140-2595

Dear Mr. Jones:

I would like to apply for the Registered Dietitian position that was advertised in the *Milwaukee Journal* on Sunday, February 25. I feel that my experience, education, and career goals are well suited for the position. I will graduate in May 2003 from the University of Wisconsin-Stout.

Clear application

I have extensive experience in both in-patient charting and diet counseling. As a student, I have learned all the proper procedures and conditions of SOAP noting as well as narrative charting and PIE charting. Through my work at Children's Hospital of Milwaukee I have worked one on one with patients for diet consults for high cholesterol, weight management, and eating disorder treatment. Much of the semester in Diet Therapy and in Skills Training was dedicated to nutritional assessment and counseling practices. Also, over the 2001–2002 school year, I worked directly with the University Counseling Center in developing and leading a weekly eating disorder support group.

Their key words at the beginning of the paragraph.

Details of work experience and classes used to create interest.

I have also had experience in nutrition education through both educational and community services. In Nutrition Education, I designed and implemented a nutrition program for the full-time University Dining Services workers. Also, during my field experience at Children's Hospital, I developed a nutrition class for 6- to 12-year-olds with attention deficit hyperactivity disorder.

Their key words at the beginning of the paragraph.

My résumé is enclosed for your review. Through my work experience and education, I am confident that I can be an asset to your company. Could I meet with you to set up an interview? You can contact me at (715) 232-1515. Thank you for your consideration.

Asks for interview.

Sincerely,

Julie Ann Gotthardt

Julie Ann Gotthardt, R.D.

enc. résumé

Select a Format

To make a professional impression, follow these guidelines:

- Type the letter on 8½-by-11-inch paper.
- Use white, 20-pound, 100 percent cotton-rag paper.
- Use black ink.
- Use block or modified block format explained in Chapter 19.
- Sign your name in black or blue ink.
- Proofread the letter carefully. Grammar and spelling mistakes are irritating at best; at worst, they are cause for instant rejection.
- Mail the letter, folded twice, in a business envelope.

Examples 20.1–20.3 show three application letters organized by skills. Two use traditional paragraphs and one uses a vertical list for emphasis.

INTERVIEWING

The employment interview is the method employers use to decide whether to offer a candidate a position. Usually the candidate talks to one or more people (either singly or in groups) who have the authority to offer a position. To interview successfully, you need to prepare well, use social tact, perform well, ask questions, and understand the job offer (Stewart and Cash).

Prepare Well

To prepare well, investigate the company and analyze how you can contribute to it (Spinks and Wells). To investigate the company, ask your contact person for some company literature, use annual reports, use descriptions in *Moody's*, items from *Facts on File, F&S Index, Wall Street Journal Index*, or *Corporate Report Fact Bank*, or a close reading of the company's Web site. After you have analyzed the company, assess what you have to offer. Answer these questions:

- What contributions can you make to the company?
- How do your specific skills and strengths fit into its activities or philosophy?
- How can you further your career goals with this company?

Use Social Tact

To use social tact means to behave professionally and in an appropriate manner. Acting too lightly or too intensely are both incorrect. First impressions are extremely important; many interviewers make up their minds early in the interview. Follow a few common sense guidelines:

- Shake hands firmly.
- Dress professionally, as you would on the job.
- Arrive on time.
- Use proper grammar and enunciation.
- Watch your body language. For instance, sit appropriately; don't give the impression of lounging.
- Find out and use the interviewers' names.

Perform Well

Performing well in the interview means to answer the questions directly and clearly. Interviewers want to know about your skills. Be willing to talk about yourself and your achievements; if you respond honestly to questions, your answers will not seem like bragging. For a successful interview, follow these guidelines:

- Be yourself. The worst thing is to get a job because people thought you were a kind of person that you're not.
- Answer the question asked.
- Be honest. If you don't know the answer, say so.
- If you don't understand a question, ask the interviewer to repeat or clarify it.
- In your answers, include facts about your experience to show how you will fit into the company.

Ask Questions

You have the right to ask questions at an interview. Make sure you have addressed all pertinent issues (Spinks and Wells). If no one has explained the following items to you, ask about them:

- Methods of on-the-job training
- Your job responsibilities
- Types of support available—from secretarial to facilities to pursuit of more education
- Possibility and probability of promotion
- Policies about relocating, including whether you get a promotion when you relocate and whether refusing to relocate will hurt your chances for promotion
- Salary and fringe benefits—at least a salary range, whether you receive medical benefits, and who pays for them

The Offer

Usually a company will offer the position—with a salary and starting date—either at the end of the interview or within a few days. You have the right to request a reasonable amount of time to consider the offer. If you get another offer from a second company at a higher salary, you have the right to inform the first company and to ask whether they can meet that salary. Usually you accept the offer verbally and sign a contract within a few days. This is a pleasant moment.

WRITING FOLLOW-UP LETTERS

After an interview with a particularly appealing firm, you can take one more step to distinguish yourself from the competition. Write a follow-up letter. It takes only a few minutes to thank the interviewer and express your continued interest in the job.

> Thank you for the interview yesterday. Our discussion of Ernst and Young's growing MIS Division was very informative, and I am eager to contribute to your team.
>   I look forward to hearing from you.

■ WORKSHEET FOR PREPARING A RÉSUMÉ

❑ *Write out your career objective; use a job title.*

❑ *List all the postsecondary schools you have attended.*

❑ *List your major and any minors or submajors.*

❑ *List your GPA if it is strong.*

❑ *Complete this form. Select only relevant courses or experiences.*

College Courses	Skills Learned	Projects Completed

❑ *List extracurricular activities, including offices held and duties.*

❑ *Complete this form for all co-ops, internships, and relevant employment.*

Job Title	Company	Dates	Duties	Achievements

❑ *List your name, phone number, current address, and permanent address if it is different.*

❑ *Choose a format—chronological or functional.*

❑ *Choose a layout design.*

■ WORKSHEET FOR WRITING A LETTER OF APPLICATION

❑ *State the job for which you are applying.*

❑ *State where you found out about the job.*

❑ *Complete this form:*

Employer Need (such as "program in BASIC")	Proof That You Fill the Need (show yourself in action: "developed two BASIC programs to test widget quality")

❑ *Select a format; the block format is suitable.*

❑ *Write compelling paragraphs:*
An introduction to announce that you are an applicant
A body paragraph for each need, matching your capabilities to the need
Select details that cause "measurable impact"—ones that cause readers to remember you because you can fill their needs
A conclusion that asks for an interview

❑ *Purchase good-quality paper and envelopes, and get a new cartridge for your printer if you produce the letter yourself.*

■ WORKSHEET FOR EVALUATING AN APPLICATION LETTER

Answer these questions about your letter or a peer's:

a. Are the inside address and date handled correctly? Are all words spelled out?

b. Do the salutation and inside address name the same person?

c. Is there a colon after the salutation?

d. Does the writer clearly apply for a position in paragraph 1?

e. Does each paragraph deal with an employer need and contain an "impact detail"?

f. Does the closing paragraph ask for an interview? In an appropriate tone?

g. Would you ask this person for an interview? Why or why not?

EXAMPLES

The following examples illustrate ways in which applicants can show how their skills meet the employers' needs.

EXAMPLE 20.1
Letter Organized by Skills (with Paragraphs)

1503 West Second Street
Menomonie, WI 54751
ABC Global Services
1014 Michigan Avenue
Chicago, IL 60605

November 3, 2003

SUBJECT: I/T Specialist–Programmer Position

I would like to apply for the I/T Specialist–Programmer Position for ABC Global Services in Chicago. I learned of this position through the University of Wisconsin-Stout Placement and Co-op Office. Because of my past co-op experiences and educational background, I feel I am an ideal candidate for this position.

I am very familiar with all the steps of the application life cycle and processes involved in each of these steps. In my Software Engineering course, I and four other students developed a Math Bowl program that is used at the annual Applied Math Conference. We analyzed the problem through an analysis document, created a design document, coded the Math Bowl program from the design document, and maintained the software. In my past co-op with IBM, I also was involved in requirements planning, design reviews, coding, testing, and maintenance for my team's projects.

I have experience with low-level languages such as C++ and Assembler Language through my work experience and course study. In my Computer Organization class, I developed a CPU simulator in C++, which manipulated the Assembler Language. During my Unisys co-op in the Compiler Products department, I developed test programs in C, which manipulated the low-level compiler code.

I have strong customer relations and communication skills. Every day I deal with students and faculty at my job as a Lab Assistant at the Campus Computer Lab. It is my job to help them learn the available software and troubleshoot user's problems.

Enclosed is my résumé for your consideration. I am very interested in talking with you in person about this position and a possible interview. Please call me at (715) 233-3341 at your earliest convenience. Thank you for your consideration.

Sincerely,

Heather Miller

Heather Miller
enc: résumé

EXAMPLE 20.2
Letter Organized by Skills (with Paragraphs)

Andy Vold
1410 8th St.
Menomonie, WI 54751

October 30, 2005

Qualityclear Graphics
4721 Grandview Boulevard
Cincinnati, OH 45202

Dear Human Resource Director:

I would like to apply for the electronic prepress position you advertised in your home page on the World Wide Web. I feel my education, work experience, and desire to work in the prepress industry make me well suited for this position.

I possess a great amount of skills in the area of prepress. I have acquired many of these skills through my studies at the University of Wisconsin-Stout, while seeking a degree in the Graphic Art Management program. These skills were also applied in my cooperative educational experiences at both General Mills, Inc., and the Banta Digital Group. While working for Banta, it was not uncommon for me to work a customer's job from the files to final film. This work included preflighting of files, scanning supplied photos, making alterations on the Macintosh, RIPping files for film output, and finally outputting of final film.

I have a working knowledge of the APR and OPI prepress formats, Scitex RIPping systems, and a number of different high-end scanning systems, including the Scitex flat bed scanner and the Hell drum scanner. I enjoy the fast paced, ever-changing prepress industry and am willing to grow and learn as the industry changes and as your company grows.

A copy of my résumé has been attached for your consideration. Through my work experience and education, I am confident that I can be an asset to your company. If you have any questions of me that are not answered on my résumé please feel free to call or E-mail me. Thank you for your time and consideration. I look forward to hearing from you.

Sincerely,

Andy Vold

Andy Vold

enc: résumé

EXAMPLE 20.3
Letter Organized by Skills (with Paragraphs)

1021 Eighth Street East
Menomonie, WI 54751

October 14, 2004

American Computer Systems
2540 Aldrich Avenue South
Minneapolis, MN 55108

ATTENTION: Human Resources Department

SUBJECT: Computer Programmer/Analyst Position

I wish to apply as a computer programmer/analyst with your company. I will graduate in December 2004 with a Bachelor of Science degree in Applied Mathematics/Computer Science with a concentration in Software Development from the University of Wisconsin-Stout.

I obtained an extensive UNIX background while interning two terms at IBM-Rochester. At IBM, I was a member of a major software development project. My responsibilities as a computer programmer were to develop software applications utilizing the UNIX operating system. I also developed several applications on UNIX workstations in a computer graphics course at UW-Stout.

I also have acquired a solid COBOL programming background. My sixteen months of internship experience involved application development utilizing the COBOL programming language. On this project, I did maintenance and new functionality programming using COBOL. Participating in a team environment, I attended regular status meetings, design reviews, and code reviews.

I am available for an interview at your convenience. I have enclosed my résumé, which provides additional information about my work experience at IBM and my education and activities at UW-Stout. If you have any questions about my application, please contact me at (715) 235-0123. Thank you for your time and consideration.

Sincerely,

Jim Duevel

Jim Duevel
Enclosure: résumé

You can use the "two-column" method to emphasize the match between the employer's needs and your capabilities. Write a standard introduction and conclusion, but in the body list the requirements in one column and the capabilities in the other.

Your requirements

Cost estimating

My skills

■ Estimated usage and cost savings of materials

■ Worked with budgeting, stock reorder, and payroll

■ EXERCISES

1. Your instructor will arrange you in groups of two to four by major. Each person should photocopy relevant material from one source in the library. Include at least the *Dictionary of Occupational Titles* and the *Occupational Outlook Handbook*. In class, make a composite list of basic requirements in your type of career. Use that list as a basis for completing the Writing Assignments that follow.

2. Analyze one of the letters in the Sample Documents section of the Instructor's Resource Manual (Examples 46–51). Comment on format and effectiveness of tone, detail, and organization.

3. Analyze this rough draft. It responded to an ad for a construction supervisor with experience in writing and negotiating bids. The person hired for this position would supervise the building of a condominium project in southeast Wisconsin.

   1126 Knapp Street
   Menomonie, Wisconsin 54751

   September 30, 2005

   P.O. Box 165
   Delavan, Wisconsin 53115

   Subject: Construction Supervisor Position

   I wish to apply for the construction supervisor position recently advertised in the September 15, 2005, issue of the *Milwaukee Journal-Sentinel*.

   I will graduate in May 2006 with a B.S. in Industrial Technology concentrating in Construction. I will also receive a Minor in Business Administration.

   I have worked in the construction field part-time for the past ten years. I recently completed a co-op with Tomlinson Construction Company, where I worked both in the office with their architect and on the job with a superintendent. My work in the office entailed preparing estimates and getting bids for electrical, plumbing, and heating from subcontractors. On the job I worked with the superintendent reading blueprints and making sure the work was being done to the contract specifications.

   I also worked as a field superintendent for McMc, where I was responsible for building a $250,000 addition on a building. I was responsible for supervising the project, writing estimates, and negotiating bids with the electrical, plumbing, and heating subcontractors to get the best possible deal for the company. As the field superintendent, I prepared weekly progress reports on all of the mining operations.

Could I meet with you to discuss this position? You may contact me at the above address or after 5:00 p.m. daily at (715) 235-9370.

Sincerely,

Kevin A. Jack

enc: résumé

---

4.   Revise this letter.

314 13th Avenue W.
Menomonie, WI 54751

February 24, 2004

Dear Mr. Reed: I would like to apply for the Production Supervisor position advertised in the Sunday, February 14, 1999 *Milwaukee Journal.*

I am a senior at the University of Wisconsin-Stout and will be graduating in May 2004. I will receive a Bachelor of Science degree in Industrial Technology with a concentration in Manufacturing Engineering. I feel the skills I now posses from attending the UW-Stout and past working experience will help me fit your needs.

I feel that I have the training and experience to be able to train your employees to make them able to do their job correctly and efficiently. For the past six years it has been my responsibility to train new employees in the Lawn Care and Landscape Management Field. I was required to plan schedules for two crews of three men daily. I was also responsible for supervising these crews to see that their work was done correctly and efficiently.

The course in Production Operations Management that I have taken has taught me how to link production and management skills. This skill that I posses could be put to use for you. I have taken a course in Quality Control and I feel that the control methods that I have learned would be of great asset to you and keeping you companies quality standards high.

I feel I have the ability to help lower the cost of manufacturing from course in Engineering Economy where we dealt with the relationship of company profits and cost reduction techniques.

These are just some of the assets that I posses. Would it be possible for us to set up an interview so that we could discuss in more detail my skills and experiences. I can be reached at (715)-235-6105 form 3:00 to 5:00 P.M. or contacted at my Menomonie address.

Sincerely,

Tim Dunford

Enclosure: résumé

---

5. Create a work experience résumé entry (pp. 515–516) for one job you have held. Select an arrangement for the four elements. Select details based on the kinds of position you want to apply for. Alternate: Create a second version of the entry but focus one version on applying for a technical position and one version on applying for a managerial position.

6. Write a paragraph that explains a career skill you possess.

7. Write a paragraph in which you explain how you will answer the needs listed in an ad.

8. Analyze an ad and yourself by filling out the third point in the Worksheet for Writing a Letter of Application (p. 527).

9. Analyze yourself by using the fifth and seventh points in the Worksheet for Preparing a Résumé (p. 526).

10. After completing Writing Assignment 2, read another person's letter. Ask these questions: What do you like about this letter? What do you dislike about this letter? How would you change what you dislike?

11. After completing Writing Assignment 1, read the ad and résumé of a classmate. Read the ad closely to determine the employer's needs. Read the résumé swiftly—in a minute or less. Tell the author whether he or she has the required qualifications. Then switch résumés and repeat. This exercise should either convince you that your résumé is good or highlight areas that you need to revise.

▨ WRITING ASSIGNMENTS

1. Using the worksheet on page 526 as a guide, write your résumé following one of the two formats described in this chapter.

2. Find an ad for a position in your field of interest. Use newspaper Help Wanted ads or a listing from your school's placement service. On the basis of the ad, decide which of your skills and experiences you should discuss to convince the firm that you are the person for the job. Then, using the worksheet on page 527 as a guide, write a letter to apply for the job.

3. Write a learning report for the writing assignment you just completed. See Chapter 5, Assignment 7, page 123, for details of the assignment.

■ WEB EXERCISE

Visit at least two Web sites at which career positions are advertised relative to your expertise. Do one or more of the following, depending on your instructor's directions:

a. Apply for a position. Print a copy of your application before you send it. Write a brief report explaining the ease of using the site. Include comments about any response that you receive.

b. Analyze the types of positions offered. Is it worth your time and energy to use a site like this? Present your conclusions in a memo or oral report, as your instructor designates. Print copies of relevant screens to use as visual aids to support your conclusions.

c. As part of a group of three or four, combine your research in part b into a large report in which you explain to your class or to a professional meeting the wide range of opportunities available to the job seeker.

■ WORKS CITED

Dictionary of Occupational Titles. 4th ed. Rev. Washington, DC: U.S. Dept. of Labor, 1991.

Harcourt, Jules, and A. C. "Buddy" Krizar. "A Comparison of Résumé Content Preferences of Fortune 500 Personnel Administrators and Business Communication Instructors." *Journal of Business Communications* 26.2 (1989): 177–190.

Hutchinson, Kevin L., and Diane S. Brefka. "Personnel Administrators' Preferences for Résumé Content: Ten Years After." *Business Communication Quarterly* 60.2 (1997): 67–75.

Parker, Yana. *The Résumé Catalog: 200 Damn Good Examples*. Berkeley, CA: Ten Speed Press, 1996.

Spinks, Nelda, and Barron Wells. "Employment Interviews: Trends in the Fortune 500 Companies—1980–1988." *The Bulletin of the Association for Business Communications* 51.4 (1988): 15–21.

Stewart, Charles J., and William B. Cash, Jr. *Interviewing Principles and Practices* 8th ed. Dubuque, IA: Brown, 1997.

Treweek, David John. "Designing the Technical Communication Résumé." *Technical Communications* 38.2 (1991): 257–260.

Focus on ELECTRONIC RÉSUMÉS

Electronic résumés are changing the job search. The candidate still submits a résumé, and the employer still reads it, but the "electronic way" has a key difference—technology intervenes to do much of the initial sorting. As a result, "keyword strategies" are very important. This section explains briefly how the sorting works, keyword strategies, and on-line, scannable, and ASCII résumés.

How the Sorting Works

Using one of the methods explained below, the candidate submits a résumé which, because it is electronic, is put into a searchable database. When an employer wants to find candidates to interview, he or she searches the database with a software program that seeks those keywords that the employer says are important. So the employer might want someone who can do Web design and know Dreamweaver and HTML programming. Every time the search program finds a résumé with those words in it, it pulls the résumé into an electronic "yes" pile, which the human can then read.

Gonyea and Gonyea explain the process this way: "If the computer finds the same word or words [that describe the candidate the company is attempting to find] anywhere in your résumé, it considers your résumé to be a match, and will then present your résumé, along with others that are also considered to be a match, to the person doing the searching" (62).

Thus, your use of effective keywords is the key to filling out such a form. As Gonyea and Gonyea say, "To ensure that your résumé will be found, it is imperative that you include as many of the appropriate search words as are likely to used by employers and recruiters who are looking for someone with your qualifications" (62).

Keyword Strategies

Keywords require a radical change in presenting your résumé. Your odds of being one of the "hits" in the search are increased by including a lot of keywords in your résumé. In addition to using keywords as you describe yourself in the education and work history sections of your résumé, you should also include a keyword section right in your résumé. Some of the major on-line résumé services, such as Monster.com, require you to add one.

Put the keyword section either first or last in your résumé, or in the box supplied by the résumé service. Use words that explain skills or list aspects of a job. The list should include mostly nouns of the terms that an employer would use to determine if you could fill his or her need—job titles, specific job duties, specific machines or software programs, degrees, major, and subjective skills, such as communication abilities. You can include synonyms; for instance, in the list below, Web design and Dreamweaver are fairly close in meaning, because you use one to do the other, but including both increases your chances of the scanner's choosing your résumé.

A short list might look like this:

C++, software engineering, HTML, programmer, needs analysis, client interview, team, Web design, Photoshop, AuthorIT, design requirements.

Remember, the more "hits" the reading software makes in this list, the more likely that your résumé will be sent on to the appropriate department.

On-Line Résumés/Job Searches

The Web has dramatically changed the methods of advertising jobs and responding to advertisements. Job-posting sites allow employers to post job notices; résumé-posting sites allow candidates to post résumés. The exact way in which sites work varies, but all of them work in one of two ways. On job-posting sites, like America's Job Bank, employers post ads, listing job duties and candidate qualifications, and candidates respond to those ads. On résumé-posting sites, like Monster.com, candidates post résumés in Web-based databases, and employers search them for viable applicants.

You have two options. You can begin to read the "Web want ads," and you can post your résumé.

"Web Want Ads" are posted at the job-posting site. For instance, America's Job Bank (*http://www.ajb.dni.us*) lists job notices posted by state employment offices, and Help Wanted-USA (*http://iccweb.com*) posts thousands of ads weekly for companies around the world in all lines of work. You simply access the site and begin to read. In addition, many of the résumé-posting services have a want ad site. For instance, Monster.com (*http://www.monster.com*) has an extensive listing of jobs in all categories. In all of these sites, job seekers can search by city, by job type, by level of authority (entry level, manager, executive). Candidates can search free of charge, but companies pay the sites to post the ads.

Post Your Résumé

Many sites provide this service; usually, it is free. Each site has you create your résumé at the site. You open an account, then fill in the form that the site presents to you. For instance, you will be asked for personal information (like name and address) and also such typical items as job objective, work experience, desired job, desired salary, and special skills. Usually, filling out the form takes about 30 minutes. The site creates a standard-looking format (like the ones discussed in Chapter 19), which is sent to prospective employers when they ask for it.

Scannable Résumés

Many use optical character recognition (OCR) software (Quible, McNair) to scan résumés. First, paper résumés are scanned, turning them into ASCII files, which are entered into a database. Second, when an opening arises, the human resources department searches the database for keywords.

Those résumés that contain the most keywords are forwarded to the people who will decide whom to interview. This development means that job seekers must now be able to write résumés that are scannable and that effectively use keywords.

Scannable résumés are less sophisticated looking than traditional ones, because scanners simply cannot render traditional résumés correctly. These documents contain all the same sections as traditional résumés but present them differently:

- Use one column. Many scanners scramble two-column text. Start all heads and text at the same left-hand margin.
- Use 10- to 14-point fonts. For "fine" fonts like Times and Palatino, use 11 to 12 points; for "thick" fonts like New Century Schoolbook, use 10 or 11 points. For heads, use 12 to 14 points.
- Use the same font throughout the document.
- Place your name and address at the top of the page, centered. If you include two addresses (campus and home), place them under each other.
- Avoid italics, underlining, and vertical lines.
- Do not fold your résumé. Mail it in an envelope that will hold the 8½-by-11-inch page.

ASCII Résumés

Often companies ask you to send your résumé by E-mail, the best way to do so is to send the résumé as an ASCII file, one that contains only letters, numbers, and a few punctuation marks but does not contain formatting devices like boldfacing and italics (Skarzenski).

Like scannable résumés, ASCII résumés maintain all the traditional sections; you just present them so that they will interact smoothly with whatever software program is receiving them.

The key items to be aware of are:

- Keep the line length to less than 65 characters. Some software systems have difficulty with longer lines.

- Use spaces, not tabs. Some software programs misinterpret tabs.

- Send the file to the receiver in two ways. You can send a file as part of an E-mail message or attached to an E-mail message. Some programs can read the message both ways, some only one way. If the recipient's program does not have the capabilities, it will not be able to read your message.

- To practice sending an ASCII file with your E-mail program, send yourself and a friend your résumé. You and the friend should be able to print out the résumé easily.

Works Consulted

Besson, Taunee. *Résumés*. 3rd ed. NY: Wiley, 1999.

Gonyea, James C., and Gonyea, Wayne M. *Electronic Résumés: A Complete Guide to Putting Your Résumé On-line*. NY: McGraw-Hill, 1996.

McNair, Catherine. "New Technologies and Your Résumé." *Intercom* 44.5 (1997): 65–75.

Quible, Zane K. "Electronic Résumés: Their Time Is Coming." *Business Communication Quarterly* 58.3 (1995): 5–9.

Skarzenski, Emily. "Tips for Creating ASCII and HTML Résumés." *Intercom* 43.6 (1996): 17–18.

Yate, Martin. *Résumés That Knock 'Em Dead*. Holbrook, MA: Adams Media, 1998.

Appendix A:
Brief Handbook for
Technical Writers

APPENDIX CONTENTS

This appendix presents the basic rules of grammar and punctuation. It contains sections on problems with sentence construction, agreement of subjects and verbs, agreement of pronouns with their antecedents, punctuation, abbreviations, capitalization, and numbers.

PROBLEMS WITH SENTENCE CONSTRUCTION

The following section introduces many common problems in writing sentences. Each subsection gives examples of a problem and explains how to convert the problem into a clearer sentence. No writer shows all of these errors in his or her writing, but almost everyone makes several of them. Many writers have definite habits: they often write in fragments, or they use poor pronoun reference, or they repeat a word or phrase excessively. Learn to identify your problem habits and correct them.

Identify and Eliminate Comma Splices

A *comma splice* occurs when two independent clauses are connected, or spliced, with only a comma. You can correct comma splices in four ways:

1. Replace the comma with a period to separate the two sentences.

Splice	The difference is that the NC machine relies on a computer to control its movements, a manual machine depends on an operator to control its movements.
Correction	The difference is that the NC machine relies on a computer to control its movements. A manual machine depends on an operator to control its movements.

2. Replace the comma with a semicolon only if the sentences are very closely related. In the following example, note that the word *furthermore* is a conjunctive adverb. When you use a conjunctive adverb to connect two sentences, always precede it with a semicolon and follow it with a comma. Other conjunctive adverbs are *however, also, besides, consequently, nevertheless,* and *therefore.*

Splice	The Micro 2001 has a two-year warranty, furthermore the magnetron is covered for seven years.
Correction	The Micro 2001 has a two-year warranty; furthermore, the magnetron is covered for seven years.

3. Insert a coordinating conjunction (*and, but, or, nor, for, yet,* or *so*) after the comma, making a compound sentence.

Splice	The engines of both cranes meet OSHA standards, the new M80A has an additional safety feature.
Correction	The engines of both cranes meet OSHA standards, but the new M80A has an additional safety feature.

4. Subordinate one of the independent clauses by beginning it with a subordinating conjunction or a relative pronoun. Frequently used subordinating conjunctions are *where, when, while, because, since, as, until, unless, although, if,* and *after.* The relative pronouns are *which, that, who,* and *what.*

Splice	Worker efficiency will increase because of lower work heights, lower work heights maximize employee comfort.
Correction	Worker efficiency will increase because of lower work heights that maximize employee comfort.

■ EXERCISES

Correct the following comma splices:

1. I propose to replace the Preene converter, this will increase production.

2. Turn the controller power on; the controller is located to the right of the terminal, there you push the POWER ON switch to the up position.

3. All reports are legal documents, if there is a problem in the process, they document the company's actions.

4. The savings are shown in the last column, the savings were calculated by subtracting the Apple price from the IBM price.

5. The purchase price of the MO5 unit is $8440 greater than that of the core unit, however, the core unit has greater maintenance cost.

6. Now hit the return key, the red light will go off.

7. We must stack merchandise on the floor, the store has become cluttered and crowded.

8. The shrink film applied around the seal doesn't snap off, instead the shrink film stays on the metal lid.

Identify and Eliminate Run-on Sentences

Run-on, or fused, sentences are similar to comma splices but lack the comma. The two independent clauses are run together with no punctuation between them. To eliminate run-on sentences, use one of the four methods explained in the preceding section and summarized here.

- ■ Place a period between the two clauses.
- ■ Place a semicolon between them.
- ■ Place a comma and a coordinating conjunction between them.
- ■ Place a relative pronoun or subordinating conjunction between them.

▪ EXERCISES

Correct the following run-on sentences:

1. I have checked all the angles I suggest that you convert to an Isohood Thermoblanket.

2. Using this plastic to construct pallet corner posts is practical the problem is cost.

3. Plastic can also be exposed to different climates this would be an advantage to shipping a product.

4. I have learned to synthesize relevant information for one project I used the algorithm technique to develop a task analysis.

5. This method consists of one operator operating two automatic turret lathes the foreman did not believe this method was possible he believed the operator would have to work continuously without idle time.

Identify and Eliminate Sentence Fragments

Sentence fragments are incomplete thoughts that the writer has mistakenly punctuated as complete sentences. Subordinate clauses, prepositional phrases, and verbal phrases often appear as fragments. As the following examples show, fragments must be connected to the preceding or the following sentence.

1. Connect subordinate clauses to independent clauses.

   a. The fragment below is a subordinate clause beginning with the subordinating conjunction *because*. Other subordinating conjunctions are *where, when, while, since, as, until, unless, if*, and *after.*

      Fragment   We should accept the proposal. Because the payback period is significantly less than our company standard.

      Correction   We should accept the proposal because the payback period is significantly less than our company standard.

   b. The following fragment is a subordinate clause beginning with the relative pronoun *which*. Other relative pronouns are *who, that, and what.*

Fragment   The total cost is $425,000. Which will have to come from the contingency fund.

Correction   The total cost of $425,000 will have to come from the contingency fund.

2. Connect prepositional phrases to independent clauses. The fragment below is a prepositional phrase. The fragment can be converted to a subordinate clause, as in the first example below, or made into an *appositive*—a word or phrase that means the same thing as what precedes it.

Fragment   The manager found the problem. At the conveyor belt.

Correction 1   The manager discovered that the problem was the conveyor belt.

Correction 2   The manager found the problem—the conveyor belt.

3. Connect verbal phrases to independent clauses.

a. Verbal phrases often begin with *-ing* words. Such phrases must be linked to independent clauses.

Fragment   The crew will work all day tomorrow. Installing the new gyroscope.

Correction   Tomorrow the crew will work all day installing the new gyroscope.

b. Infinitive phrases begin with *to* plus a verb. They must be linked to independent clauses.

Fragment   I contacted three vendors. To determine a probable price.

Correction   I contacted three vendors to determine a probable price.

■ **EXERCISES**

Correct the following sentence fragments:

1. The set-up process indirectly affects several people. Which are the pressman and the floor manager.

2. The total cost for this manufacturing change is $900,000. Because of an implementation time of six months.

3. To correct the problem is simple. Using a new three-phrase motor.

4. We do not have enough floor space. In the aisles. In the dressing rooms and in the checkout area.

5. I recommend that the inner seal be sealed on both size bottles. Before placing on the plastic cap. To make the product tamper evident.

6. I recommend you use the first design based on three criteria; which are cost, strength, and safety.

7. Push the model into the base of the fixture. Which you secured in step 1.

Place Modifiers in the Correct Position

Sentences become confusing when modifiers do not point directly to the words they modify. Misplaced modifiers often produce absurd sentences; worse yet, they occasionally result in sentences that make sense but cause the reader to misinterpret your meaning. Modifiers must be placed in a position that clarifies their relationship to the rest of the sentence.

1. In the sentence below, *that is made of a thin, oxide-coated plastic* appears to refer to the information.

Misplaced modifier	The magnetic disk is the part that contains the information that is made of a thin, oxide-coated plastic.
Correction	The magnetic disk, which is made of a thin, oxide-coated plastic, is the part that contains the information.

2. In the sentence below, the modifier says that the horizontal position must be tested but the meaning clearly is something different.

Misplaced modifier	Lower the memory module to the horizontal position that requires testing.
Correction	Lower the memory module that requires testing to the horizontal position.

■ EXERCISES

Correct the misplaced modifiers in the following sentences:

1. The bowl holds small batches of various liquids made of stainless steel holding about 30 quarts.

2. Positive displacement pumps produce a pulsating flow whose design provides a positive internal seal against leakage.

3. Make sure the hoppers are filled with plastic pellets which are empty.

4. The indexing head can be turned by pushing a button on the side of the indexing head, called a thumb lock.

Use Words Ending in *-ing* Properly

A word ending in *-ing* is either a present participle or a gerund. Both types, which are often introductory material in a sentence, express some kind of action. They are correct when the subject can perform the action that the *-ing* word expresses. For instance, in the sentence below, the *XYZ computer table* cannot *compare* cost and durability.

> Unclear   Comparing cost and durability, the XYZ computer table is the better choice.

> Clear   By comparing cost and durability, you can see that the XYZ computer table is the better choice.

■ EXERCISES

In the following sentences, an *-ing* word is used incorrectly; revise them.

1. By moving to the mall, this would increase rent by $1000 a month.

2. Looking at the two dust flow systems, the Sweeper will require less maintenance and last longer.

3. When using the optical light sensor, the light beam is directed in a way that surrounds the robot through the use of mirrors.

4. When filling out the report form, the personnel section appears first.

5. After comparing the size and weight of the two ovens, both ovens meet the criteria.

6. Reviewing the internship, visual displays, floor plans, and merchandising were my main duties.

Make the Subject and Verb Agree

The subject and the verb of a sentence must both be singular or both be plural. Almost all problems with agreement are caused by failure to identify the subject correctly.

1. When the subject and verb are separated by a prepositional phrase, be sure you do not inadvertently make the verb agree with the object of the preposition rather than with the subject. In the following sentence, the subject *bar* is singular; *feet* is the object of the preposition *of.* The verb *picks* must be singular to agree with the subject.

> Faulty A bar containing a row of suction feet pick up the paper.

> Correction A bar containing a row of suction feet picks up the paper.

2. When a *collective noun* refers to a group or a unit, the verb must be singular. Collective nouns include such words as *committee, management, audience, union,* and *team.*

> Faulty The committee are writing the policy.

> Correction The committee is writing the policy.

3. Indefinite pronouns, such as *each, everyone, either, neither, anyone,* and *everybody,* take a singular verb.

> Faulty Each of the costs are below the limit.

> Correction Each of the costs is below the limit.

4. When compound subjects are connected by *or* or *nor,* the verb must agree with the nearer noun.

> Faulty The manager or the assistants evaluates the proposal.

> Correction The manager or the assistants evaluate the proposal.

■ EXERCISES

Correct the subject-verb errors in the following sentences:

1. Everybody on the two teams produce 10% more on Mondays.

2. A series of these machines are lined up along a conveyor belt.

3. Screen printing is a method in which inks or a material such as paint are forced by the action of a flexible blade through a stencil mounted on a finely woven screen.

4. The stations that connect to the VAX is found on the second floor.

5. The reasons that the ZM monitor should be purchased instead of the Megaboom is a result from analyzing the conclusions on the previous page.

Use Pronouns Correctly

A pronoun must refer directly to the noun it stands for, its *antecedent*.

As in subject-verb agreement, a pronoun and its antecedent must both be singular or both be plural. Collective nouns generally take the singular pronoun *it* rather than the plural *they*. Problems result when pronouns such as *they, this,* and *it* are used carelessly, forcing the reader to figure out their antecedents. Overuse of the indefinite *it* (as in "*It* is obvious that") leads to confusion.

Problems with Number

1. In the following sentence, the pronoun *It* is wrong because it does not agree in number with its antecedent, *inspections*. To correct the mistake, use *they*.

Vague	The inspections occur before the converter is ready to produce the part. It is completed by four engineers.
Clear	The inspections occur before the converter is ready to produce the part. They are completed by four engineers.

2. In current practice, it is now acceptable to deliberately misuse collective pronouns in an effort to avoid sexist writing.

Technically correct	Everyone must bring his or her card.
Correct for informal situations	Everyone must bring their card.

Problems with Antecedents

If a sentence has several nouns, the antecedent may not be clear.

1. In the following case, *It* could stand for either *pointer* or *collector.* The two sentences can be combined to eliminate the pronoun.

    Vague The base and dust *collector* is the first and largest part of the lead *pointer. It* is usually round and a couple of inches in diameter.

    Clear The base and dust collector, which is the largest part of the lead pointer, is usually round and several inches in diameter.

2. In the following case, *It* could refer to *compiler* or *software.*

    Vague The new *compiler* requires new *software. It* must be compatible with our hardware.

    Clear The new compiler, which requires new software, must be compatible with our hardware.

Problems with *This*

Many inexact writers start sentences with *This* followed immediately by a verb ("*This* is," "*This* causes"), even though the antecedent of *this* is unclear. Often the writer intends to refer to a whole concept or even to a verb, but because *this* is a pronoun or an adjective, it must refer to a noun. The writer can usually fix the problem by inserting a noun after *this*—and so turn it into an adjective—or by combining the two sentences into one. In the following sentence, *this* probably refers either to the whole first sentence or to *virtually impossible,* which is not a noun.

    Vague Ring networks must be connected at both ends—a matter that could make wiring virtually impossible in some cases. This would not be the case in the Jones building.

    Clear Ring networks must be connected at both ends—a matter that could make wiring virtually impossible in some cases. We can easily fill this requirement in the Jones building.

■ EXERCISES

Revise the following sentences, making the pronoun references clear:

1. Probably the van will break down in three or four months. This is only an estimate but it is probable, due to the condition of the van. This would increase the amount of money spent on the van.

2. The stock lengths enter the gravity hoppers and they drop into a conveyor.

3. As more and more nodes are installed, it affects the time it takes for information to travel around the ring.

4. The pick-and-place robot places the part into a carton. It is sealed by an electronic heat seal device. [*Carton* is the intended antecedent.]

5. These breakdowns are only minor problems that take 1 to 2 hours to fix. This only costs the company about $1000.

6. As you can see, the T-door department has a substantially higher absentee rate than the other five departments. This shows a definite problem in this department. This is the only department that requires workers to carry materials in an awkward position.

PUNCTUATION

Writers must know the generally accepted standards for using the marks of punctuation. The following guidelines are based on *The Chicago Manual of Style* and the U.S. Government's *A Manual of Style*.

Apostrophes

Use the apostrophe to indicate possession, contractions, and some plurals.

Possession. The following are basic rules for showing possession:

1. Add an 's to show possession by singular nouns.

   a machine's parts   a package's contents

2. Add an 's to show possession by plural nouns that do not end in *s*.

   the women's caucus   the sheep's brains

3. Add only an apostrophe to plural nouns ending in *s*.

   three machines' parts   the companies' managers

4. For proper names that end in *s,* use the same rules. For singular add 's; for plural add only an apostrophe.

   Ted Jones's job   the Joneses' security holdings

This point is quite controversial. For a good discussion, see *The Chicago Manual of Style,* 14th ed. (Chicago: University of Chicago Press, 1993): 196–197.

5. Do not add an apostrophe to personal pronouns.

theirs   ours   its

Contractions.   Use the apostrophe to indicate that two or more words have been condensed into one. As a general rule, do not use contractions in formal reports and business letters.

I'll = I will   should've = should have   it's = it is   they're = they are

Plurals.   When you indicate the plurals of letters, abbreviations, and numbers, use apostrophes only to avoid confusion. *Chicago* (p. 197) and U.S. (p. 118) disagree on this point.

1. Do not use apostrophes to form the plurals of letters.

Xs   Ys   Zs

2. Do not use apostrophes to form the plurals of abbreviations and numbers.

BOMs   1990s

3. Use apostrophes to form the possessive of abbreviations.

OSHA's decision

Brackets

Brackets indicate that the writer has changed or added words or letters inside a quoted passage.

According to the report, "The detection distance [5 cm] fulfills the criterion."

Colons

Use colons:

1. To separate an independent clause from a list of supporting statements or examples.

The jointer has three important parts: the infeed table, the cutterhead, and the outfeed table.

2. To separate two independent clauses when the second clause explains or amplifies the first. Do not capitalize the first word of the second independent clause.

> The original problem was the efficiency policy: we were producing as many parts as possible, but we could not use all of them.

Commas

Use commas:

1. To separate two main clauses connected by a coordinating conjunction (*and, but, or, nor, for, yet,* or *so*). Omit the comma if the clauses are very short.

Two main clauses	The Atlas carousel has a higher base price, but this price includes installation and tooling costs.

2. To separate introductory subordinate clauses or phrases from the main clause.

Clause	If the background is too dark, change the setting.
Phrases	As shown in the table, the new system will save us over a million dollars.

3. To separate words or clauses in a series.

Words	Peripheral components include scanners, external hard drives, and external fax/modems.
Phrases	With this program you can send the fax at 5 P.M., at 11 P.M., or at a time you choose.
Clauses	Select equipment that has durability, that requires little maintenance, and that the company can afford.

4. To set off nonrestrictive appositives, phrases, and clauses.

Appositive	AltaVista, a Web search engine, has excellent advanced search features.
Phrase	The bottleneck, first found in a routine inspection, will take a week to fix.
Clause	The air flow system, which was installed in 1979, does not produce enough flow at its southern end.

Dashes and parentheses also serve this function. Dashes emphasize the abruptness of the interjected words; parentheses deemphasize the words.

5. To separate coordinate but not cumulative adjectives.

   Coordinate   He rejected the distorted, useless recordings.

   Coordinate adjectives modify the noun independently. They could be reversed with no change in meaning: *useless, distorted recordings.*

   Cumulative   An acceptable frequency-response curve was achieved.

   Cumulative adjectives cannot be reversed without distorting the meaning: *frequency-response acceptable curve.*

6. To set off conjunctive adverbs and transitional phrases.

   Conjunctive   The vice-president, however, reversed the
   adverbs   recommendation.

       The crane was very expensive; however, it paid for itself in 18 months.

       Therefore, a larger system will solve the problem.

   Transitional   On the other hand, the new receiving station is twice
   phrases   as large.

       Performance on Mondays and Fridays, for example, is far below average.

Dashes

You can use dashes before and after interrupting material and asides. Dashes give a less formal, more dramatic tone to the material they set off than commas or parentheses do. The dash has four common uses:

1. To set off material that interrupts a sentence with a different idea

   The fourth step—the most crucial one from management's point of view—is to ring up the folio and collect the money.

2. To emphasize a word or phrase at the end of a sentence

   The Carver CNC has a range of 175–200 parts per hour—not within the standard.

3. To set off a definition

   The total time commitment—contract duty time plus travel time—cannot exceed 40 hours per month.

4. To introduce a series less formally than with a colon

   This sophisticated application allows several types of instruction sets—stacks, queues, and trees.

Parentheses

You can use parentheses before and after material that interrupts or is some kind of aside in a sentence or paragraph. Compared to dashes, parentheses have one of two effects: they deemphasize the material they set off, or they give a more formal, less dramatic tone to special asides. Parentheses are used in three ways:

1. To add information about an item.

Acronym for a lengthy phrase	This Computer Numerically Controlled (CNC) lathe costs $20,000.
A definition	The result was long manufacturing lead times (the total time from receipt of a customer order until the product is produced).
Precise technical data	This hard drive (20GB, 5400 rpm Ultra ATA/66) can handle all of our current and future storage needs.

2. To add an aside to a sentence.

   The Pulstrider has wheels, which would make it easy to move the unit from its storage site (the spare bedroom) to its use site (the living room, in front of the TV).

3. To add an aside to a paragraph.

   The current program provides the user with the food's fat content percentage range by posting colored dots next to the menu item on a sign in the serving area. To determine the percentage of fat in foods, one must match the colored dot to dots on a poster hanging in the serving area. The yellow dot represents a range of 30–60%. (The green dot is 0–29% and the red dot is 61–100%.) This yellow range is too large.

A Note on Parentheses, Dashes, and Commas

All three of these punctuation marks may be used to separate interrupting material from the rest of the sentence. Choose dashes or parentheses to avoid making an appositive seem like the second item in a series.

Commas are confusing	The computer has an input device, a keyboard and an output device, a monitor.
Parentheses are clearer	The computer has an input device (a keyboard) and an output device (a monitor).

Commas are confusing	The categories that have the highest dollar sales increase, sweaters, outerware, and slacks, also have the highest dollar per unit cost.
Dashes are clearer	The categories that have the highest dollar sales increase—sweaters, outerware, and slacks—also have the highest dollar per unit cost.

Ellipsis Points

Ellipsis points are three periods used to indicate that words have been deleted from a quoted passage.

According to Jones (1999), "The average customer is a tourist who . . . tends to purchase collectibles and small antiques" (p. 7).

Hyphens

Use hyphens to make the following connections:

1. The parts of a compound word when it is an adjective placed before the noun.

   high-frequency system   plunger-type device   trouble-free process

   Do not hyphenate the same adjectives when they are placed after the word:

   The system is trouble free.

2. Words in a prepositional phrase used as an adjective.

   state-of-the-art printer

3. Words that could cause confusion by being misread.

   energy-producing cell   eight-hour shifts   foreign-car buyers
   cement-like texture

4. Compound modifiers formed from a quantity and a unit of measurement.

   a 3-inch beam   an 8-mile journey

   Unless the unit is expressed as a plural:

   a beam 3 inches wide   a journey of 8 miles

   Also use a hyphen with a number plus -odd.

   twenty-odd

5. A single capital letter and a noun or participle.

   A-frame   I-beam

6. Compound numbers from 21 through 99 when they are spelled out and fractions when they are spelled out.

   Twenty-seven jobs required a pickup truck.   three-fourths

7. Complex fractions if the fraction cannot be typed in small numbers.

   1-3/16 miles

   Do not hyphenate if the fraction can be typed in small numbers.

   1½ hp

8. Adjective plus past participle (*-ed, -en*).

   red-colored table

9. Compounds made from *half-, all-,* or *cross-.*

   half-finished   all-encompassing   cross-country

10. Use suspended hyphens for a series of adjectives that you would ordinarily hyphenate.

    10-, 20-, and 30-foot beams

11. Do not hyphenate:

    a.   *-ly* adverb-adjective combinations:

    recently altered system

    b.   *-ly* adverb plus participle (*-ing, -ed*):

    highly rewarding positions   poorly motivated managers

    c.   chemical terms

    hydrogen peroxide

    d.   colors

    red orange logo

12. Spell as one word compounds formed by the following prefixes:

anti-	co-	infra-
non-	over-	post-
pre-	pro-	pseudo-
re-	semi-	sub-
super-	supra-	ultra-
un-	under-	

Exceptions: Use a hyphen

a. When the second element is capitalized (*pre-Victorian*).

b. When the second element is a figure (*pre-1900*).

c. To prevent possible misreadings (*re-cover, un-ionized*).

Quotation Marks

Quotation marks are used at the beginning and at the end of a passage that contains the exact words of someone else.

> According to Jones (1999), "The average customer is a tourist who travels in the summer and tends to purchase collectibles and small antiques" (p. 7).

Semicolons

Use semicolons in the following ways:

1. To separate independent clauses not connected by coordinating conjunctions (*and, but, or, nor, for, yet, so*).

    > Our printing presses are running 24 hours a day; we cannot stop the presses even for routine maintenance.

2. To separate independent clauses when the second one begins with a conjunctive adverb (*therefore, however, also, besides, consequently, nevertheless, furthermore*).

    > Set-up time will decrease 10% and materials handling will decrease 15%; consequently, production will increase 20%.

3. To separate items in a series if the items have internal punctuation.

    > Plans have been proposed for Kansas City, Missouri; Seattle, Washington; and Orlando, Florida.

Underlining (Italics)

Underlining is a line drawn under certain words. In books and laser-printed material, words that you underline when typing appear in italics. Italics are used for three purposes:

1. To indicate titles of books and newspapers.

    > *Thriving on Chaos*   the San Francisco *Examiner*

2. To indicate words used as words or letters used as letters.

   That logo contains an attractive *M*.

   You used *there are* too many times in this paper.

   Note: You may also use quotation marks to indicate words as words.

   You used "there are" too many times in this paper.

3. To emphasize a word.

   Make sure there are no empty spaces on the contract and that all the blanks have been filled in *before* you sign.

ABBREVIATIONS, CAPITALIZATION, AND NUMBERS

Abbreviations

Use abbreviations only for long words or combinations of words that must be used more than once in a report. For example, if words such as *Fahrenheit* or phrases such as *pounds per square inch* must be used several times in a report, abbreviate them to save space. Several rules for abbreviating follow (*Chicago*).

1. If an abbreviation might confuse your reader, use it and the complete phrase the first time.

   This paper will discuss materials planning requirements (MPR).

2. Use all capital letters (no periods, no space between letters or symbols) for acronyms.

   NASA   NAFTA   COBOL   HUD   PAC

3. Capitalize just the first letter of abbreviations for titles and companies; the abbreviation follows with a period.

   Pres.   Co.

4. Form the plural of an abbreviation by adding just *s*.

   BOMs   VCRs   CRTs

5. Omit the period after abbreviations of units of measurement. Exception: use *in.* for *inch*.

6. Use periods with Latin abbreviations.

   e.g. (for example)   i.e. (that is)   etc. (and so forth)

7. Use abbreviations (and symbols) when necessary to save space on visuals, but define difficult ones in the legend, a footnote, or the text.

8. Do not capitalize abbreviations of measurements.

   10 lb   12 m   14 g   16 cm

9. Do not abbreviate units of measurement preceded by approximations.

   several pounds per square inch   15 psi

10. Do not abbreviate short words such as *acre* or *ton*. In tables, abbreviate units of length, area, volume, and capacity.

Capitalization

The conventional rules of capitalization apply to technical writing. The trend in industry is away from overcapitalization.

1. Capitalize a title that immediately precedes a name.

   Senior Project Manager Jones

   But do not capitalize it if it is generic.

   The senior project manager reviewed the report.

2. Capitalize proper nouns and adjectives.

   Asia   American   French

3. Capitalize trade names, but not the product.

   Apple computers   Cleanall window cleaner

4. Capitalize titles of courses and departments and the titles of majors that refer to a specific degree program.

   The first statistics course I took was Statistics 1.

   I majored in Plant Engineering and have applied for several plant engineering positions.

5. Do not capitalize after a colon.

   The chair has four parts: legs, seat, arms, and back.

   I recommend the XYZ lathe: it is the best machine for the price.

Numbers

The following rules cover most situations, but when in doubt whether to use a numeral or a word, remember that the trend in report writing is toward using numerals.

1. Spell out numbers below 10; use figures for 10 and above.

   four cycles   1835 members

2. Spell out numbers that begin sentences.

   Thirty employees received safety commendations.

3. If a series contains numbers above and below 10, use numerals for all of them.

   The floor plan has 2 aisles and 14 workstations.

4. Use numerals for numbers that accompany units of measurement and time.

   1 gram   0.452 minute

   7 yards   6 kilometers

5. In compound-number adjectives, spell out the first one or the shorter one to avoid confusion.

   75 twelve-volt batteries

6. Use figures to record specific measurements.

   He took readings of 7.0, 7.1, and 7.3.

7. Combine figures and words for extremely large round numbers.

   2 million miles

8. For decimal fractions of less than 1, place a zero before the decimal point.

   0.613

9. Express plurals of figures by adding just *s*.

   21s   1990s

10. Place the last two letters of the ordinal after fractions used as nouns:

    ⅒th of a second

    But not after fractions that modify nouns:

    ⅒ horsepower

11. Spell out ordinals below 10.

    fourth part   eighth incident

12. For 10 and above, use the number and the last two letters of the ordinal.

    11th week   52nd contract

■ WORK CITED

The Chicago Manual of Style: The Essential Guide for Writers, Editors, and Publishers. 14th ed. Chicago: University of Chicago Press, 1993.

Appendix B: Documenting Sources

Documenting your sources means following a citation system to indicate whose ideas you are using. Three methods are commonly used: the American Psychological Association (APA) system, the Modern Language Association (MLA) system, and the numbered references system, shown here by the American Chemical Society (ACS) system. All three will be explained briefly. For more complete details you should consult the *Publication Manual of the American Psychological Association* (4th ed.); the *MLA Handbook* (5th ed.); or *The ACS Style Guide*.

HOW INTERNAL DOCUMENTATION WORKS

Each method has two parts: the internal citations and the bibliography, also called "References" (APA, ACS) or "Works Cited" (MLA). The internal citation works in roughly the same manner in all three methods. The author places certain important items of information in the text to tell the reader which entry in the bibliography is the source of the quotation or paraphrase. These items could be the author's last name, the date of publication, the title of an article, or the number of the item in the bibliography.

In the APA method, the basic items are the author's last name and the year of publication. In the ACS method, the basic item is the number of the item in the bibliography. In the MLA method, the basic item is the author's last name and sometimes the title of the work, often in shorthand form.

In each method, the number of the page on which the quotation or paraphrase appears goes in parentheses immediately following the cited material. Because the methods vary, the rest of this chapter explains each.

Here is an example of how each method would internally cite the following quotation from page 18 of *The Internet Navigator* by Paul Gilster, which was published in 1993:

> As opposed to conventional geographic maps, which reveal the shapes and contours of land masses and oceans, an Internet map is like a diagram of a brain. What we see as we draw the various local and regional networks together with the high-speed backbone networks that link them is a set of clusters, places where connectivity is widespread.

APA Method

The APA method requires that you use just the author's last name and include the year of publication and a page number.

> According to Gilster (1993), "an Internet map is like a diagram of the brain" (p. 18).

To find all the bibliographic information on the quotation, you would refer to "Gilster" in the References section.

> Gilster, P. (1993). The Internet navigator. New York: John Wiley & Sons.

MLA Method

The MLA method of citing the passage requires that you include at least the author's last name with the page number.

> One authority noted that "an Internet map is like a diagram of the brain" (Gilster 18).

To find all the publication information for this quotation, you would refer to "Gilster" in the Works Cited list.

Gilster, Paul. *The Internet Navigator.* New York: Wiley, 1993.

Numbered References Method

The numbered method does not require you to use a last name, though you may. Every time you cite the source, wherever the citation occurs in your text, you place in the text the item's number in the bibliography. So if "Gilster" were the second item in the bibliography, you could use the number 2 to cite the source in the text. You also include a page number:

> One authority feels that "an Internet map is like a diagram of the brain" (2, p. 18).

And the Reference entry looks like this:

> 2. Gilster, P. (1993). The Internet navigator. New York: John Wiley & Sons.

Note: The ACS Style Guide (like all the other style guides for the numbered method) does not present a way to handle quotations. ACS assumes that references in scientific literature are to ideas in essays and that quotations are never used. However, because the method is commonly used in academia, the quotation method of the APA is added to it here.

The "Extension" Problem

A common problem with internal documentation is indicating where the paraphrased material begins and ends. If you start a paragraph with a phrase like "Kwang proved that," you need to indicate which of the following sentences come from Kwang. Or if you end a long paragraph with a parenthetical citation (Kwang, 1996, pp. 14–21), you need to indicate which preceding sentences came from Kwang. To alleviate confusion, place a marker at each end of the passage. Either use the name at the start and page numbers at the end or use a term like "one authority" at the start and the citation at the end.

> Kwang (1996) proved that laser printers cause more humor in technical writing. The crisp text makes people smile, causing them to look for other sources of happiness (14–21).

> One authority proved that laser printers cause more humor in technical writing. The crisp text makes people smile, causing them to look for other sources of happiness (Kwang, 1996, pp. 14–21). This conclusion surprised most of the researchers, but few of the office workers.

THE APA METHOD

APA Citations

Once you understand the basic theory of the method—to use names and page numbers to refer to the References—you need to be aware of the variations possible in placing the name in the text. Each time you cite a quotation or paraphrase, you give the page number preceded by *p.* or *pp.* Do not use *pg.* The following variations are all acceptable:

1. The author's name appears as part of the introduction to the quotation or paraphrase.

   Gilster (1993) is very definite: "Simply put, the Internet is changing so rapidly, with so many new databases, services, addresses, and projects, that it can't be neatly encapsulated in any one set of commands or maxims" (p. 2).

2. The author is not named in the introduction to the quotation or paraphrase.

   What is entirely clear is that the Internet "can't be neatly encapsulated in any one set of commands or maxims" (Gilster, 1993, p. 2).

3. The author has several works listed in the References. If they have different dates, no special treatment is necessary; if an author has two works dated the same year, differentiate them in the text and in the References with a lower-case letter after each date (1993a, 1993b).

   Gilster (1993a) points out that the Internet "can't be neatly encapsulated in any one set of commands or maxims" (p. 2).

4. Paraphrases are handled like quotations. Give the author's last name, the date, and the appropriate page numbers.

   Gilster (1993) says that the Internet changes so fast that you must come to see your experience with it as a daily learning process (p. 150).

5. When citing block quotations, the period is placed *before* the page parentheses. Do not place quotation marks before and after a block quotation. Indent the left margin 5 spaces and double-space. Do not indent the right margin.

   According to Gilster (1993),
   > There can be no complete printed directory of the Internet. Those who write about this globe-spanning network are destined to labor forever behind the technological wave. Simply put, the Internet is changing so rapidly, with so many new databases, services, addresses, and projects, that it can't be neatly encapsulated in any one set of commands or maxims. The more you use the Internet, the more you will realize that each day is itself a learning process. (p. 2)

6. If no author is given for the work, treat the title as the author and list the title first in the References.

> To learn Internet, it is useful to know that "the two most important parts are Web searching and cookies" ("Tips," 2004, p. 78).
>
> Tips for the Infohighway. (2004, July). <u>Cyberreal</u>, p. 78.

APA References

The reference list (entitled "References") contains the complete bibliographic information on each source you use. The list is arranged alphabetically by the last name of the author or the first important word of the title. Follow these guidelines:

- Present information for all entries in this order: Author's name. Date. Title. Publication information.

- Double-space the entire list. *Indent the first line* 5 spaces; start all other lines at the left-hand margin.

- Use only the initials of the author's first and middle names. *Note:* Many local style sheets suggest using the full name; if this is the style at your place, follow that style.

- Place the date in parentheses immediately after the name.

- Capitalize only the first word of the title and subtitle and proper nouns.

- The inclusion of *p.* and *pp.* depends on the type of source. In general, use *p.* and *pp.* when the volume number does not precede the page numbers (or for a newspaper article).

> Klein, J. (2000, June 15). Smart polymer solutions. *Nature, 405,* 745–746.
>
> Marks, P. (2000, July 1). Jet set displays. *New Scientist, 167,* 8.
>
> Tullo, A. H. (2000, June 26). Diode developers: A bright future. *Chemical and engineering news, 78,* 20–21.

- Place the entries in alphabetical order.

- If there are two or more works by one author, arrange them chronologically, earliest first.

> Klein, J. (2000, June 15).
>
> Klein, J. (2001).

Several common entries are shown below.

Book with One Author

Channell, D. F. (1991). The vital machine: A study of technology and organic life. New York: Oxford University Press.
Kidder, T. (1981). The soul of a new machine. Boston: Little, Brown.

▩ Capitalize the first word after a colon.

Book with Two Authors

Peters, T. J., & Waterman, R. (1982). In search of excellence: Lessons from America's best-run companies. New York: Harper.

Book with Editors

Ford, C. M., & Gioia, D. A. (Eds.). (1995). Creative action in organizations: Ivory tower visions and real world voices. Thousand Oaks, CA: Sage.

▩ Use zip code abbreviations for states.

Essay in an Anthology

Conger, J. A. (1995). Boogie down wonderland: Creativity and visionary leadership. Ford, C. M., and Gioia, D. A. (Eds.), Creative action in organizations (pp. 49–71). Thousand Oaks, CA: Sage.

▩ Capitalize only the first word of the essay title.
▩ Use *pp.* with inclusive page numbers.

Corporate or Institutional Author

American Telephone & Telegraph. (2002). 2001 annual report. New York: Author.

▩ When the author is also the publisher, write *Author* for the publisher.
▩ In the text, the first citation reads this way: (American Telephone & Telegraph [AT&T], 1997). Subsequent citations read (AT&T, 2002).
▩ This entry could also read

2001 annual report. (2002). New York: American Telephone & Telegraph.

Cite this entry as (2001 annual).

Work Without Date or Publisher

Radke, J. (n.d.). Writing for electronic sources. Atlanta: Center for Electronic Communication.

▨ Use *n.p.* for no publisher or no place.

Brochure or Pamphlet

Wisconsin's trumpeter swan recovery program (Publ-IE-045 90) [Brochure]. (n.d.). Madison, WI: Natural Resources Foundation.

▨ Treat brochures like books.
▨ Place any identification number after the title.
▨ Place the word *brochure* in brackets.
▨ This entry could also read

Natural Resources Foundation. (n.d.). Wisconsin's trumpeter swan recovery program (Publ-IE-045 90) [Brochure]. Madison, WI: Author.

In the text, reference this entry as Natural.

Later Edition of a Book

American Psychological Association. (1994). Publication manual (4th ed). Washington, DC: Author.

Encyclopedia/Handbook

Phone recorder. (1991). In R. Graf (Ed.), Encyclopedia of electronic circuits. (Vol. 3, pp. 616–617). Blue Ridge Summit, PA: Tab.

Posner, E. C. (1992). Communications, deep space. In Encyclopedia of physical science and technology (2nd ed.; Vol. 3, pp. 691–711). San Diego: Academic Press.

▨ In the text, refer to the first entry and all works with no author this way (note the use of quotation marks): ("Phone," 1991)

Article in a Journal with Continuous Pagination

O'Neill, M. J. (1994). Work space adjustability, storage and enclosure as prediction of employee reactions and performance. Environment and Behavior, 26, 504–526.

▨ In the article title, capitalize only the first word, proper nouns, proper adjectives, and the first word after a colon.
▨ Underline the volume number.

Article in a Journal Without Continuous Pagination

Kantner, R. M. (1994). Collaborative advantage: The art of alliances. Harvard Business Review, 72(4), 96–108.

■ Put the issue number in parentheses after the volume.

■ You could also give the month, if that helps identify the work: (1994, July–August).

Article in a Monthly or Weekly Magazine

Gordon, J. (2000, July). Introducing . . . the training portfolio. Training, 37, 42, 44–46.

■ Present discontinuous pages as shown here; the comma indicates the skipped page.

Newspaper Article

Bradsher, K. (2000, July 17). Was Freud a minivan or S.U.V. kind of guy? The New York Times, pp. A1, A16.

■ Note the use of *pp.* for "pages" with newspaper articles.

Personal Interview

(*Note: The APA Manual* suggests that personal and telephone interviews and letters should appear only in the text and not in the References. However, because these entries may be critical in research reports, a suggested form for their use in the References is given here.)

1. In the text, reference a personal communication material this way:

   I. Schmidt (telephone interview, February 14, 2004)

2. In the References, enter it this way:

   Schmidt, I. (2004, February 14). [Personal interview]

■ Arrange the date so the year is first.

■ If the person's title is pertinent, place it in the brackets.

Schmidt, I. (2004, February 14). [Personal interview. Manager of Technical Services, Wheeler Amalgamated, Denver, CO]

Telephone Interview

Schmidt, I. (2004, February 14). [Telephone interview]

Personal Letter

Schmidt, I. (2005, February 14). [Personal letter. Manager of Technical Services, Wheeler Amalgamated, Denver, CO]

THE MLA METHOD

The following section describes variations in MLA citation and explains entries in the MLA Works Cited section.

MLA Citations

Once you understand the basic theory of the method—to use names and page numbers to refer to the Works Cited—you need to be aware of the possible variations of placing the name in the text. In this method, unlike APA, each time you refer to a quotation or paraphrase, you give the page number only; do not use *p.* or *pg.*

1. The author's name appears as part of the introduction to the quotation or paraphrase.

   Paul Gilster is very definite: "Simply put, the Internet is changing so rapidly, with so many new databases, services, addresses, and projects, that it can't be neatly encapsulated in any one set of commands or maxims" (2).

2. Author is not named in introduction to quotation.

   What is entirely clear is that the Internet "can't be neatly encapsulated in any one set of commands or maxims" (Gilster 2).

3. Author has several works in the Works Cited.

   Gilster points out that the Internet "can't be neatly encapsulated in any one set of commands or maxims" (Internet 2).

4. Paraphrases are usually handled like quotations. Give the author's last name and the appropriate page numbers.

   Gilster says that the Internet changes so fast that you must come to see your experience with it as a daily learning process (150).

5. In block quotations, place the period before the page parentheses. Do not place quotation marks before and after a block quotation. Indent the left margin 10 spaces and double-space. Do not indent the right margin.

   According to Gilster,

   > There can be no complete printed directory of the Internet. Those who write about this globe-spanning network are destined to labor forever behind the technological wave. Simply put, the Internet is changing so rapidly, with so many new databases, services, addresses, and projects, that it can't be neatly encapsulated in any one set of commands or maxims. The more you use the Internet, the more you will realize that each day is itself a learning process. (2)

6. If no author is given for the work, treat the title as the author because the title is listed first in the Works Cited list.

   To learn Internet, it is useful to know that "the two most important parts are electronic mail and FTP" ("Tips" 78).

   "Tips for the Infohighway." Cyberreal July 1994: 78.

7. If the title of a book is very long, you may shorten the title when you discuss it in the text. For instance, Newton and Ford's book is entitled *Taking Sides: Clashing Views on Controversial Issues in Business Ethics and Society.* In the text, however, you may simply refer to the book as *Taking Sides.*

MLA Works Cited List

The Works Cited list contains the complete bibliographic information on each source you use. The list is arranged alphabetically by the last name of the author or, if no author is named, by the first important word of the title. Follow these guidelines:

- Present information for all entries in this order: Author's name. Title. Printing Information (including date).

- Capitalize the first letter of every important word in a title.

- Enclose article titles in quotation marks.

- Double-space an entry if it has two or more lines.

- Indent the second and succeeding lines 5 spaces.

- If an author appears in the Works Cited two or more times, type three hyphens and a period instead of repeating the name for the second and succeeding entries. Alphabetize the entries by the first word of the title.

Several common entries appear below. For more detailed instructions, use one of the *MLA Handbook,* 5th ed., by Joseph Gibaldi (New York: MLA, 1999).

Book with One Author

Channell, David F. The Vital Machine: A Study of Technology and Organic Life. New York: Oxford, 1991.

Kidder, Tracy. The Soul of a New Machine. Boston: Little, Brown, 1981.

- Only the name of the publishing company needs to appear. You may drop "Co." or "Inc."

Book with Two Authors

Peters, Thomas J., and Robert Waterman. In Search of Excellence: Lessons from America's Best-Run Companies. New York, Harper, 1982.

■ A long title may be shortened in the text, in this case to Search.

Book with Editor

Ford, Cameron M., and Dennis A. Gioia, eds. Creative Action in Organizations: Ivory Tower Visions and Real World Voices. Thousand Oaks, CA: Sage, 1995.

Essay in an Anthology

Conger, Jay A. "Boogie Down Wonderland: Creativity and Visionary Leadership." Creative Action in Organizations. Ed. Cameron M. Ford and Dennis A. Gioia. Thousand Oaks, CA: Sage, 1995. 49–71.

■ Put the inclusive pages of the article last. Do not use *Pp.* Also, for larger numbers, give only the last two digits in the second number (112–13) unless you need more for clarity (923–1003).

Corporate or Institutional Author

American Telegraph & Telephone. 2003 Annual Report. New York: Author, 2004.

■ In the text, cite this entry the first time as (American Telephone and Telegraph [AT&T]); thereafter use (AT&T).
■ This entry could also be arranged with the title first.

2003 Annual Report. New York: American Telephone & Telegraph, 2004.

■ Cite this version as (2003 Annual).

Work Without Date or Publisher

Radke, Jean. Writing for Electronic Sources. Atlanta: Center for Electronic Communication, n.d.

■ Use *n.p.* for no publisher or no place.
■ If neither publisher nor place is given, write "N.p.: n.p., 1994."

Brochure or Pamphlet

Wisconsin's Trumpeter Swan Recovery Program. Publ-IE-045 90. Madison, WI: Natural Resources Foundation, n.d.

■ If the pamphlet has an identification number, place it after the title.

Later Edition of a Book

American Psychological Association. <u>Publication Manual</u>. 4th ed. Washington, DC: APA, 1994.

Encyclopedia/Reference Work

"Phone Recorder." <u>Encyclopedia of Electronic Circuits</u>. Ed. Rudolph F. Graf. Vol. 3. Blue Ridge Summit, PA: Tab, 1991. 616–17.

Posner, Edward C. "Communications, Deep Space." <u>Encyclopedia of Physical Science and Technology</u>. 2nd ed. Vol. 3. San Diego: Academic Press, 1992.

▥ No page numbers appear in Posner because entries in the book are arranged alphabetically.

Article in a Journal with Continuous Pagination

O'Neill, Michael J. "Work Space Adjustability, Storage and Enclosure as Prediction of Employee Reactions and Performance." <u>Environment and Behavior</u> 26 (1994): 504–26.

Article in a Journal Without Continuous Pagination

Kantner, Rosabeth M. "Collaborative Advantage: The Art of Alliances." <u>Harvard Business Review</u> 72.4 (1994): 96–108.

Article in a Monthly or Weekly Magazine

Gordon, Jack. "Introducing . . . the Training Portfolio." <u>Training</u> 37.7 July 2000: 42+.

▥ If the article is printed discontinuously over many pages—as in 42, 44–46—give the first page only, followed by a plus sign: 42+.

Newspaper Article

Bradsher, Keith. "Was Freud a Minivan or an S.U.V. Kind of Guy?" <u>The New York Times</u> 17 July 2000: A1+.

▥ Identify the edition, section, and page number. A reader should be able to find the article on the page.

▥ Omit the article (*the*) in the title of the newspaper. If the newspaper is a city newspaper and the city is not given in the title, supply it in brackets after the title (e.g., <u>Globe and Mail</u> [Toronto]).

Personal Interview

1. In the text, interviews are cited like any other source: (Schmidt).

2. In the Works Cited, enter it this way:

> Schmidt, Howard. Personal interview. 14 Feb. 2005.

■ If the person's title and workplace are important, add them after the name:

> Schmidt, Howard, Manager of Technical Services. Georgia-Pacific, Baton Rouge. Personal interview. 14 Feb. 2005.

■ Use this rule for telephone interviews and letters also.

Telephone Interview

> Schmidt, Howard. Telephone interview. 14 Feb. 2005. [Add title and workplace if necessary.]

Personal Letter

> Schmidt, Howard. Letter to author. 14 Feb. 2005. [Add title and workplace if necessary.]

NUMBERED REFERENCES

The numbered method uses an arabic numeral, rather than a name or date, as the internal citation. The numeral refers to an entry in the bibliography. *Use APA form for the bibliographic entries.* The bibliography may be organized in one of two ways:

■ Alphabetically

■ In order of their appearance in the text, without regard to alphabetization (ACS suggests this method)

Numbered references are commonly used in short technical reports that have only two or three references. Many periodicals have adopted this method because it is cheaper to print one number than many names and dates. The difficulty with the method is that if a new source is inserted into the list, all the items in the list and all the references in the text need to be renumbered.

The following sample shows the same paragraph and bibliography arranged in the two different ways. Note that the author's name may or may not appear in the text.

Alphabetically

> The inclusion of phthlates in toys has caused a major controversy. According to researchers, phthlates cause liver and kidney damage in rats (2). As

a result of pressure brought by Greenpeace (1), the European Union outlawed phthlates in toys, especially teething toys, like tooth rings (2). As a result of the action, two alternative plasticizers, adipate and epoxidized soy bean (EOS), will be used more. ESO seems very promising because it has FDA approval (3). Many authorities, however, feel that the ban is ill conceived. One authority fears that the ban could politicize science (4). Another authority says that the concern is ungrounded because many earlier toxicological conferences concluded that the threats from phthlates to humans are miniscule (1).

1. Fanu, J. (1999, November 22). Behind the great plastic duck panic. New Statesman, 128, 11.

2. Melton, M. (1999, December 20). Lingering troubles in toyland. U.S. News and World Report, 127, 71.

3. Moore, S. (1999, December 1). Phthlate ban could boost demand for alternatives. Chemical Week, 161, 17.

4. Scott, A. (1999, October 27). EU warns on Sevesco directive. Chemical Week, 161, 24.

By Position of the First Reference in the Text

The inclusion of phthlates in toys has caused a major controversy. According to researchers, phthlates cause liver and kidney damage in rats (1). As a result of pressure brought by Greenpeace (2), the European Union outlawed phthlates in toys, especially teething toys, like tooth rings (1). As a result of the action, two alternative plasticizers, adipate and epoxidized soy bean (EOS) will be used more. ESO seems very promising because it has FDA approval (3). Many authorities, however, feel that the ban is ill conceived. One authority fears that the ban could politicize science (4). Another authority says that the concern is ungrounded because many earlier toxicological conferences concluded that the threats from phthlates to humans are miniscule (2).

1. Melton, M. (1999, December 20). Lingering troubles in toyland. U.S. News and World Report, 127, 71.

2. Fanu, J. (1999, November 22). Behind the great plastic duck panic. New Statesman, 128, 11.

3. Moore, S. (1999, December 1). Phthlate ban could boost demand for alternatives. Chemical Week, 161, 17.

4. Scott, A. (1999, October 27). EU warns on Sevesco directive. Chemical Week, 161, 24.

EXAMPLES

The following examples present three sample papers, one in each of the three formats. The first two (APA and Numbered) are excerpted from much longer papers. The MLA document briefly shows the use of MLA format.

EXAMPLE 1
Excerpt in APA format

MECHANICAL PROPERTIES

The mechanical properties of a film or coating describe how they will perform in the distribution environment. A thorough evaluation of edible films by a packaging engineer will include a look at their mechanical properties and a comparison of these attributes against other packaging materials. This section will describe two important mechanical properties: tensile strength and elongation.

Tensile Strength.   Tensile strength can be described as the amount of force required to break a material. Knowing a package's tensile strength can help the packaging engineer decide if the material will remain intact as it flows through packaging machinery. It will also help the engineer predict whether the material will break as it is stretched around a product. Table 4 summarizes the tensile strengths of various edible films. Banjeree and Chen (1995) found that whey protein films withstood 5.94 MPa of pressure before breaking. However, the addition of lipids to the whey film lowered the tensile strength to 3.15 MPa (p. 1681).

TABLE 4.
Tensile Strength and Elongation

Film Material	Tensile Strength (MPa)	Elongation Thickness (%)	Source
Proteins			
Whey	5.94	22.74	Banerjee (1995)
Whey/Lipid	3.15	10.78	Banerjee (1995)
Milk	8.6	22.1	Maynes (1994)
Zein	38.3	—	Yamada (1995)
Rice	31.1	2.9	Shih (1996)
Soybean	7.2	0.75	Stuchell (1994)
Polysaccharides			
Cellulose	66.33	25.6	Park (1993)
Synthetics			
LDPE	13.1–27.6	100–965	Park (1993)
PVDC	48.4–138	20–40	Maynes (1994)

The tensile strengths of cellulose and grain-based edible films have also been measured and compared to synthetic plastics. Park, Weller, and Vergano (1993) found that cellulose films exhibited a tensile strength value of 66.33 MPa. In the same study, LDPE required from 13.1 to 27.6 MPa to break (p. 1362). Yamada, Takahashi, and Noguchi (1995) discovered that zein protein films exhibit similar or higher tensile strengths

EXAMPLE 1
(continued)

than polyvinlylide chloride (PVDC) films. Shih (1996) found that rice protein films resisted breaking until 31.1 MPa of force was applied. Lastly,
Brandenburg, Weller, and Testin (1993) and Stuchell and Krochta (1994)
found that soy protein films took 7.2 MPa of force to break.

The thickness of the film can have a bearing on its tensile strength.
Park et al. (1993) found that the tensile strength of cellulose did not improve as the thickness increased. However, no direct comparison of thicknesses between cellulose films and LDPE films was made. Therefore, it is
difficult to make a true comparison. Yamada et al. (1995) discovered that
in order to achieve tensile strengths similar to PVDC, zein protein films 7
times thicker than the PVDC had to be used. Most researchers do not list
the thickness of the product when testing for tensile strength. This lack
of completeness in reporting their results will cause some confusion on
the part of packaging professionals.

Elongation. Elongation refers to the amount that a material will stretch
before it breaks. Table 4 lists the percent elongation of various edible
films. Park et al. (1993) found that cellulose elongation percentages varied widely among different molecular weights of films. Chen (1995)
along with Maynes and Krochta (1994) found that milk protein films had
significantly lower percentages of elongations than traditional plastic
films. They found that milk proteins elongated anywhere from 1 to 75
percent of their original length, whereas LDPE elongated to 5 times its
original length before breaking. It is widely believed that the structure of
proteins and the way that they crystallize negatively affects the film's
elongation properties (McHugh & Krochta, 1994).

Polysaccharides have better elongation characteristics than proteins.
Park et al. (1993) discovered that cellulose films can elongate from 10%
to 200% of their original length. They compared these figures to LDPE,
which was found to elongate 1 to 10 times its original length before
breaking. As with tensile strength, the amount of elongation is dependent on the thickness of the material. The amount of elongation should
be reported on the basis of the thickness of the sample tested.

References

Banerjee, R., & Chen, H. (1995). Functional properties of edible films
using whey protein concentrate. *Journal of Dairy Science, 78,*1673–1683.

Brandenburg, A. H., Weller, C. L., & Testin, R. F. (1993). Edible films and
coatings from soy protein. *Journal of Food Science, 58,* 1086–1089.

Chen, H. (1995). Functional properties and applications of edible films
made of milk proteins. *Journal of Dairy Science, 78,* 2563–2583.

Maynes, J., & Krochta, J. (1994). Properties of edible films from total
milk protein. *Journal of Food Science, 59,* 909–911.

EXAMPLE 1
(continued)

McHugh, T., & Krochta, J. (1994). Milk-protein-based edible films and coatings. *Food Technology, 48,* 97–103.

Park, H. J., Weller, C. L., & Vergano, P. J. (1993). Permeability and mechanical properties of cellulose-based edible films. *Journal of Food Science, 58,* 1361–1364, 1370.

Shih, F. (1996). Edible films from rice protein concentrate and pullulan. *Cereal Chemistry, 73,* 406–409.

Stuchell, Y., & Krochta, J. (1994). Enzymatic treatments and thermal effects on edible soy protein films. *Journal of Food Science, 59,* 1332–1337.

Yamada, K., Takahashi, H., & Noguchi, A. (1995). Improved water resistance in zein films and composites for biodegradable food packaging. *International Journal of Food Science and Technology, 30,* 599–608.

EXAMPLE 2
Excerpt with Numbered References

INTRODUCTION

As we move on the 21st century, the plastics industry may be witnessing a paradigm shift—a move from an all petroleum-based industrial economy to one that encompasses a broader base of biodegradable materials including plant derived starches. These starch additives contribute significantly in the total amount of degradation of the biodegradable films. The door has opened to a variety of new players, including non-resin companies each with a unique "hook" into the market.

Defining biodegradability and the compost environment will allow a better understanding to how this paradigm shift could take place. Synthetic films are causing problems in the compost environment due to their inability to biodegrade. Biodegradable starch-based polyethylene films could be used at the commercial, institutional, and residential level and, because they biodegrade, will not be a problem at the composting level. Compostability could aid in the marketability of biodegradable materials allowing an opportunity for companies to escape their old paradigms and shift to biodegradable. Companies have made strong impacts with biodegradable materials, yet they have to understand what their potential market will be and what cost factors will affect them in order to increase the demand for biodegradable.

NATURAL AND SYNTHETIC POLYMERS

Both natural and synthetic polymers can be broken down during biodegradation but what facts do we need to know about them? Natural (or bio) polymers are based on renewable resources. Natural polymers include polyactic acid (PLA), cellulosics and starches, and polyhydroxyalkanoates (PHA) (1). These natural polymers, which are derived from natural monomers, offer the greatest opportunities because their biodegradability and environmental compatibility are assured (2).

For example, PLA is composed of chains of lactic acid, which ultimately produce a product fermented from corn. When water is removed, a purified lactide remains. Cargill has developed ecoPLA, which combines naturally occurring polymers to attain properties needed to meet customers' film requirements. These films are completely biodegradable, including complete degradation of the lactide (3).

Complicating the issue is the role of synthetic components, polymers, such as polyethylene and polyester, that are made from petroleum-based feed stocks (1,3). Some experts, however, believe that synthetic components must be added to films to produce the required properties, like durability (3). But it is not clear that these blended stocks are biodegradable.

BIODEGRADABILITY ARGUMENTS

Experts disagree on whether blended films actually biodegrade. Some feel that most blends of natural starch-based raw materials and

EXAMPLE 2
(continued)

polyethylene will be completely biodegradable (4). Others doubt that polyethylene can ever completely biodegrade, even when combined with degradable additives such as starch. A major cause of their doubt is that the testing methods used to determine biodegradability do not extend over a long enough time frame (3).

BIODEGRADATION FACTORS AND STARCH

So will blended films actually biodegrade? McCarthy (5) found that polyethylene mixed with a starch-based additive, placed in a compost environment, does not completely decompose. The enzymatic reaction of the microorganisms in the soil does break down the starch and the polyethylene, and the starch portion is always completely absorbed. Sometimes the polyethylene pieces are still visible even though the starch is untraceable.

In the time since McCarthy's research there have been several attempts to find a way to cause the polyethylene to biodegrade. One is Cargill's ecoPLA, mentioned above. Another attempt is the Melitta company's new polyethylene and starch bag. The bag has properties similar to synthetic polyethylene plastic bags. It is rated as water and tear resistant. The bag will decompose into carbon dioxide, water, and humus in compost piles. But it must reach exothermic (combustible) temperatures of between 140–176°F in order to completely degrade in 40 days or less. If the exothermic temperature is not reached, it will take longer to biodegrade in the compost environment (2).

Having a completely biodegradable bag is an exciting prospect, but there is a problem: the 140–176° temperatures cannot be reached naturally. The solution to this problem is not clear.

Regardless of the problems, though, two major companies are making the shift to all-biodegradable stocks for their films, replacing non-biodegradable synthetic plastics. Cargill and Melitta's new advances have the possibility of working well under typical compost conditions because of their degradability characteristics.

REFERENCES

1. Krochta, J. M., & DeMulder-Johnston, M. (1997). Edible and biodegradable polymer films: challenges and opportunities. Food Technology 51: 61–74.

2. Colvin, R. (1995, April). Biodegradable polymers make small-scale return. Modern Plastics, 17–19.

3. Farrell, M., & Goldstein, N. (1995, November). Unraveling the biodegradable plastics maze. BioCycle, 74–79.

4. Lawton, J. W. (1996). Effect of starch type on the properties of starch containing films. Carbohydrate Polymers, 29, 203–208.

5. McCarthy, L. (1993, March). Biodegradables blossom into the field of dreams for packagers. Plastics World, 22–27.

EXAMPLE 3
Excerpt in MLA Format

NATURAL AND SYNTHETIC POLYMERS

Both natural and synthetic polymers can be broken down during biodegradation, but what facts do we need to know about them? Natural (or bio) polymers are based on renewable resources. According to Krochta and DeMulder-Johnston, natural polymers include polyactic acid (PLA), cellulosics and starches, and polyhydroxyalkanoates (PHA) (62). These natural polymers, which are derived from natural monomers, offer the greatest opportunities because their biodegradability and environmental compatibility are assured (Colvin 17).

For example, PLA is composed of chains of lactic acid, which ultimately produce a product fermented from corn. When water is removed, a purified lactide remains. Cargill has developed ecoPLA, which combines naturally occurring polymers to attain properties needed to meet customers' film requirements. These films are completely biodegradable, including complete degradation of the lactide (Farrell and Goldstein 75–76).

Complicating the issue is the role of synthetic components, polymers such as polyethylene and polyester, that are made from petroleum-based feed stocks (Krochta and DeMulder-Johnston 61, Farrell and Goldstein 74). Some experts, however, believe that synthetic components must be added to films to produce the required properties, like durability (Farrell and Goldstein 74). But it is not clear that these blended stocks are biodegradable.

WORKS CITED

Colvin, R. "Biodegradable Polymers Make Small-Scale Return." Modern Plastics April 1995: 17–19.

Farrell, Molly, and Nora Goldstein. "Unraveling the Biodegradable Plastics Maze." BioCycle Nov. 1995: 74–79.

Krochta, John M., and Catherine DeMulder-Johnston. "Edible and Biodegradable Polymer Films: Challenges and Opportunities." Food Technology 51 (1997): 61–74.

▪ EXERCISES

1. Edit the following sentences to place an APA citation correctly and/or to place an MLA citation correctly.

   a. On page 12 in his 1995 article, Mr. Adam Johnson notes that "The most controversial recycling method is incineration."

   b. In 1994, Dawn Kundera said on page 71 that computer workstations can cause significant eye and back strain on employees.

   c. Estelle Jones noted (p. 27, 1993) that "Even HCFCs can cause significant damage to the ozone layer."

   d. "Quality circles significantly increase employee morale and overall production," said Chester MacArthur in 1996 on p. 16.

2. Pick a paragraph from one of the three models in this appendix and rewrite it in one of the other two citation styles (e.g., change APA to numbered or MLA).

3. Turn these sets of data into an APA References list and an MLA Works Cited list.

   Marie O'Malley/1994/pages 17 to 21 and also pages 27 and 35/the magazine is Cyberhype/July 12/using Internet to find U.S. Census facts/Volume 4/Number 7

   Dawn Kundera/The census provides the basis for feasibility decisions/ Volume 87/pages 471–496/1995/Electronic Search/Number 3/Autumn

4. Use the following two excerpts and the information presented in Example 9.1 (p. 219) to create a brief research report on pixels. Your audience is people who are just beginning to use color in documents.

   THINKING IN PIXELS

   From Alan Simpson, *Netscape Navigator Gold 3.0 Book, Macintosh Edition. The Official Guide to the Premiere Web Navigator and HTML Editor* (Research Triangle Park, NC: Ventura, 1996); pp. 323–324.

   It's not always easy to define in pixels how large or small you want an image to be. But you can estimate by thinking of 100 pixels as equal to 1 inch. Figure the width of the average reader's screen to be about 600 pixels, or 6 inches. In other words, you can think of the 300-pixel-wide image as being about half the width of the reader's screen.

   The height of the reader's screen is a little trickier. At 640 × 480 pixels (the "least-space" scenario that most Web publishers work around), the height, technically, would be about 4.8 inches. But because Navigator's title bar, menu bar, toolbars(s), and status bar take up some of those pixels, it doesn't hurt to round that down to about 400 pixels, or 4 inches.

Of course, this is all relative. For example, if the reader is browsing at a resolution of 800 × 600 pixels, then that reader's screen is about 8 inches wide and 6 inches tall (minus the title bar, toolbars, and such). (Pp. 323–4)

COLOR BASICS

Written by Beth Mazur, and reprinted with permission from *Intercom*, the magazine of the Society for Technical Communication.

Your monitor displays thousands of points of light called pixels. Monitor resolution refers to the number of pixels that can be displayed. A standard monitor resolution is 640 × 480, which means that the monitor can display 640 pixels across by 480 pixels high (or more than 300,000 pixels). Newer monitors can display as many as 1280 × 1024, or over 1 million pixels.

The color of each pixel can be specified by an RGB value—how much red, green, and blue light is "combined" for that pixel. When all the colors are combined, the result is white. When none of the colors are combined, the result is black. All other display colors are created by using various combinations of red, green, and blue. Web images are essentially collections of RGB values which, when displayed, result in a graphic.

If all monitors displayed the same color for the same RGB value, life would be simple. Unfortunately, this is not the case. This article explains why and offers some basic suggestions for dealing with Web color.

"It's a Hardware Problem"

There are actually two hardware issues that affect monitor displays. The first is that not all monitors have the same capabilities when it comes to displaying color. Some monitors display what is called <u>24-bit color</u>. This means that each of the red, green, and blue components of an RGB value uses 8 bits (3 × 8 = 24). Computers that support 24-bit color can specify over 16 million colors by using various combinations of red, green, and blue.

Other monitors use what is called <u>8-bit color</u>. They can display only 256 colors at a time. Whether a monitor supports 8-bit or 24-bit color typically depends on the type of video card in the computer and/or the amount of memory (called VRAM) available.

In 8-bit color, you use the same RGB values as in 24-bit color, and therefore can also use millions of colors. The difference is that, in 8-bit color, you can display only 256 colors at a time. The 256 colors being used at any one time are called the <u>palette</u>. The operating system switches palettes depending on which application is active (i.e., your browser or your word processing program).

Images that use more than 256 colors have to be modified before they can be displayed on a monitor that supports only 8-bit color. The resulting image may be different from the original image—and sometimes very displeasing.

The second hardware problem is related to variations in computer and monitor hardware. If you've ever shopped for a television, you'll recognize the problem. Appliance stores may have twenty or thirty televisions lined up all showing the same images, but with variations in the color of the picture. There are many complicated explanations (all using technical words like gamma, luminance, and intensity) for this phenomenon, but the bottom line is that images displayed on different monitors will vary. (P. 5)

5. Rewrite the tensile strength section of Example 1 in order to emphasize that one film type is the best.

■ WRITING ASSIGNMENT

Find three articles on a similar topic and write a memo in which you give the gist of all three to your supervisor. Do not just summarize them each in turn; blend them so they support a main point that you want to call to the supervisor's attention. Use any one of the three methods of documenting.

■ WORKS CITED

Dodd, Janet S., ed. *The ACS Style Guide: A Manual for Authors and Editors.* Washington, DC: American Chemical Society, 1986.

Gibaldi, Joseph. *MLA Handbook for Writers of Research Papers.* 5th ed. NY: MLA, 1999.

Publication Manual of the American Psychological Association. 4th ed. Washington, DC: APA, 1994.

Focus on DOCUMENTING ELECTRONIC ITEMS

An exact standard for citing on-line sources has not been formalized. Various professional organizations recommend different methods of recording the key information. For more complete information than is presented below, consult the *Publication Manual of the American Psychological Association* (4th ed., pp. 173–178, 218–222), the American Psychological Association Web site (*http://www.apa.org*), *The Chicago Manual of Style* (14th ed., pp. 633–635), or the *MLA Handbook* (5th ed., pp. xv–xviii, 178–202, 205, 208–229).

The basic rule for citing electronic items is to provide enough information for your reader to find the document. For electronic items, in addition to the usual citation elements, you must provide two key bits of information:

1. The "path"—a URL, an E-mail address, or a sequence of menu/ screen choices—that will enable the user to retrieve the material.
2. The "date of retrieval"—the date on which you saw or copied the information—because electronic sources, like Web sites, change or disappear over time.

Here are guidelines for citing E-mail LISTSERVS, articles available through data services, articles available from on-line periodicals, and Web sites.

APA Guidelines

E-Mail and LISTSERVS.   APA recommends that you cite E-mail and LISTSERV postings in the same way as personal communication. In your text, such a citation would look like this:

> H. Schmidt (personal communication, October 1, 2004)

Notice that the first-name initial is presented first, unlike the order used in the reference list.

APA recommends that personal communications not appear in the reference list, but if you are required to include them, follow this:

> Schmidt, H. (2004, October 1). [E-mail]

LISTSERV Archives.   Many LISTSERVS have archives, where the original postings are stored more or less permanently, available to anyone who joins the LISTSERV. If you use the archived version of a

LISTSERV message (and you should, because archived messages are more accessible), put the item in the reference list. Use this form:

> Schmidt, H. (2004, October 1). A problem with white pine root systems. Logging associates of America listserv. Retrieved January 2, 2005, from the World Wide Web: http://www.laa.lsu.edu/cgi-bin/enter=laa.

Explanation: Author. (Date of original posting). Title from the subject line. Name of the LISTSERV. Date you obtained the item and the URL of the archive.

Article from an On-Line Service. Many libraries and companies' on-line services like EBSCOhost to find full-text articles. An entry in the References would look like this:

> Schmidt, H. (2002, Oct. 20). Eco-friendly logging practices. *American logger, 176,* pp. 56–70. Retrieved February 14, 2003, from EBSCOhost (Academic Search Elite) on the World Wide Web: http://search.epnet.com/comm-generic.

Explanation: Author. (Date of original publication). Article title. *Periodical title. Volume number of the periodical.* Date you obtained the article, name of the service (name of the database), and the URL of the service.

Note: Databases like EBSCOhost often present the publishing information in a Source line that does not give the complete page numbers of the article.

> Source: American Logger, 20 Oct. 2002, Vol. 176 Issue 10, p. 56, 14p.

If the source line is the only information available, use this form for the page numbers: p. 56, 14p. In the text, you will not be able to cite pages; just use the author's name and date.

Article Available from an On-Line Periodical. Treat an article from an on-line periodical like a hard-copy article. Note that you must add the date of retrieval and the URL:

> Schmidt, H. (2003, October). Consulting opportunities in white pine logging. *eLog, 10.* retrieved January 2, 2004, on the World Wide Web: http://www.elog.com/oct/articles/schmidt.html.

Explanation: Author. (Date of original publication). Article title. *Periodical Title. Volume number of the periodical.* Date you obtained the article and the URL of the periodical.

Professional or Personal Web Site—Home Page. Essential for citing Web pages is that you give the date of retrieval on which you viewed the site and the URL. Give as much of the other information as possible.

> Schmidt, H. (2002, December 31). *Schmidt logging associates.* Retrieved June 1, 2003, from the World Wide Web: http://www.schmidtlogging.com.

Explanation: Web owner, if available. (Date of last update, if available). *Title of Web site.* Date you viewed the site and the site's URL. *Note:* If the owner and date are not available, the above entry would look like this:

> *Schmidt logging associates.* Retrieved June 1, 2003, from the World Wide Web: http://www.schmidtlogging.com.

Cite this site as (*Schmidt*).

Professional or Personal Web Site—Internal Page. For an internal page of a Web site, give the URL of the document, not the home page.

> Schmidt, H. (2003, April 1). Consulting fee structure. *Schmidt logging associates.* Retrieved June 1, 2003, from the World Wide Web: http://schmidtlogging.com/fees.html.

Explanation: Web owner, if available. (Date of the last updating, if available—note that internal page updates and home page updates can be different; use the date of the page whose information you use.) Title that appears on the document page. *Title that appears on the home page.* Date you saw the information and the URL.

MLA Guidelines

E-mail. Treat E-mail like personal communication. Use this form in the Works Cited section:

> Schmidt, Howard. "Two Comments about Root Tailings." E-mail to the author. 1 Oct. 2004.

Explanation: Author. "Title (taken from the subject line)." Description of the message, including recipient. Date of the message.

In text the citation would read:

(Schmidt)

LISTSERVs. Although LISTSERVs are basically collections of E-mails, the entry for a LISTSERV posting requires more data. In the Works Cited section, use this form:

Schmidt, Howard. "A Problem with White Pine Root Systems." On-
    line posting. 1 Oct. 2004. Logging Associates of America List-
    serv. 2 Jan. 2005 <logserv-l@log.lsu.edu>.

Note: If you use the archived version of the document (and you should do so if you can), give the URL of the archive, e.g., <http://www.laa.lsu.edu/cgi-bin/enter=laa>.

Explanation: Author. "Title (use the subject line)." The phrase "On-line posting." Date of the posting. Name of the LISTSERV. Date of retrieval. <The on-line address of the LISTSERV's Web site, or if that address is not available, the E-mail address of the list's moderators>.

Article Available from an On-Line Source. Many libraries and companies' on-line services like EBSCOhost to find full-text articles. In your text, cite full-text articles by using the author's last name. Usually you cannot present a page number, because the full-text articles are seldom paginated; just skip the page information if it is not available. An entry in the Works Cited would look like this:

Schmidt, Howard. "Eco-friendly Logging Practices." *American Log-*
    ger 20 Oct. 2002: 56–70. *Academic Search Elite.* EBSCOhost.
    Austin Community College. 14 Feb. 2003 <http://search.epnet.
    com/commgeneric>. Keyword used: logging.

Explanation: Author. "Title of Article." *Title of Hard-Copy Periodical* date of original publication: page numbers, if available. *Title of database.* Title of service. Library you used to reach the on-line service. Date you retrieved the article <URL of the on-line service>. Keyword you used to find the article (optional).

Note: Databases like EBSCOhost often present the publishing information in a Source line that does not give the complete page numbers of the article.

Source: American Logger, 20 Oct. 2002, Vol. 176 Issue 10, p. 56, 14p.

If this is the only available information, use this form for the page numbers: :56, p. 14. In this case, in the text you will not be able to cite pages, just use the author's name.

Article Available from an On-Line Periodical. Treat an article from an on-line periodical like a hard-copy article. Note that you must add date of retrieval and URL:

> Schmidt, Howard. "Consulting Opportunities in White Pine Logging." *eLog* Oct. 2003. January 2, 2004 <http://www.elog.com/oct/articles/schmidt.html>

> *Explanation:* Author. "Title of Article." *Title of On-Line Periodical* date of original publication. Date of retrieval and <URL of article>.

Professional or Personal Web Site—Home Page. Essential for citing Web pages is that you give the date of retrieval on which you viewed the site and the URL. Give as much of the other information as possible.

> Schmidt, Howard. *Schmidt Logging Associates.* 31 Dec. 2002. 1 June 2003 <http://www.schmidtlogging.com>.

> *Explanation:* Web owner, if available. Title of Web Site. Date of last update, if available. Date of retrieval and <URL of the site>.
> *Note:* If the owner and date are not available, the above entry would look like this:

> *Schmidt Logging Associates.* 1 June 2003 <http://www.schmidtlogging.com>.

> Cite this site as (*Schmidt*).

Professional or Personal Web Site—Internal Page. For an internal page of a Web site, give the URL of the internal page, not the home page.

> Schmidt, Howard. "Consulting Fee Structure." 1 April 2003. *Schmidt Logging Associates* 1 June 2003 <http://www.schmidtlogging.com/fees.html>.

> *Explanation:* Author, if available. "Title of the Internal Page." Date of last updating, if available. *Title of the Entire Web Site* (from the home page) date of retrieval and <URL of the internal page, if possible>.

Index